SELLING MODERNITY

SELLING MODERNITY

Advertising in Twentieth-Century Germany

EDITED BY
Pamela E. Swett, S. Jonathan Wiesen,
and Jonathan R. Zatlin

Duke University Press   Durham and London   2007

© 2007 Duke University Press

All rights reserved

Printed in the United States of America on acid-free paper ∞

Designed by Heather Hensley

Typeset in Dante Monotype by Tseng Information Systems, Inc.

Library of Congress Cataloging-in-Publication Data appear

on the last printed page of this book.

FOR JACK, NATHANIEL, DANIEL, LEORA, AND MAX

CONTENTS

List of Illustrations ix

Foreword
Victoria de Grazia xiii

Acknowledgments xix

Introduction
Pamela E. Swett, S. Jonathan Wiesen, and Jonathan R. Zatlin 1

1. Marketing, Modernity, and "the German People's Soul":
   Advertising and Its Enemies in Late Imperial Germany, 1896–1914
   Kevin Repp 27

2. Visions of Prosperity: The Americanization of Advertising in
   Interwar Germany
   Corey Ross 52

3. Branding Germany: Hans Domizlaff's *Markentechnik* and Its
   Ideological Impact
   Holm Friebe 78

4. "Planting a Forest Tall and Straight Like the German *Volk*":
   Visualizing the *Volksgemeinschaft* through Advertising in
   German Forestry Journals, 1933–1945
   Michael Imort 102

5. Selling the "Racial Community": Kraft durch Freude and
   Consumption in the Third Reich
   Shelley Baranowski 127

6. "Die erfrischende Pause": Marketing Coca-Cola in
   Hitler's Germany
   Jeff Schutts   151

7. Lufthansa Welcomes You: Air Transport and Tourism
   in the Adenauer Era
   Guillaume de Syon   182

8. "The History of Morals in the Federal Republic":
   Advertising, PR, and the Beate Uhse Myth
   Elizabeth Heineman   202

9. "Wowman! The World's Most Famous Drug-Dog":
   Advertising, the State, and the Paradox of
   Consumerism in the Federal Republic
   Robert P. Stephens   230

10. "True Advertising Means Promoting a Good Thing
    through a Good Form": Advertising in the German
    Democratic Republic
    Anne Kaminsky   262

11. Promoting Socialist Cities and Citizens: East Germany's
    National Building Program
    Greg Castillo   287

12. "Serve Yourself!" The History and Theory of Self-Service
    in West and East Germany
    Rainer Gries   307

Bibliography   329

Contributors   347

Index   351

LIST OF ILLUSTRATIONS

REPP

FIGURE 1. Advertisement for Tietz Department Store, Berlin 31

FIGURE 2. The Wertheim Department Store, Berlin 38

FIGURE 3. Poster advertisement for Stiller shoes, 1908, Lucian Bernhard, artist 41

FIGURE 4. Poster advertisement for Priester matches, 1904, Lucian Bernhard, artist 43

ROSS

FIGURE 1. Kaloderma soap advertisement, 1927, Jupp Wiertz, artist 56

FIGURE 2. Newspaper announcement for Odol mouthwash, 1929 57

FRIEBE

FIGURE 1. R6 Reemtsma cigarette brand label, early 1920s 86

FIGURE 2. Ernte 23 Reemtsma cigarette brand label, early 1920s 87

FIGURE 3. Yellow Brand label for Reemtsma, early 1920s 88

FIGURE 4. Hans Domizlaff's design for a new *Reichsflagge*, 1932 95

FIGURE 5. Photograph of Hans Domizlaff, 1933 96

FIGURE 6. Photograph of President Paul von Hindenburg, 1933 97

IMORT

FIGURE 1. Pein & Pein tree nursery advertisement, 1936 110

FIGURE 2. Pein & Pein tree nursery advertisement, 1936 111

FIGURE 3. Pein & Pein tree nursery advertisement, 1938 112

FIGURE 4. Pein & Pein tree nursery advertisement, 1938 113

FIGURE 5. Bergmann tobacco company advertisement, 1938 118

FIGURE 6. Bergmann tobacco company advertisement, 1938 119

BARANOWSKI

FIGURE 1. A model shop floor, according to the Beauty of Labor, undated 131

FIGURE 2. Kraft durch Freude vacationers at the beach, 1939 136

FIGURE 3. Kraft durch Freude vacationers skiing, 1938 137

FIGURE 4. Tourist snapshots from a Kraft durch Freude cruise, 1938 139

FIGURE 5. The model for the KDF resort at Prora, on Rügen, 1938 140

FIGURE 6. Tourist snapshot from a Kraft durch Freude cruise, mid-1930s 142

FIGURE 7. Tourist snapshot of Norway's mountains, mid-1930s 145

SCHUTTS

FIGURE 1. American Coca-Cola advertisement translated for German consumers, mid-1930s 157

FIGURE 2. Coca-Cola advertisement, ca. 1935 158

FIGURE 3. Afri-Cola advertisement, 1938 166

FIGURE 4. Coca-Cola print advertisements from the late 1930s 171

FIGURE 5. Coca-Cola advertisement, 1937 172

DE SYON

FIGURE 1. Lufthansa advertisement, 1950s 186

FIGURE 2. Advertisement for Lufthansa service, ca. 1956 189

FIGURE 3. Two tourist brochures for Germany, early 1960s 193

FIGURE 4. American advertisement for Lufthansa, late 1950s 195

FIGURE 5. Lufthansa advertisement, 1960s and 1970s 197

HEINEMAN

FIGURE 1. Erotica catalogue, 1952 207

FIGURE 2. Erotica catalogue, ca. 1958 209

FIGURE 3. Women in the erotica industry, ca. 1963 210

FIGURE 4. Photograph of Beate Uhse, 1952 217

FIGURE 5. Photograph of Beate Uhse in uniform, 1944 218

STEPHENS

FIGURE 1. West German temperance pamphlet, 1953 234

FIGURE 2. The first widely distributed West German antidrug pamphlet, 1971 242

FIGURE 3. West German educational advertisement with John Lennon, 1972 250

FIGURE 4. Federally funded West German comic book, 1972 251

FIGURE 5. Illustrations from the comic book *Wowman*, 1972 253

KAMINSKY

FIGURE 1. East German storefront window, mid-1950s 266

FIGURE 2. East German poster, mid-1960s 267

FIGURE 3. East German mail-order catalogue, 1969 269

FIGURE 4. East German advertisement for wash basins, late 1950s 273

FIGURE 5. East German advertisement for camping, early 1970s 283

FIGURE 6. East German vacation advertisement, 1970s 284

CASTILLO

FIGURE 1. Poster promoting the East German "National Building Program for Germany's Capital," 1952 289

FIGURE 2. Photograph of architect Hermann Henselmann, ca. 1952 293

FIGURE 3. Photograph of a citizen's donation to the Werberwiese tower building project, 1952 296

FIGURE 4. A poster for the "Month of German-Soviet Friendship" in 1952 301

GRIES

FIGURE 1. Advertisement for Jet gasoline stations, 2004 308

FIGURE 2. Advertisement for the West German retail chain Konsum, 1965 311

FIGURE 3. East German retail chain Konsum, 1951 315

VICTORIA DE GRAZIA

FOREWORD

From all of the hullabaloo attending the inauguration of the International Advertising Congress at Berlin on August 11, 1929, Germany looked to be the pacesetter of twentieth-century merchandising. With its booming economy, the Weimar Republic was the fulcrum of European commerce. Its fifth largest city, Leipzig, hosted the world's oldest and biggest trade fair, its twice-yearly expositions of hundreds of thousands of craft and industrial wares attracting buyers from a hundred lands. Its capital, Berlin, was home to artistic circles bubbling over with the cultural irreverence on which the new marketing professions thrived. True, the congress's logo, "Advertising: the key to world prosperity," was an American advertising man's conceit. But a Berliner had come up with the logo design in the shape of a key so palpably phallic that it gave a jolt of visual testosterone to the whole proceedings.

That 1920s Germany stood at the forefront of world advertising culture looked plausible on other grounds as well. There were those 80 million German speakers, the largest language concentration in Europe and the most literate as well, and, if a third or more didn't live in Germany itself, that was fine too, for they still promised to be good markets for the country's export-oriented economy. There was also Germany's legacy as homeland to Gutenberg's print revolution, a legacy still visible in its global leadership in the typographic arts, lithography, and packaging design. There were the vibrantly colored posters affixed to the downtown kiosks that spoke of a merchandising tradition comfortably at home on the city streets. There was the upstart *Sachlichkeit* aesthetic, superbly combining utility and modernist beauty in an iconoclastic struggle against the rhetorical conventions of academic design. Finally, there was the multitude of German artists ready to engage with modern advertising, some out of the conviction that it represented a new avant-garde, others because it could pay handsomely. From the memoirs of the prudish Elias Canetti, a visitor to late 1920s Berlin, we have the unsettling image of Bertolt Brecht lounging at the Café Schlichter, boasting of the copy he had composed for Steyr and the automobile he had received as compensation.

But notoriously, advertising is about illusions. The disquieting reality was that the United States, not Germany, was the force driving the internationalization of advertising. It was the bedrock of the American profession, the famous 4-A's (the American Association of Advertising Agencies), that had initially promoted periodic international congresses, and the decision to hold this one, the first on the Continent for the first time in 1929, coincided with the installation in Europe's capitals of some of the biggest American advertising agencies. American-style advertising signaled the advent of an altogether new industry, whose basic unit of enterprise, the full-service agency, was capable of taking a new product and turning it into a high-profile brand, armed with the belief that advertising was a science, and the business a high-minded, reputable profession. Above all, American advertising presented itself as the mouthpiece of a new language, accustoming people to speak about the things they appeared to have in common and enriching their conversations about the things they adored or abhorred with visual images and idiomatic expressions. Abroad, as at home, American corporate advertising was in every way at the cutting edge of the capitalist dialectic of creative destruction.

The Weimar statesman Hans Luther spoke to the deep cultural disquiet created by American advertising when at the opening ceremonies he addressed his compatriots about "the need to make a home in both the world of the present and that of the future." Advertising was "the language of this new world," the former chancellor insisted. But as much as Germans will "want to learn from other lands which already possess a much richer experience in this language," there should be no doubt that "we also desire to develop the German dialect of this language and we want to do this in a German spirit and through German artistic sensibility."

With these words, Hans Luther captured a point that is central to *Selling Modernity*, namely, that advertising had to be treated as much as a cultural question as a business proposition. Advertising may appear to be about selling goods. But that is only one ambition. Whatever its form or technique—the handout or poster, the press insert, radio ditty, mail-order catalogue, or website pop-up—it has long been the expression of a complicated dialogue about the meaning of market relations, one mediated by specialists with diverse interests to balance. Advertisers themselves, as the contributors to this wide-ranging book so vividly illuminate, hankered after professional dignity, social status, and income. And these acquisitions depended in turn on cultivating business relations with clients and gaining the confidence of the public whose own growing expertise they were under constant pressure to probe, test, and master. Rightly, this book speaks in the plural of cultures of advertising—for the practices of advertising were highly rarified at the same time as they penetrated into the very interstices of societies, so much so that even as early as the 1920s, they emerged as a signally important signifier of modernity. How that happened will have to be told again and again, from myriad perspectives, lest we never fully grasp how advertising messages in the world today and on a global scale have become as inescapable an element of the societies we live in as the air we breathe.

The great virtue of this book is to speak of this cultural complexity from the perspective of the history of twentieth-century Germany. In common with a whole transnational cohort of young historians, its authors move from the premise that the visibility and power of the consumer economy in contemporary societies calls for a detailed, wide-ranging history of its origins. The main point here is that in twentieth-century Germany, this development was exceptionally fraught—out of fear that hyperaggressive modernity would eradicate time-honored traditions, internationalism was irreconcilable with local knowledge, soulless science would destroy disinterested art, and the monstrous commodification of everything would splinter apart the bonds of human community. It was also fraught because the internationalization of advertising culture spearheaded by American "best practices" took place in Europe against the background of a full-blown bourgeois commercial culture, based on craft industry, segmented regional markets, deep social fissures, abiding distress at a moneyed culture, and wracking political and racial conflict. Against this background, we have a book whose authors are in dialogue with one another and with the many voices that today speak to the history of consumer culture, so that by its end we have taken a big step toward knowing how the trends in the arts and technologies of advertising were bound up with the fate of Germany.

Reading this volume as a generalist, I was especially struck by three elements that give a particular German cast to the history of selling practices which today appear practically universal, so much so that differences really appear to be only a matter of national stereotypes—or in any case, not intertwined with the grand narrative of Europe's fall and recovery over the past century.

One element surely is the impact on advertising of the vexed tradition of thinking of culture as *Kultur*. In the land of Kant and Nietzsche, where cultural wars were fought with the semiotic equivalents of Big Berthas and Blitzkriegs, how could advertising culture not be deeply implicated? On the one hand, what could be more odious to a culture that saw the "beautiful as that which gives us pleasure without self-interest" than the crassness of publicity? On the other, what could be more attractive than a cultural form whose acolytes delighted in stripping away the hypocrisy of bourgeois aesthetics and debunking the asceticism that denied the masses all of the real pleasures of life? In sum, there were awesome cultural stakes in inventing a local vernacular: from the conflict over the "Americanization" of local practices and the engineering of big brand marketing of foreign and national products, to finding a language to legitimate the lust in sex toys.

Inevitably the second element distinguishing the history of advertising in Germany is the role played by National Socialism. How did a regime known for its mastery of political propaganda deal with the best practices of publicity? It is a surprise, surely, to hear from the mouths of some of the most distinguished advertising experts in the United States that the Nazis had done "one good job" in eliminating "advertising abuses," or that the dictatorship's regulation of the advertising profession represented "probably . . . the most advanced legislation to be found in this field." The only caveat from this American perspective of the late 1930s was that it would have been more admirable, following the American corporate model, if regulation had come about through the profession rather than top-down from the state. No doubt about it: the Nazi regime well understood that yet one other means to enhance its totalitarian grip lay in reestablishing political power over the slippery terrain of the commercial public sphere. Its claim to have purged the market of the manipulations of foreign and Semitic elements by bringing transparency and truth to the advertising profession was part and parcel of a far more ambitious politics of building a mass market based ostensibly on the public celebration of the people's needs rather than on the covert workings of the price mechanism. Advertising had a central role to play in a market that pretended to modify the class-divisive nature of cultural goods and distribute scarce resources by rewarding and depriving consumers according to their place in the *Volksgemeinschaft*'s hierarchy of utility and race. The effects on any number of levels were catastrophic, spelling the eclipse of those practices where, indeed, Germany had been leader; the persecution, exile, and death of Jewish artists and an aesthetics favoring populist realism spelled the death of German modernism, the restoration of the Gothic script, the end of Germany's superiority in the experimental typography that had yielded Bernhard Kursiv, Locarno, Ultra Bodoni, Memphis, Beton, Neuland, Prisma Capitals, and Futura in favor of the more conventionally eclectic American usage of fonts. However, for those in the profession itself, who handily continued working under the Third Reich and went on to thrive in postwar Germany, it was not a bad trade-off that, thanks to National Socialist regulatory powers, a disreputable profession of hucksters had been turned into a highly disciplined corporation of professionals, one that could be trusted to communicate wisely and effectively with a Volk that had been transmogrified from hagglers into heroes.

The third anomaly that strikes the reader is the bifurcated history of advertising as a result of Germany's postwar division. From the perspective of the 1950s, as industry picked up, we have the phenomenon of two countries working from similar legacies, yet experiencing the development of advertising cultures in ways that could not have been more distant from each other. So in the Federal Republic of Germany, advertising picked up and boomed with the miracle years. In the recognition that West Germany would be the fulcrum of the revived Western European economy, the biggest U.S. advertising firm of all, J. Walter Thompson, moved its European headquarters from London to Frankfurt in 1956, making the newly skyscrapered city the capital of continental corporate advertising. However squeamish West German political leaders were about advertising, which in its excess seemed to be inappropriate for the social market economy or a venerable *Kulturnation* (however far it had fallen from that ideal), the bottom line was that West Germany itself, as the European pivot of the Western Alliance, was a fabulous advertisement for the Western standard of living in the struggle against the totalitarian asceticism of the Soviet way of life. We have in this book marvelous evidence of the paradox that Coca-Cola flourished under the Third Reich; this fact is at least as noteworthy as the fact that it became the political signifier of the change of regime as one passed from one side of the Brandenburg Gate to the other.

And in the German Democratic Republic we have to face the paradox that austere socialism was by no means antithetical to advertising, and vice versa. In the five-year plans, there was space for advertising. After all, advertising was an art, or at least it had been, and in East German commercial design circles, it continued to touch base with Bauhaus ideas of the modernistic function of advertising; in its terse language, not only would it signal the advent of the modern, but it would tidily link consumers to supply. Very effectively, it would thereby contribute to the utopia of real existing socialism by harnessing desires to needs and needs to the constraints and possibilities of the planned economy.

Ultimately, from the vantage point of the economy of desire revealed through its advertising culture, contemporary Germany could be said to have become a completely normal Western nation. Marketing experts might highlight any number of small anomalies; likewise ethnographers, cultural tourists, and historians. But no element of German advertising is so original that we could argue that it is significantly different from the practice found in other European nations today, nor for that matter from its Madison Avenue progenitors. Meanwhile these progenitors have lost their own peculiarities, as they themselves have fallen prey in recent years to aggressive corporate takeovers by giant European-based global conglomerates.

In sum, *Selling Modernity* is to be complimented for clarifying that the reconstruction of the history of advertising, that most pivotal and fascinating dimension of market culture, cannot be treated as a linear or unproblematic process. Time and again, the contributors have developed just the right case to illuminate the ferociously contentious struggles over the meaning of market culture. The razzle-dazzle of commodity culture is at home with dismal inequality, and the champagne bubbles of advertising creativity fizzle away amid the sledgehammer destructiveness of capitalist progress. Knowing the particular turbulence experienced in the development of commercial culture in twentieth-century Germany brings us closer to comprehending the turbulence of mass consumer society generally and today as much as ever.

ACKNOWLEDGMENTS

This book has its origins in an interdisciplinary workshop on German advertising and public relations held at McMaster University in November 2003.
During a fruitful three-day meeting, European and North American scholars
representing a variety of fields (history, art history, film studies, and environmental studies) met to share their newest insights on the historical and cultural
significance of advertising and product promotion. This collection of essays,
while primarily a work of history, seeks in a modest way to draw together those
interdisciplinary interests and lay a foundation for future studies.

The workshop was possible due to the generosity of a number of institutions:
the Social Science and Humanities Research Council of Canada, the Offices of
the Provost and Vice President of Research at McMaster University, the Faculty
of Humanities and the History Department at McMaster University, the History of Medicine Unit at McMaster University, the Humanities Foundation at
Boston University, the Canadian Centre for German and European Studies, and
the Holocaust Education Foundation. The editors would also like to thank the
following graduate students for their assistance leading up to the event and for
making sure it all went off without a hitch: Heather Nelson, Steve Bunn, and
Jeff Hayton. Matt Leighninger and Said Ahmad should also be thanked for their
numerous airport runs to pick up and drop off participants.

In the two years that followed the conference, other individuals and funding
agencies contributed greatly to the completion of this book. In addition to the
sustained support of the organizations already mentioned, the College of Liberal Arts at Southern Illinois University, Carbondale, provided funds to support
the completion of the index. Our two anonymous readers at Duke University
Press offered thoughtful critiques and encouragement that have been essential

in improving the individual contributions and helping us write the introductory chapter. Lindsey Anderson put together a thorough bibliography of secondary sources while we prepared our introduction. Steve Bunn and Bradley Coates assisted in the editorial work, and Ruth Pincoe lent her expertise to the writing of the index.

We would also like to express our gratitude to those presenters and commentators from the workshop who are not represented in this volume but who helped us all think about the broader themes of the collection and improve our own analyses. We also thank Reynolds Smith at Duke University Press for believing in the project and helping us see it through to publication. Finally, Claudia Koonz was instrumental in first nudging us to pursue this larger project at a German Studies Association annual meeting in 2001, and she has continued to provide support and critiques throughout the entire process. We are most grateful.

PAMELA E. SWETT, S. JONATHAN WIESEN,
AND JONATHAN R. ZATLIN

INTRODUCTION

In 1959 economist and market researcher Wilhelm Vershofen noted a curious phenomenon in West Germany: "There are still contemporaries who fundamentally reject advertising." In the midst of the "Economic Miracle," this fact was indeed puzzling. Consumer goods were flooding shops and showrooms, and West Germans were enjoying the fruits of the country's postwar recovery. Yet at the same time, critics were denouncing advertisements as psychologically manipulative, vilifying their creators as sinister brainwashers, and dismissing advertising as an expensive and ineffective medium that drove up the price of a product. Against this backdrop, Vershofen drew attention to an odd paradox: critics of advertising were dismissing the very practice they "freely took advantage of."[1]

Today such sweeping rejections of advertising are harder to find. Companies take for granted the necessity of using advertising for the effective marketing of goods and services. Indeed, by 2004 advertising alone accounted for 1 percent of the global gross domestic product, and the figure continues to rise.[2] Advertising serves not only an essential economic function in advanced industrial societies, but plays cultural and social roles as well: European moviegoers look forward to a half hour of product promotions before a feature film; many Americans watch the National Football League's Super Bowl Championship "just for the ads"; ad slogans permeate the language of popular culture; and there are annual awards throughout the world for the best television commercials, radio spots, Internet ads, and even in-flight airline promotional films. Yet popular and scholarly critiques of advertising—its strategies, its pervasiveness, its effectiveness—have by no means disappeared.

Public unease and professional skepticism toward advertising in Germany over the past century serve as a useful starting point for a broader exploration of one of capitalism's most inventive, protean, and intrusive mediums. The ethical and economic objections to advertising reflect a long-standing ambivalence about consumer capitalism in a country that, ironically, has been home to some of its most successful expressions. In addition to examining the reception of advertising, however, the essays that compose this volume also investigate the broader political, social, and cultural work of the Germans who commissioned and created advertisements. The volume is premised on the idea that images of a company and its products not only define the retail landscape and inform consumer habits; they also reflect and contribute to the formation of individual and national identities, discourses on politics and morality, and discussions of the individual's relationship to free-market and planned economies. In their own ways, all these essays investigate how advertising served symbolic functions in the various political and ideological settings of twentieth-century Germany. Although the authors pursue different aspects of German advertising, each arrives at a similar conclusion: that advertising gave expression to the anxieties and opportunities produced by modern consumer society.

The story of advertising's ubiquity and influence is by no means unique to Germany. Indeed, much scholarly work has been done to address similar themes in other countries, most notably the United States, which was home to the greatest innovations in advertising over the past century. But Germany's turbulent history offers a uniquely illuminating case study of advertising's power to disseminate messages of economic stability and individual security during periods of intense change. Marked by the end of an empire, two world wars, two democracies, and two dictatorships, modern German history is defined in a more pronounced fashion by the ruptures and continuities found in other advanced industrial societies. At the same time, the sheer intensity and violence of these transformations set off German history as distinctly traumatic, and thus offer an opportunity to assess the power and endurance of commercial imagery in the most extreme circumstances. Amid these dramatic transformations, "the consumer" always existed as a powerful presence—one with whom the German state, private institutions, and companies regularly sought to communicate. Throughout the modern era advertisers and those who hire them have attempted to disseminate values and promote lifestyles to individuals in their capacities as citizens, shoppers, travelers, workers, and women and men. But what makes the German case so fascinating is the rapid succession of different political and economic systems and, in turn, the often blurry lines between the ideological aims of the state and corporate self-promotion. Against this tumultuous historical backdrop, the durability of successful companies and brand names stands out. We are drawn to ask how specific advertising tropes, such as the treasured "Made in Germany" stamp of quality, survived even as political and social systems failed.

This question does not mean to suggest a triumphant, liberating trajectory of brands outliving compromised ideologies. In fact, the essays in this volume call into question assumptions that innovations in advertising and the increasing use of this medium furthered the unfolding of an egalitarian consumer society based on an individual's access to greater goods and economic freedoms.[3] Nor does this volume claim to be able to "read history" through advertisements. As Roland Marchand argued in his pathbreaking work on American advertising in the 1920s and 1930s, advertisements are less a reflection of social reality than of the "fantasies and aspirations" consumers harbor or, for that matter, that image makers *want* them to harbor at given historical junctures.[4] In short, the contributors to this volume presume the *production* of advertising is itself infused with cultural and social meaning.

In addressing the theme of advertising broadly, the essays in *Selling Modernity* are informed by the explosion of literature on "consumer society" and "consumption" over the past decade. This scholarly interest reflects a profound shift in intellectual perspective away from the process of producing commodities and toward an analysis of their distribution and use. Some of the most interesting new work explores such themes as the political power of consumer boycotts, the function of gender in the purchasing act, and the relationship between notions of citizenship and the seemingly mundane act of shopping.[5] The great interest in consumption studies has reawakened scholars to the importance of material goods and their images as sites of historical meaning. Scholarship after the so-called iconic turn has manifested itself in a focus on diverse forms of imagery — from political campaign posters, to industrial design, to advertising.[6]

Though related to these scholarly trends, this volume differentiates itself from much of this recent literature in its focus on advertising as a bridge between production and consumption. Instead of emphasizing the social and political behavior of consumers and patterns of consumption, *Selling Modernity* highlights the actors who had the greatest stake in successful merchandising. "Selling" is, after all, a gerund, and one question is "Who is doing it?" Company managers, advertising executives, copywriters, graphic artists, market researchers, and salespeople — all of these actors have helped shape the depiction of a company's products, reputation, and visions of modern life. Rather than collapsing advertising into debates over the nature of consumption, the essays in this volume imagine product promotion as emerging as much out of debates internal to manufacturers and distributors as to the demands of consumers. German advertising has not been a neat exercise in economic rationality; ideology has often trumped profit seeking, and the advice of advertising and PR firms sometimes has had surprisingly little impact on corporate strategy. Any study of German advertising must approach consumers, corporate leaders, and advertisers as social actors whose motivations cannot be reduced solely to political and economic calculations.

While advertising is not only a visual medium, this volume does pay close attention to posters, flyers, and especially newspaper and magazine advertising.[7] Yet the essays are informed by an understanding of corporate communications that goes beyond just the visual presentation of a product or service. Public relations and marketing are now receiving the attention of scholars, who are revealing how companies rely on more varied ways of promoting products and reputations than advertising alone, from the use of press releases to the commissioning of company histories.[8] While this volume does not devote itself systematically to PR and marketing, its essays do consider some of these nonvisual forms of company and product promotion. Thus *Selling Modernity* hopes to challenge the understanding of advertising as "advertisements" in a narrow sense. Advertisements do represent the most obvious form of company publicity. But companies promote their products and reputation through a multitude of media. Billboards, radio broadcasts, tourism films, postcards, folk festivals, newsreels, cultural events in factories, refreshment booths at exhibitions, flag parades, airline livery, souvenirs, and the visual spectacle of the cityscape all appear as "sites of selling," where institutions—whether companies or the state—promote not only manufactured goods, but ideologies and lifestyles.

Understanding advertising and corporate communications more broadly in Germany depends to some degree on the history of transatlantic perceptions, misperceptions, and adaptations of theory and method.[9] Over the course of the twentieth century, German corporations and advertisers argued that U.S. advertising techniques must be modified to suit the particularities of German society.[10] America represented big profits and a large consuming public, but to many Germans those consuming masses also represented a feminine, soulless society.[11] In very different political contexts, corporations' attempts to translate American expertise into a German vernacular were aimed in part at shoring up Germany's economic autonomy in the face of U.S. dominance of world markets. The engagement with American methods, however, also uncovered a deep-seated ambivalence toward modernity. Corporate imagery had to sell, yet in a way that did not weaken this sophisticated, culture-rich society. The critique of modernity, and materialism in particular, cut across the German political spectrum and resided uneasily alongside the growing cross-cultural exchange between these two economic powerhouses.

This obsession with America commingled with specific attempts to work through the legacies of German authoritarianism. If cultural pessimists on the right saw advertising as the harbinger of a cultural catastrophe, with its origins in America, the left, particularly in the aftermath of World War II, also saw the medium as reinforcing culturally debilitating trends, with potentially serious political implications. The most trenchant assessments of advertising from the left were formulated by Frankfurt School theorists. Writing in American exile, Max Horkheimer and Theodor W. Adorno famously denounced the "culture industry" for subordinating artistic creation to the profit motive. In their classic work *The Dialectic of the Enlightenment* (1947), they charged advertising, along with film, radio, magazines, and various forms of popular music, with harnessing cultural references to help manufacturers promote their products and the lifestyles associated with them. This unscrupulous manipulation of cultural production subjugated the mind's freedom to the needs of the market just as surely as manufacturers yoked the body's strength to the requirements of industry.

More important, however, Horkheimer and Adorno argued that the culture industry's sophisticated marketing tools enabled it to transform even resistance to capitalism into money-making schemes. Because of its ability to co-opt dissent for the purpose of turning a profit, advertising helped stabilize the rule of "monopoly capital"; it depoliticized systemic conflicts, weakened resistance to economic injustice, and permitted the more effective "administration" of needs and desires along the way. For this reason, Horkheimer and Adorno "came to feel that the culture industry enslaved men in far more subtle and effective ways than the crude methods of domination practiced in earlier eras."[12]

Although abstract in its formulations, the Frankfurt School provided some of the most powerful assessments of advertising, which continue to inform intellectual critiques of mass culture. In a more alarmist fashion, the depiction of advertising as a form of psychological and social control also found its way into popular literature. Most famously, Vance Packard's *Hidden Persuaders* (1957), translated into German as the best-selling *Die Geheimen Verführer*, offered a dire warning that the "shock troops of the advertising world are subtly charting your inner thoughts, fears, and dreams so that they can influence your daily living."[13] Packard-inspired pundits found opponents in theorists like Ernest Dichter, whose best-selling *Strategy of Desire* (1960) offered a staunch defense of advertising through his innovations in motivational research. Dichter, an Austrian émigré writing in New York, also used psychoanalysis to understand the seemingly irrational behavior that lay behind the purchasing act. But he defended advertising as a scientific means of addressing people's latent needs and desires. According to Dichter, motivational research and its application in advertising did not "manipulate" people into purchasing specific goods or "twist their unconscious," but rather "provided a bridge between the consumer and the manufacturer."[14] Although Dichter's representation of individual needs rested on ahistorical assumptions about their transparency, his attempt to refocus the task of advertising on consumer preferences forced companies to research their target groups more carefully, rather than simply churn out new products without imagination or insight into the consumer's psyche.

These cold war–era discussions are worth highlighting as key expressions of the fertile intellectual work unleashed by the spread of advertising. As the following contributions will show, these theoretical explorations into humans' needs and vulnerabilities span the entire course of the twentieth century. But the broader point is that scholarly and popular understandings of advertising reflected larger concerns about the meanings of mass culture and social engineering in the twentieth century.[15] In Germany and abroad, advertising became a point of crystallization for a larger obsession with the implications of social equality, the erosion of high culture, and the ability of more and more people to access goods and services that were once the sole property of social and economic elites. Over the course of the twentieth century, Victoria de Grazia has argued, the bourgeois regime of European commerce succumbed to the revolutionary dynamic of America's "Market Empire," and more and more Europeans had access to consumer goods.[16] Whether this transformation was due to the sheer force of American cultural imperialism, or to some larger process of "Westernization" or "modernization," continues to provoke debate.[17] But whatever the origins, advertising was at the epicenter of what was a seismic historical shift.

From the German Empire to the Wende:
A Short Survey of German Advertising

Although the United States offered a new model, the very first rumblings of this seismic shift predate World War I and America's significant influence on the European continent and within Germany. Rapid industrialization in Germany after unification began a period of growth for advertising, and by the 1890s the major companies in Germany had begun to advertise their products in a serious way. Even then it was often the owners or, more commonly, the sons or younger brothers of owners who directed the publicity of their companies—and under that general heading the advertisement of products—rather than professionally trained advertisers. It was the members of this younger generation, already convinced of the power of mass media and at ease with the developing consumer society, who overcame their predecessors' principle that "the product sells itself" (*Die Ware lobt sich selbst*).[18]

At the start of the new century, the founding of the Werkbund in Munich (1907) ushered in a new attention to industrial design and the aesthetics of advertising.[19] Some advertisers began to call for uniform training and qualifications as a way to gain recognition for their profession, achieve status as members of the *Bildungsbürgertum*, and overcome the lingering public image of advertising as underhanded. Encouraged by larger trends toward specialization, the first trade journals and associations for advertisers emerged by the turn of the century, and the first independent ad agency was founded in Berlin in 1897.[20] Against this longing for scientific expertise, however, others set a more romantic vision of the creative artist. They argued that advertising was not something that could be taught, but that the advertiser was born with an artistic gift that had to be cultivated. By comparing themselves with artistic geniuses, and thus their work with visual art, these early advertisers hoped to access a different path to social status in Wilhelmine society.[21] All advertisers—salesmen and artists alike—could agree, however, on one thing: their work had a particular connection to the metropolis. Even those who prioritized the aesthetic aims of their work insisted that their designs unveiled a new urban worldview, and so they rejected the tradition-bound art academies as well as business-minded training.[22] This internal debate would not easily be resolved. Distracting advertisers from the task was the harsh criticism they faced from outside their own circles. In addition to old concerns about the truthfulness of ads, the new urban language spoken by advertisers contributed to their critics' distaste for the medium. Images and slogans defaced the cityscape, they complained, shouting at consumers in crass and even scandalous ways.

Historians view World War I as a watershed for modern advertising because it introduced new visual propaganda strategies and generated expressionist and dadaist art forms that thrived on shock value.[23] Yet the conflict also served to interrupt the growth of the field within Germany.[24] Advertisers in all belligerent nations could put to rest questions about their social allegiances by serving the cause of war, such as designing posters that sold war bonds. After 1918, advertisers in the victor nations improved their social standing during the transition to a peacetime economy. In contrast, advertisers in the defeated nations were tarnished by their cooperation with the old regime. In Germany, for example, their participation in state-sponsored propaganda that had deceived the public about the inevitability of victory strengthened the hand of those who criticized the manipulative intent of image makers. Furthermore, the war's toll on Germany's human resources interrupted the profession's development. Although advertisers gained useful training during the war, the curtailment of the production of nonessential goods, the conscription of many young men who would have chosen emerging career opportunities in advertising, and the economic crisis that came on the heels of defeat meant that it was 1923 before the German advertising industry regained its prewar level of production.[25]

By the end of the 1920s, however, purveyors of brand-name products, retailers, and even heavy industry, which had shown little interest in advertising before World War I, had set up in-house departments to manage their images in the marketplace. As Dirk Reinhardt notes, at the close of the decade a large retailer with five hundred men and women on its payroll was likely to employ twenty-five to thirty of them in the advertising of its wares.[26] In Berlin alone on the eve of the Depression, three thousand electric advertisements lit up the night sky.[27] Along with the extension of educational and employment opportunities after the war, interest in the science of advertising also surged. Research centers and publications were founded that examined the psychological impact of color, lighting, size, and other aspects of form and content on the consumer.[28] At the 1929 meeting of the International Advertising Association in Berlin, the German representative Dr. Alfred Knapp welcomed the growing sophistication of practitioners and called for further systematic study of the methods and impact of advertisements.[29] Science, Knapp believed, had won out over art as the bedrock of the industry.

The 1929 meeting in Berlin also capped off a decade in which German advertisers and other corporate publicity experts traveled widely and participated in both continental and transatlantic dialogues and associations. Nonetheless, many Germans still worried about advertising's effects on society, in particular the willingness of companies and ad agencies to follow styles set beyond Germany's borders, some of which had been imported by offshoots of U.S. and British agencies, such as the Berlin office established in 1927 by the American agency J. Walter Thompson. From the start of the Weimar Republic the images offered in advertisements reflected the promise of the new era: a youthful, socially mobile, and technologically modern society. If the republic was the crucible of modernity, then advertising was one language of experimentation that Germans interacted with on a daily basis during the 1920s. Yet providing the visual and textual vocabulary of the new age did not provide a secure or stable identity for the industry. Even those who supported the so-called American-style ads and consumerism demanded some recognition of German cultural traditions and worked hard to negotiate this ground. This struggle became much harder to maintain by the end of the republican era, when the economic crisis seemed to weaken the arguments for international styles and open markets, and significant decreases in expenditures on advertising resulted in large layoffs at agencies and in-house ad departments. The branches of large British and American agencies established just a few years earlier were all closed or sold off to German managers in the early 1930s because their largely non-German clientele had drastically slashed their budgets for product promotion in the collapsed German market. Throughout the Depression, advertising professionals maintained publicly that ads were the "key to the prosperity of the world,"[30] but privately many worried about the industry's future.

After the Nazis seized power, the new regime prioritized image making in all its forms, including advertising. By establishing a state ad council in 1933, the government sought to control all aspects of an industry still tarnished by claims of unethical business practices and foreign influence. The mandate of the Werberat der Deutschen Wirtschaft (Advertising Council for the German Economy) was to end debates about advertising by regulating everything from who practiced in the industry, to rate scales for tiny classified ads, to the content of ad copy and design. Under the ad council's guidance a *Deutsche Werbung* (German Advertising) would emerge to represent racial ideals and business practices thought lost to cosmopolitan decadence and greed. After the purging of Jews from the profession, the challenge posed to those who were allowed to practice as ad writers or company publicity experts was to offer images that promoted and satisfied individual desires without running afoul of the communal interests of the *Volksgemeinschaft* (racial community).[31] Though the council struggled against those within the government who challenged its authority and faced an overwhelming task controlling all advertising media, the Werberat continued working toward these goals until the collapse of the regime.

Though the Third Reich was "unabashedly productivist" in nature from its start, the implementation of the Four-Year Plan in 1936 further intensified the race to prepare for war and reduce wages and consumer goods production.[32] Yet in the same year the Führer also oversaw the plans for the opening of the Höhere Reichswerbeschule (Reich Advertising Academy). The first of its kind in Europe, raved members of the National Socialist Association of German Advertising Practitioners, the school boasted a multidisciplinary program, spanning the newest innovations in marketing techniques to art and design.[33] The Four-Year Plan found its own ways to affect the lives of Germany's advertisers. Long before the onset of hostilities, many advertisers found themselves well-trained propagandists engaged in the "struggle against waste" and other threats to the racial community. Many ad writers voluntarily incorporated such national slogans into their work; others were drafted into working for Propaganda Ministry campaigns to teach consumers how to conserve household products that were also essential to the military campaign, such as laundry detergent. The Reichswerbeschule, which the regime had touted so proudly and which sat in the heart of Berlin's most famous shopping district along the Kurfürstendamm, was destroyed by aerial bombardment in 1943. Its destruction meant little, however, since the widespread inability to produce consumer products in the last years of the war (particularly due to shortages of workers, raw materials, and transportation) meant that advertisers were doing little more than reminding consumers of their brand names in anticipation of a time when the shelves would again be full.

The immediate postwar years saw the continued scarcity of products to consume (and thus to advertise), a lack of paper and machinery necessary to produce ads, and a shortage of money to buy the few items on sale. Massive wartime damage in Germany meant the absence of a vibrant urban landscape so essential to advertising—from shopping centers, to kiosks in train stations, to the sides of buses and trolleys. Most contemporaries in the West remember the Currency Reform of 1948 as the turning point—the "Zero Hour"—for advertising, ending about five years of a relatively ad-free existence. The new Deutschmark precipitated a sudden abundance of consumer merchandise, and popular brands trumpeted their own triumphant return.[34] Having ceased production in World War II, for example, Persil laundry detergent proudly declared in 1950 that "Persil is back" ("Persil ist wieder da").[35] Along with commercial advertising, graphic designers found new work in advertising the benefits of the Marshall Plan and, a few years later, aiding government and industry campaigns to publicize the benefits of the social market economy.[36] Despite the break with National Socialism, once again a German state found itself working closely with industry to promote a particular ideology and a broader ethical vision of the economy.[37]

The messages conveyed by West German ads during this period mirror this transformation from an economy of scarcity to one of rapid growth.[38] According to Ingrid Schenk, from 1948 to 1951 ads reinforced the return to the peacetime production of goods and the passing of an era of shortages. From 1951 to 1955, advertisers tapped into the German penchant for saving, encouraging people to buy consumer durables with the assurance that "a short-term purchase could carry long-term savings," such as with refrigerators or other household appliances. In the second half of the 1950s, as the benefits of the economic boom began trickling down to the general public, ads were no longer about selling a new economic system or encouraging people to buy at all. Rather, in these years luxury items were transformed into necessities, as cars and other goods once deemed the property of the bourgeoisie now were portrayed as indispensable to a modern, more mobile consumer society. Finally, in the 1960s advertisements highlighted how these new "necessities" were even better in quality than a decade before.[39]

This schematic approach to West German product advertising is overly general, but it nonetheless reflects the reality that increasing material abundance found expression in advertisements. Newfound prosperity did not, however, mean new messages. In the conservative 1950s, advertisements drew on long-standing, transnational tropes about the family.[40] The housewife was coded as the primary consumer, and ads spoke to her desires for time-saving appliances and luxuries presumably paid for out of her husband's wages. Social reality, however, was more complicated than social values; despite images reflecting a conservative distribution of roles, women continued to enter the workforce and thus had their own need for professional attire and accessories not directly tied to their roles as homemakers and wives.[41] Likewise, in the 1950s, the so-called hidden consumer—the man—could not be underestimated in his desire for cigarettes, watches, and fancy suits.[42] Consequently, 1950s advertising was perhaps at its most creative in the fashion and cosmetics industry, providing people with outward displays of both conformity and an individuality that presumably had been absent in the Nazi years.

If the 1950s was the decade of "economic miracles" for both the nation and the individual household, it was also a time when the advertising profession itself underwent major changes. A key change was in attitude. According to Harm Schröter, in Germany there "was a new realization that production and sales could be supplemented by an *appropriate* advertisement."[43] The suddenness of this insight may be overstated, but in accordance with this increasing attention to the profitability of advertising, "American"-style full-service agencies began operation. In 1952 five of these companies came together to form the Gesellschaft Werbeagenturen (German Association of Full-Service Advertising Agencies). Like the American Association of Advertising Agencies, membership represented the highest badge of honor for an ad agency.[44] Around the same time, the American advertising firm J. Walter Thompson made its triumphant return to Germany, setting up shop eventually in Frankfurt, where it competed with German agencies for major accounts like Kodak, Pan American Airlines, Pepsi-Cola, Kellogg's, and Kraft foods.[45] J. Walter Thompson was, in turn, instrumental in founding Aktion Gemeinsinn (Community Spirit in Action), a charity initiative modeled directly after the Advertising Council in the United States. It depended upon the donations and volunteer work of advertisers to conduct socially conscious ad campaigns, from the first year's urgings to "Help the Housewife" (1959) to 1961's drive to make the public more sensitive to its oldest members.[46]

The coming of the full-service agency has been depicted as the first wave in the "Americanization" of the West German ad industry (the second being marketing).[47] Despite the arrival of an American import, advertisers themselves still complained of a lack of respect for their trade that they felt their counterparts across the Atlantic enjoyed. In response to this crisis of confidence, advertisers called upon their colleagues to create "advertisements on behalf of advertising" by selling the moral virtues and effectiveness of their profession.[48] They portrayed advertising as a noble calling, seeing themselves as pioneers who blazed new paths in the image making so essential to the material well-being of West German citizens.[49] They drew upon notions that harked back to the Wilhelmine era of the advertiser as creative genius, less affected by the bottom line than in the United States. The new economy of West Germany was still comparatively less geared toward consumer goods than in the United States, and thus advertisers perhaps felt more justified in claiming to embody a unique personality within an "old world," productionist economy. In addition, the "Made in Germany" quality ethos persisted, explicitly contrasting itself to the supposedly poorer quality mass-produced goods from across the Atlantic through its embrace of an artisanal ideal.

The tensions that defined the 1950s—a burgeoning ad industry, public skepticism toward advertisements, and advertisers' own attraction to and dismissal of America—were neither new nor confined to this decade. They persisted into the

1960s, when West Germans continued to assimilate advertising into their everyday lives, and the business world witnessed the demise of old firms that had not taken advantage of advertising.[50] During this decade, ads became more playful and creative, and more about enjoyment—enjoyment not only of the lifestyles depicted in ads but also enjoyment of the ads themselves. The 1960s saw Volkswagen, with its off-beat advertisements, become a favorite car of young people and the counterculture, yet the decade also witnessed attacks by "1968ers" on the advertising industry.[51] Cold war debates about "totalitarian" forms of psychological manipulation gave way to critiques of a so-called consumption terror (*Konsumterror*) that an overly materialist society had generated. Ads were seen as both the cause and the effect of a smug overproduction and overconsumption— a critique that carried over into the 1970s.[52]

These criticisms did not slow expansion and innovation within the industry. Already in the 1960s, for example, marketing had become a staple of company promotion, and the 1970s saw a refinement of marketing and consumer research techniques, such as pre- and posttests to diminish the risk of advertising flops. Television advertising brought increasing profits to companies, and the globalization of the ad industry during the last decades of the twentieth century indicated that "German advertising" was now inextricably bound to technological innovations in a shrinking world.

Despite the gradual adaptation of German companies to international advertising norms, we return to questions of continuity and rupture unique to German history. The years 1945 and 1948 may serve as zero hours in the imagination of the German public, but early advertisers in the Federal Republic of Germany (FRG) shed their pre-1945 traditions only slowly.[53] The Zentralausschuss der Werbewirtschaft (Central Federation of the German Advertising Industry), established in 1949 as an umbrella organization of ad agencies and professionals, easily accepted advertisers who had worked under the Nazi regime's Werberat, some even considering this earlier era as one which prioritized truth and consumer education over profit making.[54] Postwar advertising entrepreneurs like Hanns Brose, for example, saw his work on behalf of the West German economy (such as the 1950s campaign "The Scale," promoting the social market economy) as a continuation of his *Gemeinschaftswerbung* (communal advertising) under National Socialism.[55] Books on branding and marketing generated in the 1930s, such as Hans Domizlaff's *Die Gewinnung des öffentlichen Vertrauens* (Winning the Public Trust), found lasting life in the FRG.[56] Finally, advertisements that were produced during the Third Reich were often reused or updated in the postwar years.[57] These similarities and continuities are significant, as they speak to the persistence of cultural attitudes, business practices, and professional personnel from the Nazi years and before. But they also reveal the durability of advertising as a medium, the messages and techniques of which transcend specific political settings. Despite troubling continuities in ideology and personnel, advertising in the FRG no longer served a fascist state, but a more democratic political and economic order open to continued criticism about its use and abuse of commercial images.

If state-sponsored and commercial advertising thrived in West Germany despite widespread skepticism about its practices, advertising enjoyed a far more precarious position in the German Democratic Republic (GDR). Even though they enjoyed official support through the 1960s, campaigns advocating socialist commodities and lifestyles never successfully dispelled questions about their political effectiveness, economic value, or doctrinal probity. Some leaders of the Socialist Unity Party (SED) championed the use of advertising to regulate consumer demand, while others viewed it as an inherently capitalist invention that had been rendered unnecessary by economic planning.

Throughout the GDR's existence, East German critics of advertising consistently argued that it was nothing more than the business of confusing the desirable with the necessary. Capitalist commercials employed rhetorical deception to generate what one commentator termed "false or illusory needs . . . needs [that] are deformed, manipulated, and in part artificially manufactured to suggest illusions to working people about their real situation in society."[58] Western advertising concocted a shoddy caricature of the public sphere, underwritten by product placement and profit seeking rather than an egalitarian transparency. In addition to its manipulative content, communist theoreticians contended that advertising performed the vital task of stabilizing capitalist economies. Because markets were unable to regulate themselves, the argument ran, producers were forced to supplement them with noneconomic instruments to ease inventory crises and bring demand into equilibrium with supply. According to this view, advertising helped gloss over the contradictions inherent in capitalism by bringing the customer to the commodity.

The East German denigration of capitalist advertising as fraudulent yet essential had much in common with similar critiques articulated by other Soviet-style regimes.[59] What distinguished the GDR from its socialist allies was the SED's evolving response to a class enemy competing for political legitimacy in the same national space. Thus, the SED tried to discredit its capitalist competitors by recasting the GDR as a haven from the invasive commercialism of West Germany. To this end, the party maintained that socialist advertising served a primarily educational role. As an official guide to the planned economy published in 1970 put it, socialist advertisements should "arouse attention and interest," but their didactic content took precedence over their entertainment value or commercial utility; their goal was to "eliminate false ideas and errors," which they were to achieve by being "objective and truthful as well as rational and effective."[60]

Accordingly, East German ads rarely made use of emotional appeals, avoided eroticism, and refrained from exploiting children.[61] The ruling party ran ad campaigns that advocated personal hygiene (such as children's dental care), informed the population about changes in diet (including innovations in nutritional science), and sought to convince citizens to cease engaging in behavior harmful to themselves and others (such as drinking alcohol to excess).[62] Even commercials for consumer goods rarely spotlighted the products themselves, emphasizing instead the communal benefits of the social activities constructed around them.[63] For example, in a feeble attempt to foster gender equality and convince men to help women with household chores, a mail-order catalogue depicted a man standing next to a new washing machine and saying, "Now I'm washing the clothes!" Likewise, when the party finally authorized the use of TV commercials in 1959, it sought to "praise socialist lifestyles" as an alternative to the models of consumption broadcast on West German television that were attracting East Germans westward in droves.[64]

Because the line between consumer advocacy and political propaganda was murky, socialist advertising often aimed less at selling a specific product than at promoting the regime that manufactured it. Window displays, brochures, flyers, and magazine ads often featured communist political slogans alongside consumer goods and messages, such as "The Party Is Right" juxtaposed with an informational blurb like "Wear Shoes That Fit Well."[65] Well into the 1960s, the integration of political ideology into the East German sales pitch reflected the regime's political priorities and simply ignored consumer preferences. East German advertisers frequently made use of rhetorical misdirection to regulate the balance between supply and demand. The SED often tried to divert attention away from shortages by advocating the substitution of scarce for plentiful consumer goods.

At the same time that advertisers were busily perfecting their practices, however, the SED's ideological reservations about advertising reasserted themselves. A few weeks after the Berlin Wall went up in August 1961, for example, the Council of Ministers declared that "advertising and fashion shows contradict socialist society." The council slashed advertising budgets for factories in half and closed the studio that produced commercials for the cinema. Television advertising managed to escape the budget cuts, but the council made clear its suspicion that "the useful effects of many ad campaigns stand in little relation to their costs."[66]

Not two years later, however, advertising was granted a reprieve. In support of his program of economic reform, SED chief Walter Ulbricht demonstrated a willingness to harness capitalist instruments to achieve socialist ends.[67] Paradoxically, moreover, the construction of the Berlin Wall fostered the hope that economic planning would succeed now that it was no longer hampered by Western influence. As one communist official formulated it, advertising would now reach those East Germans "who still harbor doubts about socialism and try to elude ideological influence."[68] As a result, the GDR aired a record number of TV commercials.[69]

As Ulbricht's control over the party weakened toward the end of the 1960s, however, his opponents became bolder in their attempts to eliminate advertising, which they linked to the more troubling aspects of his reforms.[70] A perceived decline in the quality of the ads themselves lent credibility to their objections. By the 1960s, the radical edge of East German advertising, once sustained by links to the Bauhaus and constructivism, had given way to bald imitation of West German products, impoverished in conception as well as execution. Even the trade journal *Neue Werbung* complained about the quality of advertisements copywriters and graphic designers produced. For want of good commercials, East German television simply rebroadcast tried and true ads, even though oversaturation turned off consumers.[71]

By the 1970s, East German advertising was mired in an intellectual and political crisis. Yet it was the struggle for leadership of the party that brought about its actual demise. At the fourteenth plenum of the Central Committee in 1970, Erich Honecker and his supporters launched a full-scale attack on Ulbricht's reforms. Playing on the growing unease over the existence of advertising in the socialist state, Honecker depicted the East German advertising industry as a politically unreliable partner in the struggle against West Germany. Under Ulbricht's stewardship, Honecker alleged, advertising in the GDR had become too much like capitalist advertising.[72]

By the fall of 1971, Honecker was in control of the party apparatus, and he immediately set about dismantling the ad industry. Without warning, the only trade journal for advertisers, *Neue Werbung*, ceased publication.[73] Around the same time, a consensus developed among economic planners that advertising was no longer an effective instrument of economic control. In 1975, the Ministry of Trade and Supply issued a ban in the form of cost-cutting measures that withdrew all financing for advertisements of every kind.[74] In February 1976, East German television broadcast its last commercials, and advertising for consumer goods ceased. The East German state continued to issue information urging East Germans to improve their health as well as propaganda praising socialism and touting East German industry, such as posters and billboards promoting synthetic materials produced in East Germany. For all intents and purposes, however, Honecker's GDR functioned without commercial advertising, which distinguished it even from its communist allies.

As we now know, the political fiat against advertising did not resolve a central problem encountered by every industrialized state, namely, how to balance the needs of industry against the needs of individual consumers. If socialist advertising before 1976 failed to force consumer behavior to conform to the SED's ideological conceptions, eliminating it altogether hardly did away with the reality of East German consumer preferences. And as the revolution of 1989 made clear, the regime's failure to convince East Germans that there was something ennobling about an ascetic consumer model contributed greatly to its collapse.

Leitmotivs and Essays

The essays in this volume consider the processes by which corporate communications have been generated and the strikingly different contexts in which advertising decisions have been made in Germany throughout the twentieth century. Rather than focusing on consumers and patterns of consumption, the essays are distinguished by a shift in perspective toward the producers of product promotion. The contributors emphasize that in their search for profits, company owners, executives, and advertisers often had the most to gain in understanding the consumer market and, by extension, the importance of selling products, lifestyles, and ideologies. In their use of corporate sources, these essays have opened up the venerable topic of production along a new line of inquiry.

Along with this shift in narrative focus, moreover, has come a new methodological approach. Rather than treating "culture" and "business" as distinct, the essays bring the two together to provide a more complete context for understanding the advertising images, the motivations for producing them, and the intellectual and political discourses that surrounded them. Kevin Repp's and Corey Ross's essays, in examining professional advertising journals in Wilhelmine and Weimar Germany, remind us that advertising was not only a business practice, but also an artistic enterprise and a cultural lightning rod that drew together designers, social critics, and intellectuals, all of whom closely studied mass consumer culture, the effects of American business models, and the ethical consequences of advertising. Repp analyzes the growing fascination with racialized discourse in the Wilhelmine period, while Ross traces the growing influence of the transatlantic cultural exchange on the look and content of German advertisements.

Holm Friebe also draws our attention to the business and intellectual paradigms that informed advertising during the Weimar and Nazi periods. By examining the understudied figure of Hans Domizlaff, whose ideas about branding continue to influence German advertisers, Friebe shows how the practical world of selling products was always framed by cultural debates about mass psychology and political propaganda. Like Friebe's piece, Jeff Schutts's essay on Coca-Cola under the Nazis also demonstrates clearly how advertisers' work in the public sphere was in the service of both corporate and political persuasion. The Nazis introduced at once a communitarian and an ethnically exclusive vision of advertising's role in society, and Schutts explores the impact of this vision through the racial politics of the soft drink's marketing strategies.

Shifting to the democratic setting of the FRG, Elizabeth Heineman and Guillaume de Syon also bring unique corporate perspectives to larger political and cultural themes. In her study of erotica entrepreneur Beate Uhse, Heineman reveals the business strategies and political context that informed the controversial yet profitable trade in sex aids in postwar West Germany. We learn who the consumers of sex and hygiene products were, and we also discover how much sales depended on Uhse's biography as a former World War II pilot, family woman, and sexual reformer. Meanwhile, de Syon traces the rebirth of airline travel after World War II in the FRG and explores the particular challenges Lufthansa faced as it sought to lure holiday and business travelers back to a country deeply associated with mass murder.

As these essays demonstrate, the business of production and advertising was never far from politics — and, by extension, the state. To some degree, the omnipresence of the state in this volume reflects Germany's long tradition of workers and producers looking to the government to protect their interests or, alternatively, being forced into political servitude. Accordingly, a number of essays in this volume directly reveal how thin the boundaries were between commercial promotion and state propaganda. Michael Imort demonstrates how the social

Darwinian celebration of strength and the denigration of racial weakness in the Third Reich permeated advertisements themselves, in this case in journals aimed at foresters responsible for maintaining "healthy" forests. In her study of the Nazi party's Strength through Joy leisure travel programs, Shelley Baranowski demonstrates this cross-fertilization between advertisements and propaganda through the state's explicit use of corporate-style product promotion to sell a racially exclusive community to working-class and middle-class vacationers. In fact, all of the essays on the Nazi period reveal a mutually reinforcing cooperation between the state, the party, and the private sector in the creation of the Volksgemeinschaft.

The use of state power to influence the relationship between consumer behavior and citizenship played a key role in the GDR, as Anne Kaminsky and Greg Castillo reveal in their respective pieces. Despite its emphasis on class rather than race, the SED also harnessed advertising to realize its vision of an egalitarian consumer utopia. In her essay on advertising under Ulbricht, Kaminsky demonstrates that promoting consumer products was always subordinated to the aim of protecting the GDR's economic resources, even when this led to irrational and abrupt shifts in policy. From the vantage point of architectural history, Castillo traces the sedulously organized public relations campaign as well as the carefully calibrated exercise of coercion that accompanied the construction of a model socialist neighborhood in East Berlin, the Stalinallee. While Kaminsky and Castillo reveal the limits of communist control, Robert P. Stephens draws our attention to constraints on state power in West Germany. His discussion of federal anti-drug campaigns and the use of youth-oriented advertising reveals how ideological continuities and a lack of understanding of popular culture inhibited government attempts to craft compelling arguments against nonconforming consumer behavior.

As these essays reveal, Germany's dictatorships and democracies experienced varying degrees of success in mobilizing industry and consumers behind their ideological goals. While the Nazi state succeeded largely in turning these power blocs into conscripts for its war against Jews and "asocials," the East German state never enjoyed the same degree of authority with its citizenry. With these two dictatorships as models to discard, West German manufacturers and the government nominally rejected any coercive means of selling images, products, and lifestyles. But political messages and corporate branding together bred a form of social conformity that many observers saw as oppressive and, indeed, as a more subtle form of coercion.

Remarkably, the close relationship between the state and advertising remained largely uncontested despite the succession of failed political regimes. In fact, surprising continuities lurk beneath Germany's exceptional institutional discontinuities. While Corey Ross is the most ambitious in his periodization, calling into question the 1933 boundary by exploring the interwar period, each of the essays reveals the persistence of long-term trends against a background of social and political upheaval. In the book's final essay, Rainer Gries argues, for example, that the phenomenon of self-service shopping, which removed the sales staff from the sales pitch starting in the 1950s, straddled the ideological oppositions of capitalism and communism. In the name of economic rationality and consumer choice, West as well as East German stores began constructing the retail experience around a more direct engagement between customer and product that eventually transformed retail spaces themselves. Whether it was the strong state presence, the ambivalence toward advertising, or the persistence of tropes of "German" quality, these essays invite the reader to consider the fragility of Germany's watershed years: 1914, 1918, 1933, 1945, 1949, and 1989. Across borders and time periods, Germans remained conflicted about advertising, representing it alternately as a medium for artistic expression and a repository of modern sensibilities or as an affront to good taste and, worse, an insidious threat to Germany's cultural autonomy. As a result, the line between acceptable sales practices and crass "American materialism" was never very clear. Despite the ideological and ethical uncertainty that always surrounded advertising, however, the protean qualities of this medium endowed product promotion with a striking durability. Racialized and gendered images, for example, exhibit a stubborn persistence through Germany's advertising history. Colonialist stereotypes about "cleansing" Africans of their Africanness appeared in advertisements after Germany was stripped of its colonies and again into the 1930s.[75] Even after the demise of Nazism, West German producers continued to make use of racialized branding, as with the popular Negerkuss (Negro Kiss) chocolate marshmallow. And East German industry, despite its supposed internationalism, touted health tonics with ape-like caricatures of blacks.

Notwithstanding the peculiarities of German history, marked as they are by a particularly harrowing experience with authoritarian states, Germany nevertheless partook of a more general trend that emerged in industrialized nations over the course of the twentieth century. Simply stated, this trend entailed a drive to collapse the distance between the product and the purchaser through product promotion. German advertisers and companies always operated in a transnational setting in the twentieth century, and the globalization of advertising is proceeding apace in this new century.[76] But there are still ways in which German advertisers speak to distinct developments in the country's national history. For example, companies exploit East Germans' memories of full employment and a supposed transparency of consumer choice by repackaging their desire to escape from the grim present of economic decline and West German cultural ascendancy, selling "Ostalgia" by slapping communist-era labels on jars of capitalist-era marmalade.

Even while advertising *messages* may tap into distinctly national histories and mentalities, the medium itself faces challenges that transcend national boundaries. How do companies adapt to changing media technologies, which are increasingly marginalizing traditional print ads and television commercials? In response to this question, manufacturers are largely relying on "marketing" as a broad category, leading to the outright disappearance and/or consolidation of famous advertising agencies from the past century.[77] It is also leading to continued innovations in product promotion. For example, companies have begun to offer volunteers free samples of consumer goods, such as specialty foods and electronic devices, if the person agrees to "consume" or "talk up" the product in front of strangers or even friends, who remain unaware that their companion is surreptitiously inserting a sales pitch into their intimate banter.

This newest incarnation of an older idea — the "human being as ad" — is complemented by technological developments. For example, retailers are increasingly adopting radio frequency identification (RFID) tags, which, in contrast to UPC barcodes, can store information about a specific product that is easily retrieved at a distance, and which allows a retailer to restock shelves in a more rational and economical manner, prevent theft, and collect data on local purchasing patterns. The ease of data collection and the rather frightening prospect of using RFID devices to collect information on home use of these products, however, returns us to the familiar theme of the intrusiveness of the market.

Indeed, if the technologies and media have changed, the same questions about the relation between morality and merchandise remain. Is it possible to regulate the ethical uses of new advertising and marketing media? How might advertising be kept from exerting undo influence over a person? Europeans have been tackling such questions for many years, but given the need to remain competitive in the face of technological innovation and ever-expanding markets, the European Union has recently revoked its ban on product placement. The reality of global economic competition is muffling ethical reservations about the consequences of new advertising practices, changing the justifications put forth by the industry, and altering the rhetoric that once defined corporate communication.

In the case of the FRG, the "Made in Germany" quality stamp has lost some of its power as a marketing device. German corporations today are challenged to move beyond such nationalist tropes from the past century. But this is not easy. Throughout Germany's turbulent twentieth century, advertising—despite its critics—was often heralded as a force of both modernization and economic opportunity, inspiring consumers and producers alike. What remains to be seen, however, is whether the very idea of "selling modernity" is also destined to become an anachronism in a transnational, postmodern age.

Notes

1. Wilhelm Vershofen, "Für und gegen Werbung," *Wirtschaft und Werbung* 13, no. 3 (December 1959): 899–900.
2. www.itfacts.biz (accessed 15 April 2005).
3. See, e.g., Ludwig Erhard, "Marktwirtschaft und Werbung gehören entrennbar zusammen," *Wirtschaft und Werbung* 6, no. 12 (1952): 327–328. For more recent examples of this emancipatory view of advertising, see the essays and interviews in Kellner, Kurth, and Lippert, eds., *1945–1995: 50 Jahre Werbung in Deutschland.*
4. Marchand, *Advertising the American Dream*, xvi.
5. See Daunton and Hilton, *The Politics of Consumption*; Strasser, McGovern, and Judt, *Getting and Spending*; W. König, *Geschichte der Konsumgesellschaft*; Siegrist, Kaelbe, and Kocka, *Europäische Konsumgeschichte*; and Trentmann, "Beyond Consumerism." On consumption in Germany, see Carter, *How German Is She?*; Loehlin, *From Rugs to Riches*; Crew, *Consuming Germany in the Cold War*; Landsman, *Dictatorship and Demand*; and Confino and Koshar, "Régimes of Consumer Culture." On consumption in Britain and the United States, see Cohen, *A Consumers' Republic*; Hale, *Making Whiteness*; and McClintock, *Imperial Leather*.
6. For examples, see Ross, "Mass Politics and the Techniques of Leadership"; Betts, *The Authority of Everyday Objects*; and Julia Sneeringer, "The Shopper as Voter: Women, Advertising, and Politics in Post-inflation Germany," *German Studies Review* 27, no. 3 (October 2004): 476–501.
7. Notably absent from our discussion are radio and film advertisements—and for the later period, television spots.
8. See Kleinschmidt and Triebel, eds., *Marketing*; on PR in the United States, see Ewen, *PR! A Social History of Spin*; Marchand, *Creating the Corporate Soul*. For Germany, see Heinelt, "PR-Päpste."
9. For two introductions to this vast theme of German-American cultural perceptions, see Nolan, *Visions of Modernity*; Fehrenbach and Poiger, *Transactions, Transgressions, Transformations.*
10. For introductions to the history of American advertising, see Ewen, *Captains of Consciousness*; and Laird, *Advertising Progress.*
11. See, e.g., Lütdke, Marssolek, and von Saldern, *Amerikanisierung.*

12. Jay, *The Dialectical Imagination*, 216; Wiggershaus, *The Frankfurt School*, 344.

13. From promotional blurbs on page 1 of Packard, *The Hidden Persuaders*. On Packard, see Horowitz, *Anxieties*, 108–120.

14. Dichter, *The Strategy of Desire*, xxi. On Ernest Dichter, see Horowitz, *Anxieties*, 48–74. For more on how these debates played out in Britain, see Schwarzkopf, "They Do It with Mirrors."

15. See Gries, Ilgen, and Schindelbeck, *"Ins Gehirn der Masse kriechen!"*

16. De Grazia, *Irresistible Empire*, 153.

17. See the GHI conference papers on the Web, *The American Impact on Western Europe: Americanization and Westernization in Transatlantic Perspective*, www.ghi-dc.org (accessed 24 October 2005).

18. Reinhardt, *Von der Reklame zum Marketing*, 27.

19. For more on the Werkbund and the history of graphic design in Germany in the twentieth century, see Aynsley, *Graphic Design in Germany*.

20. For example, most graphic designers still referred to themselves as *Kunstmaler*, and it wasn't until 1913 that one journal began using the unwieldy title *Reklamekunstgewerbler*. See Lamberty, *Reklame in Deutschland*, 273–274.

21. Ibid., 266–267, 307.

22. Ibid., 308–309. As a result of this internal debate, Christiane Lamberty notes there was little to no training or literature to be found on the subject before 1910. The course offerings of the (mostly private) schools that did begin to emerge in the years preceding World War I certainly did not amount to the kind of comprehensive professional training some practitioners desired. Ibid., 271.

23. Ward, *Weimar Surfaces*, 93.

24. On German propaganda during World War I, see, among others, Welch, "Mobilizing the Masses."

25. Ward, *Weimar Surfaces*, 95.

26. Reinhardt, *Von der Reklame zum Marketing*, 33.

27. See Janet Ward's discussion of Weimar's electric advertising in chapter 2 of *Weimar Surfaces*. This statistic from 1928 comes from p. 102.

28. Reinhardt, *Von der Reklame zum Marketing*, 91–95.

29. Knapp, *Reklame, Propaganda, Werbung*, 12–14.

30. This was the slogan of the International Advertising Association, Berlin 1929. See ibid.

31. In this collection *Volksgemeinschaft* has been translated both as racial community and national community; both are acceptable.

32. Jarausch and Geyer, *Shattered Pasts*, 294–295. See also Nancy Reagin, "Marktordnung and Autarkic Housekeeping: Housewives and Private Consumption under the Third Reich, 1936–1939," *German History* 19, no. 2 (2001): 162–184.

33. For lists of those excluded from practice as well as statistics concerning the numbers of those attending the new Reichswerbeschule, see *Ruf der Werbung: Vertrauliche Mitteilungen für die Mitglieder der Reichsfachschaft Deutscher Werbefachleute*—NSRDW, vol. 13 (Berlin, 1937). On the opening of the Reichswerbeschule, see *Die deutsche Werbung*, July 1936, 666.

34. Kellner et al., *50 Jahre Werbung*, 33.

35. For other products that did the same, see ibid., 45; on the return of Persil, see Felden-kirchen and Hilger, *Menschen und Marken*, 124–125.

36. Schindelbeck and Ilgen, *"Haste Was, Biste Was!"*

37. On advertising in the immediate postwar period, see Wildt, *Am Beginn der Konsumgesell-schaft*, 206–211.

38. Kriegeskorte, *Werbung in Deutschland 1945–1965*.

39. Schenk, "Producing to Consume Becomes Consuming to Produce," 581–586.

40. On women, gender, and consumption in West Germany, see Carter, *How German Is She?*

41. See Moeller, *Protecting Motherhood*.

42. Breward, *The Hidden Consumer*.

43. Schröter, "Die Amerikanisierung der Werbung in der Bundesrepublik Deutschland," 101.

44. De Grazia, *Irresistible Empire*, 370.

45. On J. Walter Thompson's return to West Germany, see Wiesen, "Miracles for Sale," 151–178; de Grazia, *Irresistible Empire*, 234–235. On full-service ad agencies, see Schug, "Von *Newspaper space salesman* zur integrierten Kommunkationsagentur," 5–25; Schwarzkopf, "Advertising, Mass Democracy and Consumer Culture in Britain, 1919–1951."

46. For a collection of papers on Aktion Gemeinsinn, see "Organisations — Aktion Gemein-sinn, 1961 Jan–1963 Dec, A-R," Box 12, Peter Gilow Papers, General Correspondence, in John W. Hartman Center for Sales, Advertising, and Marketing History, J. Walter Thompson Company Archives, Frankfurt Office Records, Duke University, Durham, N.C. See also the specific campaign binders in the Aktion Gemeinsinn main office in Bonn.

47. Schröter, "Die Amerikanisierung der Werbung."

48. See, e.g., A. Wannamacher, "Werbung für die Werbung," *Graphik* 1, no. 11 (1949): 521–526.

49. For a good example of an autobiography in this vein, see Damrow, *Ich war kein geheimer Verführer*. See also the interviews of advertisers in Kellner et al., *50 Jahre Werbung*.

50. For example, Rheila-Perlen, Wybert-Pastilllen, and Suwa were no longer in existence. See Kellner et al., *50 Jahre Werbung*, 64.

51. On Volkswagen ads in the 1960s, see ibid., 69.

52. Axel Schildt and Arnold Sywottek, "'Reconstruction' and 'Modernization': West Ger-man Social History During the 1950s," in Moeller, *West Germany under Construction*, 426.

53. On pre- and post-1945 continuities, see Berghoff, "'Times Change and We Change with Them,'" 128–147.

54. Rücker, *Wirtschaftswerbung unter den Nationalsozialismus*, 359.

55. Schindelbeck, "'Asbach Uralt' und 'Soziale Marktwirtschaft,'" 235–252.

56. Hans Domizlaff, *Die Gewinnung des öffentlichen Vertrauens. Ein Lehrbuch der Markentechnik*, 2nd ed. (1951). The book was first published in 1939, and the most recent edition is 1982. See Holm Friebe's contribution in this volume.

57. For example, the Matheus Müller German champagne company first published an advertisement of an elegant modern woman raising her glass of MM Sekt in 1941. The image was slightly retooled in 1952 and used steadily until the mid-1960s. For more information, see the company's website, www.mm-extra.de (accessed 23 October 2005).

58. Horst Seeger, ed., *Lexikon der Wirtschaft. Volkswirtschaftsplanung* (East Berlin: Verlag die Wirtschaft, 1980), 86–87. For more on Marx's conceptualization of need, see Heller, *The Theory of Need in Marx*. For more on the SED's application of the category of need to the production and distribution of consumer goods, see Hilgenberg, *Bedarfs- und Marktforschung in der DDR*. For more on the official approach to consumerism in the GDR in the 1960s, see I. Merkel, *Utopie und Bedürfnis*, and Landsman, *Dictatorship and Demand*. On the Honecker period, see Stitziel, *Fashioning Socialism*, and Zatlin, "The Vehicle of Desire."

59. For the Yugoslavian example, see Patterson, "Truth Half Told," 179–225.

60. Hans Borchert, ed., *Lexikon der Wirtschaft. Industrie* (East Berlin: Verlag die Wirtschaft, 1970), 866.

61. See the example in Andreas Hergeth, "'Wenn die Leute lachen, sind sie bereit zu kaufen': Ein Interview mit Isabella-Margarete von Oettingen, Autorin und Regisseurin bei ttt," in Neue Gesellschaft für bildende Kunst, *Wunderwirtschaft*, 79.

62. Ibid.

63. Some planners criticized this emphasis as insufficiently educational. See Anneliese Albrecht and Hans Dietrich, "Fernsehwerbung weist Disproportionen auf," *Die Wirtschaft*, 12 December 1968, 15.

64. *Neues Deutschland*, 14 December 1959.

65. "Die Partei hat Recht" and "Trag fussgerechtes Schuhwerk." See, e.g., Kaminsky, *Kaufrausch*, 61, 114–115.

66. DY30, IV 2/610/33, p. 2, and letter to Ulbricht, 1 February 1962, 155, DY30, IV 2/610/34, Stiftung Archiv Parteien und Massenorganisationen der Deutschen Demokratischen Republik im Bundesarchiv [hereafter SAPMO-BA].

67. Baylis, *Technical Intelligence and the East German Elite*, 221–225; Kopstein, *The Politics of Economic Decline in East Germany*, 45–46, 50; Lavigne, *The Socialist Economies of the Soviet Union and Europe*, 57–58, 223–290; Alan H. Smith, *The Planned Economies of Eastern Europe*, 54–80; and Steiner, *Die DDR-Wirtschaftsreform der sechziger Jahre*, 52–55.

68. Anneliese Albrecht, "Die Funktion und Aufgaben der Werbung auf dem Konsumbinnenmarkt, die Verantwortung der einzelnen Organe bei der Lösung dieser Aufgaben und die Vorbereitung und Durchführung der Werbemaßnahmen," *MIB* 3 (1963): 8, cited in I. Merkel, *Utopie und Bedürfnis*, 220.

69. Nevertheless, commercial programming still remained surprisingly modest, rising from a mere six hours' worth of TV ads broadcast for the entire year of 1959 to 109 hours aired in 1969. Tippach-Schneider, "Moderner Einkauf," 70.

70. Officials at the Ministry for Trade and Supply, for example, ordered a halt in 1969 to all ads for consumer goods sold in the upscale Exquisit stores. I. Merkel, *Utopie und Bedürfnis*, 222.

71. For a later example, see Fred Tamme, "Ausnahmen bestätigen die Regel," *Neue Werbung*,

February 1972, 39. It is worth noting that the records of the only East German ad agency, DEWAG (Deutsche Werbe- und Anzeigengesellschaft), are closed to the public for reasons that remain unclear. This fact alone complicates attempts to reconstruct the history of advertising in the GDR, and the internal politics of the agency in particular.

72. See the stenographic notes in IV A2/2032/50, DY30, SAPMO-BA.

73. Because the archives are closed, it is unclear exactly what happened at DEWAG.

74. Anordnung zum sparsamen Einsatz materieller und finanzieller Fonds für Werbung und Repräsentation vom 23.1.1975, Anweisung Nr. 21/1975 of the Ministry of Trade and Supply, 26 June 1975. This decree was based on a decision taken by the Council of Ministers in February 1975. It is worth noting that it did allow for exceptions in extreme cases, such as when production mishaps led to a surplus of a given item and economic officials wanted to sell it off. By the 1980s, however, when Honecker's economic policies undermined the GDR's finances and further disrupted production, shortages were increasingly common. And if economic planners had learned anything, promoting products that did not exist was a sure-fire way of transforming economic into political discontent.

75. The Henkel corporation mobilized colonialist stereotypes of African savages cleansing themselves of their blackness by bathing in or drinking Henkel detergents. See cartoon in Paul Mundhenke, "Wirkungsgrenzen der Markenartikel-Insertion und deren Beurteilung durch den Vertreter," *Blätter vom Hause* 18, no. 1 (January 1938): 7–13. See also Ciarlo, "Rasse konsumieren," 135–179. Germany was not the only society that employed racial stereotypes in its advertising. See also Hale, *Making Whiteness*; McClintock, *Imperial Leather*; Richards, *The Commodity Culture of Victorian England*; Harp, *Marketing Michelin*; and Pinkus, *Bodily Regimes*.

76. They also must respond specifically to European Union regulations and restrictions on, for example, tobacco advertising, which is prohibited on television.

77. Stuart Elliott, "Advertisers Want Something Different," *New York Times*, 23 May 2005.

1
—
KEVIN REPP

MARKETING, MODERNITY, AND

"THE GERMAN PEOPLE'S SOUL"

Advertising and Its Enemies in Late Imperial

Germany, 1896–1914

The German advertising specialist has to know the German people's soul better—than the advertisements in American humor magazines.

—Ernst Growald, "Auguren-Sprüche"

Advertising had come a long way, proclaimed the director of Hollerbaum und
Schmidt, Berlin's premiere publisher of poster art, as he opened the latest
show of retail displays and modern graphic design at the Zoological Garden Exhibition Halls in February 1908. Once shunned due to a "reputation for unsound-
ness," the industry had worked hard in the past two decades to overcome German cultural prejudices that had only been sharpened by an uncritical adoption
of garish foreign models in the early days. "Unrelentingly one sought at that
time for new means of propaganda, and with just as much dexterity as energy
the German business world has understood how to make art and technical skill,
science and literature, subservient to its purposes," Growald proudly declared—
and without undermining German *Kultur* in the least.[1] On the contrary: "With
a firm gaze the applied arts have seized hold of the advantages that the tasteful
outfitting of shops offered them, and the painter and the sculptor know just the
same that they can go hand in hand with commerce and find material advantages

in this way, without needing to become untrue to their artistic ideals." As a result, modern advertising had won acceptance as a legitimate practice not only among members of the respected business community, but also from guardians of the nation's cultural heritage as well. Supervised by Professor Bruno Paul, students from the Royal School of Applied Arts had thus decorated the booths for the Exhibition, which brought together the work of more than 120 poster artists—"among them names like Döpler t[he] Y[ounger], Ernst Neumann, Julius Klinger, Lucian Bernhard"—much of it on loan from public museums or private connoisseurs such as the art critic Paul Westheim (whose collection resides at the core of the Berlin Art Library's holding of historical posters today). Mainstays of the local and national economy, AEG and Siemens, demonstrated their support with a joint exhibit on advances in the subtle and effective illumination of shop windows, while the Alliance of Berlin Specialty Stores underscored the constructive nature of this relationship on the evening after the opening with lectures on "Physics in the Service of Advertising" and "Technology in the Service of Businesses." The keynote address, however, highlighted the distance modern advertising professionals still felt the need to place between themselves and the crass hucksterism of P. T. Barnum, which many Germans continued to associate with the industry: "Science in the Fight against Crime."[2]

Far from signaling the happy acceptance of advertising as part and parcel of the "German people's soul," Growald's optimistic pronouncements in fact sought to deflect gathering resistance to what the public widely perceived to be an unhealthy, alien—and primarily American—intrusion. Like the pretentious art-show atmosphere, with critics, catalogues, and juried competition, the buoyant mantra of symbiosis between the worlds of commerce and Kultur, endlessly repeated by Growald, Westheim, Klinger, and others at the 1908 Exhibition, had emerged from years of confrontation as a defensive strategy consciously designed to "tame" the brazen Otherness of commercial modernity by rendering it in idioms suited to the particular social, cultural, and aesthetic sensibilities of a German audience. "American advertising is good for America, but not for Germany," Growald warned potential clients at the show. Or, as he put it rather more vividly a few years later, in America the advertisement could "run around all naughty and naked; in Germany she has to be decently draped in a nice little cloak."[3] At times bitter, at times playful, the engagement between advertising and its enemies in late Imperial Germany had certainly been productive. Indeed, the efforts of Wilhelmine advertisers to soothe fears of rampant "Americanization" evoked powerful visions of a Symbolist-inspired aesthetic and the "Gothic" modern that represented significant breakthroughs in the history of graphic design and commercial architecture at the beginning of the twentieth century. But by 1908 these strategies of appeasement were beginning to wear thin. Emboldened by success, and stung by campaigns that resulted in punitive taxes, police harassment, and ordinances against the "disfigurement" of urban and rural landscapes by advertising, spokesmen for the industry became increasingly resentful of the scorn with which even supposed friends and allies continued to treat the profession. Already discernible beneath the harmonious rhetoric in Growald's catalogue, this defiance burst into angry debates over the respective value of art and advertising that made headlines within weeks after the exhibition closed. As the conflict escalated, some in the business soon declared it was time to throw off the "mask of culture" once and for all.[4]

The clashes over advertising and art spilled out into many different arenas at the beginning of the twentieth century—economic and political, aesthetic and cultural—as the advent of commercial modernity directly touched on the material interests of many competing groups in Wilhelmine society at the same time that it visibly transformed the landscapes of German towns and cities. In order to explore these complex ramifications, I focus on two manifestations of fin de siècle commercial culture that seemed to gather the various elements of contention involved in these debates around particular sites laden with special significance in the eyes of contemporaries: the department store and the advertising poster. Among the most powerful motors behind the rapid expansion of the German advertising industry, department stores quickly became a concrete symbol of the new commercial order on many levels, evoking opposition from conservatives and the small shopkeepers and artisans of the *Mittelstand* as well as the cultural opponents of Americanization. At the same time, however, these conflicts produced one of the first and most successful attempts to "tame" commercial modernity for German consumption: the modern Gothic architecture of the Wertheim Department Store designed by Alfred Messel in Berlin. The successful melding of traditional cultural sensibilities and modern commercial prowess in Messel's Wertheim served as a model for the spiritualized *Sachlichkeit* advertising professionals like Growald promoted as a way to assuage the qualms of the German soul in 1908. Focusing on the so-called *Sachplakat*, or "object poster," the second part of the essay examines conflicts between advocates of the fine and applied arts that emerged from this solution, generating an increasingly visceral contempt for aestheticism on the part of advertisers and graphic artists, which in many ways anticipated the avant-garde's revolt against *l'art pour l'art* and the cult of creative genius in the epoch of high modernism that followed the First World War.

Wertheim, Tietz, and the "Idea of the Department Store"

The predicament advertisers faced could easily be seen at the grand opening of Tietz's Department Store on Leipziger Straße in Berlin, which took place the same year the Greatest Show on Earth came to town, in September 1900.[5] After pouring 3.5 million marks into the construction of the enormous, "hyper-modern," glass-and-steel emporium—instantly nicknamed "The Aquarium" by smirking locals—the ill-advised owner, Oskar Tietz, compounded his error by bringing in an entire team of American advertising consultants to prepare the city for what he hoped would be an outstanding entrepreneurial debut in the imperial capital. A barrage of press releases, posters, and publicity stunts finally culminated with a pompous opening-day address, followed by a "lighting rehearsal" intended to astonish the assembled crowds with the spectacle of the magnificent glass mansion illuminated from within by night. The result was a stream of public ridicule and denunciations so intense that Tietz's family worried for months that the venture was bound to end in bankruptcy.[6] "It's not that the Berliner is too conservative for it. On the contrary. He gladly takes to the foreign when it appeals to him. But things like American advertising are distaste-ful to him from the start," one critic sourly observed in Maximilian Harden's *Future* magazine, a review of culture and politics that was widely read by both established elites and young and struggling avant-garde artists at the fin de siècle. "Tietz's advertising was completely lacking in that discreet finesse that precisely knows the limits within which it is effective without giving offense. The public was fed up with reading the name Tietz in every tram coupé and running across Tietz automobile-wagons that had been sent out on advertising rides in every part of the city."[7] While the fate of the enterprise hung in the balance, Tietz's major competitor, Wertheim, only benefited from the public relations disaster, as its advertising was soon held up as a model of tact and restraint, favorably contrasted with the tawdry "American" rival just down the street.

The intense hostility of this response bespoke more than injured taste on the part of Berlin's overly refined critics. Five years earlier, angry mobs had resorted to violence, hurling stones, smashing display windows, and assaulting female clerks at Tietz's store in Munich, until the military was called in to suppress the outbreak, which undoubtedly owed much to the anti-Semitic slogans used to rile up shopkeepers and artisans against unwelcome competition from "outsiders."[8]

1. The brash advertising of Wertheim's competitor Tietz, mid-1890s.

Nor was Wertheim immune from this kind of agitation. Like Tietz, the Wertheim family had risen rapidly from humble beginnings as Jewish shopkeepers in the province (both started out in the small port city of Stralsund), borrowing models of large-scale commercial retail imported from abroad to become the owners of a nationwide chain of department stores by the turn of the century. Still new to German shoppers at the time, the department store was an unfamiliar sight, even in big cities, and at first the Wertheims had to fight hard to dissociate themselves from the image of the "junk bazaars," sprawling outgrowths of uncontrolled traffic in wholesale goods, often of ill repute, which, alongside consumer cooperatives, represented the only alternative to small shops for most customers.[9] Soon, however, it became apparent that the advantages of scale combined with organizational efficiency and convenience made for something qualitatively different, a juggernaut of modern consumer capitalism that threatened traditional retail with significant — many believed "unfair" — competition. If Wertheim had a reputation for tact and restraint, it was because the firm had learned to keep a low profile in order to avoid attacks from the ever-vigilant champions of small business. When the department store began advertising its status as official supplier to the Court of Wilhelm II, for instance, newspapers like *The State Citizen* and *Truth* burst out with polemics so vile that Georg Wertheim privately let it be known that he would forgo the honor of being named commercial councilor in order to avoid further attacks in the anti-Semitic press. "The Royal State Government, which would nominate Mr. Wertheim for a distinction because, say, he sacrificed 50,000 marks [in charitable donations], which with his gigantic income is a bagatelle, would *flat out mock the industrious* Mittelstand *and slap itself in the face.*"[10]

Claiming to represent the true strength and heritage of the national economy, the small shopkeepers and artisans of "the industrious Mittelstand" appealed to the state for help on many occasions in what to them seemed to be a life-and-death struggle with the large-scale structures of commercial modernity. After a legislative campaign culminated in new regulations against "unfair competition" and a nationwide tax on advertising in the mid-1890s, the movement had next trained its sights on the department store, which it branded a mortal threat to "the general welfare." At its eighth annual congress, held in October 1898, the Alliance of German Craft Associations warned "that the spread of department bazaars has made further advances, that the peril of great numbers of entirely justified livelihoods in the industrious and commercial Mittelstand being sucked dry has thereby lurched into precarious proximity." It was "urgently necessary to move against this peril as quickly as possible," the resolution advised: "The assembly, for reasons of the general welfare, especially for the preservation of a vigorous class of middling and smaller artisanry, commerce, and industry, considers an effective taxation of the large department stores to be an urgent demand."[11] The notion that a traditional way of life, indeed, the future of the entire social order was at stake only gained ground in intense public debates over the next few years, particularly after the younger generation of national economists hailed department stores and advertising as steps toward an increasingly rationalized and efficient system for the distribution of mass-produced consumer goods, which would ultimately lead Germany out of the age of late capitalism and into a socialist economy in the coming century. "Very small, ugly, wretched, crummy little retailers are seen in ever smaller numbers, and we don't *want* to see them any more," a young Werner Sombart defiantly announced at the 1899 congress of the Association for Social Policy, brashly assailing the older generation for its support of protective legislation for the Mittelstand. "From the consumer standpoint we are striving for a new configuration of the street's image. We want to have magnificent stores in our cities."[12] On the opposite side, a local shopkeeper from Breslau, where the conference was held, bitterly complained that he was being ruined by mass retail and defended the traditional German way of doing business. "I can't accept the principles that the large department stores apply," he cried. "You won't hold it against a trusty businessman from the good old days, either, if he doesn't do such repulsive advertising as the department stores do, and no one else will claim that that kind of advertising is a good quality for an honest businessman."[13]

Strangely, perhaps, high-ranking officials in the Prussian state government were inclined to take the department store's side. "There is in fact a national-economic viewpoint—and we're bumping up against it, consciously or unconsciously; in part it is even within ourselves—which is of the opinion that concentration of enterprise, reduction of merchandise costs, escalation of gross revenues is always the greatest progress a society can make," Minister of Finances and the Interior Johannes Miquel admitted to cheers of "Hear, hear!" on the Left in the Prussian House of Deputies, as he reluctantly presented a government bill calling for punitive taxes on department stores in February 1900.[14] Yet despite his own sympathy for the progressive standpoint, the minister had to submit to the noisy demands of the Mittelstand and their conservative allies in government: only the Social Democrats and a handful of Left Liberals held out against the bill, which easily passed through parliament to become the law of the land on January 1, 1901.[15] While the so-called Lex Wertheim failed to achieve its goal of "strangling" the life out of department stores with big advertising budgets, it set the tone for more than a decade of polemics and political campaigns that galvanized both sides in the struggle over large-scale retail. Joined by the League of German Agrarians, the German Artisans' Congress, Catholic Commercial Associations, and other groups resisting (or claiming to resist) the transition to modern capitalist society, the Mittelstand continued to petition the state for higher taxes on both department stores and advertising as well as harsher penalties for engaging in "unfair competition."[16] Oskar Tietz took the initiative on the other side, together with the progressive economist Julius Wernicke, founding an Association of German Department and Retail Stores with an annual operating budget of 60,000 marks and its own professional journal, *The Outfitter*, edited by one of the leading lights of the Wilhelmine reform milieu.[17]

Meanwhile, the menace of commercial invasion assumed more definite contours, as alarmist headlines about "the American Peril" began circulating in German newspapers. Inextricably entangled in the ongoing controversy over the direction the country's social and economic development seemed to be going, panic over the American Peril spread quickly in 1902, after the Berlin banker Ludwig Max Goldberger returned from a government-sponsored trip to the United States gushing about the power and vitality of the new economic structures—industrial cartels, but also department stores, advertising drives, skyscrapers, and other urban forms of organized big capital—that were now taking root in "the land of unlimited possibilities."[18] While many on the progressive and even Social Democratic side shared Goldberger's enthusiasm for the "autocratic synthesis" and "regimentalization" of American economic life, others responded with horror at the banker's suggestion that Germany strive to catch up with the new competitor if it was not to fall hopelessly behind in the age of commercial modernity. "Would this sort of Americanization of the Old World not be an outright regression of culture?" one of the leading voices in the anti–department store movement, Paul Dehn, insisted in his 1904 polemic, *Neologisms of the World Economy*. "But individual taste in the Old World is not nearly as repressed as in the New, where fashion, advertising, and last but not least the industrial spirit have led the populace to an astonishing homogeneity in the claims and needs of taste and demand," he hastened to assure his readers, with mocking superiority.[19]

Culture indeed lay at the heart of the matter for many of Dehn's readers, who resisted mass marketing and Americanization not so much for economic as for aesthetic reasons. The cultivation of individual taste was above all sacrosanct for the mandarin elites of the educated middle classes, the *Bildungsbürgertum*, whose privileged social position depended on maintaining the value of cultural capital acquired in the traditional rite of passage through Germany's prestigious institutions of higher learning, the Gymnasium and the university.[20] Such invested interest in the disinterestedness of aesthetic Kultur made the prospect of inundation by a commodified, alien, and materialistic mass culture painful to contemplate even for those who were ready to consign the Mittelstand to the dustbin of history with as little remorse as Marx had shown. Thus the progressive economist Werner Sombart, champion of "magnificent stores for our cities" in the 1899 debates at the Association for Social Policy, had always struck a tone of pessimism when it came to describing the leveling effects of modern commercial culture ever since he began investigating the rationalizing force behind "the capitalist spirit" in the early 1890s.[21] Although he continued to stress the social and economic significance of the new forms of mass retail in his 1902 study, *Modern Capitalism*, Sombart specifically designated the historic mission of department stores and advertising as "the standardization of demand and its urbanization," a process in which the "peculiar characteristics of the individual nations handed down to us are subsiding."[22] Not all of the economist's friends were as prepared to resign themselves to such a fate, however, even in the name of progress. In fact, Sombart soon became one of advertising's most outspoken enemies himself, as we will shortly see, and while he continued backpedaling into a position of cultural pessimism, many of his new acquaintances in the literary and artistic circles of the fin de siècle chose to fight back, founding organizations dedicated to preserving Germany's historic cultural legacy such as the Dürer League and the League for Homeland Protection.[23]

About the same time news of the American Peril began making headlines, cultural resistance to commercialization received a further boost from the nationwide campaign against "disfigurement" of German landscapes, which was triggered by the appearance of large and garish billboards in the picturesque valleys of the Rhine.[24] Led by the League for Homeland Protection, the movement often drew on the social anxieties of the Mittelstand and their agrarian allies, but their interests were by no means always identical, as the debate over the 1902 "Law against the Disfigurement of Regions with Exceptional Landscapes" in the Prussian House of Deputies showed. Among the few dissenting votes in the campaign's first legislative victory, delegates of the Center Party put aside their usual objections to the commercial invasion of Europe and spoke out sharply against the bill, since it thwarted the interests of small (and mainly Catholic) vintners, who desperately wanted tourists to read their signs while they rode the train down along the Rhine.[25] As state after state passed similar legislation, the movement shifted attention away from the countryside to focus on the preservation of urban landscapes, at first in quaint villages of the provinces, but eventually even in the imperial capital. After the Prussian parliament passed a second bill enabling municipalities to enact protective ordinances against "disfigurement" in 1907, the League for Homeland Protection formed local and regional "advertising committees" in order to ensure that the legislation was enforced. Furious debates at congresses of the homeland protection movement failed to dissuade its members from persisting in the assault, and leaders of the beleaguered industry joined with commercial artists and the department store lobby to found their own "fighting organization," the Alliance of Advertising Interests.[26] But it was an uphill battle. Under pressure from Police President Gottlieb von Jagow, even the liberal city council of Berlin relented in 1909, restricting "the mounting of advertising signs, display cases, lettering, and illustrations" on a long list of designated historic buildings, streets, and squares—including the bustling Potsdamer Platz—to protect the city from "damage in an aesthetic sense."[27]

Given such resistance, it should come as no surprise to find Wilhelmine advertisers and department store owners holding art shows, concerts, balls, and essay competitions, opening professional schools for the "decorative art" of window dressing—in short, doing everything conceivable to persuade a suspicious and hostile public that, in Germany at least, commerce and culture did indeed go hand in hand.[28] The task of draping highly visible signs of commercial modernity "in a nice little cloak," as Growald put it, but one that still allowed the allure of its undeniable and forbidden attractions to show through, drove commercial artists and architects to imaginative feats ranging from the ridiculous to the sublime at the fin de siècle. Nowhere was the challenge more effectively met than in the modern "Gothic" style Alfred Messel hit upon in designing the famous Wertheim Department Store on Leipziger Platz in Berlin. Under construction in several phases between 1896 and 1907, the building sprawled out along Leipziger Straße until it dwarfed the Prussian House of Lords and the Ministries of the Army, Navy, Public Works, and Agriculture that stood adjacent to it on this symbol-laden strip between Wilhelmstraße and Potsdamer Platz in the heart of the imperial capital. Certainly there was no hiding the conspicuous modernity of the emporium, one of the first genuine department stores the city had seen, and in the eyes of contemporary critics the true genius of Messel's solution was that he did not even think of trying. "This intelligent and clear-sighted architect was the first to grasp unadulterated the idea of the department store," declared the art critic Karl Scheffler in his 1910 exposé, Berlin: A City's Destiny. "The bold American spirit that haunts Berlin spurred this talent, actually more aristocratically refined than violent, toward an unconditionality of expression and let him find forms in which the rhythm and the spirit of the modern age is clear and monumental."[29]

The secret to selling modernity, Scheffler and others agreed, was to demonstrate that its forceful dynamism—the "bold American spirit"—was not an incurably alien Other, but instead could actually give new life to forms that expressed the cultural sensibilities of the German soul. Harnessing the capacities of modern construction materials, Messel had in fact broken through the false and alien façades of decadent neo-Renaissance and Baroque architecture, which had

flooded the capital in a frenzy of speculative construction after national unification in 1871. Light and strong, the towering sheets of glass and slender thrusting
columns of Wertheim marked a return to the creative fusion of Gothic and neo-
Classical motifs that graced the very best work of Carl Friedrich Schinkel, master
of Berlin's lost stylistic heritage from the days of Frederickian absolutism, the
Golden Age of "Athens on the Spree." "Within the local architectural tradition,
it points back to Schinkel's Architecture Academy, in whose puritanically severe
brick front such demands won an architectonic expression that strikes [us] as
wholly modern, spiritually kindred," the young city planner Walter Curt Behrendt reflected on Messel's work in 1911. "The Gothic, which otherwise always
feels like something capricious, like an external formal ingredient everywhere
in Schinkel's work, functions precisely in the Architecture Academy as a wholly
original element, as a *spontaneous expression of national tradition*. So too with Messel, who was the first to Gothicize the Renaissance in the Wertheim Building."[30]

While it reached back to reconnect with a local architectural tradition from
Berlin's past, Messel's Wertheim also pointed ahead to the future in a revolutionary way. Just as the pointed arches and ribbed cruciform vaulting of the Gothic
cathedral had burst the constraints of Romanesque architecture and the oppressive feudal order it had represented in the Middle Ages, the spindly columns of
the modern department store promised to smash through the "predominance
of the horizontal" and the illusion of princely sovereignty it sustained for the autonomous economic subjects of bourgeois ideology, as the new spirit manifested
itself in the collective power of labor and industry. "Here the impact of social-
political evolutions showed itself in architecture," Behrendt wrote. "The spirit
of economic organization, which will be the driving force of the coming industrial state, finally triumphed over the tired and dying culture of the Renaissance.
Thus the newly emerged art form, created by the architect's imagination led by
the will of the times, is already capable of achieving almost the significance of a
symbol."[31]

While Tietz's "Aquarium" remained an isolated relic, jarring in its surroundings, warning against the perils of an unreflective Americanism, department
stores around the country rushed to follow Wertheim's lead, transforming the
commercial landscapes of German cities with the bold vertical lines of Messel's
Gothic modern.[32] The successful translation of international mass marketing into
structures that spoke to local customers in a familiar, though still revolutionary
language did little, of course, to calm the fears of the Mittelstand or the Homeland Protection movement, which looked on in horror as the historic patchwork

2. The imposing façade of the Berlin Wertheim department store on Leipziger Platz designed by Alfred Messel. From *Berliner Architekturwelt* 1, no. 1 (1898).

of distinctive regional styles disappeared behind the monotonous repetition of Messel's masterpiece all across the land. Indeed, Police President Jagow's move to require the insertion of thick horizontal slabs in the façades of all new retail buildings in Berlin after 1907 — ostensibly for reasons of fire safety — seemed calculated to put an end to the vertical menace, and it no doubt registered the alarm of the anti-department store lobby, which had been calling for such a provision for some time.[33] Nevertheless, the impact of the new style on early modernist commercial architecture remained (and remains) profound in Germany. Monumentality, dynamism, vertical "lines of force" became powerful motifs for the younger generation, which continued to apply these principles, above all in the Sachlichkeit of modern industrial buildings, long after Jagow's demise. Among the most famous landmarks of the fin de siècle breakthrough that still stands today is the AEG Turbine Factory in Moabit, built by Peter Behrens in 1908. Later criticized for its "static" neo-Classical rigidity, the rhythmic repetition of vertical thrust in the building's naked iron beams expressed the dynamism of productive industry for those with eyes to see before World War I. Contemporaries had no trouble recognizing Messel's signature in the factory, which they described in much the same terms as Wertheim's Department Store on Leipziger Platz: a temple of modern technological advances harnessed by the collective power of German energy.[34]

Symbolism and the Sachplakat

The notion that new structures of large-scale commerce and industry would find a receptive market in Germany only if they took forms that spoke to both the modernity of their function and the historical traditions and tastes that informed the psychological needs of potential buyers stood squarely in the foreground of the Wilhelmine reception of innovations in commercial architecture. If Messel was the first to approach the idea of the department store "with the necessary Sachlichkeit," as his admirers claimed, then the sobriety or professionalism or "objectivity" they had in mind consisted not only of reinforced concrete, glass, and steel, but above all of acknowledging the very real, material significance of *subjective* factors in calculating the equation for success.[35] Nor were architects alone in applying this understanding of the psychologized concrete—a principle I like to call "funky Sachlichkeit"—to the commercial landscapes that arose in the cities of fin de siècle Germany, which often appeared anything but sobering. "Back behind, on Potsdamer Platz, the electric roof-advertisements played their brightly colored games, now in loops, now in strips that suddenly lit up and seemed to hang in the sky," wrote the novelist Max Kretzer, exploring the new magic of lighted signs as he shifted from a gritty Naturalist to a more playful Symbolist perspective after the turn of the century. "It looked as if gusts of wind were continuously storming through the air, extinguishing this gigantic fiery script at times only to bring it back to life somewhere else," as more of the signs flickered over Leipziger Straße all the way to Dönhoffplatz and Spittelmarkt at the far end. "All the colors were sprayed out, creating a brilliant painting for the astonished eye, an artificially produced, fleeting *fata morgana*, impressive enough to achieve its purpose for moments of time."[36]

Savored by an impoverished aristocrat in the novel, Kretzer's fantasia echoes in strikingly similar terms the language of Wilhelmine advertisers, who in fact undertook painstaking "scientific" experiments to determine the exact amount of time such images needed in order to impress themselves on the retina, and thereby to insinuate unbidden "suggestions" surreptitiously into the unconscious mind.[37] "It is simply impossible to walk past it without paying attention," one expert declared, analyzing the effectiveness of nighttime advertising on the same streets Kretzer described: "The alternating play of light draws the gaze of the passerby to the images and letters it paints on the walls of houses in flaming script."[38] While Symbolists explored these landscapes with an eye for capturing beauty in the experience of technologically induced hallucinations, advertising professionals insisted on "the greatest objectivity" in their own investigations of this enchanted ground at the turn of the century.[39] A "constant surveillance of the psyche of the clientele" was called for, *Modern Business* magazine demanded, "a study of the inner processes in the life of the soul that ripen into decisions to purchase."[40] Indeed, because it produced such tangible results — cold hard profits were always the bottom line — the "practical psychology" of marketing research was "proving itself vastly superior to the theoretical" branch of the science, the Viennese economist Victor Mataja argued in 1910. "The convenience-urge, sense of beauty, vanity, every trait in human nature that makes it easier to make mistakes in the calculating of economic things — in short, every peculiarity, every inclination is spied out with a keen eye and made serviceable for the purpose of acquisition."[41]

Like the department store, the flood of color and light that suddenly poured out across every available surface in German cities was widely perceived as an import from America, and even advocates acknowledged that the origins of the modern industry lay far across the waves, in "the land of advertising."[42] Yet the psychological intricacy of the new science also precluded a simple adoption of foreign models without taking into account local customs. American advertising made money in America precisely because it targeted the specific tastes, the "national character," of Americans, which most German experts agreed was loud, childish, and unabashedly obsessed with all things gigantic. In Germany, by contrast, advertising had to be "impressive but not obtrusive" if it was to appeal to the delicate aesthetic sensibilities of shoppers in the Land of Poets and Thinkers.[43] "In Berlin they are going American, and in Munich they make jokes about Berlin," one early connoisseur of poster art wrote before the turn of the century, referring to the illustrators of *Simplicissimus* and *Youth* magazine (*Die Jugend*), who developed the first distinctively native style of commercial graphics, the so-called *Jugendstil*, in the Bavarian capital in the 1890s.[44] Ten years later, however, the advantage had passed to Berlin, where the bold, sleek simplicity of the Sachplakat, or "object poster," established Hollerbaum und Schmidt as the number-

3. Classic poster by Lucian Bernhard for Stiller shoes, 1908. From Jeremy Aynsley, *Graphic Design in Germany, 1890–1945* (Berkeley: University of California Press, 2000).

one publisher of German poster art in the first decade of the twentieth century. "All of Berlin is one big poster by Lucian Bernhard," Max Brod wrote of the most renowned master of the new style for the Expressionist journal *Sturm* in 1911. There was "something very strange" about Bernhard's use of image and color, the visitor from Prague reported, "something like an idyllic steam engine, an American arcadia," which somehow compressed all the roaring dynamism of the city into smooth, minimalist forms glistening with an almost magical serenity. "And so he conquered the metropolis, the extravagantly frugal man (what else does the poster want, the department store, the vast expanse with its fast trains, *all of modern life*, other than to awaken in man the double illusion: that he throws himself tempestuously into the fray, and that at the same time he energetically holds himself together)."[45]

Brod's simile, "an American arcadia," catches perfectly in its intended paradox the challenge Wilhelmine advertisers and department store owners faced in taming the brashness of commercial modernity without losing its force in the age of the American Peril. The problem with making posters artistic, Growald repeatedly told customers at Hollerbaum und Schmidt, was that they had to shock and startle the passerby with every possible sensation, to seize attention "against the will of the observer," rather than waiting patiently for the knowing eye of the connoisseur to dwell in contemplation on subtleties of beauty and eloquence. "The visual representation must be simple and drastic, the text as short and gripping as at all possible."[46] Willfully defying traditional standards of aesthetic judgment, commercial art inevitably incurred the wrath of critics, who assailed its shows and competitions in much the same terms they would later hurl at the works of Futurists and Expressionists: "Here the drastic, the brutal application of paint, which is calculated for coarse effect at greater distances, which no longer pays heed to nature, brushes on hair in strokes of fire-engine red, faces in brown or in chalk white, carries the day," one author groaned at the first exhibit of "modern posters" held by the Association of Berlin Artists in 1897.[47] For the Symbolist Brod, by contrast, such daring disregard for the conventions of nature was precisely what distinguished the revolutionary breakthrough in Bernhard's style. "Because it has to be said once and for all that he was the first to discover the emotional effect of the black background, of black shadows," Kafka's friend thrilled, "who put thick straight-edged lines under words instead of underlining, venomous green or pale pink, who used magical twinkling stars instead of periods, and curves instead of letters."[48]

If advertising needed aesthetic appeal in order to sell, and this for Growald was always the only consideration, then it was time to rewrite the rules of aesthetics. "Art in the service of advertising," he insisted—not the other way around.[49] The Sachlichkeit of Bernhard's Sachplakat had in fact emerged quite literally from this subordination, or so the legend told. Seeking to win a competition for the best poster sponsored by Priester Match Company in 1903, Growald's star artist had achieved fame by effacing the work of his own hand, slathering a thick layer of paint over the elaborate details of an interior scene he had sketched until all that remained was this striking image: two match sticks and the firm name and address on a jet black background.[50] After signing an exclusive contract with Hollerbaum und Schmidt, Bernhard perfected the style, which relied on the use of sharp visual contrasts and increasingly bold, simple representations of the naked commodity to impress object and brand name, the hallmarks of the Berlin Sachplakat, on the eye of the beholder. "These two hieroglyphs suffice entirely," the artist told Expressionist critic Adolf Behne some years later.

> The poster should stimulate the eye through a perplexing appearance in its entirety, and already at the moment in question the passer-by should be able to extract from the poster: . . . a boot, or chocolate, or wicker furniture, or bookbinding firm! This is to be attained through impressive representation of a typical object from the appropriate branch of business. But

Priester-Hölzer

Deutsche Zündholzfabriken
Aktiengesellschaft
Centrale Berlin
C.2. Klosterstr. 99.

4. Classic poster by Lucian Bernhard for Priester matches. From *Zeitschrift für moderne Reklame*, 1, no. 1 (1904).

the passer-by, without needing to detain himself any longer, one — two — three — should also have already read the name of the firm: Schultze, Müller, Lehmann.[51]

By the time Behne published these remarks, in the revolutionary year 1919, the German avant-garde had moved far beyond commercial culture in its scorn for the elitist posturing of traditional, "disinterested," aesthetics. Condemning capitalist industry for its attempts to turn advertising into "a philosophy and an aesthetic," the critic nevertheless acknowledged the significance of the step that led to the Sachplakat. "Bernhard created the most genuine poster precisely because he threw artistic attitudes in image and script overboard, because he worked in the first place in the interests of the commercial sponsor, not out of artistic ambition."[52]

As Behne's contempt for "artistic ambition" so clearly announced, the felicitous marriage between commerce and Kultur that Growald and others had celebrated eleven years earlier did not last for long, if indeed it was ever consummated at all. Shortly after the Exhibition closed in February 1908, advertising came under sharp attack from one of its former champions, Werner Sombart, who had eloquently formulated the progressive arguments in favor of large-scale commercial retail, which lobbyists continued to use on behalf of department stores and advertising for decades to come.[53] Now ensconced as a leading expert at the new Berlin Commercial College, the economist suddenly retracted his claims as to the legitimacy of advertising as an instrument even for achieving objective material gains, let alone for the advancement of culture.[54] A storm of ridicule forced his resignation from the editorial board of *Tomorrow*, the high-brow culture magazine in which he had published the attack—and which depended on sales of advertising space to finance its publication. But Sombart continued his broadside against the industry in Harden's *Future*, aiming directly at the most vulnerable point in Wilhelmine marketing strategy. Echoing the Homeland Protection movement's rhetoric on "disfigurement," he particularly took issue with the claim that advertising posed no threat to distinction in the fine arts, and thus to the cultural capital of the Bildungsbürgertum. "Exactly the same thing is happening with commodities as with artistic and literary achievement; the larger the circle of consumers, the more the judgment of most people lacks independence," Sombart snarled. "Or do they really want to maintain that even in the fields of art and literature the best manifestations are those that, thanks to a slick advertising, have found the widest circulation?"[55]

Coming just as cultural resistance to department stores and advertising ignited a fresh round of agitation against commercial "disfigurement"—in Berlin, the city council was just beginning debates over the local ordinance—this unexpected attack from an old ally was the last straw for frustrated spokesmen of the industry across the country, who began questioning the rights of aesthetes and snobs to pass judgment on their enterprise.[56] "Why should a contemporary citizen who earns his bread through the painting of linen and paper be ashamed to lend his energy to a branch of industry?" one author demanded in the progressive newspaper *Plutus*, which published a series of outraged responses to the economist's act of betrayal. "We see precisely in the career of the artist a career like any other. Every career, after all, is a remuneration of intelligence. Mr. Sombart should not encourage the arrogance of artists vis-à-vis businessmen, which unfortunately exists, with articles like this."[57] Ill will between the two sides continued to build, however. Furious at the notion that painting was "a career like any other," the art critic Fritz Stahl whipped up local resentment against the commercial graphics industry to such an extent that by 1910 Berlin painters were trying to break up attempts to organize on the part of their better-paid colleagues with shouts of "Fight, fight!"[58] Masters of the Sachplakat like Bernhard and Julius Klinger, who had seen their work transform the metropolis, grew increasingly impatient with the antiquated idealism of those who preferred to sacrifice all on the altar of l'art pour l'art in splendid isolation rather than lend a hand toward building the collective monuments to a new and powerful age. "We don't consider ourselves artists 'by the grace of God'; we want rather to work together on the tasks that life gives us," Klinger proclaimed in 1912, "and it lies in [the nature of] our times that the adornment of department stores and eateries has grown just as important for our everyday lives as the pomp of city halls and houses of God once were in former times."[59]

Forged in decades of struggle between advertising and its enemies, the defensive strategies of Wilhelmine mass marketing had produced remarkable new forms of commercial art at the turn of the century—Messel's Americanized Gothic, the "idyllic steam engine" of the Sachplakat, memorable among them. But as it collapsed into open warfare in the last few years of Europe's longest peace, the misalliance between commerce and Kultur gave birth to what was oddly perhaps its greatest legacy. Familiar strains from a very unfamiliar voice, the revolt against l'art pour l'art, aestheticization, and the cult of artistic genius began not among leftist critics of capitalism and mass consumer culture who picked up the refrain in the age of Weimar, Bauhaus, and Neue Sachlichkeit. Instead, it was the spokesmen of capitalist industry who insisted on redefining culture in material terms, who rejected flat out the aura of "disinterested" art. "No! The German advertising system of our day certainly no longer has any need to disguise the lack of its right to exist behind a mask of culture," fumed the editor of Modern Business, Hans Weidenmüller, responding in April 1914 to the latest patronizing speech on the need for better taste in advertising. "Does [the salesman] want to moonlight for the 'aestheticization of the public'? Does the 'Idea of the Beautiful' have a special value if harnessed to the cart of business earnings? Certainly not!" Productive labor alone—not idealism, not aesthetics—bestowed genuine cultural value in the modern world: "German Kultur is no temple of beauty and scholarship lifting itself high above the common daily labor of the gainfully employed multitude; no, the totality of this everyday work, as it is performed from the day laborer to the college instructor composes in its valuable, mature parts the overall conception of culture."[60]

Notes

1. Ernst Growald, "Vorrede," in *Augur: Reklame-Handbuch und Ausstellungs-Katalog*, ed. Ernst Growald (Berlin, 1908), 7. The opening epigraph quotation is from Growald's "Auguren-Sprüche," in the same volume, 84.

2. Growald, "Vorrede," 8–9.

3. Growald, "Auguren-Sprüche," 84; Ernst Growald, "Amerikanische und deutsche Reklame," in *Die Reklame: Ihre Kunst und Wissenschaft*, ed. Paul Ruben (Berlin: Paetel, 1914), 1: 61. The convergence of art and commerce was addressed at many advertising exhibitions but received special attention in the 1908 catalogue.

4. See note 51.

5. On Berlin's disillusionment with Barnum as personification of "Humbug" and his association with advertising as "amerikanischer Bluff," see "Quodlibet-Schaufenster: Eine Betrachtung," *Moderne Geschäft* 5, no. 20 (October 1913): 4; Maximilian Harden, "Barnum," *Zukunft* 31, no. 9 (May 1900): 321–325; Alfred Kerr, *Wo liegt Berlin? Briefe aus der Hauptstadt, 1895–1900*, ed. Günther Rühle (Berlin: Siedler, 1997), 589–590.

6. Tietz, *Hermann Tietz*, 60–62; Plutus, "Tietz," *Zukunft* 35, no. 3 (April 1901): 125–128; "Warenhaus Hermann Tietz," *Propaganda* 4, no. 1 (October 1900): 9–12; Maximilian Harden, "Wertheim und Tietz," *Zukunft* 32, no. 13 (September 1900): 537–545; Kerr, *Briefe*, 615–618; Paul Göhre, *Das Warenhaus* (Frankfurt: Rütten und Loening, 1907), 7–9, 116–117.

7. Plutus, "Tietz," 127.

8. Tietz, *Tietz*, 44–45. On anti-Semitism and the Mittelstand, see Volkov, *The Rise of Political Anti-Modernism*. Among Tietz's advertising ploys that raised particular hackles in Harden's *Zukunft* was the ostentatious granting of days off for Jewish holidays; Plutus, "Tietz," 127.

9. For an overview of the development of German department stores and their late arrival in Germany, see Gerlach, *Das Warenhaus in Deutschland*, 38–64; Ladwig-Winters, *Wertheim*, 25–36; Julius Wernicke, *Kapitalismus und Mittelstandspolitik* (Jena: Fischer, 1907), 531–709; Gustav Stresemann, "Die Warenhäuser": Ihre Entstehung, Entwicklung und volkswirtschaftliche Bedeutung, *Zeitschrift für die gesamte Staatswissenschaft* 56 (1900): 696–733; Georg Buß, "Das Warenhaus: Ein Bild aus dem modernen Geschäftsleben," *Velhagen und Klasings Monatshefte* 21 (1906–1907): 601–616.

10. "Vom Warenhaus Wertheim," *Die Wahrheit*, 28 August 1908, emphasis in the original. See also other newspaper clippings in the Prussian police dossier: Inhaber der Firma A. Wertheim, 1906–1918; A Rep 030, Titel 94, Nr. 14311, Landesarchiv Berlin.

11. Quoted at the 1899 *Verein für Sozialpolitik* debates over department stores and other forms of large-scale commercial retail: *Verhandlungen der am 25., 26. und 27. September 1899 in Breslau abgehaltenen Generalversammlung des Vereins für Sozialpolitik (Schriften des Vereins für Sozialpolitik)* (Leipzig: Duncker und Humblot, 1900), 88: 199–200. For overviews of the Mittelstand's role in the legislative campaigns against department stores, see Julius Wernicke, "Der Kampf um das Warenhaus und die Geschichte des Verbandes Deutscher Waren- und Kaufhäuser e.V. bis Ende 1916," in Gerson Bach et al., eds., *Pro-*

bleme des Warenhauses: Beiträge zur Geschichte und Erkenntnis der Entwicklung des Warenhauses in Deutschland (Berlin: Verband Deutscher Waren- und Kaufhäuser, 1928), 15–
17; Louis Leopold, "Der Verband Deutscher Waren- und Kaufhäuser," Zeitschrift für die
gesamten Staatswissenschaften 17 (1917): 8–16; Walther Jäh, "Die Großbazaare und Warenhäuser, ihre Berechtigung und ihre Besteuerung," Schmollers Jahrbuch 24 (1900): 292–
306.

12. Werner Sombart, "Die Entwicklungstendenzen im modernen Kleinhandel," in Verhandlungen, 154.

13. Verhandlungen, 208.

14. Stenographische Berichte über die Verhandlungen des Hauses der Abgeordneten, 26–27 February 1900, 1883-1887.

15. Biermer, "Warenhäuser und Warenhaussteuer," in J. Conrad et al., eds., Handwörterbuch
der Staatswissenschaften (Jena: Fischer, 1911), 611–612. See also note 9.

16. Biermer, "Warenhäuser," 604; see also Gerlach, "Warenhaus," 62; Hermann Schmidt,
"Organisation und Propaganda in der Politik," in Ruben, Die Reklame, 1: 138.

17. Leo Colze (pseud.), Berliner Warenhäuser: Nachdruck der Erstausgabe von 1908, ed. Detlef
Bluhm (Berlin: Fannei und Walz, 1989), 62–63; Leopold, "Verband," 1–5. For a quick
overview of activities on the part of the Association of German Department and Retail
Stores in these years, see Wernicke, "Kampf," 27–44.

18. Ludwig Max Goldberger, Das Land der unbegrenzten Möglichkeiten (Berlin: Fontane,
1903). For overviews of the contemporary literature and debates on the American Peril,
see Paul Arndt, "Die amerikanische Gefahr," Nation 19 (1901–1902): 756–758; Friedrich
Hertz, "Wissenschaft und Praxis," Plutus 1, no. 39 (September 1904): 763–765; Paul Dehn,
Weltwirtschaftliche Neubildungen (Berlin: Allgemeiner Verein für deutsche Literatur,
1904), 254–275; Max Vosberg, "Die amerikanische Gefahr," Zukunft 51, no. 3 (April 1905):
105–110; Ludwig Max Goldberger, "Die amerikanische Gefahr," Preußische Jahrbücher 120
(1905): 1–33; Georg Bernhard, "Amerika," Plutus 2, no. 47 (November 1905): 893–895;
Georg Bernhard, "100 Prozent," Plutus 3, no. 1 (January 1906): 1–3; Georg Bernhard,
"Umschau: Furcht vor Amerika," Plutus 3, no. 8 (February 1906): 143–144; Wilhelm Bode,
"Die amerikanische Gefahr im Kunsthandel," Kunst und Künstler 5 (1907): 3–6; chapter on
"Die amerikanische Gefahr" in Adolph Donath, Psychologie des Kunstsammelns (Berlin:
Schmidt, 1911); Otto Corbach, "Politik u Handel," Die Aktion 1, no. 14 (May 1911): 419–
421. For historical analysis, see Schmidt, Reisen in die Moderne; Pommerin, Der Kaiser und
Amerika, 207–220.

19. Dehn, Neubildungen, 212, 241.

20. For the classic expression of this view, see Ringer, Decline of the German Mandarins. For
an excellent survey of recent debates, see Sperber, "Bürger, Bürgertum, Bürgerlichkeit,
Bürgerliche Gesellschaft."

21. Elsewhere I have discussed at length the development of Sombart's views on the capitalist spirit; see Repp, Reformers, Critics, and the Paths of German Modernity, 148–183.

22. Werner Sombart, Der Moderne Kapitalismus (Leipzig: Duncker und Humblot, 1902), 2:
311–326.

23. For an overview of these circles, see Kratzsch, Kunstwart und Dürerbund; Viehöfer, Der

Verleger als Organisator; Rollins, *A Greener Vision of Home*; Applegate, *A Nation of Provincials*.

24. On the campaign against "disfigurement," see Ludwig Pickardt, "Der Kampf um die Streckenreklame," in Ruben, *Die Reklame*, 1: 23–38; A. von Oechelhaeuser, "Die Auswüchse des Reklamewesens," in Ruben, *Die Reklame*, 2: 1–39; Victor Mataja, *Die Reklame: Eine Untersuchung über Ankündigungswesen und Werbetätigkeit im Geschäftsleben* (Leipzig: Duncker und Humblot, 1910), 469–471; *Stenographischen Berichten* 19, no. 1 (February 1902): 987–1006, and no. 4 (April 1902): 4488–4515. Similar campaigns against outdoor advertising also played a significant role in French debates over aesthetics and politics in this period; see Jeffrey Weiss, *The Popular Culture of Modern Art: Picasso, Duchamp, and Avant-Gardism* (New Haven: Yale University Press, 1994), 52–70.

25. *Stenographische Berichte*, 1 February 1902, 998–1002.

26. Oechselhaeuser, "Auswüchse," 3–7.

27. "Vorlage zur Beschlußfassung betreffend, Ortstatut zum Schutz der Stadt Berlin gegen Verunstaltung," Landesarchiv Berlin, A Rep 00–02/1, Nr. 1581.

28. The most important private school for advertising as an art was the Higher Professional School for Decorative Arts founded in 1910 by the Museum for Art in Commerce and Industry in conjunction with the Deutsche Verband für das kaufmännische Unterrichtswesen, Verband der Berliner Spezialgeschäfte, Verband künstlerischer Schaufensterdekorateure, and the Werkbund; S. Müller, *Kunst und Industrie*, 126–127; Simon Rector, "Der Verband künstlerischer Schaufensterdekorateure," *Moderne Geschäft* 5, no. 24 (December 1913): 17. For more examples of the attempt to emphasize the artistic and cultivating qualities of advertising, see Th. Cordier, "Pariser Plakate," *Reklame* 5, no. 15 (August 1895): 258–260; "Die Kunst auf der Straße," *Reklame* 5, no. 17 (September 1895): 301; A. Wiedemann, "Schaufenster-Dekoration," part 1, *Reklame* 7, no. 3 (February 1897): 35–36; part 2, no. 4 (February 1897): 52–53; part 3, no. 8 (April 1897): 217–218, and part 4, no. 10 (May 1897): 146–148; Reinhold Weinhold, "Die Berliner Plakat-Säulen in ihrer Sommer-Toilette," *Reklame* 7, no. 12 (June 1897): 179–180; W-d, "Die Kunst der Schaufenster-Dekoration," *Reklame* 7, no. 13 (July 1897): 194; "Reklamekunst," *Propaganda* 3, no. 1 (October 1899): 1–4; Die Zigarre, "Die Fortschritte unserer Schaufenster-Dekorationen," *Reklame* 10, no. 11 (June 1900): 101; Mil Richter, "Weltanschauung," *Propaganda* 4, no. 2 (November 1900): 37–41; Wernicke, *Kapitalismus*, 554; Conrad Alberti, "Die Entwicklung Berlins und des Kaufhauses N. Israel," *Israel-Album* (1902): 74–75; Göhre, *Warenhaus*, 10–12; Ferdinand Avenarius, "Reklame und Kultur," *Kunstwart* 22, no. 5 (December 1908): 257–269; Mataja, *Die Reklame*, 120–121; Osthaus, "Schaufenster," 59–69; Hans Weidenmüller, "Die Durchgeistigung der geschäftlichen Werbearbeit," *Jahrbuch des Deutschen Werkbundes*, 1913, 70–74; Pritschow, "Kaufmann," 14–16; "Kunst im Handel," *Moderne Geschäft* 5, no. 24 (December 1913): 12–14.

29. Scheffler, *Berlin: Ein Stadtschicksal*, 204–205. The physical and symbolic expansion of Wertheim was a subject of frequent commentary at the time. "Erected on a 16,700 m² site, the Wertheim Department Store displays a ground-floor surface area of 14,000 square meters and thus exceeds that of the German Reichstag building, which measures 11,200 m² by 2800 m²," one popular writer wrote in 1906. "Combined its six floors con-

tain a useable surface area of 80,000 m², not much smaller that that of the Königsplatz";
Buß, "Warenhaus," 606. For more on the construction and physical expansion of Wertheim on Leipziger Platz, see Ladwig-Winters, *Wertheim*, 42–48; Behrendt, *Alfred Messel*, 62–87.

30. Behrendt, *Messel*, 103–104, my emphasis.

31. Ibid., 65–66.

32. For more on the enthusiastic contemporary admiration for Messel as inventor of the "new Gothic" and the Wertheim on Potsdamer Platz as "Urtyp" of Berlin commercial architecture at the fin de siècle, see "Warenhaus Hermann Tietz," 10–11; Scheffler, *Berlin*, 204–205; Alfred Wiener, "Geschäftsbauten und Reklame," in Ruben, *Die Reklame*, 89; Alfred Wiener, "Warenhaus," in Ruben, *Die Reklame*, 49–50; Hans Jaretzki, "Reklame und Architektur," in Ruben, *Die Reklame*, 126–127; Buß, "Warenhaus," 607–608; Osborn, "Stadt und Warenhaus: Ein Beitrag zur boden- und baugeschichtlichen Entwicklung," in Bach et al., *Probleme des Warenhauses*, 128; Posener, *Berlin auf dem Wege zu einer neuen Architektur*, 369–380, 453–464; Klaus Strohmeyer, *Warenhäuser: Geschichte, Bluete und Untergang im Warenmeer* (Berlin: Wagenbach, 1980), 75; Gerlach, *Das Warenhaus in Deutschland*, 103–105. Posener's stridently partisan claim that Messel's "glass beam construction was never built a second time, not even by Messel" (Posener, *Berlin*, 376), is sharply contradicted not only by the contemporary reception, but also by a walk around present-day Berlin, where the considerable remnants of fin de siècle commercial architecture attest to the widespread imitation of his style, upon which Göhre and others remarked at the time. The unmistakable echoes of Messel's beams in the façades currently being added to Berlin's existing commercial buildings, which together with the burst of new construction are once again giving the city proper an increasingly uniform appearance, seem to bear out Walter Curt Behrendt's claim that Messel stands second only to Schinkel as shaper of Berlin's urban physiognomy (Behrendt, *Messel*, 103–104).

33. Wernicke, *Kapitalismus*, 701. See also Wiener, "Warenhaus," 50; Wernicke, "Kampf," 21–22; Gerlach, *Warenhaus*, 106; Posener, *Berlin*, 376; Hans Schliepmann, "Vom Straßenbilde," *Berliner Architekturwelt* 6 (1904): 75.

34. Fritz Hoeber, *Peter Behrens* (Munich: Müller und Rentsch, 1913), 111–112; Gropius, "Die Entwicklung moderner Industriebaukunst"; Posener, *Berlin*, 376; Jeffries, *Politics and Culture in Wilhelmine Germany*, 104–108, 128–131; Müller, *Kunst*, 52–56, 59–62; Goerd Peschken, "Peter Behrens: AEG Buildings," in Scheer et al., *City of Architecture, Architecture of the City*, 84–85.

35. The quote is from Scheffler's introduction to Behrendt, *Messel*, 15–16. Powerful emotional, even quasi-religious impulses are connected with Messel's direct and "sachlich" style by many observers in both the professional and the popular press at the time; Leo Nacht, "Moderne Schaufensteranlagen," *Berliner Architekturwelt* 6, no. 10 (1904): 339–340; Oskar Bie, "Alfred Messel," *Zukunft* 20, no. 2 (1909): 750–751; Göhre, *Warenhaus*, 13–14; Joseph August Lux, *Ingenieurästhetik* (Munich: Lammers, 1908), 8, 24–29.

36. Max Kretzer, *Söhne ihrer Väter* (Leipzig: Elischer Nachfolger, 1908), 31–32.

37. Hans Weidenmüller, "Zwangsmäßige Blickführung bei Werbsachen," *Das moderne Geschäft: Zeitschrift für Schaufenster-Dekoration, Geschäfts-Ausstattung und Reklame: Kaufmän-

nisches Fachblatt für Handels-Wissenschaft, Statistik und Organisation 6, no. 1 (January 1914): 3–4. See also August Endell, "Vom Sehen." *Neue Gesellschaft* 1, no. 4 (26 April 1905): 45–47. The general consensus about the parallels between advertising and hypnotic "suggestion" in the fin de siècle trade literature is discussed in Mataja, *Die Reklame*, 26–27, 332–339; Wilhelm Münch, "Psychologie der Mode."*Preußische Jahrbücher* 89 (1897): 1–26. For a more subtle analysis of the organs for unconscious "intellectual reception," see Bernhard Wities, "Das Wirkungsprinzip der Reklame: Eine psychologische Studie," *Zeitschrift für Philosophie und philosophische Kritik* 128 (1906): 138–154.

38. Alfred Damitsch, "Aussenreklame," *Plutus* 11, no. 26 (June 1914): 511. The topos of illuminated advertising as fiery script is a common theme in advertising trade journals from the turn of the century; see Fred Hood, "Strassenreklame in Paris," *Propaganda* 3, no. 10 (July 1900): 325.

39. The quote is from Ernst Growald, "Die Kunst im Dienste der Reklame," in *Die Reklame*, 1: 94, and it follows immediately after an extended discussion of the parallels between advertising and "mass suggestion"; ibid., 91–94.

40. A. Poiret, "Das Milieu und seine Wirkung," *Modernes Geschäft* 5, no. 20 (October 1913): 1–2.

41. Mataja, *Die Reklame*, 167–168.

42. The identification of America as "the land of advertising" came early; "Propaganda des Detaillisten," *Propaganda* 3, no. 8 (May 1900): 273. See also Philip Berges's series of articles, "Reklamewissenschaftliche Spaziergänge durch Amerika," *Reklame* 5, nos. 1–9 (January–May 1895); "Wie man in Amerika annonciert!," *Reklame* 5, no. 1 (January 1895): 2–3; Eugen Zabel, "Reklame in Berlin," in Albert Kühnemann, ed., *Groß-Berlin: Bilder von der Ausstellungsstadt* (Berlin: Pauli Nachfolger, 1896–97), 242–243; drr, "Amerikanische Schaufensterreklame," *Propaganda* 3, no. 7 (April 1900): 220–222; Georg Bernhard, "100 Prozent"; Scheffler, *Berlin*, 197–200; Joseph Adler, "Mode und Literatur," *Aktion* 3, no. 49 (December 1913): 1138–1139; Joseph Adler, "Die Hamburg-Amerika Linie," *Aktion* 4, no. 20 (May 1914): 426. Mataja particularly emphasizes the role of America in pioneering psychological research on advertising; Mataja, *Die Reklame*, 332–339. For examples of warnings against the direct importation of American advertising, see Growald, *Der Plakat-Spiegel: Erfahrungssätze für Plakat-Künstler und Besteller* (Berlin: Kampffmeyer'sche Zeitungs-Verlag Salomon, 1904), 77; Growald, "Auguren-Sprüche," 84; "Amerikanische Reklame und deutsches Publikum," part 1, *Moderne Geschäft* 5, no. 20 (October 1913): 13; part 2, no. 21 (November 1913): 12–13; Ernst Growald, "Amerikanische und deutsche Reklame," in Ruben, *Die Reklame*, 1: 63–68.

43. "Eindringlich aber nicht aufdringlich"; "Amerikanische Reklame und deutsches Publikum," 13.

44. Oscar Bie, "Moderne Zeichner," *Westermanns Monatshefte* 91 (1901–1902): 387.

45. Max Brod, "Berlin für dem Fremden," *Sturm* 1, no. 46 (January 1911): 368.

46. Ernst Growald, "Das Plakat, sein Zweck und seine Eigenschaften," in *Der Plakat-Spiegel*, 9–10. Others went so far as to insist that advertising and art were for that very reason mutually exclusive, "since the essence of all art, even applied, is discretion; all advertis-

ing, though—even the 'discreet'—has to be concerned with standing out." Leon Zetlin, "Götze Reklame," *Plutus* 5, no. 22 (May 1908): 437.

47. "Moderne Plakate," *Die Reklame* 7, no. 15 (August 1897): 229.

48. Brod, "Berlin," 368.

49. Ernst Growald, "Die Kunst im Dienste der Reklame," in *Augur*, 95.

50. Meggs, *A History of Graphic Design*, 249–251. For more on Bernhard and the Sachplakat, see Friedrich Plietzsch, *Lucian Bernhard* (Hagen: Fuhfus, 1913); Robert Höser, "Lucian Bernhard," *Zeitschrift für moderne Reklame*, no. 1 (1904): 18–21; Henatsch, *Die Entstehung des Plakats*, 136–142; Schindler, *Monographie des Plakats*, 116–118; Ursula Zeller et al., *Bernhard: Werbung und Design im Aufbruch des 20. Jahrhunderts* (Stuttgart: Institut für Auslandsbeziehungen, 1999).

51. Adolf Behne, "Alte und neue Plakate," in *Das politische Plakat* (Charlottenburg: Verlag "Das Plakat," 1919), 6–7.

52. Ibid., 8.

53. Sombart's analysis of department stores and advertising in the 1902 edition of *Modern Capitalism* formed the backbone of much of the pro-industry lobby literature; see especially Göhre, *Warenhaus*, 101–120; Wernicke, *Kapitalismus*, 550–552.

54. Werner Sombart, "Die Reklame," *Morgen* 2, no. 10 (1908): 281–286.

55. Werner Sombart, "Ihre Majestät die Reklame," *Zukunft* 63 (1908): 475–487.

56. Johannes Steindamm, "Zu Sombarts Reklame," *Morgen* 2, no. 19 (1908): 599–601; Edmund Edel, "Kunst, Kultur und Reklame," *Morgen* 2, no. 19 (1908): 601–605; A. Jacoby, "Amoklauf," *Morgen* 2, no. 19 (1908): 606–608; Ernst Growald, "Sombart über Reklame," *Plutus* 5, no. 14 (April 1908): 276–278; H. Dose, "Sombart der Reklamefeind," *Plutus* 5, no. 17 (April 1908): 337–338; Karl Kujath, "Reklame, Volkswirtschaft und Aesthetik," *Plutus* 5, no. 19 (May 1908): 376–378; Leon Zetlin, "Götze Reklame," *Plutus* 5, no. 22 (May 1908): 433–437; Julius West, "Die Wirkung der Reklame," *Plutus* 5, no. 26 (June 1908): 511–512; Ferdinand Avenarius, "Reklame und Kultur," *Kunstwart* 22, no. 5 (December 1908): 257–266. For overviews of the debate, see Mataja, *Die Reklame*, 59–61; H. Pritschow, "Vom Kaufmann und Künstler: Ein Wort zum gegenwärtigen Stand der kaufmännischen Reklame," *Moderne Geschäft* 5, no. 21 (November 1913): 14–15.

57. Kujath, "Reklame, Volkswirtschaft und Aesthetik," 378.

58. Simon Rector, "Der Verband künstlerischer Schaufensterdekorateure," *Moderne Geschäft* 5, no. 24 (December 1913): 17.

59. Quoted in Sebastian Müller, "Deutsches Museum für Kunst in Handel und Gewerbe," in Hesse-Freilinghaus et al., *Karl Ernst Osthaus*, 321.

60. Weidenmüller, "Für Deutschlands erste Werbehochschule"; Weidenmüller, "Braucht die Reklame eine Kulturmaske?," *Moderne Geschäft* 6, no. 7 (April 1914): 5.

2

COREY ROSS

VISIONS OF PROSPERITY

The Americanization of

Advertising in Interwar Germany

In interwar Germany, as elsewhere in Europe, "Americanism" was a catchword for nothing less than modernity itself. As a young nation unencumbered by the ballast of tradition, America represented a land of seemingly unlimited opportunity, the epitome of utilitarian efficiency and technological innovation, a sign of things to come. With America's growing economic and cultural influence after World War I, Europeans increasingly projected their hopes and fears about their own future onto the United States, which in many respects served as an embodiment of the challenge posed to European societies by modernity.

Nowhere were these hopes and fears more apparent than in the ambivalent responses to the transference of American consumer culture to Europe. Widely celebrated for its promise of material abundance and "democratization of consumption," American material civilization was simultaneously decried for what critics saw as its brutally rational erosion of cultural traditions, quashing of individualism, and threat to social stability.[1] American mass consumption and marketing practices presented a challenge to European consumption regimens at a variety of levels, including traditional patterns of craft production and local merchandizing, rigidly class-bound hierarchies of consumption and taste, and ingrained notions about the relationship between art and commerce.[2]

Though this transatlantic cultural exchange affected Europe as a whole, responses varied from country to country. Obviously, the ability to emulate

American consumer society depended on hard economic factors such as productivity, the size and strength of markets, and the infrastructural prerequisites for large-scale trade and distribution. In economic terms, Germany, with its large markets, advanced industries, and highly developed infrastructure, represented relatively fertile soil in spite of the deleterious effects of war and reparations. Yet social and cultural factors also shaped responses to the "Americanization" of consumption and marketing, and in this regard Germany not only boasted what was arguably the strongest native advertising tradition in Europe, rooted in long-lived and relatively well-organized efforts at a synthesis of art and commerce, but was also gripped after the war by a wide-ranging discourse on propaganda and "mass psychology" that powerfully molded conceptions of advertising and publicity.

This essay analyzes the appropriation and adoption of American advertising practices in interwar Germany primarily against this social and cultural backdrop. It approaches this as a two-directional, albeit rather asymmetric, process of exchange, inquiring first into how and why Germans looked to American advertising for guidance, but also considering the effects of U.S. advertisers' attempts to penetrate European markets during the 1920s and 1930s. After briefly describing German perceptions of advertising in the United States, I trace the efforts to transpose U.S. techniques and organizational models to Germany before finally considering some of the reasons for the increasing emulation of certain aspects of American marketing in the 1930s, including a number of parallels to National Socialist propaganda techniques and specific measures introduced by the regime after 1933. As we will see, the selective appropriation of U.S. advertising practices was molded by a wide range of factors during the interwar years, albeit with quite different underlying aims after the Nazi takeover. That the ongoing process of Americanization in many ways made its greatest advance amid the "Germanization" rhetoric of the Nazis testifies to both the continuing fascination with the United States as a model of modernity as well as to the complexity of the indigenous impulses that shaped Germans' engagement with it.

Germany Looks to America

The general acceptance of U.S. leadership in the realm of advertising was part and parcel of America's undisputed economic preeminence after World War I. With its rationalized industries and abundance of raw materials, the U.S. economy was more productive, generated higher real wages, and sustained a market for consumer goods that was deeper and broader than markets in Europe — that is to say, it was a "mass" market in the sense that it transcended both social and geographic barriers. Advertising functioned as the currency that bound together this sprawling, anonymous market of goods; it was the oil for the machinery of mass consumption in the United States. Just as the thoroughly rationalized American enterprise represented the cutting edge of production, so, too, were marketing techniques in the United States widely perceived as synonymous with "modern" advertising. As one of the participants of a 1928 "study trip" to the United States put it, "There is an unbelievable amount to learn from this people, which is not burdened by an excess of tradition and is therefore unfamiliar — in the best sense — with the law of inertia."[3]

What, more concretely, distinguished the U.S. advertising scene from Europe's, and why were German advertisers so keen to emulate certain aspects of it? After all, advertising could hardly be considered primitive in Germany. Advertising turnover and revenues rose exponentially over the two decades before World War I, and Germany was home to some of the most innovative and skillful graphic designers anywhere (as U.S. advertisers privately admitted).[4] One clear difference about advertising in the United States — and indeed the one that probably impressed Germans the most — was its sheer scale, which translated into colossal profits for the most successful agencies: J. Walter Thompson, Erwin Wasey, and Ayer and McCann. In the late 1920s it was estimated that roughly three times as much was spent on advertising in the United States as in Germany.[5] This was directly related to another significant difference insofar as it reflected a greater willingness on the part of American industry to invest in advertising. German advertisers, who constantly bemoaned the supposed ignorance of German firms about the importance of modern publicity, greatly desired the kind of societal recognition they thought their American counterparts enjoyed, and explicitly latched on to the "Truth in Advertising" campaign with which American advertisers had previously tried to improve their professional image.[6] The need to "advertise for advertising" (make "Reklame für die Reklame") to overcome the deep-rooted skepticism about advertising's economic benefits was a constant theme of the various advertising exhibitions throughout the 1920s and beyond, and was also one of the primary motives for staging the International Advertising Association's 1929 World Advertising Congress in Berlin.[7]

Not only was it considered easier to drum up business in the United States, but the actual creation and dissemination of advertising messages also faced fewer hurdles. The advertising sector in the United States was considerably more organized than in Europe. In particular, the standardization of formats and sizes made it far easier to place the same advertisement in several periodicals at once.

The relative transparency of circulation figures for American newspapers, monitored by an independent auditing bureau, also took a lot of the guesswork out of price negotiations. By contrast, German advertisers continuously decried the "circulation swindle" (*Auflagenschwindel*) and "rate embezzlement" (*Tarifuntreue*) of the German press throughout the 1920s; publishers were generally loath to publish accurate circulation figures so long as there was no compulsion for their competitors to do likewise.[8] Moreover, the American advertising profession was under tighter self-regulation than in Germany, where "serious" advertisers saw themselves in a constant rearguard action against the excesses of fly-by-night swindlers who had swarmed into the advertising business during the years just after the war.[9]

In addition, American advertising techniques were themselves somewhat different. For one thing, the United States was well ahead in the use of "scientific" market analysis, which was deemed an integral component of any "rationalized" sales machinery. Indeed, market analysis first took hold in Germany after 1925 as part of broader efforts at rationalization during the brief economic upswing of the late 1920s, and from the beginning Americans were closely involved.[10] The very rationale underlying the expansion of market analysis—namely, the deliberate attempt at a more accurate targeting of advertising messages in order to tap new markets—was moreover directly related to the development of a unique new means of framing and disseminating these messages in the United States. Whereas the poster-style advertisement (characterized by a striking or "yelling" image geared toward grabbing attention and devoid of much or any explanatory text apart from the brand name) remained a mainstay of marketing throughout Europe during the 1920s, American advertisers since the turn of the century had developed a new editorializing style for the mass circulation press that relied as much on textual argumentation as on imagery.[11]

Often described as "salesmanship in print," this new advertising genre was characterized by "hard-selling copy full of reasons and arguments in place of rhymes and slogans."[12] Pioneered by firms like J. Walter Thompson and Erwin Wasey in national weeklies like the *Saturday Evening Post* and *Ladies' Home Journal*, the new editorializing style was deliberately geared toward the mass of subbourgeois consumers to whom, it was believed, it was easier to sell the usefulness of a product rather than its image. Whereas the aesthetic appeal of the artistic poster may have suited urban bourgeois sensibilities, such symbolic representations were considered inappropriate for appealing to the practical and use-oriented mind-set of most "ordinary" consumers. Simply displaying the product, however cleverly, was not enough. The average middle-income consumer needed a more

1. Kaloderma Soap poster by Jupp Wiertz, 1927. Courtesy of Deutsches Historisches Museum, Inv.-Nr. P73/3439.

concrete reason to part from hard-earned money—hence the development of "the new 'reason why' approach."[13] Also occasionally dubbed the "capitalist realist" style, this new genre of editorializing advertisement sought to persuade consumers to purchase a product by describing its benefits and by arguing why consumers should partake of them, often enlisting celebrity testimonials or scientific data to back up their claims.[14] Instead of grabbing attention by means of symbolic representation, they sought to generate need by means of argumentation. Accordingly, this style of advertising tended to be more consumer-centered than product-centered. As the journal *Printers' Ink* remarked, it represented a shift from the "factory viewpoint" to a focus on "the mental process of the consumer."[15] Geared toward the socially and geographically diverse markets in the United States, the use of editorializing copy was commonly regarded in Germany as the quintessentially American style of advertising.[16]

Warum küßt er mich nicht?

Die schönste Frau wird nicht begehrt, wenn unreiner Atem ihrem Munde entströmt. Eine kräftige Mundspülung mit Odol verbürgt frisch-duftenden Atem.

Odol-Zahnpasta n. wie Odol nach streng wissenschaftlichen Grundsätzen aufgebaut. Odol-Zahnpasta wird von uns nicht in schweren Bleituben, die zwar billig, aber scheußlich sind, geliefert, sondern – ohne Preiserhöhung – in reinen Zinntuben. Es gibt keine bessere Zahnpasta als Odol-Zahnpasta. Odol-Zahnpasta verhütet Zahnbelag und hat köstlichen Geschmack.

2. This Odol mouthwash advertisement, 1929, is an early example of the text-rich style. From *In aller Munde: Einhundert Jahre Odol* (1993), 110. Courtesy of the Odol-Archive in the Deutschen Hygiene-Museum Dresden.

The huge scale of American advertising, its modicum of cultural legitimacy and recognition, and its relatively high degree of organization and new techniques of communication were all objects of intense interest in Weimar Germany and served, at least implicitly, as benchmarks for the development of the profession in Europe as a whole. Yet despite the frequently overenthusiastic paeans to U.S. advertising methods, there were no serious calls for their wholesale adoption in Germany. As one might expect, some of the stereotypes about the supposed superficiality and low educational standards of Americans played a role here: "That Germany with its much more skeptical populace differs in many respects from the United States with its more naïve and volatile masses—this hardly requires additional proof."[17] But apart from this more or less universal assumption, there were also a number of other factors that conditioned the response to U.S. marketing techniques in Germany.

Most obvious were the aforementioned craft traditions in Germany. Embodied in such renowned organizations as the Werkbund and Dürer-Bund, the wide-ranging efforts of industrialists and artists to raise the design quality of consumer goods and to elevate popular tastes had led to an enormous expansion of artistically inspired advertising before 1914, associated above all with Lucian Bernhard in Berlin and Ludwig Hohlwein in Munich.[18] Despite being weakened by the war and events that followed (in particular, the plummeting advertising budgets of business firms and the rise of more utilitarian marketing approaches in the wake of rationalization), such efforts continued to exert a strong influence on advertising in the 1920s. Granted, the general trend toward a more "advertising-technical" (werbetechnisch) as opposed to purely "artistic" orientation was clear enough and found institutional expression in the founding of the Bund deutscher Gebrauchsgraphiker and the dissolution of the Verein der Plakatfreunde (a leading proponent of artistic advertising before 1914) shortly after the war.[19] Yet a certain predilection for the artistically inspired poster was by no means abolished by these developments, merely weakened—and indeed, in many eyes not weakened nearly enough. As Hanns Kropff complained in 1924, advertising was still by and large judged according to artistic rather than purely marketing criteria: "They [artists] seldom concern themselves over whether their work is good from an advertising standpoint. They draw or paint a design and then fill the precious space with it. And the odd thing is that the commissioning firm accepts and publicizes the design simply because the artist says it is good and because it was made by *him*. Advertising is produced not for the person paying for it, but rather for the reputation of the artist."[20]

American advertisers largely agreed with this assessment. As late as 1928 J. Walter Thompson representatives were struck by the degree to which artistic merits still prevailed over purely marketing criteria as the primary standard for evaluation. Although a layout could be very effective in psychological terms, it still would not necessarily be regarded as good in Germany: "Merely to fill the space is apparently enough, provided the advertising is striking in appearance."[21] Moreover, this predominance of "clever art" designed to attract attention reflected, in American eyes, a German emphasis on the medium over the message, which in turn meant a reduction of the perceived importance, amount, and quality of editorializing copy. The Germans' traditional artistic focus led them, according to Thompson representatives, to regard the essence of American advertising as consisting merely of *more* copy, thus blinding them to the fact that it was also *different* copy with a different purpose.

Apart from Germany's craft traditions, the remarkable fascination with propaganda and mass psychology after World War I—nourished by the notion that the war was lost because of a "failure of nerves" on the home front instead of military defeat—also shaped the appropriation of American advertising techniques. During the early 1920s there appeared a veritable flood of studies on the nature of propaganda, on its deployment during the war, on the contemporary uses of propaganda abroad, on the distinction between propaganda and advertising, and on the relationship between propaganda and public opinion.[22] What bound together this vast body of literature was above all its predication on the basic concepts and language of mass psychology, whose supposed "laws" were seen to hold the key to effective propaganda. Whether or not one ever actually read Gustav Le Bon's classic *Psychologie des foules*, all of the seminal works in this discourse—including *Mein Kampf*—reflected its basic tenets: the conceptualization of the masses as irrational and dangerous, feminine and seducible; the threat posed by "massification" (*Vermassung*) to elite values and traditional authority; the masses' controllability via suggestion; the appeal to emotion over reason; the power of action and violence; the prioritization of image over word and of form over content; and of course the desire of the masses to invest loyalty in others.

In terms of its Americanizing tendencies in the sphere of commercial advertising, this discourse on propaganda and mass psychology was somewhat ambivalent. On the one hand, its pseudo-scientific pathos tended to reinforce the gradual trend away from "artistic" conceptions of advertising toward more explicitly psychological approaches, and in this sense ran parallel to current notions of "mass manipulation" in the United States. Building on Hugo Münsterberg's introduction of *Psychotechnik* before the war, the rapid expansion of applied psychology and industrial psychology during the early 1920s was one of the primary outgrowths of Germany's rationalization efforts. "Advertising psychology" (*Werbepsychologie*) was an integral part of this expansion; it was frequently discussed in the main professional journals and given institutional expression in 1920 with the establishment of the Institut für Wirtschaftspsychologie at the Berliner Handelshochschule.[23] The first synthetic works on advertising psychology soon followed; their heavy reliance on recent research findings from the United States was symptomatic of American leadership in the field.[24]

Yet, on the other hand, the strong predominance of mass psychology in the German advertising discourse also hindered the adoption of certain American techniques, namely, the editorializing ad. For the dominant understanding of the mass public as passive, feminine, and seducible tended to encourage a particular "school" of Werbepsychologie which held that "exerting an effect on the psyche of an individual within the mass is most successful when it appeals to the most primitive instincts and desires."[25] In this view, advertising was closely associated with "suggestion" or even hypnosis.[26] As one contemporary commentator put it, advertising was most effective in the form of a "momentary suggestion . . . whose hypnotic power nonetheless continues to work long afterwards."[27] This rhetoric of suggestion not only reflected the current conception of public communication as largely monologic and manipulative, but also indirectly reinforced the continued dominance of a producer-oriented approach to marketing goods in Germany. Insofar as the editorializing style of American advertising was more consumer-oriented and therefore relied on different psychological mechanisms from that of suggestion (i.e., playing on insecurities, appealing to the desire for participation and social acceptance), the categories and presumptions of mass psychology that underpinned the entire German discourse on propaganda in the 1920s represented a barrier to its appropriation in Germany.

In addition to this narrowing of the psychological framework, the clear prioritization of image over text hardly encouraged the adoption of a more "argumentative" style of advertising characterized by long copy. The notion that pictures were more powerful than words was essentially a given, and was based on the related assumption that appeals to emotion (which were associated with images) were more effective than appeals to reason (associated with text). As the *Berliner Illustrierte Zeitung* put it in 1921, "What interests the masses of people are matters of sensory perception. The formation of their opinions proceeds from the visual appearance of life and its occurrences, not through intellectual consideration and speculation."[28] The rising popularity of the cinema and the current intellectual fascination with film as "a new turn toward the visual" only further reinforced this understanding of imagery as "the genuine mother tongue of humankind."[29]

To sum up so far, in spite of the widespread fascination with American marketing techniques and in spite of the gradual emergence of scientific over artistic methods of advertising, the stunning visual image continued to hold its own in Germany, even in press announcements. Not only was the mass consumer market (for which American advertising techniques were devised) simply less developed in Germany, but the survival of older craft traditions in the guise of modernized *Gebrauchsgraphik* and the general prioritization of image over argument meant that U.S. marketing methods were adopted selectively at best. In the sphere of advertising, as in many other spheres, America served more as a general *chiffre* for modernity, a kind of foil against which to perceive and make sense of the rapid societal transformations within Germany itself, than as a source of ready-made new advertising techniques.[30] Put somewhat differently, although "modernization" and "Americanization" were often conflated, German advertisers nonetheless distinguished the two and, so far as possible, strove for the former over the latter. As former chancellor Hans Luther put it in his address to the World Advertising Congress in 1929, "If we do not wish to decline as a people, then we must make our home within the new and ever-changing world. Advertising is a language of this new world. We want to learn from other countries that already possess a greater familiarity with this language. We also want, however, to develop the German dialect of this language and to do this with a German sense of intellectuality and art appreciation."[31]

America Comes to Germany

In the meantime, as German advertisers were looking to the United States for new ideas, American firms were busy penetrating European markets to an unprecedented degree after World War I.[32] After the currency reform and stabilization in 1924, Germany's markets increasingly attracted the attention of American corporations, whose advertising agencies began to establish contacts and eventually to found their own branch offices in Germany.[33] This was part of a wider pattern of European penetration whereby U.S. advertisers generally gained a foothold in Britain before moving to the main cities on the continent. As a rule, they initially came to Europe to market brand-name products for U.S. firms, for the most part consumer durables (especially automobiles) and personal hygiene products. The basic rationale was to offer U.S. clients the usual all-round service and methods *en locale*—something which local agencies could not offer because of a lack of familiarity with U.S. techniques and which the smaller American export companies employing "canned" copy could not offer because of a lack of familiarity with local conditions.[34] What this added up to was the erection of small outposts of U.S. advertising in Europe: full-service agencies employing market analysis for conceiving their campaigns and (often, not always) American editorializing style for executing them. As one of the main proponents of these methods within the United States and by far the largest American advertising organization in Europe, J. Walter Thompson in many ways epitomized this development.

It is difficult to judge the Americanizing influence exerted by these small outposts in Germany. Undoubtedly the Germans watched with interest. There was no shortage of discussion about the arrival of the American agencies, which over time managed to gain a base of local clients. The Americans, for their part, also entered with great optimism and a certain degree of missionary zeal, regarding the German market, along with the British, as one of the two most promising in Europe.[35] But in a variety of ways, the landscape of the German advertising industry did not readily lend itself to U.S.-style advertising campaigns, and the presence of American agencies trying to execute such campaigns through German newspapers and with German craftsmen did not dramatically change how most of the latter did business.[36]

One of the biggest barriers was the structure of the German media, in particular the lack of a national press. The *Berliner Illustrierte Zeitung* was the only publication remotely approaching the circulation figures of the big American weeklies; the average newspaper circulation in Germany was only 50 percent that of England. The vast bulk of newspapers served a distinctly local readership. This was true even of the large Berlin dailies (*Berliner Morgenpost, Berliner Zeitung, Berliner Lokal-Anzeiger*), which were rarely read outside of the capital. Compounding this problem was the aforementioned lack of price and size standardization. In 1927, J. Walter Thompson's Berlin office dealt with 135 papers with 101 different size formats, few of which were willing or able to cite reliable circulation figures — all in all, a recipe for considerable difficulty with both placement and price negotiation.[37] If Americans found placing advertisements in Germany difficult, creating them in the first place was hardly any easier. As already noted, German artists and printers were by and large accustomed to eye-catching imagery adorned with the overconspicuous, yelling script typical of the poster-style announcement. Most were therefore unfamiliar with the requirements of American-style advertisements, with their dense layout, decorative titles, and blend of different script styles and sizes. Moreover, composing the editorializing texts that the American firms swore by created a number of difficulties. Within the German media such texts were widely regarded as vacuous and stupid: Kurt Tucholsky, for one, unsparingly mocked the tastelessness and didacticism of advertising copy.[38] Yet a far more immediate problem was the language barrier. Early attempts to translate U.S.-style copy into German were anything but successful. In view of the supposed genius of American advertisers, Germans understandably took considerable delight in pointing to the "propagandistic grotesque" of clumsily translated slogans like "Frage den, der einen hat" (for Packard's classic "Ask the man who has one"), or the downright excruciating "Der vollkommenste Buick je gebaut!" ("The most refined Buick ever built!").[39]

The only solution was to get natives to write copy, but first they needed to learn how to do it. Or, more precisely, first they had to be sold on the idea, for the skepticism toward long editorializing copy was shared even by many German employees within the American branch offices. As one Thompson representative in Berlin complained in 1927, "All the old nuts had to be cracked. Long versus short copy. The use of slogans. Large logotypes. Featuring the trade mark. Catchy rather than specific, selling head lines. As a result in Germany we now have our own way. No slogans. Copy as long as we wish to make it. Logotypes as small as we wish to use them. No trade marks. And copy as we wish to write it." Such experiences frequently made American advertisers "long for . . . 'the ease of advertising in America,'" in particular "for newspapers that have standard rates—for typographers that have some type assortment—for hand letterers who letter gracefully rather than heavy and black and deadly—for clients slightly more grounded in advertising fundamentals."[40]

The language barrier, different advertising traditions, a different skills base, a different media structure—all of these factors caused problems, but hardly unexpected ones. Though it took some time, the American agencies did learn to work quite effectively within the German environment. What they did not reckon with, or at the very least underestimated at first, was how the different social context in Germany rendered some of their techniques ineffective even once they were satisfactorily realized against the odds just mentioned. U.S. advertising firms generally believed in, or at least assumed, a kind of universal set of advertising principles. The operating assumption was that "Markets Are People—Not Places," and that people with money and a desire to spend it could and should be sold to anywhere: "The world market is just like the national market in its fundamentals and that basic fact should never be forgotten in adapting sales policies to meet foreign conditions."[41] Thus it was consternating to discover that tried and true methods sometimes had to be reconsidered.

Thompson's German marketing campaign for Pond's beauty cream offers a useful illustration. Having successfully employed the "personality testimonial" for their Ponds campaign in the United States, Thompson quickly discovered that it did not work in Germany "for some strange reason."[42] Representatives fumbled for explanations for quite some time. John Watson, reporting back after a European tour in 1930, suggested that residual *bildungsbürgerlich* values were the reason: "The mass of the population of German women are not beauty-mad the way they are here—virtues of the mind seem to be still at a premium in Germany—so it is a little hard to get an angle on them." Getting an angle was made all the more difficult by the fact that the high society from which testimonials were usually drawn was all but nonexistent in Germany and was in any event not admired as in the United States: "There is no interest whatever in society or smartness or any of the standards, activities, or practices for which it stands."[43] Nor were testimonials from "new" celebrities any better: "The interest in stage and screen personalities in Germany is not nearly so great either in extent or intensity in Germany as in America. Actresses are not regarded in the same way as in America as persons to be admired and imitated."[44] Having discovered that cosmetics per se were largely frowned upon, that social emulation marketing was inapplicable and that disposable incomes in Germany were too small to mount the standard "two creams" campaign (selling cold cream and vanishing cream in tandem), Thompson executives sought to market the cold cream alone by appealing to what they perceived as a "movement towards naturalness and simplicity" in Germany.[45] They attributed this trend to the realization that economic reconstruction after the war was possible only through hard work and simple living, which encouraged a rejection of materialism and superficiality. In addition, the immense popularity of sport and the idealization of bodily health and strength powerfully influenced notions of beauty: "The German man admires, and the German woman aspires, to a type of beauty that is somewhat masculine." Clearly, an emphasis on health as opposed to cosmetic beauty promised the best results—hence the new campaign's focus on the theme of "naturalness." The editorializing text argued that Pond's cream was based on the hygienic principles of cleanliness and protection, and distinguished between "artificial" cosmetics that merely hid skin blemishes and Pond's, which catered to the "natural" needs of skin. As usual, scientific data were mobilized in support of the message, in this case the classic "dirty cotton-ball" test and "pore-breathing" arguments. After early setbacks the revamped Pond's campaign proved remarkably effective, even in the dire economic situation of the early 1930s. Sales for the period from January to May 1932 were up 6.9 percent over the previous year, and an aggressive local campaign in Hamburg increased sales by a whopping 158 percent.[46]

Though it took a long time to find the right arguments, this campaign can be interpreted as a victory of the American editorializing ad rather than as a sign of its limitation. Such successes, in particular the detailed market analysis underlying them, did indeed bring recognition to the American agencies from German firms.[47] Yet broadly speaking, German advertisers remained skeptical about the appropriateness of U.S.-style marketing in the German context. The supposed naïveté of American consumers, the incomparably longer distances that advertising messages had to travel in the United States, the relatively homogeneous American public—an array of arguments were mounted against imitating U.S. practices in Germany, even by those quite open to Americanisms in principle.[48] In spite of the many paeans in professional journals, by no means did the majority of German advertisers consider the organizational form or techniques of the U.S. agencies superior, let alone adopt them in their day-to-day operations. During the 1920s local advertising conventions were adjusted, not displaced, by exposure to American marketing methods, which were only very selectively appropriated. The firsthand observation of American agencies in Germany did little to change this, since the foreign agencies had failed to land any real coups besides perhaps the impressive campaigns for Chrysler (which was, as one article pointed out with some satisfaction, run by the leading English firm William Crawford) and for Palmolive soap (whose international advertisements were not specially devised for Germany).[49] As *Seidels Reklame* put it in autumn 1931, shortly before most of the agencies radically scaled down or closed their German offices altogether, "For the time being, the branch offices of the American agencies have yet to produce the proof that their methods and practices are better than those of our own experts." In the final analysis, experience and talent were still deemed paramount: "With the best will in the world, America, too, cannot perform any miracles [*kann . . . mit keinem anderen Wasser kochen*]."[50]

Between Americanization and Germanization:
Advertising in the 1930s

Though it is difficult to document, let alone quantify, there can be little doubt of the increasingly American appearance of German advertising over the early and mid-1930s: in the expanding use of text, of consumer-centered argumentation, of color printing and photography.[51] There are a number of possible explanations for this, not least advances in photography and printing, the sheer length of exposure to American marketing styles, as well as the contingent of German advertisers who had acquired firsthand experience while working for U.S. agencies, some of whom were to found their own companies or run subsidiary affiliates of American firms after the general exodus of 1932–1933.

But apart from developments within the advertising milieu itself, there were also a number of wider changes in German society that reinforced this trend. By the end of the 1920s there was a growing recognition that the future of marketing lay in selling branded products to an increasingly national and socially diverse market, as was already largely the case in the United States. There was, accordingly, a growing impatience with the traditional focus on "a limited number of so-called transport hubs, while the bulk of the millions living in the small towns and the countryside are neglected and in some cases totally excluded." For it was in the "provinces" that one found "the millions of future purchasers who have yet to be won over and persuaded." Along with this changing perception of the market came the recognition, just as in the United States several decades earlier, that selling new products to a first generation of consumers required some degree of "instructive explanation" and "psychological persuasion": "The aim is to open up new markets and win over new segments of society, to penetrate regions which have yet to see the light as to how important proper bodily hygiene, hair care, dental and skin care are for the well-being, self-improvement and personal performance of the individual." In other words, these "future masses of purchasers . . . must first be awakened."[52] With the foreseen outward and downward expansion of the market for consumer goods, the American "capitalist realist" style, with its emphasis on utility and reasoned arguments—its shift from the "factory viewpoint" to "the mental process of the consumer"[53]—would almost naturally come into its own: "For far too long we have told the masses that we wanted to sell them something . . . until one day it dawned on us how crude, misguided and undignified this policy of masters and followers, of rulers and subjects has been in the realm of commercial propaganda."[54]

Another development that may, at least indirectly, have contributed to the increasingly Americanized look of advertising over the early 1930s was the very visible success of Nazi propaganda. While I would not want to argue any chain of causality here, there were certain parallels between National Socialist propaganda techniques and American marketing methods that may have contributed to a subtle shift in perception. This is not to say that Nazi propaganda had a "capitalist realist" look or feel to it. Quite the contrary: stunning imagery was absolutely central, and the emphasis on a highly emotive "pictorial language" (*Bildersprache*), against the arguments for a more persuasion- and conviction-based form of propaganda by the "Strasser wing" of the party, was what most singled out the movement's image and most impressed advertisers at the time.[55] As the renowned advertiser Ernst Growald remarked in 1932, "Hitler's success rests in large part on the excellent advertising [*Reklame*] that is especially effective in view of the fact that his opponents possess nothing remotely as effective as a counterweight. The advertising fetish of the Nazis is the swastika, which is propagated better than any factory or trade symbol ever was."[56] National Socialist propaganda certainly represented in this sense a "revolt of images."[57]

But it was also more than that. For while the use of emotive imagery and brand symbols reflected conventional advertising wisdom at the time, other aspects of Nazi propaganda showed parallels with a more specifically American style: namely, in the combination of emotional imagery with a degree of concrete explanation. Throughout its electoral campaigns the Nazi movement also laid considerable emphasis on verbal appeals to the concrete interests and desires of various social groups. Like an editorializing advertisement, these appeals were couched in a popular idiom and distilled down to a few basic points and sought to explain why people should give Hitler their votes. This mixture of imagery and argumentation was precisely what advertising experts were currently recommending for successful political electioneering. However indispensable "suggestive publicity" (*Suggestivwerbung*) was "for any grand-style propaganda," persuasive arguments could not be wholly abandoned. Effective propaganda, in other words, was characterized by a combination of suggestive and persuasive propaganda, a symbiosis of the poster and the flyer, of image and text.[58]

Whatever similarities one might discern between National Socialist propaganda and the editorializing style of American advertisements can perhaps be related to the fact that they were trying to accomplish somewhat similar tasks. The primary aim of the large American agencies was to open up new markets for consumer goods, overcoming geographical barriers and traditional social hierarchies of taste and in the process constructing new consumer identities centered on participation in the purchase of commodities. The Nazis, for their part, aimed at opening up whole new constituencies for their ideas, breaking down older electoral allegiances and constructing new political identities revolving around participation and social entitlement based on nation and race. Both campaigns, whether selling unfamiliar products to new consumers or selling novel policies to new constituencies, required a mixture of emotional appeal and explanation. Moreover, they also required targeting audiences and varying their messages accordingly. One size did not fit all. Celebrity testimonials by Lady Mountbatten or Mrs. Reginald Vanderbilt sold Pond's cream in Sweden but were a nonstarter in Germany.[59] Railing against big capital and Jewish department stores went down well in small Protestant towns but was generally avoided as propaganda in the urban centers. Just as the American agencies swore by market analysis over the "clever idea," so too did the Nazi leadership emphasize organization and deliberation over spontaneous strokes of genius.[60]

Such speculative parallels aside, the real breakthrough for the American editorializing style ironically came *after* the Nazi takeover and the departure of the U.S. agencies, as commercial marketing techniques increasingly mirrored those in the United States despite the official denigration of all "foreign" advertising influences. There was nothing paradoxical about the timing, for in many ways it reflected the Nazis' new propaganda requirements after acquiring power in 1933. As the focus switched from national revolution to consolidation, there was a dramatic shift away from the agitation of the "period of struggle" toward a more subtle, more omnipresent, and more persuasion-oriented brand of state propaganda.[61] In the realm of commercial advertising, triumphant pronouncements that "there will be no place in the future for vacuous imitation of foreign advertising that does not correspond to the German character" and nationalistic jubilation over the supposed end of "the era of uncritical adulation of American 'models'" provided but thin cover for the fact that Germans continued to study and were increasingly adopting American advertising methods.[62] Of course, this was true of only some aspects. The *Gleichschaltung* of professional bodies and the clear distinction between advertising consultants (*Werbeberater*) and brokers (*Werbevermittler*) meant that the full-service agency model never had a chance to develop, unlike in the rest of Europe.[63] In addition, certain new 1930s genres like the comic strip ad remained marginal, and there was a complete ban on radio advertising after December 1935.[64] Yet the quintessentially American style of print advertising was clearly on the rise. Some of the reasons for this were essentially structural. The establishment of reliable circulation figures and precise size and format standards greatly enhanced market transparency for print advertising and helped make it more profitable. A new requirement for explicit written authorization to quote or cite public personalities also removed some of the suspicion and odium attached to testimonial ads.[65] As in other European countries, the press was also becoming more centralized, which made national marketing campaigns easier.[66] At the same time, national campaigns grew in importance with the expansion of chain stores and increasing centralization of sales networks. All of these factors, in conjunction with new restrictions and charges on postering, contributed to the far-reaching eclipse of the poster by newspaper advertisements.[67]

In addition to such "secular" changes, the rise of American marketing techniques in the mid-1930s may also have been related to their affinity or at least compatibility with certain ideas about advertising that were rather specific to the Nazis. Press advertisements in the United States were geared toward a relatively broad and homogeneous market of "ordinary" people with sufficient purchasing power to participate in the consumption of goods. Though the economic preconditions of the American model of consumption were first achieved in

Germany in the 1950s, images of a society of mass consumption in which the "little people" participated clearly resonated with National Socialist visions of social integration and entitlement for all "people's comrades."[68] As *Die Reklame* put it in July 1933, "It is precisely the new *Volksgemeinschaft* which sweeps away both snobbish aestheticism on the one hand and crass materialism on the other, and which, by bridging class differences and therefore also distinctions of taste, works towards a grand and unambiguous appreciation for authenticity, beauty and propriety that is held in common by all Germans."[69] Advertising, so it was argued in markedly Fordist language, served the common good by stimulating demand and raising consumer expectations, which were themselves seen as a hallmark of German cultural superiority over the relative primitiveness of other peoples.[70]

Though the consumer Volksgemeinschaft remained a mirage, the constant invocation of social harmony and the common good nonetheless had an impact on how advertising was conceived and carried out in the Third Reich. Above all, the ideological straitjacket of the Volksgemeinschaft, which imposed upon the advertising sector a mythical community of interests between producers and consumers, had a number of concrete effects. For one thing, the Nazis wasted little time in cleaning up marketing practices with a raft of tightened regulations against misleading, exaggerated, or dishonest sales pitches—to general applause both within and beyond the profession.[71] But more important for our purposes here, the myth of a community of interests shaped perceptions (at least in published opinion) about the very nature and function of advertising, which indirectly encouraged a more Americanized, editorializing look and feel to mass circulation press advertisements.

The aim of advertising could no longer simply be to boost sales for a particular firm regardless of the wider ramifications. While there was nothing wrong with increasing sales per se, this was justified only insofar as it brought a real benefit to consumers and served the higher aim of strengthening the German economy. Within this framework, the role of advertisers was not merely to sell goods for producers, but to act as a kind of honest broker, even consumer educator. As *Die Reklame* exclaimed in May 1934, "More than ever before, the honest and capable advertiser nowadays wants to substantiate and explain to consumers out of inner conviction why they are well served by this or that product! He wants to conceive of himself as a stimulant and harbinger of new needs [*Bedürfnisse*]." Assuming the role of honest broker required the adoption of new methods: "Only advertising that shows the consumer how to satisfy certain needs sufficiently and economically will have any justification in the future. Any advertisement so bereft of positive sales arguments that it only screams the product's name into the world with grandiose expenditure will increasingly be rejected as an unjustifiable waste of money." Though based on totally different ideological premises, the parallels between this Nazified conceptualization of good marketing practice and the American editorializing style are fairly obvious. Indeed, apart from the pious calls for responsibility toward both consumer and producer, the overall recommendations could just as easily have originated from a J. Walter Thompson or Erwin Wasey handbook: "Do not just propagate the name, but also the product—do not merely place an ad for the producer, but also for the consumer—do not simply write, but also explain and convince."[72]

This move toward an understanding of advertising for the "common good" was accompanied by a shift in the underlying premises of advertising psychology away from the previous emphasis on manipulating basic instincts toward appeals to consumers' desires (though whether this more subtle means of persuasion also represented a "less inhumane" brand of advertising psychology is highly debatable).[73] Insofar as advertisers were already realizing the limitations of a product-centered approach in the early 1930s, Nazi attacks on the cynical manipulation of the consumer merely accelerated an existing trend. In place of the "crude stimulants such as suggestion, deception, etc." that characterized the previous "epoch of 'suggestion competition,'" by the mid-1930s leading advertisers were calling for a new emphasis on persuasion based on consumer wishes: the desire for beauty, health, and social acceptance.[74] As Hanns Kropff, arguably the leading proponent of this shift, put it in 1936, "The drum-beater, the sales cannon" needed to be replaced by the "factually prepared salesman who listens attentively to the consumer in order to find out his wishes"—a task made considerably easier by the expansion of consumer research in the Third Reich.[75] Armed with such knowledge, "the new salesman . . . does not try to bring about a sudden sale through suggestion, but rather will work with the earnest tools of persuasion."[76] What this meant more concretely was spelled out two years earlier in a series of articles juxtaposing ineffective suggestive versus praiseworthy persuasive advertisements. Although these articles do not (for obvious reasons) explicitly recommend a wholesale adoption of American advertising techniques, they nonetheless read as nothing less than a full-blown argument for Americanization. Virtually all of the illustrations juxtapose a suggestive German poster-style announcement against a persuasive American editorializing ad.[77] "Hard-selling copy full of reasons and arguments" was, in other words, not only more ideologically palatable than the traditional poster style, it was also deemed more effective. By the mid-1930s, American "salesmanship in print" had found a new home in the Nazi Volksgemeinschaft.

This is certainly not to say that National Socialist advertising policies were singularly "modernizing" or future-oriented, as of course other aspects of advertising in the Third Reich ran counter to the Americanizing trends discussed above. Strict party control amounted to a loss of professionalization in many regards; radio advertising, which boomed in the United States in the 1930s, was marginal before 1935 and banned thereafter; and of course the efforts to reintroduce *Fraktur* and to Germanize advertising images were anything but modernizing (insofar as they affected mainstream marketing). Nor is it to posit any simple chain of causality between Nazi propaganda and advertising policies on the one hand and the rise of the American-style editorializing ad on the other. Rather, their relationship is more appropriately conceived as one of parallels and mutual influence, whereby the former was in many ways remarkably compatible with the latter.

The fascination shown toward American advertising methods in interwar Germany was due to the fact that American advertisers had by this time acquired far more experience than their European counterparts in communicating with mass publics. Their techniques and practices were observed with interest because they represented, at least in many eyes, the future of advertising. But American marketing techniques were not adopted wholesale, and patterns of appropriation were influenced by a wide range of economic, political, social, and cultural factors. In the Weimar Republic, German advertisers may frequently have indulged in uncritical adulation of the American model, but in practice they tended to adopt only those methods that suited the German context in the here and now. Under the Nazis, this selective appropriation of American techniques remained the rule, though for different reasons than before. Whereas the Weimar modernizers tended to view the United States as a kind of rough guide for the construction of a society of abundance, thus perceiving the adoption of American advertising methods as an integral part of this project, the Nazi leadership possessed its own unique blueprint for the future.[78] For them, visions of a consumer Volksgemeinschaft were predicated first and foremost on the acquisition of "living space," which initially required a policy of accumulation and sacrifice. For the time being, therefore, the Nazis operated according to autarkic, not Fordist, principles. Thus advertising in the Third Reich was—well before the outbreak of war—ultimately oriented more toward steering consumption (*Ver-*

brauchslenkung) than stimulating it (*Bedarfsweckung*), and American advertising styles were emulated, whether deliberately or otherwise, only insofar as they supported this goal. For the Nazis, Americanism in advertising, as in all other spheres, was a means to an end only.[79]

Notes

1. See especially Lüdtke, Marssolek, and von Saldern, *Amerikanisierung*; also Fehrenbach and Poiger, *Transactions, Transgressions, Transformations*; Gassert, "Amerikanismus, Antiamerikanismus, Amerikanisierung"; Kroes, *If You've Seen One, You've Seen the Mall*; Richard Kuisel, *Seducing the French*.

2. See above all Victoria de Grazia, "The Arts of Purchase: How American Publicity Subverted the European Poster, 1920–1940," in Kruger and Mariani, *Remaking History*, 221–257, on whose arguments this essay consciously seeks to build.

3. "Amerika," *Die Reklame* (hereafter DR), 21, no. 17 (1928): 624. The trip was organized by the Verband Deutscher Reklamefachleute and included visits to several major cities as well as the 1928 International Advertising Association convention in Detroit.

4. See the comments in J. Walter Thompson Company Archives: Staff Meeting Minutes Collection, 1927–1938 (hereafter JWT Staff Meeting Minutes), Box 2, Staff Meeting 10 September 1929, 3, Rare Book, Manuscript, and Special Collections Library, Duke University.

5. See Alfred Knapp, "Wege und Ziele der Organisation des Werbewesens," in *Reklame, Propaganda, Werbung: Weltorganisation* (Berlin: Verlag für Presse, Wirtschaft und Politik, 1929), 11ff., which estimates annual advertising expenditure in Germany at around RM 2 billion and around RM 6 billion ($1.5 billion) in the United States.

6. See, e.g., Max Pauly, "Truth in Advertising," DR 16, no. 135 (1921): 135–137.

7. See DR 22, no. 5 (1929): 160; Arthur Stamper, "Die wachsende Wertung der Reklame," *Seidels Reklame* (hereafter SR) 6, nos. 1–2 (1921): 1–2. This was also, of course, a concern before World War I: see Kevin Repp's chapter in this volume. As Alfred Knapp, general secretary and treasurer of the Welt-Reklame-Kongress put it, the aim was to raise the "economic and social standing" of the advertising profession in Germany, and in general "to gain for advertising the recognition of its importance that it deserves within the framework of the national economy." Knapp, "Wege und Ziele," 16, 11.

8. "Die Wahrheit in der Auflagennennung," SR 9, no. 7 (1925): 297–298; "Der VDR nimmt zur Auflagennennung und Auflagenkontrolle Stellung!," DR 19, no. 3 (1926): 119; Hans Traub, "Auflagenkontrolle und Leseranalyse," DR 23, no. 20 (1930): 626–628; Fritz Wille, "Die Auflagenkontrolle und ihre Durchführung," DR 24, no. 1 (1931): 27.

9. See the comments of Ernst Growald and Johannes Steindamm in SR 5, nos. 1–2 (1920): 1.

10. It is telling, for instance, that the first firm to carry out detailed market analysis in Germany was J. Walter Thompson. Equally telling is the fact that the first standard German-language work on the subject was the product of a collaborative German-American effort: Hanns Kropff and Bruno Randolph. *Marktanalyse: Untersuchung des Marktes und*

Vorbereitung der Reklame (Munich: Oldenbourg, 1928). The first study on market analysis specifically related to the German context was Armin Kiehl, *System der Markt-Analyse: Die Praxis kontinentaler Untersuchungen* (Lübeck: Coleman, 1929). See generally Reinhardt, *Von der Reklame zum Marketing*, 46–48.

11. See generally de Grazia, "The Arts of Purchase," especially 230–257.

12. Quotes from Marchand, *Advertising the American Dream*, 10. See also Lears, *Fables of Abundance*.

13. Marchand, *Advertising*, 10.

14. De Grazia, "The Arts of Purchase," 236.

15. Quoted in Marchand, *Advertising*, 11.

16. See the remarks in Paul Knoll, "Das Anzeigenwesen des Ullsteinhauses," in *50 Jahre Ullstein, 1877–1927*, ed. Verlag Ullstein (Berlin: Ulstein, 1927), 303–328, especially 322.

17. L. Richard, "Reklame-Agenturen nach amerikanischem System!," SR 15, no. 10 (1931): 409.

18. On the Werkbund generally, see Campbell, *The German Werkbund*; also F. J. Schwartz, *The Werkbund*. On the emergence of the Kunstplakat, see Reinhardt, *Von der Reklame zum Marketing*, 49–76; Lamberty, *Reklame in Deutschland*, 321–377.

19. Reinhardt, *Von der Reklame zum Marketing*, 77–78.

20. H. Kropff, "Götterdämmerung der deutschen Reklamekunst," DR 17, no. 10 (1924): 674–675, emphasis in original. It is no coincidence that Kropff was one of the first German advertisers to use the American-style editorializing ad, most notably in his highly successful mid-1920s campaign for Elida soap. See Reinhardt, *Von der Reklame zum Marketing*, 221.

21. This and the following quotes from JWT Research Reports, Microfilm Collection 16mm, reel 232, A. E. Hobbs, "Advertising in Germany," January 1928, 1.

22. Just a sampling: Johann Plenge, *Deutsche Propaganda. Die Lehre von der Propaganda als praktische Gesellschaftslehre* (Bremen: Angelsachsen-Verlag, 1922); Edgar Stern-Rubarth, *Die Propaganda als politisches Instrument* (Berlin: Trowitsch und Sohn, 1921); Kurt Hesse, *Der Feldherr Psychologus: Ein Suchen nach dem Führer der deutschen Zukunft* (Berlin: E. S. Mittler, 1922). Hermann Schmidt, *Das politische Werbewesen im Kriege* (Berlin: Arbeitsbund für Werbelehre, 1919); Hermann Schmidt, *Das politische Werbewesen in der Umsturzzeit* (Berlin: Arbeitsbund für Werbelehre, 1919); Ludolf Knesebeck, *Die Wahrheit über den Propagandafeldzug und Deutschlands Zusammenbruch* (Berlin, 1927); Georg Huber, *Die französische Propaganda im Weltkrieg gegen Deutschland, 1914 bis 1918* (Munich: Pfeiffer, 1928); Wilhelm Ernst, *Die anti-deutsche Propaganda durch das Schweizer Gebiet im Weltkrieg, speziell die Propaganda in Bayern* (Munich: Beck, 1933); Hans Thimme, *Weltkrieg ohne Waffen: Die Propaganda der Westmächte gegen Deutschland, ihre Wirkung und ihre Abwehr* (Stuttgart: Cotta, 1932); Wilhelm Prosch, "Die Propaganda. Ihre Anwendung in der Politik und ihre Bedeutung für Deutschlands Wiederaufstieg," Ph.D. diss., Hamburg, 1924; Hans Domizlaff, *Propagandamittel der Staatsidee* (Hamburg: Hanseatische Verlagsanstalt, 1932). See Ross, "Mass Politics and the Techniques of Leadership."

23. Reinhardt, *Von der Reklame zum Marketing*, 87–92. The first director of the institute was

Prof. Walter Moede, who was also editor of the main applied psychology journal *Prak-tische Psychologie* and its successor *Industrielle Psychotechnik*.

24. Most influential in this regard was the study by Theodor König, "Die Psychologie der Reklame." Not only did the bulk of relevant studies (on memory and repetition, form and shape recognition, color and placement effect) build on experimental psychological approaches pioneered in America (in part by Münsterberg), but also the application of psychological principles in advertising was considered to be further developed there: witness the person of John Watson, professor of psychology at Johns Hopkins University and founding father of behaviorism, who worked as a vice president for J. Walter Thompson during the 1920s and 1930s.

25. Christoph v. Hartungen, *Psychologie der Reklame*, 2nd ed. (Stuttgart: Poeschel, 1926), 5.

26. See the standard work by Mataja, *Die Reklame: Eine Untersuchung über Ankündigungswe-sen und Werbetätigkeit im Geschäftsleben*, 4th ed. (Leipzig: Duncker und Humblot, 1926), 26–28; also Helene Stückel, "Suggestion in der Reklame," *DR*, no. 145 (February 1922): 62; generally Reinhardt, *Von der Reklame zum Marketing*, 93–96.

27. G. Schultze-Pfaelzer, "Die Hauptformen öffentlicher Werbung," *SR* 7, no. 12 (1922): 256.

28. *Berliner Illustrierte Zeitung*, no. 41 (1921), cited in Walter Schmitt, *Das Filmwesen und seine Wechselbeziehungen zur Gesellschaft. Versuch einer Soziologie des Filmwesens* (Freudenstadt: Oskar Kaupert, 1932), 113.

29. Bela Balazs, *Der sichtbare Mensch*, 2nd ed. (Halle: Knapp, 1926), 27.

30. See generally Nolan, *Visions of Modernity*.

31. Quoted in Knapp, *Reklame, Propaganda, Werbung*, 3–4.

32. For an interesting contemporary overview, see "Europe as a Market," *Atlantic Monthly* (1930): 400–409.

33. For an excellent overview of the U.S. agencies and their organizational forms in Ger-many, see Schug, "Wegbereiter der modernen Absatzwerbung in Deutschland," espe-cially 39–42. See also the brief description in Reinhardt, *Von der Reklame zum Marketing*, 127–128.

34. See the discussion in Box 2, Staff Meeting 8 October 1929, 1–2, JWT Staff Meeting Min-utes.

35. Box 1, Staff Meeting 20 December 1927, folder 80, JWT Staff Meeting Minutes.

36. Compare the emphasis on the "modernizing" impact of the U.S. agencies in Schug, "Wegbereiter."

37. Main Newsletter Series, JWT Newsletter no. 192, 15 November 1927, 482, JWT Newsletter Collection.

38. Willett, *The New Sobriety*, 137. See also the derision of the "canned advertising pitch" in J. G. Faber, "Amerika du hast es besser!," *SR* 15, no. 10 (1931): 406.

39. *DR* 19, nos. 15–16 (1926): 729–730; "Deutsche Sprache, dichterische Freiheit und Buick-Wagen!," *DR* 19, no. 20 (1926): 980–981.

40. These quotes are from JWT Newsletter, no. 192, 15 November 1927, 482.

41. News Bulletin Series, 1922–1931, JWT News Bulletin no. 135, July 1928, JWT Newsletter Collection; Clement Watson, "Markets Are People—Not Places," 3.

42. This and the following quote from Box 3, Staff Meeting 9 December 1930, 5, JWT Staff Meeting Minutes.

43. Microfilm Collection, 16mm, reel 224, "Memorandum on Pond's in Germany: Review of Spring 1932, Recommendations for Fall 1932," 2, JWT Research Reports.

44. Ibid., 12.

45. A survey of four hundred women in Berlin and Cologne in August 1929 found that even among users of cold creams, 68 percent still used no cosmetics as a matter of principle. Microfilm Collection, 16mm, reel 224, "Pond's Investigations in Germany: Comparison of Results of Two Consumer Investigations," 1, JWT Research Reports.

46. Quotes and sales figures from Microfilm Collection, 16mm, reel 224, "Memorandum on Pond's in Germany: Review of Spring 1932, Recommendations for Fall 1932," 3–5, JWT Research Reports.

47. Box 4, Staff Meeting 27 October 1931, 10, JWT Staff Meeting Minutes.

48. See, e.g., the reactions of participants on the VDR (Verband Deutscher Reklamefachleute) study trip to the United States in 1928: DR 21, no. 17 (1928): 624.

49. L. Richard, "Reklame-Agenturen nach amerikanischem System!," SR 15, no. 10 (1931): 409–410.

50. Ibid.

51. In this sense Hartmut Berghoff's assertion that continuities between the Weimar Republic and Nazi periods outweighed discontinuities requires qualification, though I would wholly agree with his argument with respect to vague notions of "Germanness" and "honesty" in advertising styles, which changed far less than the National Socialist ideologues liked to claim. Hartmut Berghoff, "Von der 'Reklame' zur Verbrauchslenkung. Werbung im nationalsozialistischen Deutschland," in *Konsumpolitik*, 97. See also Reinhardt, *Von der Reklame zum Marketing*, 220–230.

52. Quotes taken from H. W. Brose, "Die Königin unter den Werbeträgern," DR 22, no. 24 (1929): 908–910.

53. Quoted in Marchand, *Advertising*, 11.

54. Brose, "Die Königin unter den Werbeträgern," 908.

55. On the disputes within the NSDAP (National Sozialistische Deutsche Arbeiter Partei), see Paul, *Aufstand der Bilder*, 51–53. Apart from the KPD (Kommunistische Partei Deutschlands),which used similar techniques, the Nazis' political opponents despised these appeals to emotion as sheer demagoguery and by and large sought to counter them with appeals to reason (Sergei Chakotin's belated efforts for the SPD [Sozialdemokratische Partei Deutschlands] notwithstanding). See Harsch, *German Social Democracy*, 177.

56. Ernst Growald, "Reklame-Fetische an die Front!," SR 16, no. 9 (1932): 319. See also I. G. Faber, "Nationalsozialistische Werbung," SR 16, no. 8 (1932): 299–301; Heinz Bachmann, "Psychologische Fundamentalfehler," SR 16, no. 8 (1932): 304. See also Holm Friebe's essay in this volume.

57. So the fitting title of Paul, *Aufstand der Bilder*.

58. Erich Kwilecki, "Die Propaganda für die Präsidentenwahl," DR 25, no. 9 (1932): 269.

59. Out of the eight advertisements in Thompson's 1932 Pond's campaign in Sweden, five were testimonials. Microfilm Collection, 16mm, reel 232, "Pond's 1931 and 1932," JWT Research Reports.

60. Paul, *Aufstand der Bilder*, 57. This was reflected in, among other things, the establishment of the Reichspropagandaleitung at Hitler's behest, and also in the title of chapter 11 of *Mein Kampf*: "Propaganda und Organisation."

61. The Nazis were acutely aware by November 1932 that their agitational propaganda style had exhausted its possibilities. See Paul, *Aufstand der Bilder*, 106–108, also 263; see also Bussemer, *Propaganda und Populärkultur*.

62. Quotes from "Deutsche Werbung für deutsche Arbeit!," *SR* 17, no. 5 (1933): 145; W. Lüders, "Sünde wider die Natur!," *SR* 17, no. 6 (1933): 194. On the continuing interest in American advertisements, see "Originelle Muster amerikanischer Werbung," *DR* 27, no. 19 (1934): 628–629; O. v. Halem, "Amerikanische Werbung," *SR* 18, no. 8 (1934): 258–260.

63. See Reinhardt, *Von der Reklame zum Marketing*, 128; de Grazia, "The Arts of Purchase," 249–250.

64. Berghoff, "Von der 'Reklame' zur Verbrauchslenkung," 96.

65. Ibid., 88.

66. The number of newspapers decreased dramatically, from about four thousand in 1933 to only 977 in 1944: Koszyk, *Deutsche Presse*, 369. Of course, this centralization in Germany resulted not only from commercial trends, but also from political bans on certain periodicals.

67. From 1934 to 1938, advertising volume rose by 35 percent in German newspapers and by 47 percent in magazines: Reinhardt, *Von der Reklame zum Marketing*, 201, also 188–189, 256–257. By 1937, 87 percent of advertising expenditure in Germany was on newspapers: de Grazia, "The Arts of Purchase," 257 n. 37.

68. See generally Baranowski, *Strength through Joy*; also Baranowski's contribution to this volume.

69. Emil Endres, "Die neue Gesinnung in der Werbung," *DR* 26, no. 12 (1933): 382.

70. "Advertising shows the consumer what new and more beautiful things the world can offer him if only he exerts himself to offer the corresponding amount of effort for it." Paul Blankenburg, "Wirtschaftswerbung und nationalsozialistische Weltanschauung," *SR* 19, no. 9 (1935): 326. See also Fr. Mayer, "Deutsch werben," *SR* 18, no. 3 (1934): 118.

71. See Berghoff, "Von der 'Reklame' zur Verbrauchslenkung," 87–92; also generally Rücker, *Wirtschaftswerbung unter dem Nationalsozialismus*.

72. Quotes from "Setzt sich eine neue Werbeauffassung durch?," *DR* 27, no. 10 (1934): 295–297.

73. Reinhardt, *Von der Reklame zum Marketing*, 99.

74. Blankenburg, "Wirtschaftswerbung und nationalsozialistische Weltanschauung," 326; Reinhardt, *Von der Reklame zum Marketing*, 99. An influential work along these lines is Hanns Kropff, *Psychologie in der Reklame als Hilfe zur Bestgestaltung des Entwurfs* (Stuttgart: Poeschel, 1934).

75. Above all by the Nürnberg Institut für Marktforschung, the Gesellschaft für Konsum-

forschung, and the Institut für Konjunkturforschung. See generally Berghoff, "Von der 'Reklame' zur Verbrauchslenkung."

76. H. Kropff, "Psychologie in der Werbung," SR 20, no. 12 (1936): 444.

77. H. Kropff, "Suggestion, Glaube und Überzeugung in der Reklame," SR 18, no. 7 (1934): 227ff.; no. 8 (1934): 263ff.; no. 9 (1934): 302ff.; no. 10 (1934): 355ff. Quote from no. 7 (1934): 227. On Kropff's Americanizing predilections, see also note 20.

78. Nolan, *Visions of Modernity*; for the pan-European perspective, see Maier, "From Taylorism to Technocracy."

79. See Gassert, *Amerika im Dritten Reich*, 26–27.

3

HOLM FRIEBE

BRANDING GERMANY

Hans Domizlaff's *Markentechnik*

and Its Ideological Impact

In the history of advertising and political propaganda in modern Germany, one man stands out as both a practitioner and a theoretician. Hans Domizlaff, who was born in 1892 in Frankfurt am Main and died in Hamburg in 1971, enjoys a broad appeal today. If, as Domizlaff emphasized again and again, "one must be patient until the time has come for a brand to grow in fertile soil," then the brand *Domizlaff* is now well established.[1] His central work from the 1930s, *Wie man das öffentliche Vertrauen gewinnt. Ein Lehrbuch der Markentechnik* (How to Achieve Public Confidence: A Manual of Brand Technique), was republished several times in West Germany, most recently on the occasion of his hundredth birthday. This book can be found in most university libraries, and his theoretical and practical approach to branding is continually being revisited by the Institut für Markentechnik in Geneva. Wherever his name appears, Domizlaff is remembered as "the godfather of German branding," "the inventor of 'brand technique,'" and an "Urfaust of advertising." The last expression was coined in the 1960s by economist Ernest Dale, who wrote, "If there ever was an 'Urfaust' in management, advertising and marketing thought, it is Hans Domizlaff. He is one of the immortal managerial 'symbolists.'"[2] Although his ideas continue to influence German advertisers and the business world more broadly, the full impact of his reactionary and antidemocratic ideas, fully conceived before World War II, has yet to be recognized.

Since World War II, a number of works from outside the field of marketing science have provided insight into Domizlaff's political and private persona.[3] This essay, however, offers a close reading of his early texts—and the concept of "brand technique" in particular—in order to place Domizlaff's ideas within the intellectual currents of Weimar Germany. Domizlaff, this essay argues, can be identified as an agent of a "conservative revolution" within marketing. In the waning years of the Weimar Republic, he attempted to merge a reactionary ideology with a modernist surface culture. This was most evident in his recommendation to redesign national propaganda—to relaunch the brand *Germany* even before the Nazis did so with such terrifying consequences.

The Brand Domizlaff

Although Domizlaff is currently celebrated as a pioneer in his discipline, his reputation in his own time, especially in the years prior to World War II, was unremarkable. Domizlaff's reemergence in the world of German marketing may be explained in part by an underdeveloped sense of historical memory in this field, where, according to Ursula Hansen and Matthias Bode, "time only exists as the universal presence on the periphery of the future and, therefore, is marked by ahistoricity."[4] Moreover, throughout his life, Domizlaff engaged in what might be called a strategic self-positioning, whereby success would be achieved in an unorthodox manner. Wrote Domizlaff, "The paths a good propagandist follows are often elusive and hard to recognize or judge from the outside."[5]

In a portrait written in 1963, the journalist Willi Bongard still wondered why a man "who influences and often seduces millions of consumers each day" had never been the subject of much public interest: "It is strange enough that this man, in spite of the number of publications, has remained more or less unknown to the public eye."[6] Indeed, with one exception (which will be discussed below), Domizlaff's books were largely unrecognized upon publication, both by the general public and among professionals and theorists in the still developing academic field of marketing in Germany. In the very first compendium of literature on branded products from 1940, his name does not appear once.[7] In Eugen Leitherer's comprehensive bibliography of trade and marketing literature from 1961, Domizlaff also goes unmentioned.[8] Finally, in a 1953 essay on the history of German economic advertising, there is a single, rather offhand allusion to Domizlaff's political opportunism and his talent for creating a "personality cult."[9]

During the Weimar and post–World War II periods, this ignorance of Domizlaff's work was accented by an at times mutual hostility between German advertisers (and academics) and Domizlaff himself. This tension was very likely deliberate on Domizlaff's part. Known as a maverick and a loner, he was also a typical autodidact, studying philosophy and art history in Paris, London, and Leipzig, but never completing a degree. After a short intermezzo as a set designer at the Leipzig Theater, he found his way into advertising. His ambitions always exceeded the boundaries of the nascent field of advertising. He considered himself an artist, a philosopher, and a genius, who wound up in the advertising industry by accident. This might actually be regarded as a typical *deformation professionelle*, although, according to Rainer Gries, Volker Ilgen, and Dirk Schindelbeck, "like many professionals in advertising, Hans Domizlaff aimed for something greater: He wanted to be an artist or author, but remained an advertising man and executive consultant all his life."[10]

Domizlaff avoided close contact with other professionals in his field, rarely contributing to debates carried out in advertising magazines. His books were published either by small publishing houses or as private publications or even hand-distributed as manuscripts. In this manner, he could cultivate a myth that his insights were a kind of secret knowledge available only to a chosen few. Being an outsider in his profession and self-made mass psychologist, he nevertheless possessed a powerful ability to convince executives to implement his ideas. In 1921 he met Phillip Reemtsma of the Erfurt-based tobacco company Reemtsma, where, in his first job as a brand technician, he gained practical experience and tested his ideas. By 1933 Domizlaff had found his way to Siemens, where he had full responsibility for the company's corporate design.

Domizlaff's book *Brevier für Könige* (Breviary for Kings) is, in its form, content, and mode of distribution, typical of his self-promoting tactics.[11] Dedicated to "my royal friend"—implicitly the young successor at the top of the Siemens hierarchy, Ernst von Siemens—the book was given to only a select group of people in the 1930s, and not actually published until 1950.[12] It is a Machiavellian-inspired guide to ruling a "kingdom" (any sphere of interest, a company as much as a state) according to the principles of a secret science of mass psychological governance. Notwithstanding its gesture toward Germany's elites, the author was sorely disappointed that the plan to convince political and economic leaders of the text's value by word of mouth was a failure. The publisher admitted as much in the introduction to the 1950 edition: "Despite all efforts, the author's hope to confidentially educate the ruling statesmen and business leaders has proven illusory; hence the only remaining option is to create interest through public debate. However there is a risk that putting the book in the hands of lay-persons may lead to misunderstandings and false allegations."[13] Publicity, it appears, had been a means to an end in the eyes of Domizlaff. His true intention was to gain influence over an elite group of political and economic leaders. As feared, such "misunderstandings" grew in the Federal Republic. Although his operating base, the Institut für Markentechnik (founded in 1954 in Hamburg), was in operation until his death in 1971, Domizlaff slid into "growing isolation" due to his increasingly radical and antidemocratic vision of secretly establishing an *Unternehmerstaat*, a regime led by conspiring business leaders.[14]

In the last decades of his life, Domizlaff withdrew to the loneliness of his farm near Hamburg, spending his time cultivating animals and pursuing his passion for sailing, on which he wrote a number of quite successful pieces of nonfiction. He did not live long enough to witness his rediscovery as a mastermind of "holistic" branding. Some of today's most fashionable management doctrines and the contemporary boom of "biologistic" approaches in business theory indeed seem to have revived the concept of *Markentechnik*, spawning catchy terms like the "genetic code of a brand."[15] Such trends unwittingly call upon reactionary intellectual traditions of the late nineteenth century and early twentieth.

Psychotechnique and Mass Psychology

Before World War I, product design and advertising were the cooperative undertakings of industry and art, with the latter including graphic design and architecture. The overall objective was "aesthetic coherence," an ideal expressed most clearly in the discussions and practical works of the Werkbund, an association for applied arts founded in 1907. The programmatic idea of *Sachlichkeit* (objectivity) stood at the heart of this alliance between art and industry. As Frederic J. Schwartz has written, "The members of Werkbund were trying to set up a world in which art and economics would speak the same language."[16]

Advertising witnessed a wave of professionalization and customization in the 1920s, fostered by the economic recovery after 1923 and manifesting itself in an independent advertising industry and the establishment of in-house advertising divisions. As Corey Ross makes clear in his essay in this volume, advertising changed dramatically in the Weimar years due to the adoption of more advanced standards from America, often at the expense of artistic ambitions in product design and advertising. The urge to analyze and improve the efficiency of advertising meant artists were replaced by (on the whole) well-trained psychologists or "psychotechnicians." The standard for successful advertising changed from "aesthetically coherent" to "psychologically effective."[17] The term "psychotechnics" was coined by the German Harvard professor Hugo Münsterberg, whose book *Grundzüge der Psychotechnik* (Basics of Psychotechnique) paved the way for the foundation of applied psychology in Germany.[18] After the war, psychotechnics, based mainly on behavioristic lab experiments, became widespread in Germany: "By 1922, 170 German firms had separate divisions devoted to psychotechnics. Its practitioners became the first business consultants of the twentieth century and found lucrative employment consulting for German firms intent on modernizing their procedures."[19]

The emergence of psychotechnics in German advertising reflected a new open-mindedness among corporate executives and may explain Domizlaff's career boost in 1921, when he became the head of advertising at Reemtsma before the age of thirty without having ever studied psychology. The scientization of advertising, however, was not on his agenda. By this time, Domizlaff's unique understanding of mass psychology had already developed out of his own idiosyncratic philosophy.[20]

The most comprehensive introduction to Domizlaff's philosophy can be found in his 1946 book *Analogik*, which the author claimed to have "conceived at the age of 18."[21] No less humble than this assertion was the book's subtitle, *Denkgesetzliche Grundsätze der naturwissenschaftlichen Forschung* (Mental Laws of Scientific Research). Chapter titles such as "Rationality," "Life," and "Human Being" allude to the comprehensive nature of the book's contents. Rationality is overruled in favor of an intuitive perception of the world based on metaphors and analogies. Most metaphors in the text are taken from biology. Illness, fashion, religion, ideologies, and even mathematics become *Ideenorganismen* (idea organisms) or *Großorganismen* (giant organisms), antagonizing each other, manifesting their wild, omnivorous character. Monsters, hopelessly crammed together, populate Domizlaff's world. But masses arise as giant organisms only when crowds are held together by the same idea or focus, similar to ant or bee populations.

This mixture of antirationalism, biologism, and social Darwinism was popular in the interwar era and was associated with a range of thinkers, such as Friedrich Nietzsche and Oswald Spengler. It is rather difficult to reconstruct Domizlaff's sources, since he never used quotations or citations in any of his books, possibly to prevent any questioning of his originality. His somewhat cynical antirationalism may have been deduced from Nietzsche, who regarded humans as driven purely by instincts. Spengler, strongly influenced by Nietzsche himself, might have been the basis for Domizlaff's organic view of social phenomena, as well as for his ambivalence toward technology. Moreover, Nietzsche might have provided the morphological epistemology, which juxtaposes Gestalt against the rational, hard factual laws of science. Ernst Jünger, ideologically close to Spengler, illustrated this esoteric form of reality perception in his 1932 essay *Der Arbeiter*: "From the moment one starts to conceive in terms of Gestalt, everything becomes Gestalt. Hence, Gestalt is not an additional factor to be detected. Rather the world turns into an arena for Gestalten and their interactions in the twinkling of an eye."[22] Gestalt is Domizlaff's chosen synonym for giant and idea organisms, and it serves to secure those concepts against any rational questioning.

The main influence for Domizlaff's mass psychology, however, was clearly the French physician Gustave Le Bon, whose book *The Crowd* was originally published in 1895 and was translated into German in 1908.[23] Le Bon used his experiences during the mass disturbances and mob riots of the Paris Commune of 1870–1871 to generalize about all mass phenomena. The term *Massenseele* (mass soul), also used by Domizlaff, originates in Le Bon's work.[24] Masses form an instinctively driven unity, in which individual thinking is abandoned. Accordingly, mass psychology and individual psychology are based on different principles and have little in common.

The notion of the mass as a unitary subject was quite common during the Weimar era, and Le Bon's mass psychology was widely influential. Sigmund Freud, for example, referred extensively and, for the most part, positively to Le Bon in his *Group Psychology and the Analysis of the Ego* from 1921. But unlike Le Bon, he argued that "the contrast of individual and social or mass psychology, which appears meaningful at first sight, loses much of its sharpness at closer inspection."[25] Freud located the typical characteristics of the mass soul in the subconscious of the individual mind.

Departing from Freud's insight, Domizlaff categorically separated the individual and the mass psyche. He insisted that many "typical mistakes in the critique of advertising" were based on the nonobservance of this distinction.[26] The concept of a *Massengehirn* (mass brain), which also figures prominently in his Markentechnik, was central to Domizlaff's thinking: "When dealing with individuals the existence of a superimposed mass psyche is hardly recognizable. When it comes to examining larger groups of people, though—and in Markentechnik we only deal with masses—the existence of a Massengehirn is immediately apparent."[27] As with Le Bon, the mass is characterized by impulsivity, irritability, and irrationality.[28] In other words, the mass exhibits animalistic traits: "To get a better idea we can assume that the mass has preserved a higher level of instinct, like many inferior organisms."[29] Domizlaff reiterates this point elsewhere: "The rationality of giant organisms lies on a much lower level than even the most unintellectual human being. Instead the comparison to animals applies."[30]

Consequently, whenever he comes in contact with a mass, the mass psychologist has to find nonrational ways of communicating in order to cope with the animalistic features of the giant organism: "Individuals can be won over with rationalism. Animals and masses need to be influenced by means of dressage."[31] Indeed, the work of the mass psychologist resembles a battle with a hungry beast rather than a dialogue between human beings. The ultimate purpose of the brand idea is to evoke a very special need in the consumer—almost an addiction—that can be satisfied only by the matching branded product.[32] It becomes clear that "winning public confidence," the highest aim of Markentechnik, has a pathological character; Domizlaff indeed refers to a "psychosis of confidence."[33]

Historian Dirk Reinhardt has referred to the "inhumane tendencies" of (applied) psychology in the 1920s and its regard for the individual human being as an easily manipulated object, driven only by baser human instincts.[34] If Reinhardt is correct, then Domizlaff's mass psychology marks a sinister variety of this trend. For Domizlaff, the mass is a resonating body, whose vibes need to be met by the mass psychologist. At the same time it is erratic and threatening, a dangerous mob resisting the psychologist's influence.

While Domizlaff sees his view of mass psychology as unquestionable, he fails to explain why those principles, analyzed by Le Bon during actual mob gatherings, should also apply to the virtual mass of consumers, the target group of mass-produced brand-name items. Domizlaff's mass psychology could be interpreted in terms of Freud's psychology of the individual, adapted to fit the expanding environment of mass markets and surface culture. Yet Domizlaff holds to the mass psychological foundation with a stubbornness that has important implications for his Markentechnik, both theoretically and, to a limited extent, for his very own practice as a brand manager.

During the Weimar era, as Reinhardt points out, "people's ambition to stand out of the mass—no longer divided by class—grew steadily," and "the meaning of a seemingly individual lifestyle, as well as its definition by specific habits of consumption increased."[35] Domizlaff, in contrast, insisted on the value of his idea of one single homogeneous mass, controlled by one single "mass brain." "There may be thousands of different commodities," he wrote, "but the vast mass of consumers . . . is always the same."[36]

Domizlaff argued that human beings are to be addressed either as rational individuals or as part of the mass, driven by baser human instincts; *tertium non datur*. Accordingly, he completely ignored the techniques adopted during the mid-1920s, largely by branches of U.S. advertising and market research agencies, such as identifying target groups and taking the consumer's individual needs seriously.[37] For Domizlaff, all sociodemographic differentiations are leveled out: "In general, [the existence of] pronounced individual social groupings is very uncommon. But even in the exceptional case that two groups can be separated, with one mainly consisting of those with higher education and the other made up of workers, practical experience shows no relevant deviation in their mass psychological features."[38]

The only differentiation Domizlaff allows for is ethnic. Germany's position lies between the "easily infected peoples of the south" and the "stubborn individualistic population of the north." If one proceeds from this mass psychological logic, the need to capture "the entirety of a geographically divided mass of people derives from the necessity to avoid any effects of negative interference."[39] Hence, the famous statement made by Kaiser Wilhelm II on the eve of World War I, "I know no parties anymore; I know only Germans," can be translated into Domizlaff's vocabulary: I know no target groups, just the German mass brain.

Natural Brand Building and Brand Personality

"Food for thought" for the mass brain is Domizlaff's definition of a brand, though the concept is not restricted to branded products only. And like anything else, the brand is subject to biological conditions and the laws of nature. Even the historical evolution of the branded article industry ensued "spontaneously," like "a product of nature." Therefore, the "laws of natural brand building," as conceived by Domizlaff, are bound by the verities of natural science: "The laws of brand building are laws of nature."[40]

Although man-made, brands are living creatures, according to Domizlaff's conception of idea organisms. One of the central ideas of Markentechnik is that the product itself, including all aspects of its composition, yields the "brand idea" (*Markenidee*). Once the brand idea encounters the instinct of the mass, it becomes alive and spreads like a virus: "An idea . . . can become a self-contained life form within the mass psyche, approximating the image of millions of microbes as carriers. This explains the autonomous life of brands, which can grow on their own strength, regardless of the critical reasoning of individuals, as if they were living creatures themselves." In a way, Hans Domizlaff could be called the inventor of

ERNTEN 27 BIS 30 + MUSTERCIGARETTEN + MISCHUNGSNUMMER R6 o/M

Diese Cigaretten werden in den neuen Fabrikationsanlagen des technischen Muster betriebes in Altona-Bahrenfeld hergestellt. Ihre Lieferung ist zunächst beschränkt. Der ungewöhnlich zarte und reine Charakter dieser Mischung beruht darauf, daß sämtliche Tabake zweimal fermentiert werden. Die Cigarette wird ausschließlich ohne Mundstück hergestellt. Die Hauptprovenienzen stammen aus folgenden Distrikten.

Djumaja, Nevrokop, Cavalla, Xanthi,
Akkissar, Sindirgi, Ayassoluk, Samsun.

Die Cigaretten sind Muster der doppelten Fermentation und neuer Fabrikations methoden, die zugunsten der Tabakqualität die Nebenkosten der Herstellung auf das denkbar geringste Maß herabsetzen ließen

REEMTSMA CIGARETTENFABRIKEN G.M.B.H. ALTONA-BAHRENFELD

1. Domizlaff's R6 cigarette label for Reemtsma from the early 1920s. From Cigarettenfabriken H. F. and Ph. F. Reemtsma, eds., *Tabago* (Hamburg, 1960).

"viral marketing." Yet the image of the brand as a disease hardly fits alongside the morphological approach of its creator, as when Domizlaff insists, "One shouldn't make the mistake of comparing brands to plants or even human beings." Moreover, the anthropomorphization of the brand—the core idea of Markentechnik—reveals a striking irony in Domizlaff's thinking. Whereas people lose their humanity and individuality within the mass, brands turn into complex personalities, leading Domizlaff to proclaim that "a brand has a face just like a human being," and that "changing a single feature of the face leads to a notion of alienation and critical questioning."[41]

This concept of "brand personality" (*Markenpersönlichkeit*) remains the central pragmatic contribution of Domizlaff's Markentechnik today. Marketers worldwide deal explicitly with "brand personalities."[42] Nonetheless, one cannot easily connect this concept with Domizlaff's own work as a brand designer, specifically at Reemtsma after 1923. The typical "style" of Reemtsma was a Sachlichkeit, rooted in the product itself. The cigarette R6, created by Domizlaff in 1923 within the space of two days and two nights (according to him), was given its name simply because it was the sixth brand in the Reemtsma product portfolio.[43] On its box, the company advertised its new production process rather verbosely, praising its "double fermentation." The product Ernte 23 (Harvest 23)

2. Domizlaff's Ernte 23 brand label for Reemtsma. From Cigarettenfabriken H. F. and Ph. F. Reemtsma, eds., *Tabago* (Hamburg, 1960).

was named after the tobacco harvested in 1923. The Gelbe Sorte (Yellow Brand) simply referred to the color of the packaging. All brand-name typefaces combine discreet arabesque and sans serif majuscules. Baroque ornaments, typical of the Wilhelmine period, are strangely blended with Weimar's modern, sober Sachlichkeit.

In search of their personalities, these brands are characterized by their decidedly impersonal images. In comparison to competing cigarette brands during the Weimar period, this contradiction is glaring. In these early days of branding, most cigarette brands were carriers of secondary meanings, which often found their origins in the sphere of culture. Legendary brands such as Manoli's Dandy and Suggestion borrowed from fashion vogues and philosophical concepts and became icons of a modern lifestyle, even before World War I. Cigarette brands like Dada, Simplizissimus, and Logik, all introduced around 1920, took their cues from the current trends in art, literature, and philosophy. Hans-George Böcher has written of these brands, "The branded article carries something like a missionary character: Its brand name and design can be read as a proof of taste, attitude, even as an artistic credo of its consumer."[44]

In this context, brands designed by Hans Domizlaff actually appear as "natural" products, insofar as they lack any connection to a contemporary cultural or symbolic reference system. They are neither male nor female, neither young nor

3. Domizlaff's early 1920s design for Reemtsma's Yellow Brand. From Cigarettenfabriken H. F. and Ph. F. Reemtsma, eds., *Tabago* (Hamburg, 1960).

old, and have only one thing in common: they reflect the bold and ornamented *Jugendstil* of the Wilhelminian era. Today's elaborate concept of "brand personality" demands a unity between the attributes suggested by the brand on the one hand, and the consumers' values on the other. Domizlaff's definition of brand personality, however, is all about the producer. The concept falters the moment the brand's characteristics converge with the producer's characteristics, which include production processes as well as the Gestalt of the founder and entrepreneur. But this is exactly what Domizlaff had in mind when talking about natural brand building. The brand is the icon of the heroic inventor's or entrepreneur's personality: "A branded article is the product of a personality and is therefore best marked by the personal stamp of this personality." For this reason, Domizlaff rejects any "fantasy names" as brand names. He pleads for the founder's name as the one and only name for his brand: "The human mind accepts and admires people far more than impersonal titles." The rigidity of this approach culminates in his apodictic verdict: "One company has one brand, two brands are two companies."[45]

The idealization of the heroic founder as origin of the brand and the strict "one company, one brand policy" did not readily correspond to the economic realities of the Weimar Republic. In another context, Domizlaff writes about the multibrand policy of companies, which was already commonplace in the 1920s: "Look at those corporations that rule several empires from a single center. They are soulless creatures, mechanistic money-machines, which laboriously pay dividends but show no rhythm in development or stability in times of crises."[46] While Domizlaff was unfaithful to his own maxim in his work for Reemtsma (because of the company's multibrand strategy), he received his second chance to put his theories into practice at Siemens, where after 1933 he created a consistent corporate identity, establishing the Siemens style. Domizlaff's ultimate achievement at Siemens was to apply the name of the founder (Domizlaff deeply admired Werner von Siemens) to their consumer electronics line, which had been formerly branded by the fantasy name Protos.

The seemingly modern concept of Markentechnik conceals a deeply nostalgic core at which lies a profound mistrust of Western liberalism and individualism. This nostalgia was partly conserved during the Third Reich but ultimately replaced Western management standards after World War II. It resembles more closely the well-organized world of heraldic signs and symbols than modern concepts of branding and advertising.

Markentechnik and the Conservative Revolution

"Markentechnik is the art of creating mental weapons in the struggle for truthful performances and new ideas for winning public confidence," proclaims Domizlaff in the introduction to his textbook. Thus, Markentechnik is, like any war strategy, a *Geheimwissenschaft* (secret science). Consequently, Domizlaff develops his concept not as a how-to manual, as the name may suggest, but as an *ex negativo* critique of the advertising practices of his day by rejecting all "contradictions in style."[47]

The main style in advertising was, in his eyes, dominated by a lurid craving for sensation rooted in the fairground style of earlier times. "The primitive ways of funfairs still find their equivalents in most ads created by today's industry." He condemns those ideas aimed at quick sales as fueling mistrust and even rejection in the long run. In contrast, his understanding of Markentechnik is tailored to suit the reputation of the honorable salesman, who does not need to force his goods upon the customer. Rather, he relies on the high quality of his stock to develop loyal, regular customers: "The Markentechnik way is the way of unobtrusive noblesse and self-confident dignity with a strong awareness of the necessities of each market."[48]

Domizlaff demonstrates the process of natural brand building through the modern tale of salesman Hermann Schmidt, who begins as a small trader of exclusive, high-quality chocolate and becomes the owner of a fictitious chocolate brand without any help of primitive "fairground" advertising methods, or any advertising at all. Markentechnik covers everything from product innovations to packaging design, according to Domizlaff, but first a brand must prove itself viable on its own. Even then, advertising should always remain as low-profile as possible, because "the best advertising is the advertising you don't need."[49]

The image of a brand designer rejecting advertising so explicitly may appear strange. But given the sometimes excessive advertising of the 1920s, it actually is almost progressive. In fact, the radical antihumanism of his mass psychology is put into broader perspective when Domizlaff pleads for a matter-of-fact style in advertising, featuring "only ideas derived exclusively from the brand product itself."[50] The main impulse behind this strategy, however, seems to be a profound distrust of modern Western surface culture techniques. And it should not be forgotten that this style arises from mass psychological strategies. A rational pitch is part of the tactic, simply because, "compared to animals, giant organisms need a certain superficial coat of rationality in order to be convinced."[51]

The stylized ideal of the honorable salesman and the prioritization of "the house's reputation, which owns the brand as a symbol," are evidence of Hans Domizlaff's preference for a preliberal economic order of trade guilds and protected markets, which were still partly in operation in the Kaiserreich. Hence, Domizlaff's Markentechnik can be read as a defense strategy against modern liberalism, its global influences and its ability to establish competitive markets. In small town life and perfect villages, Domizlaff finds the ideal escape. Large cities, on the contrary, are insidious manifestations of the decadence of modern life, which expresses itself in a decay of style: "The city dweller is familiar with the smart salesman of many impersonal businesses, who has taught him to be a sober critic. When he comes to smaller towns he tends to misinterpret the decent manner of local merchants as a sign of weakness. . . . This style, however, is by no means provincial or out-dated, but honorable and convincing."[52]

Hamburg, deeply influenced by its long tradition of trade dynasties, is the only large city Domizlaff can accept. Berlin, the vibrant heart of Weimar's surface culture, seems like a modern Babylon to him: "Berlin is a fairground and its citizens are blunted and suspicious by those fairground methods." Undoubtedly, the origin of this decadent style, disguised as the "smart art of selling" and the "celebrated technique of great salespeople," is the United States. Domizlaff saw the "rough methods" of the Americans as unsuitable to Europe and its "older culture." American sales tactics were "a kind of black magic developed at the funfairs, practiced just to dig the salesman's own grave."[53]

Despite this sweeping condemnation of American techniques, some of Domizlaff's contemporaries were more sympathetic to—or at least intrigued by—the United States. During the 1920s and 1930s, Carl Hundhausen studied American methods of public relations on location. Friedrich Schönemann, a revanchist at heart, eyed the sophisticated art of mass persuasion in the United States with envy.[54] To Domizlaff, however, the adaptation of American techniques was tantamount to the decline of the nation: "For some time now the American approach has become exemplary for German advertising. Only experts recognize that the German mentality provides very different conditions for advertising campaigns than the American mentality." Given these differences in mentalities, Domizlaff deduces the superiority of his Markentechnik to advertising, or, even worse, *Reklame* (the older term for "shouting" billboard advertising): "Perhaps America is different; I don't know the conditions there very well. But for Germany the overwhelming importance of brands compared to advertising will probably prevail forever."[55]

The self-constructed conflict between advertising and Markentechnik, as well as Domizlaff's rejection of advertising in general, fits neatly into the larger discourse that structured ideological debates at the time. As advertising stood opposed to Markentechnik, so did Zivilisation's rival Kultur. This classic topos of German intellectual development was especially prevalent during the Weimar period. Thomas Mann's World War I essay *Reflections of a Non-political Man* set the tone by introducing the differentiation between German Kultur and Franco and Anglo-Saxon Zivilisation as synonymous with the conflict between Geist and Politik.[56] Throughout the 1920s the adherence to this dichotomy and to the irrational depths of German Kultur formed the basis for the conservatives' struggle with the forces of modernism. Janet Ward has referred to the Weimar years as a "stunning moment in modernity when surface values first ascended to become determinants of taste, activity and occupation—a scene of functioning that shows us there was in fact a time, when the new was not yet old, modernity was still modern and spectacle was still spectacular."[57] In this context, Domizlaff's Markentechnik can be judged as a desperate attempt to fight the modern, to turn back time and reanimate tradition.

It is clear that Hans Domizlaff is not representative of his profession in the Weimar era. Yet he *is* representative of distinct intellectual currents in the Weimar

Republic, and he is the only person to have translated them into the language of marketing. The bricks of Domizlaff's Weltanschauung resemble the ideology of the diffusely conservative, antidemocratic lobby of the time. First, there is the contempt for the masses, manifested in mass psychology. This attitude found its way into the thinking of moderate intellectuals, yet it remained of special interest to conservative intellectuals. Their loudly voiced disdain for the masses served to discredit democracy, and therefore the form of government and the republic itself.

Second, the pervasive references to the organic, suggesting an organically organized state, fit perfectly into this context. "One of the indispensable elements of anti-democratic thinking is the word organic," writes Kurt Sontheimer. The myth of an organic body, expressed in an organic form of state, was held up against the overly complex and "massified" democracy. "The objective of these mystified terms is to weaken the existing order and provoke a willingness for a better order according to those myths."[58]

Domizlaff's rejection of advertising draws accordingly from the ideological arsenal of the "national reactionary circles" of the early 1930s. As Uwe Westphal notes, "With an eye to the traditional small and medium businesses, the massive advertising of the recent years came under attack; it was accused of destroying national German identity by means of unleashed competition and of betraying German interests, especially those of the middle class in favor of the interests of international capital."[59]

It is easy to accuse Domizlaff of sympathizing with fascist ideals, and of anticipating Nazi propaganda, as Gerhard Voigt's essay *Goebbels als Markentechniker* (Goebbels as Brand Technician) suggests.[60] It was Domizlaff himself who added fuel to this interpretation by circulating the myth that Hitler personally reviewed his book *Propagandamittel der Staatsidee* in the Nazi party organ *Völkischer Beobachter*, and by spreading the anecdote that Goebbels had reassured him that he knew every word of it by heart.[61] A recent book on Goebbels portrays this myth as fact, and a recent article in *Der Spiegel* even draws strong psychological parallels between Goebbels and his "teacher of advertising," Domizlaff.[62]

It may seem as if National Socialism and its propaganda machine served as the practical adaptation, transformation, and radicalization of Domizlaff's ideas. But it is more appropriate to place the ideology of Markentechnik in the context of the "conservative revolution." This movement served as one of the enablers and precursors of the Nazi regime, but it did not share all aspects of its ideology. As Sontheimer points out, National Socialist ideology comprised manifold antidemocratic currents. It was an open, often contradictory system representing fragments from the conservative revolution as well as from National Bolshevism, Revolutionary Nationalism, German Nationalism, and Deutsch-Völkische ideologies.[63] What really separated National Socialism from the conservative revolutionaries was that leading Nazis, namely Hitler and Goebbels, had a practical vision of building a mass organization and gaining power, whereas the conservative revolution was marked by theoretical concepts debated among small, elitist circles with few real-world connections. On their agenda was nothing less than a revolutionary rejection of the achievements of Western liberalization since the French Revolution and the "reestablishment" of an organic and eternal state that had never existed before. The difficulties of this seemingly ambitious and radical program—expressed in the paradoxical terms "conservative" and "revolution"—are immediately clear. The conservative revolution was a romantic utopian project that participated in the political sphere only insofar as the National Socialists borrowed some of their rhetoric.[64]

Although little is known about possible personal connections or exchanges between Hans Domizlaff and exponents of the conservative revolution, the diffusion of—and internal tensions within—this intellectual environment can be found in Domizlaff himself. Gries, Ilgen, and Schindelbeck characterize his inner contradictions precisely: "In Hans Domizlaff we see mental structures of the 19th and 20th century colliding. Warm hearted, he looks back on pictures of the good old times, culminating in the icon of the senile Kaiser; with ice-cold rationality he tries to fill the power vacuum after the monarch's resignation by replacing it with a cigarette box designed to create a similarly strong psychosis in the consciousness of the mass."[65]

In the end, the paradoxes and ambiguities of Markentechnik are identical to the paradoxes and impossibilities of the conservative revolution, which tried to realize premodern ideals through modern methods. With reference to conservative and subsequent National Socialist ideologies, Jeffrey Herf has employed the term "reactionary modernism" to explain "the embrace of modern technology by German thinkers, who rejected Enlightenment reason."[66] In some ways, Domizlaff embodied this phenomenon, using modern surface techniques in order to restore the premodern state.

Branding Germany

The Markentechnik concept was never restricted exclusively to branded products. If a brand possesses the potential to turn into a character, then, conversely, a person—or, according to *Analogik*, any giant organism—can also turn into a brand. It is irrelevant what kind of person triggers the psychosis of confidence; it could be a heroic entrepreneur or a charismatic leader of a state (a "king," to use Domizlaff's language). Domizlaff notes in *Brevier für Könige*, "All words and actions a king performs in public must follow the single purpose of creating a favorable image. In business vocabulary this is called creating brand value. The people's psychological dependency on the king's brand value is the ultimate aim of all mental instruments of power."[67]

In the precarious situation of the early 1930s, when democracy was already eroded to such an extent that "Back to Weimar!" no longer appeared to be an option, Domizlaff undertook his only attempt to intervene actively in the political sphere.[68] In his manuscript *Propagandamittel der Staatsidee*, distributed in 1931 and published in 1932, he clearly articulates his thoughts and attempts to influence the Weimar government, which he accuses of having neglected the people's needs for simple symbols. He suggests a complete relaunching of the brand *Germany*, including a consistent corporate design based on the ideas of mass psychology. Turning as always to the eternal laws of mass psychology, he ignores the actual causes and symptoms of the political crisis, already apparent in 1931, declaring that states "develop organically on their own, as soon as the instincts of the Volksgemeinschaft come to life."[69]

Domizlaff's wide-ranging catalogue of strategies was not confined to the head of state and its symbols. Rather, the *Führer-Idee* (leader idea) should be extended to the entire appearance of the state, including design templates for written materials and a uniform dress code for parliament members.[70] An empowered *Werbeleiter des Reiches* (advertising leader for the Reich), based on the archetype of the censor in the Roman Empire, should supervise the adherence to these guidelines—a job for which Domizlaff considered himself a suitable candidate.[71]

Even though the book's tenor is totalitarian, it contains some passages that seem to correspond with a modern notion of a state and an enlightened conception of "branding nations," for example, increasing citizens' loyalty to the state by addressing them politely in official letters. Domizlaff's main focus, however, lies in his proposal to achieve a consistent national corporate identity through the new design of the Reich's flag. The origin of this proposal was the so-called *Flaggenstreit* (flag debate) in the Weimar Republic and the contested uses of symbols in the young republic. The Weimar constitution designated the little-known colors of the 1848 Paulskirche, black-red-gold, as the official tricolor of

VORSCHLAG EINER VERWENDUNG
DES REICHSWAPPENS ALS DEUTSCHE NATIONALFLAGGE

REICHSFLAGGE PREUSSISCHER STAATSANGEHÖRIGER
Als Beispiel einer Nationalflagge mit dem Abzeichen
der Landeszugehörigkeit

FLAGGE DER DEUTSCHEN REICHSBEHÖRDEN, ARMEE UND MARINE

4. Hans Domizlaff's design for a new *Reichsflagge*. From Hans Domizlaff, *Propagandamittel als Staatsidee* (Hamburg, 1932).

the republic, which replaced the imperial black-white-red. As a compromise, the latter colors were kept on some official flags, such as the Reich's trade flag. The pluralism of flags resulted in a rejection of the new flag as the state's symbol. The official flag was associated with governmental parties, especially the Social Democrats. The conservatives held on to the colors of the Wilhelmine era, while the Communists preferred revolutionary red. In short, the Weimar Republic suffered from a "domestic confusion of symbols."[72]

Domizlaff's suggested solution was to use an archetypical sign, instead of a modern symbol, to represent the state, which would be recognized by the mass brain's consciousness: "The eternal value of the state does not require a contemporary, i.e. a conceived-as-modern symbol, but rather a flag that reassures the consciousness of age-old traditions. There is only one solution: The German *Reichswappen* (a black eagle on a golden or yellow field), which is partly still used today, must become the one and only tradition-bearing flag—one that can bring

Hans Domizlaff, der Verfasser des Buches „Propagandamittel der Staatsidee", am Steuer seiner Jacht

5. "Hans Domizlaff, author of the book *Propagandamittel als Staatsidee*, at the wheel of his yacht." From *Die Reklame*, January 1933.

an end to this disastrous turmoil among the German Volk."[73] The traditional eagle on a yellow background, dating back to the medieval era and first used by Friedrich Barbarossa, was the ultimate conservative revolutionary's answer to the inner disruption of the modern state: a regression into a mythic world of symbols, resurrecting the pomp and glory of the fallen monarchies.[74]

In 1932, Domizlaff introduced his plans to Reich Chancellor Heinrich Brüning, but failed to convince him.[75] Despite this failure, Domizlaff's public and professional reception reached its peak in 1932. The January 1933 issue of *Die Reklame*, the leading publication for Germany's advertising professionals at the time, is a remarkable testament to this. The editor announced a new direction in publishing policy with the goal of covering the interactions of politics, economy, and advertising more broadly in the future.[76] A positive review of *Die Propagandamittel der Staatsidee*—accompanied by a symbolically charged picture of Hans Domizlaff steering his yacht—defended the idea of creating a politically independent Reichs-Werbe-Zentrale (Reich advertising headquarters). Its aim would

Reichspräsident Paul von Hindenburg

6. President Paul von Hindenburg. From *Die Reklame*, January 1933.

be to separate out the "commonly shared, the unifying and the collective values" from the "political party confusion." In support of this concept, the review was followed by a long Domizlaff-inspired article searching for "advertising traits in the figure of the Reich President." In the article, eighty-five-year-old Hindenburg was celebrated as a "patriarch of the people" and depicted as the perfect focal point for the mass soul: "In the figure of Hindenburg, the Reich President has truly become the 'solid rock in the flood of events' because of an inner calling. We hope and wish with confidence that he will remain so for a long time. Advertising humanity has found its most noble and natural incarnation."[77] The accompanying pictures of the Reich president depict the elderly general as upright, taciturn, and determined. A brand personality full of dignity and honor — character traits that Domizlaff found essential for a statesman — Hindenburg is the last reflection of a long-lost monarchist Germany, the conservatives' last hope to cling to.

As we know, this attempt by parts of Germany's advertising profession to ditch all modernist claims in favor of Domizlaff's approach never really matched the political realities and the agenda of the key players. Less than two years later Hindenburg was dead, and a mighty censor in no need of counseling controlled all matters of propaganda, as well as the entire advertising industry. Meanwhile the flag's new design was quite a bit more modern than Domizlaff had suggested. After World War II, former chancellor Brüning wrote to Domizlaff about propaganda during the final days of the Weimar Republic: "The Nazis had young, mostly unknown artists full of ideas who were identified and strongly patronized by Goebbels. It would have been a misjudgment on the part of Hitler to neglect his natural talent and his extraordinary understanding of the mass psychological necessity for a new method of propaganda."[78]

A recent interpretation of Joseph Goebbels as the first-ever spin doctor and creator of the "brand Hitler" highlights the propaganda minister's strikingly modern edge. As Lutz Hachmeister writes, "Joseph Goebbels stands for a specific modernity in National Socialism, which historians long failed to acknowledge. . . . His biography builds the bridge from the totalitarian and mythical concept of the 'Third Reich' to very contemporary approaches toward 'campaigning' and 'political marketing.'"[79] As we know, this was a modernity that violently outperformed Domizlaff's own superficially modern concept of brand technique. Though ignored by the regime, Domizlaff continued to write in seclusion. After the war, his branding ideas eventually took hold in a setting Domizlaff himself would never have predicted: in the vibrant consumerist democracy of West Germany.

Notes

This essay was translated from the German by Holm Friebe and Pamela E. Swett.

1. Domizlaff, *Die Gewinnung des öffentlichen Vertrauens*, 104.
2. Meyer, *Begegnungen mit Hans Domizlaff*, 147.
3. As a selection: *Das größere Vaterland—Ein Aufruf an die Intellektuellen* (Hamburg: Wolfgang Krüger Verlag, 1946); *Vorsicht Dämonen! Eine Warnung an die deutschen Intellektuellen* (Hamburg: Wolfgang Krüger, 1948); *Idealisten—Eine schauspielerische Darstellung seelischer Gemeinschaftskräfte* (Hamburg: Hans Dulk, 1953); *Nachdenkliche Wanderschaft* (Hamburg: Hans Dulk, 1950). See also Gries, Ilgen, and Schindelbeck, *"Ins Gehirn der Masse kriechen!"*
4. Hansen and Bode, *Marketing und Konsum*, 3.
5. Hans Domizlaff, *Typische Denkfehler der Reklamekritik* (Leipzig: Verlag für Industrie-Kultur, 1929), 13.
6. Bongard, *Männer machen Märkte*, 235.

7. Georg Bergler, *Das Schrifttum über den Markenartikel*, 2nd ed. (Berlin: Dt. Betriebswirte-Verlag, 1940).

8. Leitherer, *Geschichte der Handels- und Absatzwirtschaftlichen Literatur*.

9. Schmiedchen, *Kurzer Beitrag zur Geschichte der deutschen Wirtschaftswerbung*, 38–40.

10. Gries et al., "Ins Gehirn der Masse kriechen!" 47.

11. Hans Domizlaff, *Brevier für Könige: Massenpsychologisches Praktikum* (1950; Hamburg: Dulk, 1952).

12. Bongard, *Männer*, 241.

13. Domizlaff, *Brevier*, xxi.

14. Deichsel, *Und alles Ordnet die Gestalt / Hans Domizlaff*, 185. Deichsel was a dedicated follower of Domizlaff's Markentechnik approach.

15. See, for example, Brandmeyer, *Achtung Marke!*, 129.

16. F. J. Schwartz, *The Werkbund*, 8.

17. See Reinhardt, *Von der Reklame zum Marketing*, 89.

18. Hugo Münsterberg, *Grundzüge der Psychotechnik* (1913; Leipzig: Johann Ambrosius Barth, 1920).

19. Ward, *Weimar Surfaces*, 96–97.

20. Domizlaff's Markentechnik, Willi Bongard writes, "is only to be understood against the background of his mass psychology." Bongard, *Männer*, 244.

21. Ibid., 240; Hans Domizlaff, *Analogik—Denkgesetzliche Grundsätze der naturwissenschaftlichen Forschung* (Hamburg: Wolfgang Krüger, 1946).

22. Ernst Jünger, *Der Arbeiter—Herrschaft und Gestalt* (Hamburg: Hanseatische Verlagsanstalt, 1932), 32.

23. Gustave Le Bon, *The Crowd: A Study of the Popular Mind* (New York: Macmillan, 1896). The German-language edition is *Psychologie der Massen* (1911; Stuttgart: Körner, 1982).

24. Le Bon, *Psychologie*, 9.

25. Freud, *Massenpsychologie und Ich-Analyse*, 13: 73.

26. This critique of the industry was reflected in the title of his first book on the subject: Domizlaff, *Typische Denkfehler der Reklamekritik*.

27. Domizlaff, *Gewinnung*, 136.

28. Le Bon, *Psychologie*, 19.

29. Domizlaff, *Gewinnung*, 141.

30. Domizlaff, *Brevier*, 190.

31. Ibid., 191.

32. Domizlaff, *Gewinnung*, 163.

33. Ibid., 45.

34. Reinhardt, *Reklame*, 96.

35. Ibid., 449.

36. Domizlaff, *Gewinnung*, 87.

37. Reinhardt, *Reklame*, 46–47.

38. Domizlaff, *Gewinnung*, 151.

39. Ibid., 151, 152.

40. Ibid., 86.

41. Ibid., 147, 59, 92, 91.

42. See, e.g., Eugen Leitherer, "Geschichte der Markierung und des Markenwesens," in Bruhn, *Die Marke*, 54–74.

43. Bongard, *Männer*, 239.

44. Hans-Georg Böcher, "Von 'Leibniz' bis 'Du darfst!': Die Marke als Devise," in Bruhn, *Die Marke*, 169–170.

45. Domizlaff, *Gewinnung*, 59, 58, 85.

46. Ibid., 110.

47. Ibid., ix, 13.

48. Ibid., 16, 43.

49. Ibid., 94.

50. Ibid., 114.

51. Domizlaff, *Brevier*, 191.

52. Domizlaff, *Gewinnung*, 28, 38–39.

53. Ibid., 39, 41–42.

54. Friedrich Schönemann, *Die Kunst der Massenbeeinflussung in den Vereinigten Staaten von Amerika* (Berlin: Deutsche Verlags-Anstalt Stuttgart, 1924).

55. Domizlaff, *Denkfehler*, 63, 80.

56. Thomas Mann, *Betrachtungen eines Unpolitischen* (1918; Frankfurt: S. Fischer, 1985), 31.

57. Ward, *Weimar*, 2.

58. Sontheimer, *Antidemokratisches Denken in der Weimarer Republik*, 322, 326.

59. Westphal, *Werbung im Dritten Reich*, 20.

60. See, e.g., Posiadly, "Imagewerbung für den Staat"; Gerhard Voigt: "Goebbels als Markentechniker," in Haug, *Warenästhetik*, 231–269.

61. Gries et al., *Gehirn*, 61.

62. Michael Wildt, "Goebbels in Berlin," in Hachmeister and Kloft, *Das Goebbels-Experiment*, 74; "Die Marke Hitler," *Der Spiegel*, July 2005, 60–72.

63. Sontheimer, *Antidemokratisches Denken*, 171–172.

64. Ibid., 148–156.

65. Gries et al., "Ins Gehirn der Masse kriechen!" 68.

66. Herf, *Reactionary Modernism*, 1.

67. Domizlaff, *Brevier*, 43.

68. Sontheimer, *Antidemokratisches Denken*, 383.

69. Hans Domizlaff, *Propagandamittel der Staatsidee* (Hamburg: Hanseatische Verlagsanstalt, 1932), 11.

70. Ibid., 28.

71. His ambitions were even supported for a time by publisher Hermann Ullstein. See the letter from Hermann Ullstein to Domizlaff of 27 January 1931, reprinted in Deichsel, *Gestalt*, 98. In this letter Ullstein mentions having supported Domizlaff's promotion, but also critically questions his suggestions for the rebranding.

72. Friedel, *Deutsche Staatssymbole*, 20.

73. Domizlaff, *Propagandamittel*, 45.

74. Friedel, *Staatssymbole*, 16.

75. In a 1948 letter to Domizlaff, Brüning expressed his regret for not having considered his ideas, citing the political situation at the time. Letter from Heinrich Brüning to Hans Domizlaff of 2 July 1948, reprinted in Deichsel, *Gestalt*, 88.

76. *Die Reklame*, January 1933, 1.

77. Ibid., 4–5, 6

78. Deichsel, *Gestalt*, 88.

79. Hachmeister and Kloft, *Goebbels-Experiment*, 7.

4

MICHAEL IMORT

"PLANTING A FOREST TALL AND STRAIGHT

LIKE THE GERMAN *VOLK*"

Visualizing the *Volksgemeinschaft* through Advertising

in German Forestry Journals, 1933–1945

The Nazis' "Thousand-Year Reich" lasted twelve years. For much longer than that, from 1925 to 1959, Elias Canetti worked on his masterpiece, *Masse und Macht*, in which he attempted to understand the visceral connection between the two phenomena of "crowds and power," a connection that formed one of the most resilient yet least understood foundations of the Nazi regime. In the work that gained him the 1981 Nobel Prize for Literature, Canetti argued that, for Germans, there was one symbol that more than any other represented that connection: the forest. In the most famous passages from *Crowds and Power*, Canetti writes, "The crowd symbol [*Massensymbol*] of the Germans was the army. Yet the army was more than just the army: it was the marching forest. In no other modern country has the affinity for the forest [*Waldgefühl*] remained as alive as it has in Germany. The parallel arrangement and rigidity of the upright trees, their closeness and quantity fill the heart of the German with a deep and mysterious delight. To this day he loves to go into the forest where his forefathers lived, where he feels at one with the trees."[1]

Fifty years after the publication of *Crowds and Power*, Canetti's attempt to categorize "the German" and identify a universal symbol for him appears arguably problematic. In this essay, I do not intend to debate the theoretical merits and shortcomings of Canetti's essentializing ideas as such. Instead, I want to focus on Canetti's choice of the forest as the essential German "crowd symbol" that underlies the superficial symbol of the army. Why the forest? For anyone not immersed in the canon of German cultural and intellectual production, this may appear an odd choice. While non-German audiences may be aware of the mythical allure of the Black Forest or the ubiquitous forest symbolism of Grimms' fairy tales, they often dismiss them as just that: myth and fable, without any import in the real world of politics and power.

By contrast, I argue that the forest has in fact often formed an important element of German political discourse.[2] Most recently, this was exemplified by the prominent role that the specter of *Waldsterben* (forest dieback from acid rain) played in the ascent of the German Green Party into mainstream politics and, eventually, government. I examine the role of the forest in German advertising discourses during the Nazi period, particularly the way the Nazis used forest symbolism to conflate advertising and propaganda with the goal of teaching Germans about their role in the new German *Volksgemeinschaft*, or "national community." While the Nazis' mastery of propaganda is well documented, less has been written about the cultural and social history of advertising during the Nazi regime.[3] Even less examined are the efforts by the National Socialist regime to mandate a new organizational structure for the advertising sector with the goal of inserting its message into mainstream advertising.[4] I take a synoptic view of these developments and examine them in conjunction rather than in isolation from one another.

After a brief examination of how the Nazi state "coordinated" propaganda and advertising, I analyze advertising imagery from three academic forestry journals to illustrate how propaganda and advertising were increasingly conflated in practice. In the first case study, I demonstrate how advertising in forestry journals illustrated Nazi propaganda by visualizing the forest as an analogy of the German Volksgemeinschaft. In the second case study, I investigate how advertising gave the spatially dispersed readership of forestry journals clues as to how to behave properly as *Volksgenossen*, or "national comrades." Together, these analyses show that the Nazis not only created overt propaganda to further their cause, but frequently piggybacked their political message on innocuous commercial advertising campaigns.

The Coordination of the German Media and Advertising Industry

The Nazis lost very little time in bringing all sectors of the "consciousness industry" under their control. On 25 March 1933, Goebbels bluntly acknowledged the purpose of his new Ministry of Propaganda: "The task of the ministry is to execute the mental mobilization of Germany."[5] Consequently, all media in the National Socialist state were placed under the control of the Reichskultur-kammer (Reich Culture Chamber) to "coordinate" cultural production in all its facets. The Reichskulturkammer comprised seven chambers for the various cultural professions, and only accredited members of the chambers were permitted to work in their respective professions. Moreover, individuals who were denied membership or were expelled because of their Jewish faith or oppositional views were criminalized, as their expulsion was entered into their police record.[6] In the print media, the direct and total state control was further solidified by the Schriftleitergesetz (Editors Law) of 6 April 1933, which bound editors in duty to the state and made them personally liable for the content of articles appearing in their publications. Meanwhile, Nazi cover firms were clandestinely buying up many newspapers and publishing houses, while others were simply merged, expropriated, or shut down by decree. In a similar fashion, other media sectors, such as broadcasting and film, were brought under direct control of the Nazis within a few months of their taking power.[7]

In the advertising sector, the "coordination" was codified on 12 September 1933, when the Gesetz über Wirtschaftswerbung (Commercial Advertising Law) gave the Nazis control over all aspects of commercial advertising in Germany. To exercise that control, a new body was created under the auspices of Goebbels's Propaganda Ministry: the Werberat der deutschen Wirtschaft, or Advertising Council for the German Economy. It fell within the purview of the Werberat to grant or deny advertising practitioners the all-important official accreditation and thus control who was able to work in advertising in Germany. Likewise, the Werberat collected the *Werbeabgabe*, a mandatory 2 percent levy on all printed advertisements that was used to cross-finance state propaganda. Finally, the mission of the Werberat was to implement and enforce new regulations regarding the content, form, and means of advertising, such as the official "Guidelines for the Design and Execution of Commercial Advertising" published by the Werbe-rat on 1 November 1933, according to which "advertising must be German in its ethos [*Gesinnung*] and expression.[8] It must not violate the morality of the German Volk, in particular its religious, patriotic, and political sentiment and aspiration."[9]

As a result of the new laws and regulations, the Nazis controlled not only all channels of official propaganda, but also had the power to muzzle any commercial advertising they deemed inappropriate. The German advertising industry initially welcomed the interventions because it hoped that the new state control would bring higher standards and an increased degree of professionalism to the industry and thus enhance its credibility among the public.[10] Yet, while the purview of the Werberat certainly expanded over time, it did not always have the means to enforce its own regulations. For example, in 1934 the Werberat prohibited the display of posters of any sort in shop windows, but within days the German Football League had successfully undermined this directive by arguing that the ban did not extend to advertising for sporting events. In a similar fashion, other interest groups were at times able to ignore or bend regulations issued by the Werberat.[11]

Like all other print publications, academic forestry journals were made to conform to the goals of the National Socialists. Three journals in particular — *Deutsche Forst-Zeitung, Der Deutsche Forstwirt,* and *Deutsche Forstbeamtenzeitung* — exemplify this development. These journals shared a number of characteristics, most of which relate to their multiple functions, frequent publishing schedule, and dual readership profile. To begin with, the editorial boards of these journals were "coordinated" by the Nazis immediately after January 30, 1933. Hence, we may safely regard their content as state-sanctioned. In addition, in the numerous cases where editorials elaborated on political rather than professional issues, we may also consider them vehicles of official propaganda. Furthermore, these journals traditionally also served as paraofficial law gazettes for the forest administration and trade publications for the lumber trade. As such, they enjoyed the widest possible circulation among the forestry sector. To properly reflect fluid market conditions, they appeared weekly or semiweekly, which enabled them to respond swiftly to current affairs both within and outside the forestry sector. Next, they provided an important platform for exchange among academically trained foresters who were dispersed across Germany and thus spatially isolated from their discursive community. Hence, in addition to technical articles, they also carried articles of general interest and political commentary. Finally, they contained advertising sections that catered to two very distinct audiences: the (invariably) male professional reader and his need for professional, political, technical, and trade information; and the female homemaker residing in the dispersed foresters' households. This dual readership of male professionals and female homemakers allows for a parallel analysis of multiple advertising discourses.

"Eternal Forest — Eternal Volk": The Role of Advertising
in Visualizing the German Volksgemeinschaft

The seeds of the "natural" analogy between forest and Volk were planted in the late nineteenth century by *völkisch* authors who claimed that the German "race" was particularly *bodenständig,* or "rooted in the soil," because it had gone through millennia of coevolution with its primary environment: the surrounding forest. As a result, the argument continued, Germans had developed a strong affinity for the forest that ensured the latter's continued thriving in Germany. In turn, the enduring exposure of Germans to the forest environment ensured that their *Bodenständigkeit,* or "rootedness," was passed on to the next generation, thus forming an "eternal" cycle of mutually formative influence that had long since been broken in such nations as England and France, where the forest had been cleared or altered. In this vein, the popular novelist and social historian Wilhelm Heinrich Riehl insisted in his *Natural History of the German People as a Foundation for Social Policy* of 1854 that the German forest was indispensable because it sustained "the pulse of the life of the Volk, so that Germany may remain German."[12]

In the early twentieth century, völkisch authors recast the supposed interconnectedness of German forest and people as a normative analogy, in which the structure of the forest served as a model for the restructuring of the German nation into a Volksgemeinschaft. This "national community" of Germans was to be based on "racial" kinship rather than political citizenship and structured by occupational estates rather than social classes. To völkisch writers, the Volksgemeinschaft represented the only "truly German" form of social organization, and völkisch foresters insisted that the forest was the perfect model for such a restructuring of the German nation. One of the first to express this idea was the Prussian forester Rudolf Düesberg, who argued in his 1910 book, *The Forest as Educator,* that "the social order of the forest must become a model for the economic and social institutions of the German people."[13] This "social order of the forest" was based on the following three tenets: that the individual tree was ephemeral, while the collective stand was eternal; that trees formed uniform strata that performed different functions within the stand, for example, dominant canopy and serving understory; and, finally, that while some layers were more valuable than others, each layer was equally important for the functioning and well-being of the collective as a whole.

Transferring this organic "social order of the forest" to the political realm of a rapidly modernizing Germany, Düesberg demanded that, because "the ephemeral lifespan of the individual is irrelevant" compared to that of the forest or nation, "the individual must sacrifice himself for the welfare of the collective."[14] Thus, individual Germans were to serve the nation by working as part of their "proper" occupational estate just as individual trees served the stand within their distinct canopy layers. Düesberg's ideas were warmly received by völkisch activists who were disenchanted with the increasing individualization of German society, but it was not until the tumultuous years of the Weimar Republic that his conclusions were discussed as particularly apt. For example, the forester Eduard Zentgraf explicitly "updated" Düesberg's ideas to the critical political situation of the year of the Hitler coup in his 1923 *Forest and Volk*.[15] Beginning in the early 1920s, völkisch foresters became increasingly insistent that the forest should be seen as the "natural" model for a restructured "New Germany." They urged their readers to recognize the many "parallels between forest and nation such as . . . canopy layers and social stratification; care of the forest edge and *Grenzlanddeutschtum*;[16] natural reseeding and eugenics; . . . forest organism and Volk organism."[17] Years before the Nazis' ascent to power, they concluded that "it is the path to the Volksgemeinschaft that the forest shows those who are willing to open their eyes."[18]

Not surprisingly, this viewpoint assumed the status of virtual dogma when the National Socialist state declared a Volksgemeinschaft its official goal. After 1933, the coordinated forestry journals ran an endless string of articles with the programmatic title "Forest and Volk" or a close variation thereof.[19] In these articles, the alleged parallels between forest and Volk were conjured up to educate the Volksgenossen about their proper place in the Volksgemeinschaft. In short, ordinary citizens were to see themselves as uniform members of the rank and file (the serving understory layers), while the party brought forth the leaders (or dominant canopy). Regardless of where one's "proper" station happened to be, everyone had to serve the greater good. As a forester by the name of Dörr stated in one of those articles, "The forest is our master. Egalitarianism is not the way of nature. The strong oak tree does not refuse to form a community of life [*Lebensgemeinschaft*] with the simple herbs. Strong and weak belong together, each supports the other, and all subordinate themselves to the common good. That is also the way it should be in a true Volksgemeinschaft, which is a dream no longer but has now become reality."[20]

The forest was to teach Germans about their role as Volksgenossen, and no one was more candid about what that meant for the individual German than Hermann Göring, the second in command in the Nazi hierarchy. As early as 1934, Göring had wrested jurisdiction over forestry affairs from the German *Länder* and created a new centralized Reich Forestry Office under his control. In a programmatic speech at the opening ceremonies of the 1935 convention of German foresters, the self-anointed "Reich Master of Forestry" bluntly declared, "Forest and people are much akin in the doctrines of National Socialism. The people is [*sic*] also a living community, a great, organic, eternal body whose members are the individual citizens. Only by the complete subjection of the individual to the service of the whole can the perpetuity of the community be assured. *Eternal forest and eternal nation are ideas that are indissolubly linked.*"[21] In the tightly edited articles that appeared in the forestry journals, Göring and the "lesser" authors thus frequently drew analogies between the ideal type of the German forest and the Volksgemeinschaft: both were supposed to comprise more or less uniform individuals who were to draw their raison d'être from their place in the functionally stratified collective.

Advertisements visually complemented these propaganda texts and so reinforced their message. Literally flanking the articles on the forest-Volk analogy were advertisements for nurseries, tools, and machinery that were ostensibly of a commercial character yet embodied the imagery that the textual propaganda could only imply, for example, rows upon rows of straight, tall, strong, and uniformly shaped trees "in formation" and similar representations of the "German" ideals of collective order, uniformity, and strength. For an example of this visualization we may look to a series of advertisements placed by one of the largest nurseries in Germany, Pein & Pein, which illustrates the conflation of propaganda and advertising messages in a variety of ways.

In most of their advertisements in the three journals between 1935 and 1938, Pein & Pein followed a similar composition pattern that clearly emphasized the layered and collective character of the depicted forest stand and so visualized the desired functional stratification of the Volksgemeinschaft. Although the advertised product was saplings, young stands appeared only occasionally, and then as mere silhouettes looming in the background. Instead, the advertisements were dominated by mature trees in the foreground that were drawn in considerable detail. Yet, while this detail clearly identified the species to which the trees belonged (mostly pine), it did not allow for distinguishing one individual from another, as they were almost identical in size and shape. Moreover, they were invariably rendered in symmetrically spaced clusters. The result of this particular combination of perspective, level of detail, and uniformity was that the trees had a collective rather than individual presence. This impression was reinforced through the repetition of stereotypical characteristics: perfectly straight, tall, and healthy dominant trees standing in a symmetric spatial arrangement.

Such an arrangement is reminiscent of a unit of soldiers ready for inspection, the analogy most aptly expressed in Elias Canetti's characterization of the German army as "the marching forest."[22] The analogy of forest and army would have been rather familiar to the contemporary readers of such advertisements, who were witnessing the increasing militarization of public discourses in mid-1930s Germany. In fact, in a 1936 propaganda film, *Ewiger Wald* (Eternal Forest), the interchangeability of trees and soldiers was made glaringly obvious when the director used the new technique of fading to dissolve images of one into the other. The arrangement of trees in the Pein & Pein advertisements reflected this analogy and visually represented trees as placeholders for individual Germans as mere subunits of a larger collective entity. This gave visual expression to Göring's insistence on "the complete subjection of the individual to the service of the whole," which in itself was but a variation on the National Socialist propaganda mantra "You are nothing, your Volk is everything!"

Several of the Pein & Pein advertisements stressed not only the collective character of the forest (and, by extension, the Volksgemeinschaft), but also the presence and mutual interdependence of at least two distinct functional strata: dominant canopy trees and serving understory trees. The flawless dominant trees (or "leaders" of the Volk) were surrounded by a "bodyguard" of serving trees. In silviculture, serving trees are used to shade the lower trunks of dominant trees (those that have been selected for the production of knot-free saw wood) and thereby prevent the formation of light-induced branches that could result in future knots (remnants of such "nuisance" branches are visible in Figure 1). Transferred to the realm of the Volk, this subservient yet indispensable stratum represented the many Volksgenossen who were told to serve their nation by working to their best capacity in the particular occupational estate to which "fate" had assigned them, thus enabling the elite to perform their important leadership tasks for the benefit of all. As Dörr had written, "Strong and weak belong together, each supports the other, and all [are] subordinate to the common good." By praising the importance of such serving strata, the Nazis tried to woo the blue-collar population away from the leftist parties and into acquiescence with the National Socialist regime.

As early as 1934, a forester by the name of Fuchs in yet another "Forest and Volk" article had a priori transferred the idea of serving strata to the Volksgemeinschaft: "By recognizing the importance of so-called 'serving trees' for the forest, we also accept the importance of this question for the life of the Volk."[23] Yet Fuchs did not stop at axiomatically postulating a forestlike occupational stratification of the German Volksgemeinschaft and who was to play what role in it; he also questioned just who was to be allowed to play a role at all. Fuchs raised

1. "Frugal, fast-growing pines." Pein & Pein advertisement, *Der Deutsche Forstwirt* 18, no. 18 (1936): 232.

the "racial question," that is, What sort of "genetic inheritance" made trees and humans worthy of being called German? He argued that, because of foresters' experience with purging stands of the least desirable trees to foster the more desirable, they more than any other profession were able to appreciate the importance of "eliminating all *mentally* or physically deficient."[24] Why would a forester make such a leap from forest-thinning practices to human mental capacity? Arguably, Fuchs's reasoning reflected the heightened emphasis on eugenics that the Nazis pursued immediately after coming to power. It is worth noting that this article appeared in 1934, less than a year after the Sterilization Law of 14 July 1933, which led to the forced sterilization of hundreds of thousands of Germans for reasons such as "feeblemindedness," schizophrenia, epilepsy, and homosexuality. While the Sterilization Law did not single out "racial" groups and was applied universally, the Nuremberg Laws on Citizenship and "Blood Protection" of 1935 added the concept of "racial purity" to the equation: now the state could legally persecute individuals on the basis of their genetic and "racial" heritage.

Werbung Eberwein

Ödland *muß Wald werden!*

Pein & Pein G.m.b.H.
Forſtpflanzen · Forſtsamen · Lohnanzucht
Halstenbek i. Holstein Fach 101
Älteste und größte Forſtbaumschule im bedeutendsten Anzuchtgebiet Deutschlands

2. "Unproductive lands must become forest." Pein & Pein advertisement, *Der Deutsche Forstwirt* 18, no. 16 (1936): 204.

Just as Fuchs's article did, the advertisements under examination in this section reflected this increasing racialization of everyday life. They subtly visualized the "racial question" raised by Fuchs and others and so underscored the propaganda message of the articles. To do this, some advertisements did not depict forests at all but showed the antithesis of German forestry: heath that bore neither field nor forest. Dotting the so-called unproductive lands were a handful of birches and junipers, species that foresters considered unproductive at best and noxious at worst. The advertisements made it very clear that such a situation was untenable: "Unproductive lands must become forest," one advertisement simply declared (see Figure 2), while another explained that "unproductive lands [are] something we cannot afford in the battle for autarky."[25] The "racial question" was introduced by rendering the few visible trees not only as clearly belonging to "unproductive" species (itself a slanderous term in the National Socialist lexicon), but also as crooked, forked, and stunted: a visual allusion to their "racial" deficiency. Pein & Pein offered to supply the "racially sound" sap-

3. "Healthy, vigorous trees only from racially pure and site-adapted seedlings." Pein & Pein advertisement, *Der Deutsche Forstwirt* 20, no. 44/45 (1938): 576.

lings that were supposedly necessary to rectify this deplorable situation and, in another advertisement, showed what the transformed landscape could look like. Once again we see the now familiar clusters of perfectly shaped dominant trees with their attendant serving trees, juxtaposed with remnants of the heath for better contrast (see Figure 1).

Similarly, the racial question was addressed in several other Pein & Pein advertisements that combined most of the characteristics just examined (see Figures 3 and 4). These advertisements showed a picture-perfect "German" forest (comprising all the elements discussed above) in the process of being harvested by strapping teams of men and horses. The advertisement text credits "racially pure" saplings with having created this highly desirable (and profitable) forest, but the aspect to emphasize here is the interesting way the advertisements reflect the tension between Modernist and Romantic aesthetics that was so characteristic of the contradictory self-identification of the Third Reich. The Modernist

4. "Bountiful harvest only from healthy, site-adapted seedlings." Pein & Pein advertisement, *Der Deutsche Forstwirt* 20, no. 92 (1938): 1140.

aspect is created by the gargantuan dimensions of the trees, their rigid straightness, and the stark symmetry of their arrangement. By contrast, the lumberjacks felling those Modernist forests are wearing traditional garb and using none of the mechanized technology that was sweeping German forestry in the 1930s, such as the chainsaw and motorized skidding equipment. This contrast is all the more surprising as one would normally expect natural elements such as the forest to be associated with the Romantic perspective and cultural elements such as workers and their implements with the Modernist perspective, as in the case of an advertisement for Stihl chainsaws, for example, which appeared in the same journal.[26]

In short, the juxtaposition of propaganda articles on the "Germanness" of the forest and its lessons for the creation of the Volksgemeinschaft with advertisements such as the Pein & Pein series suggests some striking parallels in the way forest and Volk were conceptualized by their respective authors. Such an interpretation of advertisements as visualizing the concept of the Volksgemeinschaft may appear tenuous to a twenty-first-century reader not steeped in the iconography of the Nazi state. It is worth remembering, however, that contemporaries would have been surrounded by similar messages in virtually every domain of their everyday lives, whether in education, entertainment, or, as in this case, advertising. Moreover, the use of the forest as an analogy of the Volk had a long-standing tradition, making such interpretations of the forest as inherently German almost a matter of common sense. This symbolic analogy was exactly what Canetti was trying to express when he called the forest-as-army the "crowd symbol" of the German nation. When Germans thought of the forest, they thought of it as the *German* forest, with all of its attributes, such as order, uniformity, and strength, transferring to the nation. Ultimately, the Nazis could and did use the forest as a symbol for the German Volksgemeinschaft precisely because it had been firmly established as a symbol of Germany and Germanness for more than a century. All they had to do was extend the suggestive trajectory from *forest* to *German* and further to *Volksgemeinschaft*.

How prevalent was this association, and how much effort was required to remind readers of it? For an answer we may turn to such a mundane publication as a school textbook on biology. In the foreword to the 1936 edition, the eminent natural historian Konrad Guenther dispels any doubts over the applicability of biological tenets gleaned from the forest to the life of the Volk: "The analogies that arise at every opportunity—between the community of the forest and the Volksgemeinschaft, between order in the forest and order among the Volk—are so obvious that they need not be pointed out individually."[27] Similarly, the introduction to the 1936 art exhibition *Der Wald* (The Forest) in Berlin praised the power of the visual arts to intuitively express the "natural" similarities between the forest and the Volk: "What the man of science or the natural philosopher can scarcely put in words about the phenomenon of the forest, the artist sometimes succeeds in expressing surprisingly well: subordination of the individual to the whole, multitude in unity, the circle of dying and becoming, struggle for survival and the necessity to live together."[28] Operating within such an environment where the analogy between forest and Volk was all but taken for granted, the creators of the Pein & Pein advertisements did not have to drop too many hints as to the message they wanted to convey. At the same time, this absence of "obvious" propaganda elements makes it all the more difficult for a twenty-first-century reader to decipher how superficially "innocent" advertising is actually laced with propagandistic symbolism.

How common was this conflation of advertising and propaganda? Was it intentional, tolerated, or accidental? While it is difficult to say with any certainty exactly how individual advertisers made day-to-day decisions under tight regulatory restrictions, we can see the conceptual environment in which advertisers operated by looking at some of the theoretical writings that informed the German advertising industry in the 1930s. As Corey Ross shows in his essay in this volume, the 1920s represented a tumultuous time for German advertising theorists and professionals. Trying to adopt American methods without becoming "Americanized" proved a challenge that extended far beyond the actual industry and often brought up larger political and sociocultural issues. One reason for this challenge was the politicization of German society during the Weimar Republic, when politics spilled into every aspect of life. In the field of advertising, this is mirrored in the permeability between the theories of advertising and propaganda in the works of Hans Domizlaff.[29]

In the 1920s, Domizlaff developed the idea of branding products in Germany, eventually arguing that the task of advertising a branded product was to "win the trust of the public."[30] In the 1930s, however, he also applied the ideas of branding and public trust to the state. In his *Breviary for Kings*, for example, Domizlaff suggested that a leader could use techniques akin to those of effective advertising to control the "mass soul" of those in his realm, whether that be a company, an organization, or a state. For the allegorical king to win and retain the role of leader, he had to move the public to place the same trust in his acts and symbols as they would in a successful brand product.[31] Similarly, in a 1932 publication entitled *Propaganda Means of the Idea of the State*, Domizlaff adapted the idea of branding to the state itself, suggesting that the state and its symbols, such as the flag, could be equated with a brand and needed to be promoted in a similar fashion.[32] With this argumentation about the parallels between advertising for a product and for a political idea, Domizlaff punctured the already taut membrane between advertising and propaganda. It is not surprising that Goebbels was reputed to have known Domizlaff's *Propagandamittel* by heart.[33] The outright unwillingness of the Nazis to maintain any meaningful distinction between propaganda and advertising is further illustrated by the marching orders Goebbels gave to the Werberat "to submit all German commercial advertising to a unified will, to end the organizational fragmentation caused by excessive individualism, and to *implement* advertising according to the requirements of the new German state."[34] The wording leaves no doubt that, through the Werberat, the state aimed not only to restructure the sector and impose its will on all advertising venues, but also to create advertising by and for itself—in other words: propaganda. Like propaganda proper, advertising was thus just another way to "execute the mental mobilization of Germany" demanded by Goebbels.

Within months of the Nazi takeover of the German government, we thus find a situation where the control over both official propaganda and commercial advertising was increasingly bundled in the hands of a few individuals and institutions. In our example of the Pein & Pein enterprise, this focus is exemplified by the company's owner, Ernst Pein, who was also the appointed Reich leader of the coordinated Reich Association of Seed Producers and Forest Nurseries (Reichsverband der Forstsamen- und Forstpflanzenbetriebe). With such personal overlap between commerce and officialdom, it is hardly surprising to find a corresponding blurring of the line between advertisement and propaganda.

This raises the question of whether we can find a similar conflation of propaganda and advertising once we move beyond the tightly organized audience of professional foresters and into the context of less specific advertising discourses. To test this assumption, the next section examines advertisements that were directed at a more general audience and that appeared alongside the professional advertisements in the forestry journals. These advertisements were directed both at foresters in their capacity as plain citizens, and at the general readership that was liable to pick up and peruse the weekly publications in the Forsthaus. These more general advertisements were more explicit in their message and openly combined propaganda and advertising. Advertisements could be used to admonish the newly minted Volksgenossen to act in appropriate ways.

"Golden Rules": Advertising Teaches
Volksgenossen Proper Conduct

Not all advertisements in forestry journals were concerned with the forest or the profession of forestry. Many dealt with questions of a more general nature. What was the correct attitude of Volksgenossen toward their work and coworkers? What constituted proper behavior on the job and in social situations? What was an appropriate form of leisure consumption, and when was an acceptable time for it? Three different advertising campaigns launched by tobacco companies between the years 1938 and 1942 illustrate how these questions were posed and simultaneously answered. The nature of the advertised product suggests that these advertisements were placed in the forestry journals not to enrich the professional discourse of foresters, but to reach the reader as a private individual faced with the task of negotiating the new everyday realities of a National Socialist Germany under the exigencies of war. Accordingly, such advertisements gave the reader more or less subtle hints how to act and consume in a wartime economy without running afoul of the new standards of Nazi propriety.

A series of advertisements placed by the Bergmann tobacco company during the years 1938 and 1939 are particularly illustrative. Each advertisement suggested that readers had a choice between emphasizing *Form* or *Inhalt* (content) in their own private and work lives. In their artwork, the advertisements ridiculed those who dressed fashionably and behaved in a seemingly affected manner, suggesting that they chose form over content and, by extension, superficiality over deep values. By contrast, those who dressed and behaved in a more sensible and "natural" manner, whether as workers, intellectuals, or women, were depicted as choosing honest content over pretentious form. (Tellingly, this tripolar division also suggests that women were seen as unlikely to fall into either of the first two categories.) The ultimate product message was of course the claim that Bergmann cigarettes identified those who smoked them as individuals who had made the right choice; they were "deep" and honest, content-oriented individuals who cared more about the flavor of a cigarette than about its packaging or cachet.

Yet the advertisements also contained less than subtle political messages, for example, the suggestion that those who chose form over content were out of step with the spirit of the times and thus could face trouble at the workplace. Conversely, those who chose content over form were represented as possessing a positive attitude and work ethic, which ultimately enabled them to perform their work in a way that was in the best interest of the Volksgemeinschaft. This message was spelled out in an advertisement that appeared in 1938, in which the company chided those who wasted their energies on superficialities while expressing its "great respect for those who tackle their work with joy and energy. Consequently, the Bergmann Company employs no bellyachers, and a brisk spirit prevails at all times" (see Figure 5). This was a thinly veiled admonishment to workers everywhere to display the "proper" attitude at work lest they be accused of being out of step with the times or, even worse, sabotaging workers' morale—a charge that could easily lead to draconian sanctions in Nazi Germany.

A second advertisement in the same series with the telling caption "Golden Rules" (see Figure 6) disapproved of accumulated wealth and conspicuous consumption as foreign to the German Volksgemeinschaft by suggesting that a stereotypical fat-cat capitalist is literally outweighed by a bookwormish intel-

5. "Form or Content: That's the Question." Bergmann advertisement, *Deutsche Forstbeamtenzeitung* 7, no. 20 (1938): 753.

lectual: placed on opposite ends of a balance arm, the "content" of the slender thinker easily counterbalances the massive "form" of the financier, who is drawn as an overweight "suit." The newspaper grasped by the latter further suggests that he makes his money through "unproductive" stock market speculations rather than "honest" work, an impression reinforced by the dollar sign on his bursting moneybag, both symbols that Nazi propaganda often used to signify "Jewish capitalism." By contrast, the slender figure of the thinker is strikingly reminiscent of the Poor Poet, a stereotypical German man of letters made famous by the homonymous 1837 painting by Carl Spitzweg. Finally, in a third advertisement (not reproduced here), fashion-obsessed women are criticized for their "un-German" vanity by ridiculing a woman drawn in an haute-couture outfit.[35] While she is clearly hoping to impress her mate with her frilly dress, the man remains utterly unimpressed, for, as the copy tells us, he is wise enough to prefer "inner values" over "outward appearances," both in women and "in all other things." To contemporaries, the ridiculing of fashion was a thinly disguised stab at the alleged superficiality and degenerateness of French *Zivilisation* that völkisch authors for decades had been dismissing as inferior to "deep" German Kultur.[36]

In its advertisements, the Bergmann tobacco company thus gave some gen-

Goldene Gesetze.

In der Schule haben wir den schönen Satz gelernt: „Was man an Kraft erspart, das geht an Weg wieder verloren". Und das Leben lehrte uns entsprechende Abwandlungen: „Was man an Geld gewinnt, das geht an Geist, was man an Form gewinnt, das geht an Inhalt wieder verloren".

Gerade diesen letzten Satz haben wir uns von Anfang an mächtig hinter die Ohren geschrieben. Wir haben also unser ganzes Können darauf konzentriert, unsere Zigaretten mit appetitlich-frischem Tabak zu füllen, - die richtige Form hat sich dann ganz von selbst eingestellt.

Haus Bergmann **Privat**
„so appetitlich frisch "

6. "Golden Rules." Bergmann advertisement, *Deutsche Forstbeamtenzeitung* 7, no. 25 (1938): 997.

eral advice about how to behave as an employee and consumer in late-1930s Germany. The values recommended for adoption were commonly associated with the stereotypical deep German character: a strong work ethic coupled with a sense of duty and pride in the nonmonetary rewards of work, as well as a preference for the simpler things coupled with a voluntary limitation of one's material consumption. In the context of a German economy that was preparing for war, such advice was intended to bind individuals together and to forestall or suppress any grumblings by labeling them as greedy or unpatriotic bellyachers who violated the common good.

This message became increasingly blunt as Germany rushed into World War II. In the early years of the war, the Hanewacker company advertised its chewing tobacco as an alternative to smoking in workplaces where open flames were prohibited.[37] Evidently, the forest in the summer was such a location where, as one of the advertisements declared, "as we all know, smoking is strictly prohibited—regardless of the fact that it does not behoove us to smoke in the forest in the first place."[38] One can easily appreciate the fire threat posed by smoking in the forest and thus agree with the prohibition, but why would smoking be particularly inopportune for foresters? One hint could be found in an accompanying image of a forest clearing with silhouettes of deer, which suggested that smoking might scare away the game that foresters (who as a rule were also hunters) might want to stalk. In another advertisement that ran several weeks later, however, this explanation is not applicable. Here, the image of a sowing farmer in the foreground and a team of horses plowing in the background is set against a rising sun. The text states, "There are many occasions in the life of a man where it is not proper for him to smoke. Just think of your work, the cinema or the theater! How fortunate are those who turn to Hanewacker in such situations!"[39]

There are two messages folded into this advertisement. The first is the obvious textual one that smoking is restricted in some public entertainment places. The second is contained in the artwork showing archetypal German farmers working the land. While the traditional farmer might be imagined as smoking a pipe, the Romanticizing image of the peasant who is rooted in the soil is clearly at odds with the idea of cigarette smoking, a habit that was associated with urban dwellers and intellectualism. Foresters were thus subtly reminded that cigarette smoking was inopportune for them because they, like farmers, were part of the most bodenständige estate. By itself, this would already have meant discouraging cigarette smoking, but it was amplified by the function that farmers and foresters were assigned by the Nazis: both "estates" were made public role models as the most naturally National Socialist of all Germans. As such, foresters had a role model function to fulfill, and the advertisements reminded them of the heightened responsibility they bore within the Volk.

A third series of tobacco advertisements appeared in four consecutive issues of the *Deutsche Forst-Zeitung* in 1942. Commissioned by the Palm cigar company, these advertisements clearly showed the effects of the wartime shortages on advertising. Instead of trying to sell more cigars, they actually gave advice on how to ration them. Hartmut Berghoff calls such seemingly counterintuitive forms of advertising "frugality and admonishment advertisements," that is, advertisements that reminded the consumer to be parsimonious with the valuable resources that went into making the goods he or she was about to consume.[40] In fact, the advertisements were very frank about the supply shortages in Germany, which was partly due to the increasing need to acknowledge the difficult supply situation that all readers lived through every day; denying the reality of scarcity would have irritated, rather than placated, consumers. The advertisements published by the Palm cigar company turned this necessity into a virtue, however, and tried to appeal to customers by giving them advice on how to make the most of their precious supplies: "Chain smoking: a thing of the past. These days, one thinks thrice before lighting one's Palm cigar, enjoying it in peace and quiet after dinner rather than at work or in the street car."[41] This message of deferment and awareness was repeated often: a cigar should be smoked only when one "has the time to savor its wonderful aroma in peace," which might not be easy: "Dear smoker, remain steadfast in the morning—even if the Palm cigar tempts you—and wait until after work to smoke."[42] The dual message of all Palm advertisements was that working and smoking (and, by extension, leisure) did not go together: the Volksgenossen should focus first on one and then on the other, but not mix the two.

In all of these tobacco advertisements, consumers were given clear indications of what they should and should not be doing. Some of these messages were tied to the proper use of the actual product being advertised, that is, when and where it was appropriate to smoke, while others addressed more general behaviors, such as one's demeanor at the workplace and the voicing of criticism. Of course, this message was not limited to tobacco advertisements, but could be found in connection with other products as well. Adhesive bandages, for example, served as a foil for raising the issue of absenteeism.[43] Still, the advertisements just discussed had at least an ostensible product message on which the propaganda message was piggybacking. The final examples of advertisements, however, illustrate that over the years of the Third Reich the political message became more candid and the tone increasingly urgent. This shift in tone is expressed most poignantly in the advertisements that forestry journals ran for themselves, in their own attempts at increasing their circulation.

In 1934, the *Deutsche Forstwirt* encouraged readers to advertise on its pages by lowering its rates and "thus debunking the excuse that rates are too high," hinting that the placement of advertisements could be interpreted by the authorities as "a contribution to the economic recovery."[44] A year later, in 1935, the *Deutsche Forstwirt* warned foresters not to underestimate the demands that the new political realities could bring for them and recommended itself as a trustworthy guide: "Don't miss anything in our eventful times. You must at all times be informed about the economic, political, and cultural aspects of life so as to have a clear idea of all the measures and instructions you are required to initiate. Your professional journal is a valuable help and advisor that is indispensable every hour of every day."[45] By 1936, the tone had become more forceful, as the journal flatly demanded to be read: "Reading a high-quality professional journal is a necessity—recruit those professional comrades still standing on the sidelines!"[46] Finally, by 1937, the readers were asked to denounce outright those who continued to evade the reach of the journal by "passing on the addresses of friends and professional comrades who still do not read *Der Deutsche Forstwirt*."[47] Readers were well advised to follow these thinly veiled exhortations to toe the party line, lest they be accused of "standing on the sidelines," which would have immediate consequences for their professional careers and even personal lives.

Parallel to these exhortations directed at the professional, the advertisements directed at the female homemaker showed a similar increase in urgency. Early on, the advertisements still appealed to the pride and "diligence of the German woman" in their efforts to sell sewing machines.[48] Soon, however, the tone became more politically explicit. In 1935, diligence had been replaced by duty as the most important virtue the German homemaker was expected to cultivate, in this case by reading the magazine *The German Rural Woman*: "Avoiding mistakes is a national duty at a time when the Fatherland is fighting for economic freedom and independence. Every homemaker, and every rural homemaker in particular, must join in this great task. Avoiding mistakes in every task in house, farm, and garden helps foster the wealth of the nation."[49] Once the war had begun and foodstuffs became ever harder to obtain, advertisements such as one for a "simple food" cookbook focused on the duty of the homemaker as the person primarily responsible for feeding the family and the corollary effects on the whole nation: "An important task for you as homemaker is the most appropriate use of all apportioned foodstuffs because it affects the health of your family and ultimately the perseverance of the home front."[50] In a similar vein, an advertisement for children's shoes mentioned the quality of the shoe brand only as a segue to reminding women of their alleged responsibility to teach children both proper consumptive behavior and manners: "If you were fortunate enough to obtain Trommler shoes for your children, you will surely see to it that their durability is not reduced wantonly through improper use."[51] The accompanying illustration made it clear that a mother could forfeit entitlement to the apportioned children's shoes simply by allowing her children to slip on their Trommler shoes without opening the laces and using a shoehorn. The advertisement demonstrated that the control of the state had reached even into the smallest aspects of everyday life. According to another ad from 1942, "These days, laundry hints are more than good advice: they have become commandments."[52] This language left nothing to be desired in terms of clarity. At no time could the reader be in doubt of what was demanded of him or her.

These advertisements, if one can still use that term, jettisoned any allusions to the desires and dreams of the consumer; instead, they badgered the reader with politically motivated advice on how to make the most of the situation and the reduced availability of everyday products. Even more than their earlier counter-parts, they served to complement the official state propaganda in delineating the safe boundaries of public discourse and behavior for the Volksgenossen. After reading what such advertisements had to say about one's national duty, there was little latitude for the individual German to plead ignorance. In a some-what less heavy-handed manner, these advertisements thus performed one of the functions of propaganda: to inform the citizenry of the expectations of the state — and the consequences of not meeting those expectations.

Conclusion

In a dictatorial regime such as the Nazi state, we should not be surprised to find a blurring of the line between political propaganda and commercial advertising. The parallel analysis of propaganda and advertising directed at two distinct audi-ences of German forestry journals demonstrates how subtle yet extensive the overlap between those two discourses could be. I have argued that this overlap was brought about intentionally by the National Socialists so that advertisements could in fact perform the function of propaganda or at least supplement it. The juxtaposition of advertisements with editorials and articles makes clear how this was achieved by drawing on the established analogy between forest and Volk so that one could serve as code for the other. This analogy worked because, after more than a century of literary, artistic, and musical romanticization of the for-est as German, the public was very familiar with the connotations of the forest as the symbol of Germany and Germanness. In essence, the forest had become accepted as what Canetti called the "crowd symbol" of the German nation long before the rise of the Nazis. All they needed to do to mobilize this analogy for their purposes was to extend that symbolism from *Volk* to *Volksgemeinschaft* and use the forest to provide visualizations for those concepts.

. We also have seen that even seemingly innocuous advertisements for forest saplings could carry an implicit political and even racist message that was visible to the reader only if he or she was steeped in the contemporary discourse. For twenty-first-century observers of the Nazi period (or any other historical period, for that matter), it is thus of paramount importance to deconstruct the advertis-ing within the contemporary context so as to identify its hidden messages. As we have seen, this can take a considerable effort. If we truly hope to understand the workings of the Nazi regime, however, this effort is indispensable.

Notes

1. Canetti, *Crowds and Power*, 185, 190, 197.

2. See also Michael Imort, "A Sylvan People: Wilhelmine Forestry and the Forest as a Symbol of Germandom," in Lekan and Zeller, *Germany's Nature*, 58–80, as well as Michael Imort, "'Eternal Forest—Eternal Volk': Rhetoric and Reality of National Socialist Forest Policy," in Brüggemeier, Cioc, and Zeller, *How Green Were the Nazis?*, 43–72.

3. On propaganda, see, e.g., Welch, *The Third Reich*; Gellately, *Backing Hitler*. For a discussion of the historiography of advertising in twentieth-century Germany, see Rainer Gries, Volker Ilgen, and Dirk Schindelbeck, "Kursorische Überlegungen zu einer Werbegeschichte als Mentalitätsgeschichte," in Gries, Ilgen, and Schindelbeck, *"Ins Gehirn der Masse kriechen!"*; Dussel, "Wundermittel Werbegeschichte?"; and Hartmut Berghoff, "Konsumregulierung im Deutschland des 20. Jahrhunderts. Forschungsansätze und Leitfragen," in *Konsumpolitik*. For analyses that focus on advertising during the Nazi regime, see Westphal, *Werbung im Dritten Reich*; Reinhardt, *Von der Reklame zum Marketing*; and Hartmut Berghoff, "Von der 'Reklame' zur Verbrauchslenkung. Werbung im nationalsozialistischen Deutschland," in *Konsumpolitik*. For a cultural history approach, see Bussemer, *Propaganda und Populärkultur*.

4. On the Werberat, see, e.g., Rücker, *Wirtschaftswerbung unter dem Nationalsozialismus*.

5. Goebbels on 25 March 1933, in a speech on the future of German broadcasting, quoted in Sywottek, *Mobilmachung für den totalen Krieg*, 23.

6. Frei, *National Socialist Rule in Germany*, 64–65.

7. For accounts of the alignment of the media, see Sywottek, *Mobilmachung für den totalen Krieg*; also Welch, *The Third Reich*.

8. See Rücker, *Wirtschaftswerbung unter dem Nationalsozialismus*, 175–278.

9. Cited in Heinrich Hunke, *Die neue Wirtschaftswerbung: Eine Grundlegung der deutschen Werbepolitik* (Hamburg: Hanseatische Verlags-Anstalt, 1938), 75. Note how the singular form of "sentiment" and "aspiration" aptly expresses the Nazis' insistence on uniformity.

10. Berghoff, "Von der 'Reklame' zur Verbrauchslenkung." See also the discussion by Ross in this collection regarding Berghoff's assertions about the continuities between the Weimar Republic and the Nazi period.

11. See Rücker, *Wirtschaftswerbung unter dem Nationalsozialismus*, 103–174.

12. Wilhelm Heinrich Riehl, *Die Naturgeschichte des deutschen Volkes* (Leipzig: Kröner, 1854). The book is also available in an abridged English translation by David Diephouse, *The Natural History of the German People* (Lewiston, N.Y.: Edwin Mellen Press, 1990). See also the role of the forest in the "German writings" by Paul de Lagarde, *Deutsche Schriften* (Göttingen: Dieterich'sche Universitätsbuchhandlung, 1878). For an example of a völkisch forester's perspective, see Franz von Mammen, "Heimatschutz im Walde," in *Heimatschutz in Sachsen*, ed. R. Beck (Leipzig: Volkshochschulverlag, 1909).

13. Rudolf Düesberg, *Der Wald als Erzieher. Nach den Verhältnissen des preußischen Ostens geschildert* (Berlin: Paul Parey, 1910), 138.

14. Ibid., 41.

15. Eduard Zentgraf, *Wald und Volk* (Schriften zur politischen Bildung, hrsg. von der Gesellschaft "Deutscher Staat," Heft 10) (Langensalza: Hermann Beyer, 1923).

16. This term is best translated as "the Germandom of ethnic Germans living just beyond the current borders of Germany" and represents an irredentist reference to, among others, Alsace and Lorraine.

17. Theodor Künkele, "Die außerfachlichen Aufgaben des Forstbeamten," *Silva* 14, nos. 52/53 (1926): 413.

18. Walther Schoenichen, "Im Namen der Staatl. Stelle für Naturdenkmalpflege in Preußen," in *Vom grünen Dom: Ein deutsches Wald-Buch*, ed. Walther Schoenichen (Munich: Georg D. W. Callwey, 1926), 205.

19. For example, Fritz Loetsch, "Wald und Volk," *Allgemeine Forst- und Jagdzeitung* 109 (May 1933): 170–171; Fuchs, "Wald und Volk," *Der Deutsche Forstbeamte* 2, no. 19 (1934): 345–348; Holle, "Deutscher Wald, deutsches Volk," *Der Deutsche Forstwirt* 17, no. 65 (1935): 785–787; Holle, "Deutscher Wald—Deutsches Volk!," *Deutsche Forstbeamtenzeitung* 1, no. 18 (1935): 453–455; Hermann Göring, "Deutsches Volk—Deutscher Wald," *Zeitschrift für Weltforstwirtschaft* 3 Sonderheft Deutschland (1935–1936): 651–661; Eduard Krca, "Wald und Volk," *Sudetendeutsche Forst- und Jagdzeitung* 37, no. 19/20 (1937): 185–186; Schmidt "Deutscher Wald—Deutsches Volk," *Deutsche Forst-Zeitung* 7, no. 18 (1938): 659–660; and Curt Francke, "Wald und Volk," *Der Deutsche Forstwirt* 25, no. 97/98 (1943): 401–403.

20. Forstmeister Dörr, "Der Kampstüh: Vom Werden und Vergehen des deutschen Waldes," *Der Deutsche Forstwirt* 16, nos. 44–45 (1934): 454.

21. The quote is taken from the official English translation of the speech in Göring, *Deutsches Volk—Deutscher Wald*, 656, grammar and emphasis in the original.

22. Canetti, *The Crowd in History*, 195–196.

23. Fuchs, "Wald und Volk," 345.

24. Ibid., emphasis added.

25. *Der Deutsche Forstwirt* 18, no. 16 (1936): 204; *Der Deutsche Forstwirt* 18, no. 20 (1936): 260.

26. See, e.g., *Der Deutsche Forstwirt* 23, nos. 71/72 (1941): 553.

27. Konrad Guenther, foreword to Hugo Keller, *So lebt die Waldgemeinschaft: Eine Bildreihe in 3 Heften. 1. Heft: Biologische Gemeinschaftskunde* (Leipzig: Verlag Ernst Wunderlich, 1936), xii.

28. Richard Bertold Hilf, "Der Wald des Künstlers: Zur Kunstausstellung 'Der Wald,' Berlin, 6. Juni bis 12. Juli 1936," *Forstarchiv* 12, no. 13 (1936): 250.

29. On Domizlaff, see Holm Friebe's essay in this collection.

30. Thus the title of his book: Domizlaff, *Die Gewinnung des öffentlichen Vertrauens.*

31. Domizlaff, *Brevier für Könige*, first circulated in manuscript form in the 1930s.

32. Domizlaff, *Propagandamittel der Staatsidee.*

33. Dirk Schindelbeck, "Hans Domizlaff oder Die Ästhetik der Macht," in Gries et al., *"Ins Gehirn der Masse kriechen!"*

34. Cited in Westphal, *Werbung im Dritten Reich*, 166; emphasis added.

35. *Deutsche Forstbeamtenzeitung* 8, no. 1 (1939): 21.

36. On the attempt by the Nazis to create an Aryan female image, see Guenther, *Nazi "Chic"?*

37. On the Nazis' antismoking campaign, see Proctor, *The Nazi War on Cancer.*

38. *Deutsche Forst-Zeitung* 11, no. 14 (1942): 209.

39. *Der Deutsche Forstwirt* 22, nos. 85/86 (1940): 675.

40. Berghoff, "Von der 'Reklame' zur Verbrauchslenkung."

41. *Deutsche Forst-Zeitung* 11, no. 6 (1942): 89.

42. *Deutsche Forst-Zeitung* 11, no. 4 (1942): 57; *Deutsche Forst-Zeitung* 11, no. 7 (1942): 105.

43. *Deutsche Forst-Zeitung* 10, no. 21 (1941): 362.

44. *Der Deutsche Forstwirt* 16, no. 52 (1934): 527.

45. *Der Deutsche Forstwirt* 17, no. 101 (1935): 1213.

46. *Der Deutsche Forstwirt* 18, no. 79 (1936): 980.

47. *Der Deutsche Forstwirt* 19, no. 51 (1937): 567.

48. See, e.g., *Der Deutsche Forstwirt* 16, no. 90 (1934): 975.

49. *Der Deutsche Forstwirt* 17, no. 81 (1935): 980.

50. *Der Deutsche Forstwirt* 22, nos. 39/40 (1940): 336.

51. *Deutsche Forst-Zeitung* 11, no. 7 (1942): 108.

52. *Der Deutsche Forstwirt* 24, nos. 91/92 (1942): 443.

5

SHELLEY BARANOWSKI

SELLING THE "RACIAL COMMUNITY"

Kraft durch Freude and Consumption in the Third Reich

A dvertising in the Third Reich wavered between autarky and international-ism. On the one hand, as Hartmut Berghoff has argued recently, it adopted German folk motifs, absorbed Nazi racial iconography, and eschewed what it termed "Jewish" or "American" materialism. On the other, it borrowed freely from international fashions, unable to escape their allure. Moreover, continues Berghoff, advertisers sold "deprivation" and "enticement" both, in keeping with the Nazi regime's own contradictory approach to mass consumption, which delayed material gratification to benefit rearmament while simultaneously promising a future of abundance.[1] The paradoxes of advertising that Berghoff describes underscored the fragility of the Nazi regime's intention to create a unified "racial community" (*Volksgemeinschaft*). To be sure, the Third Reich privileged collective over individual needs and the containment of consumption to enable the expansion that would ensure Germany's biological survival and continental domination. Nevertheless, Nazism also sought the unreserved commitment of its population, which it believed was crucial to eliminating the social divisions that imperiled its imperial ambitions. As a result, the regime's sensitivity to the individual and collective desires embedded in an emergent consumer culture sat uneasily with its disciplined and militarized image of the nation. Well before its ascension to power, in fact, the electoral success of Hitler's movement derived as much from its Americanized techniques of self-promotion and its promises of upward mobility as from its condemnations of mass consumption and mass culture.[2]

After 1933, the huge leisure organization Strength through Joy (Kraft durch Freude, or KdF) embodied the Nazi regime's difficult navigation between the claims of rearmament and its desire for popular loyalty, its restrictions against consumer goods in the present and its assurance of a materially comfortable future. As arguably the most popular Nazi social program, one that explicitly promoted the racial community through programs ranging from mass tourism to bettering the work environment, KdF muted the contradictions inherent in the Nazi dilemma. The organization's endeavors catered to the immediate desires of Germans by delivering the consumption of cultural experience leveraged through economies of scale, which in turn yielded bargain-basement prices for its services. Contrary to Berghoff, however, who argues that Strength through Joy was but a "virtual reality of imagined consumption," KdF's version of consumption was very real. It conjoined claims to material luxury with the nonmaterial values of community, producing inexpensive products that preserved Nazism's economic priorities while simultaneously persuading its participants that the regime had improved their standard of living.[3] Although KdF formally adhered to the regime's proscriptions against "un-German" advertising, its desire to sell the "community" through pleasure linked material well-being to the themes of social harmony and racial exclusivity.

Harmonizing Work and Leisure: KdF's "High" Standard of Living

Founded in November 1933 as a subsidiary of the German Labor Front (Deutsche Arbeitsfront), Strength through Joy mushroomed into a multifaceted purveyor of leisure activities and workplace improvements. Deploying subsidies from the Labor Front and the purchasing power of its potentially vast clientele, whom it encouraged to save toward the purchase of its offerings, KdF negotiated blocks of inexpensive tickets to cultural events and sites such as operas, concerts, the theater, and museums. In addition to its extensive sports programs, KdF managed some three hundred adult education programs, which offered courses ranging from the study of foreign languages to photography, history, and geography.[4] Then there was its most widely publicized program, tourism, which became its most profitable arm, earning 80 percent of its total income. In a little over a year after KdF's founding, the organization had pumped over 68 million Reichsmarks into the economy.[5] By 1938, according to the best estimate, some 43 million Germans, many of them repeat travelers, had availed themselves of KdF's weekend excursions, domestic tours, ski trips, and Baltic and Mediterranean sea cruises.[6] Following the launch of the Volkswagen project in 1937, a Labor Front undertaking in which KdF's director, Bodo Lafferentz, sat on the board, well over three hundred thousand Germans enrolled in savings plans toward the purchase of the "KdF Wagen."[7] Strength through Joy directed its offerings to a working-class audience, hoping that by granting workers access to the cultural practices of the middle classes and bettering the conditions of their labor, it would suppress class conflict and integrate workers into the nation. Although KdF's tourism did allow more workers to travel than did the package tours of the Socialists during the Weimar Republic, salaried employees and civil servants were overrepresented in its longest and most costly vacation trips. Nevertheless, KdF reached a mixed so-cial constituency and thus lent support to the Nazi regime's claim to have muted class divisions.[8]

Strength through Joy's leaders, many of whom had been influenced by a com-bination of Taylorism, industrial psychology, and the palliative corporate social policies of the 1920s, aggressively grabbed political space that other Nazi leaders or institutions ignored, promoting a "higher" standard of living for workers while accepting the constraints on the consumption of material goods that the regime imposed.[9] Yet to KdF's promoters, which included the Labor Front's leader, Robert Ley, KdF was no mere leisure organization. Rejecting what they saw as the artificial distinction between work and leisure, in which leisure amounted to little more than an escape from the drudgery of labor, KdF leaders stressed the harmony between them. Purposeful, spiritually uplifting, and restorative recre-ation would enhance the joy in work, raise productivity, and eliminate the class conflict that had so poisoned Weimar labor relations. On the shop floor itself, Strength through Joy's division, the Beauty of Labor (Schönheit der Arbeit), advocated improved healthfulness and aesthetics through on-site concerts and art exhibits, company investments in lighting, cleanliness, and ventilation, and the provision of recreational facilities, shower and changing rooms, and attrac-tive canteens.

Taken together, KdF's programs embodied, in the view of its promoters, the Nazi regime's commitment to raising German living standards in the broadest sense, that is, aesthetically and spiritually, not just materially. Such standards would be superior not only to that which the left advocated at home and abroad, that is, the collective provisioning of goods according to need rather than indi-vidual "performance" to benefit the "racial community," but also that embodied in the alleged "materialism" of American consumerism, which in the regime's view encouraged insatiable desires for tangible mass-produced goods. In Feb-ruary 1934, three months after KdF's founding, Robert Ley cast the regime's promised benefits in terms of the "honor" they could receive. Rather than giving workers what they really desired—comradeship with their countrymen and the respect that their skills deserved—Socialists, Communists, and trade unions stirred up class hatred with their demands for higher wages and a shorter work-day as the only means of improving the lives of wage earners. Instead of the rank materialism, individualism, and class conflict of the past, Ley concluded, community, courage, and obedience constituted the mantras of the present.[10] Strength through Joy's promoters and even the regime's emissaries followed suit. To a British audience in 1936, the German consul to Liverpool stated that the new social order in the Third Reich valued not "money and possessions" but "performance and achievement." Strength through Joy stood for the principle that workers deserved more than just material advantages. They were to experience the elevation provided by the spiritual values of the racial community.[11] Similarly, the Labor Front functionary Theo Hupfhauer argued that the "standard of life" was measured not merely in the number of material goods that one possessed but more particularly by the degree to which workers shared in the total creative product of the nation, including its artistic heritage.[12]

*Advertising Antimaterialism: KdF Advertising
and the Discouragement of Desires*

Because of Nazism's opposition to materialism, it is no surprise that much Strength through Joy advertising and promotion conformed to the Nazi regime's desire to sustain a modest, autarkic, or "German" consumption that discouraged the immediate and unlimited gratification of desires. The organization's most overtly productivist program, the Beauty of Labor, testified to Nazism's rejection of cosmopolitanism, beginning with its determined and, by its own lights, successful, campaign to eradicate inappropriate advertising from the work-place.[13] Instead, the aesthetic that it advocated in its brochures, instructional films, traveling exhibits, and its glossy periodical *Schönheit der Arbeit* and through numerous shop floor functionaries envisioned uncluttered surroundings, abundant light, the welcoming intrusions of nature in the workplace—plants on the inside and green spaces outside—cheerful dining rooms decorated with folk-loric and peasant motifs, and recreational facilities. Although such improvements were consistent with proposals circulated throughout the industrialized world by modernizing plant designers, architects, and industrial psychologists, the Beauty of Labor's aesthetic transmitted distinctly Nazi objectives. Thus the Beauty of Labor obsessed over cleanliness, or "squeaky cleanliness" (*peinliche*

1. "Let spring into the factory." A model shop floor, according to the Beauty of Labor. From *Schönheit der Arbeit*, undated issue. Author's collection.

Sauberkeit), less because it was a sign of godliness than because it signified social integration and racial purity. Not content with spotlessly clean work environments that would triumph over their opposites (grime, darkness, cramped and unhealthy conditions), the Beauty of Labor strove to cleanse the bodies of workers by lobbying employers to install or improve showers and changing rooms. Taken together, the clean bodies of workers testified to the eradication of the plague of class conflict from the social body. A clean and neatly attired body, like a clean and ordered shop floor, would incline individual dispositions toward a comradeship with the nation, which would dissipate Marxist disorder, social upheaval, and proletarian internationalism. According to one KdF periodical, the "'dirty' worker . . . should according to Marxist theory not become clean and well-dressed. Rather he should remain, so to speak, a walking advertisement for the infamous lie of the class struggle."[14] Fusing the ideological baggage of imperialism, which linked cleanliness and whiteness, and Nazism's racial hygiene, the Beauty of Labor used cleanliness to divide those spared the regime's racial purges, including workers whom bourgeois notions of cleanliness had once denigrated, from Nazism's victims, whose "asocial" slovenliness merited forced sterilization and social death.[15]

The Beauty of Labor pursued its goals beyond the industrial plant in its initiative, instituted in 1936, to prettify the German countryside in anticipation of the arrival of thousands of foreign visitors to the summer Olympic Games in Berlin. Detailed guidelines for the Beautiful Village (Das schöne Dorf) project demanded "cleanliness and order," even in work buildings, and consistency in agricultural style, landscape, and furnishings to reify villages as "typically" German. The touristic purposes became evident as well in the argument that village entrances should be made more attractive, like calling cards extended to visitors. The village cemetery was to be the German cultural site par excellence, for it was to eschew foreign vegetation such as cypress trees, in accordance with the dominant trend in landscape design during the Third Reich.[16] Tombstones were to conform to the general tenor of the graveyard as a whole. Peasant living quarters and farm structures were to avoid garish colors and styles, abstain from the use of urban building materials, such as concrete retaining blocks, and strive instead for a subdued coherence in keeping with their natural surroundings. Whitewashed houses complete with window boxes and climbing roses, trimmed shrubbery, and mended and painted fences would lift rural spirits and heighten the commitment of locals to maintaining the soil as an honorable calling. The Beauty of Labor's putatively successful crusade to eliminate advertising from factories encouraged an equally persistent effort to remove it from the countryside, where advertising had become sufficiently pervasive as to turn up in cemeteries.[17] Villages could permit "good, healthy" advertising, by which was meant advertising that did not contribute to the "urbanization" (Verstädtlichung) of the soil. Like the exteriors of residences and work buildings, rural advertising was to shun abrasive colors and remain understated in size, proportion, and frequency of appearance. It should be devoid of "foreign" images and represent the sensibilities of local artists and craftsmen, who instinctively understood and represented rural values. No advertisements were to be posted on doors, trees, or bridges, and only modest ads were allowed on the exteriors of shops.[18]

Likewise, KdF's promotion of its domestic and foreign tourism bowed willingly to the regime's expectations of austerity and sacrifice for the good of the racial community. Leveraging a 75 percent reduction in fares from the German Railroad, KdF trains crisscrossed the country with eight hundred to one thousand vacationers each, who had paid remarkably little for their trips compared to the cost of commercial tours and even that of the social tourism of the left.[19] Championed as a means for Germans from one region to get to know their countrymen from another, tourists stayed as guests in private accommodations, which, in addition to promoting conviviality, also kept the cost low for KdF tourists, while generating supplementary income for their hosts. Communal celebrations accompanied the departures and arrivals of KdF trains, while "community evenings" joining hosts and guests became standard fare on the night before tourists left for home or for another destination.[20] Partially the result of pressure from commercial tourism interests, who objected to the intrusion of KdF mass tourism in well-established spas and resorts, yet consistent with its communitarian purposes, KdF's domestic tourism specialized in tours to less well-traveled locales and especially to economically hard-pressed border regions, which benefited significantly from the infusion of much-needed revenue.[21]

Strength through Joy's choice of tourist destinations, such as the Rhine, the Black Forest, and the Baltic seacoast, frequently exploited the Romantic awe of nature. Yet sights of significance to the regime's ultranationalism and revisionism, be they the monument to Hermann the Cheruscan, who repelled the Romans, medieval towns with half-timbered buildings such as Rothenburg, or Danzig and the Tannenberg memorial, encouraged an identification with past victories of the ethnic community.[22] Germans, especially workers, would come to appreciate the German past and feel a common bond with their countrymen, thus freeing themselves from the imprisonment of class that Marxism had once imposed on them. Workers whose nationalism could not help but be awakened by touring with Strength through Joy, argued Ley, would abandon Marxist internationalism and no longer yearn for Moscow.[23] Cruises expanded on KdF's domestic agenda, inculcating not only nationalism and racism, but also visions of a future German imperium overseas. Agreements with Fascist Italy and Salazar's Portugal, which quickly translated into the popularity and propaganda success of its Italian and Madeira cruises, allowed for ceremonies of fascist unity in Strength through Joy's ports of call. They also, in the eyes of KdF promoters, presented the opportunity for vacationers to observe racial differences firsthand in the poverty of southern Italy and Lisbon and in the dark skins of locals in Libya, Italy's recently pacified colony.[24]

Strength through Joy's use of tourism to promote the racial and national community drew its inspiration from the regime's antimaterialism and distrust of individualism, which it believed would clash with its racialized variant of collectivism. Evoking the "front experience" of World War I, KdF's communitarianism called for the regimentation of tourists, whom it unceasingly warned to observe punctuality, obey tour directors, attend to their assigned places on trains and at inns, and eschew self-centeredness, especially the sort that would aggravate class distinctions. "Attention work comrades [*Arbeitskameraden*]," exhorted the instructions attached to a voucher for a nine-day inland vacation. "Unconditional obedience to the directions of the tour leader is required. He is responsible for the smooth functioning of the trip. Support him during the trip with discipline and comradeship." Those who failed to obey would be sent home immediately.[25] Mornings onboard ship caricatured Nazism's populist militarism, beginning with a blast of the trumpet from a cabin steward, followed by calisthenics on deck until breakfast, followed in turn by a flag parade accompanied by the ship's orchestra.[26] Monthly programs and brochures borrowed from the language of tourism to transmit Strength through Joy's redefinition of the standard of living in less commercial and material terms. Indeed, explained one monthly bulletin, "Our vacation trips are not commercial undertakings, but an occasion for the highest idealism."[27] Vacation trips were to provide recreation, self-discipline, and a sense of community, insisted Ley, and not become opportunities for hedonistic "orgies."[28] Consistent with the edification and spiritual uplift embedded in the classical Greek and imperial Roman ruins that KdF featured as sightseeing destinations abroad, KdF eschewed the materialist quest for personal pleasure. Instead, one was to contemplate the sublime, cultivate comradeship with one's fellow tourists, improve one's education by studying ancient art and architecture, regain one's equilibrium in preparation for the return to work, kindle one's historical consciousness, broaden one's horizons by leaving one's village or region to visit exotic locales, and especially experience an unthreatening form of fantasy. According to its periodicals, the KdF trip was "magical," "like a dream" or "long buried childhood dream," a "fantasy" of adventure and discovery that had now come true. Taken together, KdF trips were "unforgettable experiences" that encouraged tourists to transcend the everyday world.[29] In short, although a purchasable consumer good—a concatenation of images, promised experiences, and services—the seeming nonmateriality of Strength through Joy tourism packaged dream worlds and sold them as commodities.

Materialism through the Back Door:
Accommodating Consumer Desires

Nevertheless, a closer look at KdF's operations and marketing reveals an equally persistent willingness to accommodate what Nazism claimed to reject: individualism, materialism, and consumer expectations for personal freedom, comfort, and fun. Such a strategy was not unusual for commercial advertising during the Third Reich; thus it is not surprising that a Nazi Party organization that was in business to deliver leisure to its clientele should have behaved similarly. Strength through Joy's accommodations undoubtedly increased the numbers who flocked to its outings and vacation trips. Despite its reputation as the tour provider for the masses, garnered in visions of third-class train compartments loaded with vacationers and from the fears of commercial tourism interests that its hordes of tourists would compromise the social tone of established spas and resorts, KdF did allow time in its schedules to encourage individual exploration. A former communist raved about his one-week trip to Austria, the total cost of which did not exceed the normal roundtrip train fare to the same destination. For side trips and special events, tour organizers secured significant price reductions, and in any case, there was no obvious pressure to participate in them. Tourists enjoyed a good deal of personal freedom, for the only sign of the trip's official character was the swastika on the locomotive and the staged receptions that greeted the KdF train on its arrival in each village along the way.[30] With the exception of Norway, where currency regulations and a strong leftist resistance on land kept tourists aboard ship, tourists either signed up for excursions on land or set out on their own, the only restriction being the requirement that they return to ship by nightfall. In fact, the relative freedom of KdF vacationers, which middle-class tourists could more easily take advantage of, became a source of social division, as working-class tourists could not afford the cost of extras.[31] Moreover, even the Gestapo and SD (Sicherheitsdienst) agents who were assigned to KdF trips to prevent the infiltration of dissidents and the exposure of tourists to foreign antifascists, assumed roles as tourists and tour leaders. An agent aboard an extended Mediterranean cruise reported on the "unforgettable impressions" that ancient Athens left with vacationers, testifying to the manner in which business and pleasure conjoined.[32] Without denying their repressive function, agents just as often acted as informal ombudsmen for tourists, relaying in their reports complaints about food, entertainment, and accommodations, along with their more political assessments.

The degree to which Strength through Joy's tourism reflected and anticipated popular desires became clearer still in its advertising. For all its opposition to materialism and commercialism, its monthly magazines and tour brochures undermined or at least qualified them, while simultaneously remaining faithful to Nazi priorities. Cartoons conveying the fun that tourists would enjoy or their trips often satirized imaginary hosts whose exoticism encouraged caricature and

Meer und Strand sind so das rechte Urla
ziel für alle, die es lieben, in der woge
See zu schwimmen, den ziehenden W
nachschauend im Sand und in der Sonn
liegen und bei frohem Spiel in freier N
den Tag zu verleben. Hier ist wirkliche
gebundenheit und Sorglosigkeit. Gerade
unsere Arbeitskameraden mit Familie sind
Fahrten an die See besonders geeignet.
An der Ostsee werden wieder die pom
schen Badeorte Kolberg, Henkenhagen, Z
Lubmin u. a. besucht. Ganz besonders ern
ki auch Zoppot, das hervorragende S
Danzigs. Über die Fahrten an die Sam
küste berichten wir an anderer Stelle.
Neben der Insel Fehmarn und der K
Bucht an der mecklenburgischen Küste kon
in diesem Jahre erstmalig Sachsenurl
nach der Insel Rügen. Nicht lange
dann wird das große KdF.-Seebad bei M
auf Rügen fertiggestellt sein und wöche
20000 deutschen Arbeitern mit ihren F
lien Freude und Erholung spenden.
Unterkunftsorte unserer Fahrten befinde
ganz in der Nähe des im Bau befindl
KdF.-Bades. Es sind Sassnitz und Le
etwas weiter abliegend Breege. Die
die Insel Rügen typischen Kreidefelsen
Stubbenkammer mit dem Königsstuhl k
von dort aus leicht besucht werden.
Auch die Nordsee konnte diesmal in
Reiseprogramm einbezogen werden. Die
zigartigen Inseln Juist und Norderne
ostfriesischen Inselgruppe sind für drei Fa
unseres Gaues belegt.
Ostsee: 119, 132, 144, 170, 183,
196, 228, 233, 236, 239, 263, 286,
302, 313, 323, 327, 332, 344, 355,
Nordsee: 156, 203, 207, 360.

2. KdF vacationers at the beach. From *Die Deutsche Arbeitsfront*. NS Gemeinschaft "Kraft durch Freude," Gau Sachsen, *Urlaubsfahrten*, 1939, 20. Author's collection.

blatant racism. Thus, an African chieftain, "Wahatupa," armed with his spear and human bone but naked save for his loincloth, delivered a warning to his tribe as a snake lay coiled in the background: "No one should eat a KdF vacationer on my watch. We too have to show that we're cultured." Or they depicted dangerous beasts tamed by naïve, if intrepid, tourists. "But Freddie," protests a cartoon wife to her horrified cartoon husband as she swings contentedly on a huge python draped over a tree bough, "you told me that giant snakes aren't poisonous."[33] Furthermore, KdF periodicals increasingly resorted to images similar to those of commercial tourism to entice vacationers. Half- and full-page scenic panoramas, advertisements depicting young, healthy sun worshippers frolicking on the beach, well-groomed and prosperous couples on the ski slopes, and insouciant shuffleboard players aboard ship and announcements of snapshot contests promised modern comfort and a break from daily routine. Although conforming to the regime's emphasis on leisure as crucial to raising productivity, rising family

Winterfreuden
in luftiger höhe

3. On the slopes. KdF increasingly pitched its tour promotions to young women. From *Die Deutsche Arbeitsfront*. NS Gemeinschaft "Kraft durch Freude," Gaudienststelle Bayerische Ostmark, *KdF-Urlaub 1938*. Author's collection.

incomes demanded sophisticated sales pitches to KdF's prospective clientele, an audience whose expectations KdF gleaned partially from surveys distributed to its tourists.[34]

KdF's choice of models implicitly testified to another irresistible benefit: Nazism's vision of what racial purity should look like. Flawless complexions, handsome faces, symmetrical and well-proportioned physiques were not the only striking feature of KdF ads. The prominence of young, attractive, and apparently single women testified to Strength through Joy's dependence on a constituency that had grown significant during the interwar period, this despite the prudish anxieties of tour directors and agents regarding the behavior of women who took advantage of the freedom that travel gave them. Anything but the "Gretchen" stereotype attired in dirndls, female models exuded the naturalness and freedom of the racially superior. Whether packing for their trip, waving from the window of the smoking compartment of their train (an indication that

KdF was willing to borrow potentially subversive images from commercial advertisers),[35] frolicking at the beach, or gazing from the ski slopes, models bespoke middle-class status in recognition of the female salaried employees who flocked to KdF tourism. In keeping with the Nazi regime's artistic standards, KdF eschewed Hollywood-style sensuality when depicting women in bathing suits, shorts, or short-sleeved blouses. Announcements of snapshot contests discouraged the submission of women in alluring poses and recommended instead natural and unforced poses that radiated fitness, good health, and controlled fecundity. In addition to demonstrating the physical characteristics of the racially acceptable, KdF's female models evoked a disciplined prosperity for a deserving nation.

Moreover, KdF promotions promised creature comforts as a reward for the frugality of participants who saved for its products, thus capturing and mitigating the tension between delayed gratification and future bounty. Ads and articles that encouraged workers to put money away for a "KdF Wagen" emphasized not merely the car's low cost, high gas mileage, and ease of maintenance, but also its speed and the comfort of its upholstery. One article depicted well-dressed parents and their happy well-adjusted children departing from their single-family home, combining comforting images of domesticity with modernity. "Papa" drives the Volkswagen out of the garage, ready for a family outing, while his wife and children bound out the door in anticipation.[36] The promotion for Strength through Joy's two newest cruise ships, the *Wilhelm Gustloff* and the *Robert Ley*, launched in 1938 and 1939, respectively, conveyed KdF's increasing attraction to luxury. The *Wilhelm Gustloff*, named after the Swiss Nazi Party leader whom a Jewish medical student assassinated, had twenty-five hundred square meters of deck space and featured a swimming pool, gymnasium, and cinema. To eliminate the class demarcations of other ships, the cabins of both ships were arranged along the decks on the outside. Each contained separate sleeping quarters, with living space complete with table, sofa, chair, and built-in wardrobe.[37] The *Robert Ley* possessed a two-story theater, five thousand square meters of deck space, a gymnasium, a swimming pool painted with mermaids riding atop dolphins, and cabins that at least equaled the *Wilhelm Gustloff* in comfort. Its dining room, consisting of attractively set tables for four, encouraged intimate conversation rather than mass travel.[38] Like the luxury liner that catered to the wealthy, the *Robert Ley* amounted to the *Bremen* for the working classes. In interviews with the press, Ley projected a fleet of twenty KdF ships, as well as an enlarged harbor at Bremen complete with a hotel that would accommodate more than three thousand, a

4. A KdF tourist's photo album: snapshots from a cruise to Norway on the ship *Der Deutsche* (1938). Author's collection.

train station, a huge garage, and an entertainment center for tourists waiting to embark on their cruises.[39] The comfort fetish illustrated in such promotions spoke to KdF's sensitivity to the proclivities of its clientele, whose photo albums included snapshots and postcards of the ships' dining rooms, cabins, reading rooms, and decks.

No Strength through Joy tourism project better illuminates its paradoxes than its resort at Prora, scheduled to open in 1940 on the inlet between the resort towns of Sassnitz and Binz, on the Baltic island of Rügen. The first of five projected resorts on the Baltic and North Seas, the KdF Seebad Rügen was to provide an inexpensive one-week vacation to twenty thousand working-class holidaymakers, thus addressing KdF's most persistent problem: the underrepresentation of workers in its tours.[40] At first glance, the accommodations at Prora suggested a cross between the barracks and the assembly line, in which small guestrooms, identical in size, were lined along antiseptic and utilitarian hallways. The focal point of the Rügen project, an enormous multipurpose hall, underscored the politicized, indeed plebiscitary, potential of vacations from the point of view of

5. "The model for the KdF resort at Prora, on Rügen." From Reichsamtsleitung Kraft durch Freude, *Unter dem Sonnenrad: Ein Buch vom Kraft durch Freude* (Berlin: Verlag der Deutschen Arbeitsfront, 1938), 129. By permission of The Center for Research Libraries, Chicago.

the Nazi regime. In addition to serving as the site for musical and stage perfor-mances, the structure would accommodate parades, demonstrations, and other forms of live propaganda.

The selling of Rügen, however, belied the appearance of fascist regimenta-tion. The island's reputation as a summer resort for the prominent and well-off testified to KdF's desire to open the cultural practices of the middle and upper classes to "lesser-earning *Volk* comrades." Unlike the innovative plans in the 1920s for the Berlin "Thermal Palace," which envisioned a spacious indoor beach and swimming area, the Rügen project was to take workers directly to the seaside at low cost.[41] Strength through Joy periodicals bragged endlessly about the resort's unparalleled amenities. Despite the modest size of the guestrooms, each one faced the beach and came equipped with central heating, hot and cold running water, and comfortable upholstered furniture. In addition to two huge swim-ming pools, one of them enclosed, heated, and with a wave-making machine, a pier would permit cruise ships to dock, while the resort's train station was constructed to handle up to three thousand workers and their families each day. Other on-site recreational facilities—bowling alleys, billiard rooms, a cinema, a large restaurant and other cafés—would allow each vacationer to pursue his or her fancy. To reassure prospective consumers, Strength through Joy promised its clientele that accommodating the masses would not entail the sacrifice of the satisfaction of family or individual desires. Each vacationer would claim fifteen meters of beach to himself or herself, not including the space available in the woods behind the resort that stood ready for exploration or contemplation. The variety of entertainment would disperse vacationers to such a degree that no one would feel cramped or regimented.[42]

Community and Individualism: The Experiences of KdF Tourists

What did KdF tourists actually experience? In light of Strength through Joy's intention to sell the racial community through vacation travel and thus realize one of the Nazi regime's most important political objectives, it is fair to interrogate KdF's popular reception. To be sure, although tourists generally followed KdF's directives, they resisted its most egregious attempts at regimentation. Yet KdF's simultaneous appeals to community and its sensitivity to individual preferences accorded with the expectations of tourists, which in turn paralleled the regime's desire to have its cake and eat it. Tourists took Strength through Joy's cut-rate accommodations and services in stride. Carefully composed photo albums, diaries, and tourist testimonials in Strength through Joy's monthly magazines and company periodicals expressed appreciation for the friendliness of hosts, the comfort and cleanliness of private lodgings, and especially the putative community that transcended class divisions.[43] For Maria Förster, occupation unspecified, a cruise around the Italian peninsula fulfilled a long-time yen to travel and the triumph over social barriers. "It is strange how quickly every mistrust fell," she exclaimed, "for it lasted only a few hours, and then what emerged was a great and trusting comradeship. . . . Here sits the factory worker next to the young office employee, the country woman next to the city woman. There are no differences."[44] For a Krupp ironworker, a cruise also fulfilled a lifelong dream realized only under National Socialism. From the departure of his train from Essen to his return to the same station, vacationers behaved like a family rather than a collection of strangers. The conviction that the democratization of tourism was at hand did not stop with the departure of his cruise ship from Hamburg. Observing the opulent and well-staffed yacht of an "American millionaire" caused the worker to ask, "Will this woman with all her money be happier than we who are on this marvelous trip? I hardly think so." As for the English Channel and the Isle of Wight, he commented that "almighty Albion" was certainly beautiful, but no place was as captivating and orderly as Germany. Lying in a deck chair, the ironworker recalled the words of the Social Democratic Party boss Philipp Scheidemann, who once promised workers a future of tourism and automobiles. Nevertheless, only Hitler had come through.[45]

By the same token, however, tourists were eager to assert themselves as individuals, experience pleasure and release, flout KdF's restrictions, accumulate

6. "Mannheimers on *The Monte Olivia* with KdF in Norway." From the photo album of Erich Wagner, Mannheim, undated (mid-1930s). Author's collection.

things, and assert their class prejudices. Allusions to class and regional tensions appeared frequently in the surveillance reports of the Gestapo and SD, as well as references to the resentment of the excesses of party officials, who, especially on the cruises, claimed special privileges with a lack of subtlety unsurprising in a new elite that faced few checks on its authority. Tourists violated currency regulations by smuggling goods purchased with marks, crossed borders without authorization to buy souvenirs, and trafficked in cigarettes and other trinkets exchanged for hard goods. Not surprisingly, alcohol became the lubricant of transgression. Thus, the Rhine River trip for twelve hundred employees of the Edel Steel Works in Ueringen resulted in an orgy of destruction to the steamer, the costs for which the firm had to absorb.[46] And much to the dismay of the regime's spies and KdF tour leaders, vacationers often resisted politicization, much like the middle-class tourist who snapped, "Don't bother me with politics. I don't want to have anything to do with them."[47] Notwithstanding the subversive messages that KdF advertising deployed, women tourists bore the brunt of criticism for such *unvölkisch* behavior in SD and Gestapo eyes, emerging not just as physical objects of surveillance, but also as a discourse that testified to the regime's ambivalence toward consumption and its suspicion of materialism. Gendered assumptions of the irrationality, frivolousness, and self-absorption of women yielded the view that female travelers could not grasp the real purposes of KdF tourism, especially young and single women who journeyed without a husband or chaperone. Female dress became a weapon in the class warfare that Strength through Joy sought to curtail, particularly on the cruises, where evening dances, costume parties, and other kinds of entertainment offered opportunities for display to those who could afford it. "A group of female passengers showed a taste for the sort of jewelry and attire," according to an agent, "which cannot be considered appropriate for a KdF vacation trip."[48] In addition, in official eyes, female travelers were soft touches for souvenir and kitsch sellers and, worse still, flagrant in their propensity for illicit sex that violated not only bourgeois norms but also the regime's racial codes. The actions of some of the women on a Mediterranean cruise were "shameless," according to an agent. One got drunk in the company of a Greek officer, wobbling unsteadily as she returned to her ship loaded down with the money and gifts that her short-term companion had given her. Chastised for swapping their cigarettes with Arabs in Tripoli, several female vacationers insolently retorted that at least their trading partners were not Jews, betraying their willingness to exploit Nazi racial hierarchies to achieve individual ends against the proscriptions of tour directors. Ignoring warnings that their deportment did not conform to that which the "master race" demanded, the women gaily posed for snapshots with locals.[49]

Nevertheless, KdF's accommodations to the individualism and materialism of its tourists yielded positive benefits for the regime, despite the occasional unruliness of vacationers. The manner in which Germans, or at least those whom the regime's repression did not directly impact, underscored the "positive" achievements of National Socialism resided in no small measure in the touristic assessments as to Germany's standard of living compared to that of other nations. Because Strength through Joy's tourists, when traveling outside Germany, journeyed most often to economically less well-developed states with large impoverished regions, or, as in the case of Poland, traversed through them, comparative reflections on the relative well-being of Germans became a consistently lively topic of conversation. A trip from Berlin to Königsberg through the Polish Corridor aroused great interest, according to an agent, for no one could help noticing the deteriorating train stations, unkempt and untended forests, and the poverty-stricken misery that ended only upon the train's approach to Danzig.[50] The Portuguese soldiers who begged for cigarettes grabbed the attention of tourists on a cruise to Lisbon and Madeira, as did the grinding poverty of Madeira's fishing villages.[51] If German passengers occasionally praised Mussolini's or Salazar's determination to improve the lives of their citizens, they persisted in comparing the putative filth of local conditions to the "high" living standards that they were accustomed to in Germany.[52] Tourist judgments, furthermore, frequently resorted to racial stereotypes, which, if hardly unusual among travelers from the wealthy industrialized world, generally matched the expectations of KdF tourism promoters as to the values that they hoped to inculcate. Thus, a civil servant from Stettin in Pomerania commented on the "southern nonchalance" (*Lässigkeit*) that characterized the majority of Portuguese as he observed the raggedly clothed children who begged from tourists in the Lisbon harbor.[53] Nor were tourists averse to making comparisons that trivialized the Nazi regime's repression, such as the passengers on a cruise to Italy who contrasted the grime of Naples and Palermo with German "cleanliness." Every complainer, they opined, should be forced to live in the miserable living quarters that they observed there, which were nonetheless "better than a year in a concentration camp."[54]

To be sure, fewer tourists traveled abroad with KdF than participated in its domestic tours. Nevertheless, the number who took sea voyages was significant, having peaked at 140,000 in 1939, and such numbers almost certainly sufficed to have created a ripple effect.[55] The dissemination of first-person travel accounts in factory newspapers and libraries and in KdF's widely distributed literature became instruments for circulating the retrospectives of tourists. Moreover, the manner in which the media popularized travel during the Weimar era, the travel accounts on the radio, the slick advertising of package tours, and short film clips of cruises almost certainly stimulated the desire of KdF tourists to recount their experiences to a larger public.[56] Finally, the informal exchanges that occurred between vacationers and acquaintances, postcards sent from vacation spots, and the display of photo albums, commemorative pins, and luggage labels assured the even wider impact of tourists' judgments. Carefully composed snapshots depicted fun, relaxation, pleasure, and camaraderie aboard ship, as well as panoramic views that mimicked the visions of natural beauty laid out in KdF brochures. The painstaking arrangement of such albums suggests their authors' intention not merely to engage in private recollections of a special time, but also to share their experiences of enlightenment, self-expression, and well-being.

Even working-class tourists could not resist discovering the differences in the standard of living between Germany and the ports of call that they visited.

7. "Panoramic snapshot by an anonymous tourist of the mountains of Norway," undated (mid-1930s). Author's collection.

Having witnessed the poverty in Portugal on a cruise to Madeira, some workers announced that they would under no circumstances change places with the Portuguese.[57] Commented the author of a report on his cruise to the same destination in a KdF periodical, the Portuguese with whom he and his comrades came into contact could not believe that the Germans were workers because they appeared to be so well dressed. Only when the tourists showed their hands to their hosts did the latter become convinced.[58] Although acknowledging the recent suffering in Germany, workers aboard a cruise to Italy expressed satisfaction with the Nazi government, having observed up close just how Italian workers lived.[59] Even recorders of tourists' impressions with a very different viewpoint, such as the undercover agents of the German Social Democratic party in exile (Sopade), arrived at similar conclusions. Workers on a cruise to Portugal, noted one such observer, were astonished at the terrible living conditions there: "All working-class vacationers were very satisfied with their trip, even the one-time Social Democrats."[60]

Strength through Joy's ability to reconcile sacrifice and expectation and Spartanism and luxury, which it conveyed through its advertising and its practices, significantly aided the Nazi regime's quest for popular legitimacy. While KdF insisted that its participants comply with its ideological purposes, it succeeded because it accepted something less than the rigid martial discipline and self-denial envisioned in the regime's ideal of the racial community. Thus, the same tourists who sought sexual adventure or engaged in other means of transgression also explored the ruins at Pompeii or the Acropolis, absorbed the contents of guidebooks, and celebrated their fellowship with each other, taking advantage of the flexibility the KdF provided to combine seriousness of purpose with fun. During a period in which scarcity was more evident than prosperity, KdF helped to persuade the majority of Germans whom the terror did not directly affect that an improved economy, rising living standards, the possibility of experiencing pleasure, and the commitment to social opportunity defined the Nazi regime.[61] If the mixed messages of KdF's advertising and the desires of its tourists abetted the materialism and individualism that the regime condemned, both became vehicles to deepening the popularity of the Third Reich.

Notes

1. See Hartmut Berghoff, "Enticement and Deprivation: The Regulation of Consumption in Pre-War Nazi Germany," in Daunton and Hilton, *The Politics of Consumption*, 165–184; and "Von der 'Reklame' zur Verbrauchslenkung: Werbung im nationalsozialistischen Deutschland," in *Konsumpolitik*, 77–112.

2. See Corey Ross's essay in this volume.

3. Berghoff, "Enticement and Deprivation," 173, 177.

4. Otto Marrenbach, *Fundamente des Sieges: Die Gesamtarbeit der Deutschen Arbeitsfront von 1933 vis 1940* (Berlin: Verlag der Deutschen Arbeitsfront, 1940), 343.

5. Hasso Spode, "Arbeiterurlaub im Dritten Reich," in Sachse et al., *Angst, Belohnung, Zucht und Ordnung*, 295; Schoenbaum, *Hitler's Social Revolution*, 104 n. For further details regarding KdF's finances and income, see Buchholz, "Nationalsozialistische Gemeinschaft 'Kraft durch Freude,'" 213–235; Frommann, "Reisen mit 'Kraft durch Freude,'" 21–36.

6. See the table in Hasso Spode, "'Der deutsche Arbeiter reist': Massentourismus im Dritten Reich," in Huck, *Sozialgeschichte der Freizeit*, 295.

7. Smelser, *Robert Ley*, 171.

8. See Keitz, *Reisen als Leitbild*, 252–253. For further details on the participation of workers, see Baranowski, *Strength through Joy*, 67–72.

9. For the emergence of KdF, see ibid., chapter 2. KdF's only serious rival was Alfred Rosenberg's National Socialist Cultural Community, yet by 1937 it too was subordinated to Strength through Joy.

10. Robert Ley, "Nicht um Lohn — um die Ehre!," in *Durchbruch der Sozialen Ehre: Reden und Gedanken für das schaffende Deutschland* (Berlin: Mehden Verlag, 1935), 88–103.

11. Deutsches Konsultat, Liverpool an das Auswärtige Amt, 27 May 1936, R48527, Auswärtiges Amt-Politisches Archiv, Bonn.

12. "The Standard of Life of the Individual Depends on the Creative Efforts, the Joy in Work,

and the Achievement of the Community," *German Addresses for Committee X, World Congress "Work and Joy," Rome 1938* (Berlin: Buchdruckwerkstätte, 1938), 3–10.

13. Anson Rabinbach, "The Aesthetics of Production in the Third Reich," in Mosse, *International Fascism*, 211.

14. "Sauberkeit und Ehre gehören zusammen," Nationalsozialistische Gemeinschaft (NSG) Kraft durch Freude, Gau München-Oberbayern, *Kraft durch Freude*, April 1937, 17; "Sauberkeit im Betrieb ist eine Notwendigkeit," NSG Kraft durch Freude, Gau Hessen-Nassau, *Kraft durch Freude* 4, no. 4 (April 1937): 10–12.

15. On the relationship between cleanliness and imperialism, see Burke, *Lifebuoy Men, Lux Women*, 17–62; McClintock, *Imperial Leather*, 207–231; Richards, *The Commodity Culture of Victorian England*, 119–167. The literature on Nazi racial policy has proliferated, especially over the past two decades. For a summary statement, see Burleigh, *The Third Reich*, chapters 4 and 5.

16. Joachim Wolsche-Bulmahn and Gert Gröning, "The National Socialist Garden and Landscape Ideal," in Etlin, *Art, Culture, and Media under the Third Reich*, 79.

17. NSG, KdF Kreiswart, Kreis Hannover an alle Orts-und Betriebswärte der NSG, "Kraft durch Freude," 2 December 1936, 122a, VIII, 180, Niedersächsisches Hauptstaatsarchiv, Hannover.

18. "Die Werbung im Dorf," Landesarchiv Koblenz, Bestand 714, no. 5406.

19. Spode, "Arbeiterurlaub," 317–319; Keitz, *Reisen als Leitbild*, 142.

20. For a good summary of the mechanics of KdF's domestic tours, see Bruno Frommann, "Reisen im Dienste politischer Zielsetzung: Arbeiter-Reisen und 'Kraft durch Freude'-Fahrten," Ph.D. diss., University of Stuttgart, 1993, 143–154.

21. For a nuanced analysis of KdF's relationship to commercial tourism, see Semmens, *Seeing Hitler's Germany*, 98–128. As for KdF's impact on impoverished regions, see Baranowski, *Strength through Joy*, 198–200.

22. On Rothenburg, see Hagen, "The Most German of Towns." On continuities and discontinuities of Nazi tourist culture and practice in general, see Semmens, *Seeing Hitler's Germany*, 42–71.

23. "'Kraft durch Freude': Leistungen des Deutschen Sozialismus," *Siemens-Mitteilungen*, no. 156 (December 1934): 235, Siemens-Archiv Munich.

24. For further details, see Baranowski, *Strength through Joy*, 202–212; Liebscher, "Mit KdF 'die Welt erschließen.'"

25. Teilnehmerkarte für UF 82/39, Kraft durch Freude, Gau Magdeburg-Anhalt, Abteilung Reisen, Wandern und Urlaub.

26. *Krupp: Zeitschrift der Kruppschen Werksgemeinschaft*, "Mit 'Kraft durch Freude' auf dem Dampfer 'Oceana' nach England," 1 July 1935, 373, Historisches Archiv Krupp, Essen. See also Frommann, "Reisen im Dienste," 243.

27. This statement appears in a lengthy description of KdF's rules, NSG Kraft durch Freude, Gau Pommern, *Monatsprogramm* no. 1 (December 1934): 5–9.

28. Rede des Reichsorganisationsleiter Pg. Dr. Ley am 11 July 1938 auf dem Schiff "Wilhelm Gustloff," R58, no. 944, Bundesarchiv, Berlin-Lichterfelde (hereafter BAL).

29. Good examples of such language can be found in NSG Kraft durch Freude, Gau Pom-

mern, *Monatsprogramm 1934/35*; "Spar für Deinen Urlaub," NSG Kraft durch Freude, Gau Schwaben, *Jahres-Urlaubsprogramm 1935* (Berlin: Verlag des Deutschen Arbeitsfront, 1935); G. Müller-Gaisbert, *Volk nach der Arbeit* (Berlin: Verlag Richard Carol Schmidt, 1936), 294–300.

30. Bericht über die Lage in Deutschland, Nr. 16, July 1935, in Stöver, *Berichte über die Lage in Deutschland*, 680–681.

31. Baranowski, *Strength through Joy*, 264–265.

32. Bericht des SS-Unterstumführers Prieb über die Teilnahme an der KDF, Auslandsfahrt nach Dalmatien, Griechenland mit dem Dampfer "Oceana" vom 6. bis. 18. November 1936, R58, no. 950, 284, BAL. See also Baranowski, *Strength through Joy*, 280–281.

33. "Das Lacht der Urlauber," NSG Kraft durch Freude, Gau Süd Hannover-Braunschweig, *KDF Monatsprogramm*, June 1939.

34. Report on Strength through Joy submitted by Hugh R. Wilson, Ambassador to Germany, to President Franklin Delano Roosevelt, August 1938, German Diplomatic Files, box 32, Hugh R. Wilson: March–November 1938, Franklin D. Roosevelt Library, Hyde Park, New York (www.fdrlibrary.marist.edu).

35. Hartmut Berghoff, "'Times Change and We Change with Them': The German Advertising Industry in the Third Reich—Between Professional Self-Interest and Political Repression," in Church and Godley, *The Emergence of Modern Marketing*, 141.

36. "Ein Traum wird Wirklichkeit mit dem KDF Wagen," NS-Gemeinschaft Kraft durch Freude, Gau Süd Hannover-Braunschweig, *KDF-Monatsheft* (July 1939): unpaginated.

37. "Eine Fahrt mit dem 'Gustloff': Flaggschiff der deutschen KDF-Flotte," *Deutsche Wechruf*, 30 June 1938; "Auf Wiedersehen im Salzkammergut: Eine unvergeßliche Nordseefahrt für österreiche KDF-Fahrer," *Niedersächsische Tageszeitung*, 26–27 March 1938. Both are found in the VVP 17, no. 2456, Niedersächsisches Hauptstaatsarchiv, Hannover. See also Marrenbach, *Fundamente des Sieges*, 358–360.

38. "Wissenswertes vom schönsten KDF.-Schiff 'Robert Ley,'" NS-Gemeinschaft Kraft durch Freude, Gau Mainfranken no. 4 (May 1939): 5; Die Deutsche Arbeitsfront, NS-Gemeinschaft "Kraft durch Freude," Reichsamt Reisen, Wandern und Urlaub, *KDF-Schiff "Robert Ley"*: *Die "Bremen des deutschen Arbeiters,"* DB 72.12, Institut für Zeitgeschichte, Munich.

39. Die Deutsche Arbeitsfront, NS-Gemeinschaft "Kraft durch Freude," Reichsamt Reisen, Wandern und Urlaub, *"KDF-Schiff 'Robert Ley'"* (Berlin: Verlag der Deutschen Arbeitsfront, 1939); "Der Bau von zwanzig KDF.-Schiffen geplant. Vier grosse KDF. Bäder an der Ostsee-1940 mit KDF nach Tokio/Eine Unterredung mit Dr. Ley," *Hannoverscher Anzeiger*, 3 March 1936, VVP 17, no. 2456, Niedersächsische Hauptstaatsarchiv, Hannover.

40. For detailed accounts of the resort, see Rostock and Zadniček, *Paradies Ruinen*; Hasso Spode, "Ein Seebad für Zwantzigtausend Volksgenossen: Zur Grammatik und Geschichte des Fordistischen Urlaubs," in Brenner, *Reisekultur in Deutschland*, 7–47; Baranowski, *Strength through Joy*, 223–231.

41. Gert Gröning and Joachim Wolschke-Bulmann, "The *Thermenpalast* (Thermal Palace): An Outstanding German Water-leisure Project from the 1920s," in Anderson and Tabb, *Water, Leisure, and Culture*, 141–147.

42. Reichsamtsleitung Kraft durch Freude, *Unter dem Sonnenrad: Ein Buch von Kraft durch Freude* (Berlin: Verlag der Deutschen Arbeitsfront, 1938), 129–130.

43. In one such diary, recounting a stay in an "idyllic" village in the Bayerische Ostmark, the writer warmly complimented her hosts, the Larks family, for her "pretty, clean" guest-room and the quality of food that the hostess served at breakfast. Anonymous diary in author's personal possession.

44. "Kameraden erleben Italien: Eine KDF.-Seefahrt 'Rund um Italien' von Maria Förster, NSG Kraft durch Freude, Gau Mainfranken," *Kraft durch Freude*, no. 1 (January 1939): 1, Historisches Archiv Krupp, Essen.

45. A. Christiansen, "Mit 'Kraft durch Freude' auf dem Dampfer 'Oceana' nach England," *Krupp: Zeitschrift der Kruppschen Werksgemeinschaft* 26, no. 19 (July 1935): 373, Historisches Archiv Krupp, Essen.

46. Bericht über die Lage in Deutschland, Nr. 19/20, January–February 1936, in Stöver, *Berichte über die Lage in Deutschland*, 680–681.

47. Bericht über die 45. Urlaubsreise mit M.S. Monte Olivia nach Norwegen, 13–21 July 1936, R58, no. 948, 4, BAL.

48. Reisebericht über die "Frühlingsfahrt nach Italien, Tripolis, und Madeira," der NS-Gemeinschaft "Kraft durch Freude" der Deutschen Arbeitsfront (Reichsamt für Reisen, Wander und Urlaub), 10–31 March 1939, R58, no. 950, 649, BAL.

49. Bericht über die Reise Dalmatien-Griechenland mit der Reichsbahn und dem Dampfer "Oceana," 2–15 March 1939, R58, no. 950, 626, BAL; KDF Frühlingsfahrt nach Italien, Tripolis und Madeira auf dem Dampfer "Stuttgart," 11–30 March 1939, R58, no. 950, 586, BAL.

50. Bericht über die KDF-Reise U.F., Nr. 4306, 29 June 1939, R58, no. 947, 177, BAL.

51. Bericht über die KDF-Herbstfahrt nach Madeira, Tripolis und Italien des M.S. "Wilhelm Gustloff," 12–31 October 1938, R58, no. 950, 293–294, BAL.

52. Bericht über die KDF-Seereise mit Dampfer "Oceana," 2–12 March 1938, BAL R58, no. 949, 13–14; Bericht über die Teilnahme des SS-Hauptsturmsführer Mulde, 2–12 March 1939, R58, no. 950, 71, BAL; Bericht über die Rund um Italienfahrt der KDF mit dem Schiff "Oceana," 1–12 December 1938, R58, no. 950, 447-8, BAL. Cf. Liebscher, "Mit KDF 'die Welt erschließen,'" 61–71.

53. Otto Kühn, "Mit 'Kraft durch Freude' nach Madeira 1936," MS 127, Institut für Zeitgeschichte, Munich.

54. Bericht des SS-Oberscharführer Otto-Wilhelm Wandesleben über die stattgefundene KDF-Reise nach Italien, 6–18 November 1938, R58, no. 950, 384, BAL.

55. Spode, "Arbeiterurlaub," 295; Marrenbach, *Fundamente des Sieges*, 355.

56. Keitz, *Reisen als Leitbild*, 95–111; Sandoval, "Film Representations of German Holiday Cruises," 19–21.

57. Bericht über die Reise des K.d.F.-Schiffes "Der Deutsche" nach Madeira, 21 March–7 May 1938, R58, no. 950, 241–242, BAL.

58. "Wir deutschen Arbeiter in Madeira," NS Gemeinschaft "Kraft durch Freude," Gau Sachsen, *Kraft durch Freude* (May 1935): 2–4.

59. Betr.: Bericht über die Rund um Italienfahrt, der KdF mit dem Schiff "Oceana," 1–12 December 1938, R58, no. 950, 449, BAL.

60. *Deutschland-Berichte der Sozialdemokratischen Partei Deutschland (Sopade)*, July 1935 (Frankfurt: Petra Nettlebeck), 848–849.

61. For a comparable argument, see Jeff Schutts's essay in this collection.

"DIE ERFRISCHENDE PAUSE"

Marketing Coca-Cola in Hitler's Germany

Toward the end of World War II a commotion broke out among a group of German prisoners of war disembarking from a ship in Hoboken, New Jersey. Restoring order, the American guards demanded an explanation. One of the soldiers captured from Hitler's Third Reich pointed to a familiar red sign overlooking the harbor: "We are surprised that you have Coca-Cola here too."[1] When the incident was reported in the *Reader's Digest*, Americans found the anecdote a surprising contrast to the patriotic marketing that had linked the soft drink to the Allied war effort.[2] "It was news to them," noted Hamilton Burke Nicholson, the president of The Coca-Cola Company in the early 1950s, "that something they consider 'so typically American' was considered indigenous to other countries."[3] In fact, many Americans found it unsettling to learn that, in the words of the popular Coke historian Mark Pendergrast, "while the soft drink came to symbolize American freedom — all the good things back home the GI was fighting for — the same Coca-Cola logo rested comfortably next to the swastika."[4]

Today there remains an aftertaste of scandal to the revelation that Coca-Cola "refreshed" Nazi Germany. "I was shocked," reported the British satirist Mark Thomas. He had associated the Coke brand with pleasant images — sports, Santa Claus, teenagers on a hillside teaching the world to sing — not despotic regimes. "You discover this huge history of the company that is hidden," he noted, "hidden because we're constantly swamped with images of advertising." In an effort to counter the sugar-coated "Cokelore" nourished by such marketing, Thomas partnered with artist Tracey Sanders-Wood in 2004 to create the "Coca-Cola

Nazi Advert Challenge," an international exhibition of pseudo–Nazi Coke ads created by contemporary artists. In their effort to conjure Coke's German past and "show the brand for what it really is," most of the artworks coupled Coke trademarks with Nazi symbols.[5]

Mark Thomas's surprise notwithstanding, Coca-Cola already has an established iconic role in German history: it is a totem of West Germany's "Americanization" during the 1950s. This "Coca-Colonization" has been commemorated by a Coke bottle encased in the standing exhibit at the Haus der Geschichte in Bonn.[6] As the state museum for contemporary history underscored with a special Coca-Cola exhibition in 2002, the soft drink can be seen as a sort of lubricant to Germany's postwar development of "freedom and democracy."[7]

Coca-Cola's role as the antithesis to National Socialism also was rehearsed in the first academic work to address the soft drink's presence in Hitler's Germany. Hans-Dieter Schäfer used Coke's 1930s German advertisements and sales figures to help identify within the Third Reich a "state-free sphere" of modern consumerism and "on-going Americanization" that decoupled Nazi "ideology from praxis." Noting that "guests were encouraged to drink 'ice-cold Coca-Cola' from the wall of the Sportpalast where Goebbels gave his speeches," Schäfer argued that "peaceful cosmopolitanism mitigated the militaristic, racist rhetoric used by the Third Reich to demonstrate its power."[8] However, whereas other scholars suggested that a retreat into such American-style popular culture offered Germans a site of *Resistenz* (the "static" of nonconformity) to the smooth functioning of Nazi social control, Schäfer argued that the "split consciousness" engendered by such consumerism served to stabilize the Hitler regime: "Instead of undermining Nazi legitimacy, this [Americanism in the Third Reich] strengthened control over the oppressed."[9]

Some historians were quick to question Schäfer's assertions, especially as his project rode a wave of scholarship that sought to reevaluate the "modernity" of the Third Reich.[10] This debate questioned whether "Nazism had paved the way for a liberal-democratic society in post-war West Germany."[11] Whereas in the 1960s scholars argued that the Nazis "revolutionized" German society with their pursuit of a militarized, racially defined *Volksgemeinschaft* (national community), by the 1980s at issue was whether Hitler was intentionally "progressive" and to what degree the Holocaust could be deemed "modern."[12] Tangled up with these controversies was the problem of categorizing the Third Reich's nascent consumer society.

Instead of joining in this attempt to encompass both Auschwitz and ice-cold

Cokes within a new and improved concept of modernization, this essay takes the term "Coca-Colonization" literally when analyzing Coca-Cola's marketing in Nazi Germany. In examining the actual dynamics involved in the internationalization of Coca-Cola (company, beverage, and icon), this approach reveals that Coke's success under Hitler demonstrates the process of cultural "creolization"—a narrative of Coca-Cola's "Germanization" as much as Germany's "Americanization" or "modernization."[13] As an earlier Coke scholar observed of the German POW anecdote: "The reason Coca-Cola people like this story so much is that it sums up the biggest secret of the drink's success abroad. *People of other lands tend to regard it as theirs because their own people produce it.*"[14]

Indeed, Coke's international expansion was facilitated by adapting the decentered franchise structure that had allowed it at the turn of the century to conquer the continentwide American market. By drawing from local resources (sugar, glass, capital, entrepreneurial enthusiasm—everything but the flavor-concentrate), Coca-Cola could appear "indigenous" wherever it was bottled. As H. B. Nicholson insisted, "In France, it is a French business. In Italy, it is an Italian business."[15] Consequently, the Germans who manufactured and brought Coca-Cola to market in the Third Reich were able to infuse it with enough "German character" that it became, as noted in another analysis of those confused POWs in New Jersey, a "symbol" of the German *Heimat*, or idealized fatherland.[16]

In seeking to understand better what Germans under Hitler associated with the Coca-Cola trademark, this case study of Coca-Colonization takes a closer look at Coke's advertising and public relations in the Third Reich. In deciphering the creole of Coke images and Nazi principles, it corroborates Schäfer's thesis that Coca-Cola buttressed Nazi ideology, whichever "ization" course one chooses to plot the soft drink's growing popularity.

In April 1929, when Coca-Cola was first produced in Germany, there was no reason to doubt that it was an "American" product. Back in the United States, then under Prohibition, Coke easily claimed the title of "*the* national drink"; Canada Dry Ginger Ale, its nearest competitor at the time, sold only one-third as much.[17] Moreover, the expatriate behind the new German bottling franchise, Ray Rivington Powers, with his commanding bulk, flashy car, expensive clothes, and loud jovial personality, fully embodied the local stereotype of "a true American."[18] However, despite his remarkable talents as a salesman, Powers alone did not establish Coca-Cola in Germany. The new soft drink was blocked from distribution in the established German beverage market by a formidable wall of cultural and commercial barriers. These ranged from the infamous "German thirst" for alcohol and a belief that it was unhealthy to drink anything "ice cold" to the subservience of barkeepers to local breweries and their unwillingness to pay bottle deposits.[19]

Consequently, Coca-Cola could not simply advertise itself into a German market share as Wrigley's Spearmint chewing gum had done a few years earlier. Instead, Powers realized, "Product distribution is the basis for a good business, it must precede advertising."[20] What Coca-Cola needed was a legion of local entrepreneurs who could effectively promote it at the grassroots level to both retailers and consumers. Ironically, the onset of the Great Depression facilitated the recruitment of such men. Powers assembled the *Coca-Cola Familie* of dedicated German franchise-holding wholesale distributors who found in Powers's enthusiasm and Coke's modest but guaranteed per-unit profit the motivation necessary to successfully launch the new soft drink. During the economic slump from 1930 to 1933, while in the United States Coca-Cola sales dropped over 20 percent, Coca-Cola GMBH, the new German Coke subsidiary, increased Powers's meager first year's sales figures almost twelve-fold (from 9,439 to 111,720 cases).[21] This was an especially remarkable achievement considering that overall German soft drink consumption was cut 60 percent by a devastating tax introduced by Chancellor Heinrich Brüning in 1930.[22]

Nonetheless, with the tax lifted by Hitler, even the 2.5 million Cokes sold in Germany in 1933 constituted a mere trickle compared to the coming flood. However "real" Germany's overall economic recovery was following the Nazi seizure of power, the Third Reich brought increased prosperity to Coca-Cola GMBH and its affiliates.[23] In 1938, after seeing Coke sales in Germany roughly double nine years in a row, The Coca-Cola Company in Atlanta reported:

> The growth in volume of our business in Germany has been one of the most spectacularly successful chapters in the Company's history. . . . During 1937, [company bottling] branches in operation, outside Essen [Coca-Cola GMBH's headquarters], rose from 6 to 13, concessionaires increased from 230 to 425, the roster of employees doubled, retail outlets approached 50,000, retail sales exceeded 55,000,000 units, the Company became the largest consumer of sugar in the beverage industry, the persons in Germany deriving their principal income from its product passed 5,000, and the product itself was by a wide margin the largest selling non-alcoholic beverage in Germany.[24]

A year later, despite the outbreak of World War II, Germans spent 25 million Reichmarks on over a hundred million ice-cold Cokes. Promised "Die erfrischende Pause" (a direct translation of Coke's definitive American slogan from 1929, "The Pause that Refreshes"),[25] what did these German Coca-Cola consumers imagine they were purchasing?

Any effort to define Coca-Cola must begin with a look back at the soft drink's origins. "It took two men to invent Coca-Cola," noted Frederick Allen in his history of Coca-Cola. "Legend credits [John] Pemberton with being the father of Coca-Cola, but [Frank] Robinson was the father of the *idea* of Coca-Cola."[26] In other words, in 1886 the Atlanta pharmacist Pemberton concocted the "secret formula" in his legendary backyard kettle, but Robinson, a Yankee bookkeeper come south with a printing press, stirred up the public's desire to drink it. The Harvard business historian Richard Tedlow explained, "Coca-Cola was advertising incarnate. Remember that Frank Robinson chose 'Coca-Cola' as a name, similar to other advertising names, thinking that the two C's would look well in advertising.'"[27] In addition to coining the name and drafting the famous trademark, Robinson pioneered innovative marketing techniques that complemented Coke's intrinsic "refreshing" qualities as the soft drink claimed its American market. Within a few years, these promotions ranged from free-sample coupons and direct mailings to enticing "Coca-Cola Girl" calendars and the never-ending display of the trademark on signs, buildings, and "dealer helps" that ranged from serving trays and thermometers to pencils, baseball score cards, and Japanese fans.[28] All this advertising, noted Samuel Candler Dobbs, Robinson's successor in the shaping of Coca-Cola's image, "claim[ed] nothing for Coca-Cola that it did not already have, but pound[ed] everlastingly into the public mind through printed display, the words 'Drink Coca-Cola, Delicious and Refreshing, 5 cents.'"[29] This brief message effectively summarized "the *idea* of Coca-Cola": here was a good product ("delicious") that could change the life ("refreshing") of anyone (just 5 cents) who would *drink Coca-Cola*.

The "Reminder Advertising," manifested in the novelties and point-of-sale trademark signs, complemented "Reason Why Advertising," such as posters and print ads, which presented in "words and pictures the delicious and refreshing quality of Coca-Cola."[30] This latter, more elaborate advertising sought to endow Coca-Cola with positive associations by endlessly depicting the consumption of the soft drink within agreeable contexts—in the words of the Coca-Cola historian Pat Watters, "pleasant people in pleasant places doing pleasant things as a pleasant nation went pleasantly on its course."[31] Consequently, noted Judith Williamson in *Decoding Advertisements*, "you clearly do *not* 'drink [Coca-Cola] for what it is': you drink it in order to become like the signifier in the advertisement, the distorted mirror-image that confronts you in the person or people shown in the ad."[32] Arguing that "the language of *modern* advertising" was born when ads shifted from identifying the product to representing the context of consumption, Pasi Falk concurred, "Coca-Cola depicted the world of pleasure."[33]

For most of the 1930s, while Coca-Cola GMBH focused on building its distribution system and propagating "the idea of Coca-Cola" throughout the Third Reich, Germans saw the same "world of pleasure" in Coke's advertising images as did Americans, albeit less frequently and with German texts. "Everything that we needed, we got from over there," noted Hubert Strauf, a pioneer in German advertising who was involved with Coca-Cola throughout his career. "We were thereby totally under American control, and besides we didn't have any money to do our own [advertising]. . . . The Americans always told us to only translate the ads."[34] In 1929, Strauf helped create Coca-Cola's first German promotional material, a small brochure explaining "Was ist Coca-Cola?" Powers and his salesmen handed out these flyers on the street and wherever the soft drink was available. Max Keith, the German businessman who ran Coca-Cola GMBH from the mid-1930s until 1968, recalled, "Our main activity in the field of advertising was to distribute folders . . . we had millions and millions of these prospectuses. An unbelievable amount. . . . Attractive, inexpensive advertising."[35] Typically with cover images drawn from American Coke ads and a puzzle or useful information inside to help ensure that their reminder to "Trink Coca-Cola" was seen more than once, such brochures remained for years, next to point-of-sale signs and translated American posters, the mainstay of Coca-Cola's German advertising. They were, the company explained to its dealers in 1935, "the most direct form of advertising you can use. . . . Brochures not only present the 'Coca-Cola' trademark to the public. . . . With them, we can explain why one should drink 'Coca-Cola.'"[36]

Consequently, Coca-Cola's fundamental German advertising profile in the 1930s was that which had been conceived for American audiences by Archie Lee, Norman Rockwell, Haddon Sundblom, and the other artists and admen commissioned by The Coca-Cola Company in Atlanta. In Germany as in the United States, Coca-Cola appeared to be the preferred beverage of respectable hard-working men, attractive sporty women, boys in straw hats heading off to their favorite fishing hole, and, every winter, a jolly Santa Claus decked out in Coca-Cola red.[37] Nonetheless, although, at least to discriminating viewers, the impossibly radiant smiles on these idealized Coke drinkers may have signified "America" as much as the pleasure of an ice-cold Coke, the Coca-Cola GMBH employees who were involved with advertising did their best to "somewhat Ger-

1. "Four Seasons." Like most of Coca-Cola's German advertising in the mid-1930s, this panel representing the four seasons simply added German text to illustrations created in the United States. From Peter Zec, ed., *Mythos aus der Flasche: Coca-Cola Cultur im 20. Jahrhundert* (Essen: Design Zentrum Nordrhein Westfalen, 1994), 75.

manize things."[38] The word Strauf used in 1991 to describe the process was *umpolen*, to switch or reverse polarity.[39]

In general this process was too subtle to be significant, but a couple of early instances were noteworthy. In 1935 a special Christmas brochure had Sundblom's iconic American Santa remind Germans, in a direct translation, "Thirst knows no season." On the back of the flyer, a more primitive illustration reported, "Something about Christmas Trees." The relatively substantial text, in Gothic type, concluded, "So the Christmas tree is a truly German creation."[40] Thus, while attempting to mimic the cover slogan's American success in encouraging winter soft drink consumption, the brochure also sought to integrate this new habit into established German holiday traditions. A similar switch can be seen with the posters and brochures created for Mardi Gras. As noted in *Coca-Cola Nachrichten*, Coca-Cola GmbH's newsletter for the Coca-Cola Familie, "In many areas of Germany *Karneval* or *Fasching* [the northern and southern German

2. "Suffering from a hangover? Ice-cold Coca-Cola helps" (ca. 1935). In Germany, Coca-Cola advertising claimed that the soft drink could cure headaches and keep one sober. From Anne Hoy, *Coca-Cola: The First Hundred Years* (Atlanta: Coca-Cola Company, 1986), 93.

terms for the holiday] are the highpoint of recreational life for the entire year. For months before, old and young, the poor and the wealthy, look forward to this joyful *Volksfest* [people's festival]."[41] During the 1930s, countless Coca-Cola holiday brochures, posters, and postcards "Germanized" standard images of festive Coke drinkers with an overlay of confetti and masks. Moreover, the text to such promotional materials tried to directly tap into the German thirst for alcohol: "If you are losing yourself in Mardi Gras celebrations but want a clear head in the morning, then slip in fresh and enjoyable 'Coca-Cola' breaks!"[42]

Although American Cokelore reports that Asa Candler, the founder of The Coca-Cola Company, bought Coke's secret formula from Pemberton because the soft drink relieved his headaches, an ability to cure hangovers was not touted in American advertising for what was often called "The Great National Temperance Drink."[43] In Germany, however, Coca-Cola's ability to rid one of *Katzenjammer*, or "screeching cats," colloquial German for the consequences of a night of hard drinking, became an advertising theme that extended beyond the brief Karneval season. By 1935 this selling point could be found throughout the growing catalogue of low-cost Coca-Cola publicity materials produced in Germany, not only brochures and postcards but also simple print ads and slides that were projected before the feature in movie theaters.

Moreover, it was claimed in Germany that Coca-Cola could help beer, wine, and schnapps drinkers "stay sober." One of the short rhymes propagated to the general public suggested, "Viel Bier allein im Magen, das kann kein Mensch vertragen; drum soll das Bier bekömmlich sein, stülp eine Coca-Cola hinterdrein" (roughly, No one can handle a belly full of only beer; to settle your stomach, top off with a Coca-Cola).[44] In 1935 Coca-Cola GmbH announced "the fact that ice-cold 'Coca-Cola' lessens the effects of heavy drinking of alcoholic beverages and often even eliminates them."[45] Capitalizing on this "fact," the Coca-Cola Familie tried to convince proprietors of bars and restaurants that "Coca-Cola even helps to sell more beer."[46] In 1935, an article in *Coca-Cola Nachrichten* elaborated:

> The proprietor can easily see that Coca-Cola is an in-between drink that is consumed before, during and after alcohol. Since it disappears from the table in just a couple of minutes, it can be sold cheaper than anything else that he sells. "Coca-Cola" is not a competitor with other beverages. Just the opposite, after drinking it the customer is anxious to drink more, ordering another bottle or a different drink and consuming it with delight. Coke settles the stomach and clears the head. After enjoying a Coca-Cola, some guests will drink more beer and wine than they would have consumed otherwise.[47]

This unique Coke attribute could also help defuse the traditional German prejudice that soft drinks were only for women and children. "With [the Katzenjammer-themed advertising] exactly those men who drink a lot of alcohol can be won over to drinking Coca-Cola," insisted *Coca-Cola Nachrichten* in 1934. "At first the afflicted will probably only want to drink Coca-Cola when he truly has a hangover, but by and by he will develop a taste for Coca-Cola, and can become a proper Coca-Cola drinker."[48] Less than a year later, a journalist from the Rhineland wrote Coca-Cola GmbH to recount exactly such a story, noting how even those who had once teased him for drinking Coke now drank it themselves. Explaining his stressful life at the newspaper, he reported, "I can't imagine a workday without this delicious drink."[49]

These examples demonstrate that, in ways both trivial and pragmatic, Coca-Cola GmbH did ease Coke's German launch by reversing polarity in the strange new soft drink's advertising. Moreover, as scholars seek to identify the role Coke played in German history, these developments might easily be tossed into the pen with those trying to pin down the greased pig labeled "modernization." As *Coca-Cola Nachrichten* observed in 1935, "In general, drinks without alcohol are more positively received in the modern times of technology and sports."[50] Max Keith later elaborated, "I would say that the time was just right for a good refreshing beverage because the need developed—the requirements of the people were much higher than in the past. They had to work harder, had to work faster, the technical equipment they had to handle required soberness."[51]

Nonetheless, however modern they were, Coke's Germanized selling points do not in themselves explain the soft drink's growing popularity in the Third Reich. Germany had other "indigenous" soft drinks, and American images remained predominant in Coca-Cola GmbH's burgeoning spectrum of advertising materials.[52] In fact, within the context of the challenging early years establishing Coke's German market, Coca-Cola GmbH's first advertising director observed, "Most often the value of print advertising for our product is somewhat overstated."[53] Instead, "Exhibitions and *Außenverkäufe* [concession sales at special events] are the best and cheapest advertising," insisted *Coca-Cola Nachrichten* in 1935. "There, 'Coca-Cola' drinkers are made, and that, in the end, is the goal of our entire propaganda."[54]

"Since the National Socialists became leaders of the economy," noted the German Coke newsletter in 1937, "fairs and exhibitions have assumed a decidedly more important role in economic and most especially cultural relations."[55] This phenomenon has not escaped the attention of scholars, who have examined both the Third Reich's small-town celebrations and its grandiose events, like the spectacular Nazi party rallies.[56] For Coca-Cola GmbH, however, "Our interest in representation at fairs is determined primarily by the opportunity to recruit new [Coke] drinkers."[57] Another article in 1935 insisted, "Wherever many people gather, Coca-Cola should also be present—ice-cold, of course, and at an affordable price and in sufficient quantities. We should make this such a habit that people will notice we are absent if for some reason we aren't there."[58] The logic of participating in such events had been evident since 1929, when initial batches of German-made Coca-Cola were carted off to a local regatta and the nearby docking of the *Graf Zeppelin*.

Not only did sales at such venues circumvent the traditional drinking establishments controlled by the breweries, but out in the field the Coca-Cola Familie could build consumer demand by personally explaining to fellow Germans Coke's "köstlich und erfrischende" (delicious and refreshing) qualities. Moreover, an added benefit was the possible burnishing of Coke's image through the informal tie-in to prestige events and, as with the celebrated airship, symbols of Germany's greatness and promising future.[59] However, the logistics involved in setting up concession stands at such events were formidable, from obtaining the necessary licenses to carting ice through masses of people. After a successful appearance at the 1935 Leipzig Trade Fair, Coca-Cola GmbH established a special department to assist the Coca-Cola Familie in taking advantage of Außenverkäufe opportunities, both large and small.[60] Additionally, *Coca-Cola Nachrichten* published lists of upcoming events, as well as countless articles with helpful tips.

Außenverkäufe became part of the weekly routine for the entire Coca-Cola Familie. As Else Bürfent, the wife of the Coca-Cola distributor in Bonn, recalled in 1991, "There we were on Sundays, wherever there was something happening, setting up our stand on a soccer field."[61] Meanwhile, Coca-Cola GmbH mastered the skills and connections to make such Coca-Cola kiosks a "natural" part of any major public event, from the Nuremberg Nazi party rallies to Munich's beer-soaked Oktoberfest.[62] Consequently, most Germans in the 1930s sampled their first Coke not at their usual bar or restaurant but outside watching a marching column of Nazi Brownshirts or their favorite sports team.

The range of Coca-Cola's Außenverkauf activities is suggested in the contrast between a couple of the most high-profile events. In 1938 Coca-Cola GmbH's hometown hosted the National Garden Exhibition. For the occasion, the company built a fifteen-meter-long service counter inside a large round kiosk, appropriately inscribed "Die erfrischende Pause."[63] While this monument to Coke's *Erfrischungsdienst*, or "refreshment service," was intended to last forever, Coke's presence at another national event was fleeting. In 1937 a Coca-Cola truck accompanied the first *Deutschlandfahrt*, a 3,200-kilometer world-class bicycle race that was meant to become Germany's equivalent of the Tour de France.[64] Whereas in postwar Germany the slogan "Wo Sport ist, ist Coca-Cola" (Wherever there are sports, there is Coca-Cola) was an obvious truism, during the 1930s Coke was still establishing this precedent in Europe.[65] With an extra dose of drama, *Coca-Cola Nachrichten* reported:

Who knew how much endless effort would be needed to convert the bike racers into *Freunde* [friends, i.e., Coke drinkers], as many were not familiar with our drink. Might no one want to try the beverage, unsure whether it was all right to drink an ice-cold drink when the glowing sun was forcing sweat from the pores? At the first care-station in Crossen the difficulties initially seemed insurmountable. Meaning well, one was reluctant to risk handing an ice-cold "Coca-Cola" to one of the over-heated racers. Shyly, someone made the first move. It tasted good. More was drunk, and then down went the rest in big swallows. It was a miracle. A drawn-out "ahh" encouraged the others to follow suit. And as it became clear that despite the oppressive heat there were no bad side effects, the bottles went briskly from hand to hand. The first part of the battle for "Coca-Cola" had been won.[66]

At the end of the race two weeks later, where the banner at the finish line was marked with the Coca-Cola trademark, many of the racers were wearing Coca-Cola sun visors. More important, from newsreels to magazine articles, "a mountain of news reports about the Deutschlandfahrt enthusiastically reported the good qualities of our drink, proving that in a short time 'Coca-Cola' had become the sportsman's drink."[67] In 1998, Walter Oppenhoff, the German attorney who had incorporated Coca-Cola GmbH in 1930, recalled, "Sports provided a means by which to introduce Coca-Cola, a way to spread the word."[68] However, Coca-Cola's presence at such high-profile sporting events also could bring unwanted consequences, as was demonstrated by the company's experience at the most famous Außenverkauf opportunity of the 1930s, the 1936 Berlin Olympic Games.

Although many new policies in the Third Reich benefited Coca-Cola (e.g., mandatory bottle deposits, drunk-driving laws, and regulations limiting the breweries' control of drinking establishments), Hitler's fanaticism about the health of the Volksgemeinschaft's "German germ plasma" was a double-edged sword. Whereas the Nazi campaign against so-called Genußgifte focused primarily on the consumption of tobacco and alcohol, and thus encouraged soft drink consumption, the "pleasurable poison" caffeine was also targeted.[69] Despite Coca-Cola's advertising claim that it was "Rein und Gesund" (pure and wholesome), there were periodical demands from Nazi party headquarters in Munich that Coca-Cola be investigated and regulated. Here, however, the Third Reich's chaotic "polycratic rule" played to Coke's advantage.[70] Whenever the Health Ministry was ordered to "finally do something against Coca-Cola," the well-connected Oppenhoff worked with sympathetic Prussian bureaucrats to arrange for the case to be forwarded to some forlorn administrative department. Over sixty years later, the self-satisfied attorney recalled, "For over a year the files would not return."[71] By that time, the health-conscious Nazi who had initiated the action typically would have moved on to other concerns.

However, regarding caffeine, such bureaucratic obstructionism came to an end during the 1936 Olympics. Although Schultheiss, a Berlin brewery, enjoyed an exclusive concession to quench the spectators' thirst, Nazi authorities authorized Coca-Cola GmbH to provide supplementary "refreshment service" from sidewalk stands outside the Olympic venues. Nonetheless, according to German

Cokelore, Dr. Leonardo Conti, one of the Nazi party's most senior medical doctors, became concerned about Coca-Cola when his children became agitated after drinking the soft drink at the games.[72] Whether or not the anecdote is true, that summer there was enough official concern over the caffeine in soft drinks that Coca-Cola GmbH was ordered to affix paper labels to its bottles declaring Coke *koffeinhaltig*, or "caffeine-containing." (In 1938 such labeling became mandatory in Germany and remains so today.) To protect Coke's image and sales, Keith wanted to launch an advertising campaign to explain that Coke was harmless. Instead, Robert Woodruff, the legendary "Boss" of The Coca-Cola Company who attended the Olympic Games with a contingent of executives from Atlanta, forbade the German subsidiary from responding: "You must *never* engage in defensive advertising. It simply gives dignity to your opponents and prolongs the issue."[73] Instead, Coca-Cola GmbH produced a series of promotional brochures with an Olympic tie-in. Filled with information on the world-record holders, the schedule of the games, and the best transportation routes to the Berlin stadiums, "the brochures have a value that will prompt everyone to tuck one away [for later reference]."[74] *Coca-Cola Nachrichten* urged the Coca-Cola Familie, "Use these brochures not only in your clients' bars and kiosks, take advantage of any opportunity to distribute them at sports fields and gatherings of every kind."[75]

Although Coca-Cola enjoyed only middling sales at the Berlin Olympics, 1936 was a milestone year for Coca-Cola GmbH, with distribution established throughout Germany and annual sales surpassing 1 million cases.[76] The company in Essen reported, "Not only has our business grown over the last year, most of our concessionaires have seen a similar evolution in their own businesses."[77] With Germans pausing for Coke's "Erfrischung" over seventy-five thousand times a day, the strange soft drink had established a niche within the Third Reich's *Trinkkultur*, or drinking culture. However, this was not a time for the Coca-Cola Familie to rest on its laurels. As one senior German Cokeman reminded the annual conference of Coca-Cola's wholesale distributors the following April, "After victory the solider tightens down his helmet."[78] An article in *Coca-Cola Nachrichten* elaborated:

> Does a commander going to war know beforehand if he will be victorious? He can only take care of two things. First, that he has at his disposal troops that are strong enough and equipped with the best equipment, and then that his people are infused with enough desire to win and optimism to carry them forward with enthusiasm and confidence in victory. Exactly the same is true in advertising. Advertising is not for scaredy-cats and pes-

simists. It is a manly, active, aggressive matter. Only he who gambles wins, and the world belongs only to the courageous.[79]

While most of the speeches at the conference that spring emphasized Coke's familiar marketing plan (e.g., Außenverkäufe, extensive customer service to retailers, and the endless need for advertising), there was also an undercurrent of defensiveness that revealed that Coke's recent success had come at a price: envy from others in the beverage industry. Competitors sought to discover the "secret formula" behind Coke's achievement.[80] For example, before it was deterred by Oppenhoff's legal posturing, Sinaclo AG, Germany's first producer of a brand-name soft drink, tried to market a new flavor called "Cola-Cola."[81] While the phenomenon of other beverage producers attempting to ride on Coke's coattails was familiar from its American experience, Coca-Cola GmbH's challenges within the Third Reich had a unique aspect. Whereas in the United States Coke's most vexing problem had involved the government's Progressive-era inquiry into the soft drink's "purity" as a food, in the Third Reich Coke's ethnic-national qualities were also questioned. Moreover, whereas in America Coca-Cola's advertising had enlisted Uncle Sam to demonstrate the company's patriotism during its confrontation with a crusading government official ("Pure Food and Drug" watchdog Harvey W. Wiley), in the Third Reich Coca-Cola integrated itself into the programs of the Nazi government in order to help demonstrate its German character against "slander" made by a competitor.[82]

By the late 1930s Coca-Cola's success in Germany had brought it not only new Freunde, but also the attention of potential Feinde (enemies). In August 1936 a meeting of the Brewers' Association of Central Baden reported, "We especially will watch the market-brawling advertising of the soft drink 'Coca-Cola' in order to counter it whenever possible."[83] A few months later Parzhamer Venus-Quelle, a Bavarian bottler of natural spring water, complained to state authorities, "Domestic springs will have trouble marketing their product, if they can do so at all, because a foreign company such as the Coca-Cola industry has spread its product like an avalanche."[84] In January 1937 the company's proprietor wrote the Food and Agriculture Ministry in Berlin, "For your orientation, enclosed is some information about the Coca-Cola Export Corporation. It would be interesting to know whether Jewish capital is active in Coca-Cola GmbH."[85] While the letter's attachment has been lost, it was probably a postcard-size photograph of some bottle caps that noted in Hebrew that Coca-Cola was kosher. Initially, the proposition that the soft drink was "Jewish/American dreck" (*jüdische/amerikanische Gesöff*) appeared to be a potentially serious threat to Coke's hard-won German success.[86]

The kosher Coke propaganda originated with Karl Flach, the proprietor of the Cologne-based firm F. Blumhoffer Nachfolger (Bluna), which produced Coca-Cola's most tenacious "German alternative." Around the same time that Powers was setting up his bottling operation, Flach was touring the United States, where he observed firsthand Coke's popularity. After taking over Bluna in 1931, he began to redirect the company's activities from the production of bottling machinery and generic soft drink flavorings to the promotion of Afri-Cola, his new brand-name soft drink.[87] By capitalizing on the firm's long-standing ties to the German beverage industry, Flach soon had Afri-Cola added to the product lines of several local bottlers. Nonetheless, sales of the soft drink were slow to take off. In part, this was because the manufacturer-distributors of Afri-Cola had little incentive to push the product more than their traditional beverages. Not only were such established firms not as "desperate" as some of the initial members of the Coca-Cola Familie, but Flach's franchise structure did not entail exclusive regional distribution rights to motivate the same *Kleinarbeit* (attention to detail) in advertising and customer service.

However, Coca-Cola GmbH's success in the mid-1930s provided the incentive for renewed activity on Afri-Cola's behalf.[88] By the late-1930s Afri-Cola had copied most aspects of Coca-Cola marketing. Not only did "Warum Afri-Cola?" (Why Afri-Cola?) brochures echo those that asked, "Was ist Coca-Cola?," but Afri-Cola's advertising also emphasized that "summer or winter" and "always best ice-cooled" it was the "delicious-enlivening refreshing drink" for everyone. Additionally, it was claimed, "Afri-Cola goes into the blood and has, among other effects, a neutralizing influence on alcohol's after-effects."[89] While Flach's was often less sophisticated than the advertising produced in Atlanta and Essen, he soon had a small but full spectrum of Afri-Cola promotional materials that mirrored those of Coca-Cola GmbH. These ranged from trademark-bearing glasses, ice coolers, and delivery vehicles to slides for movie theater ads and loud-speaker trucks that spread soft drink jingles. Moreover, after March 1937, *Afri-Post*, a four-page company newsletter, reported on Afri-Cola's latest marketing efforts and reminded bottler-distributors of Flach's business plan. These policies, like the publication itself, again followed Coca-Cola's example (e.g., sales contests and a company "school" for dealers, a set price, dealing only in cash, codified "commandments" of customer service).[90] By 1938, Afri-Cola's turnover, reported Wal-

3. "Afri-Cola . . . always refreshing, good and German!" While emphasizing that it was a German product, Afri-Cola's advertising and marketing strategies mimicked those of Coca-Cola. From *Afri-Post*, November–December 1938.

ter Oppenhoff to Atlanta, "is doubtless the largest sale of an alcohol-free beverage in Germany outside of Coca-Cola." He estimated Flach's sales to be half that of Coke's, and suggested "more than 90% [of Afri-Cola's success was] built up on the back of Coca-Cola G.M.B.H., and particularly by means of the untrue allegation that Coca-Cola is Jewish."[91]

While on another visit to the United States in early 1936, Flach took part in a Coca-Cola bottling plant tour that had been organized for the German Labor Front. Here he was able to pick up a souvenir that he thought might help undermine Coke's German market share: Hebrew-inscribed bottle caps intended for the Jewish community in New York. Back in Germany, Flach began to show his discovery to others in the beverage community and had a photograph of the bottle caps made into the aforementioned flyer.[92] Oppenhoff obtained a court injunction against the photograph's distribution.[93] However, Flach continued to show it around privately, often coupled with the claim that The Coca-Cola Company was run by an American Jew, Harold Hirsch. This apparently was a misunderstanding of the Atlanta attorney's role as a director on the company's board.

For Afri-Cola, such guerilla activity was part of a larger war:

Have you ever thought about it, my dear AFRI-Friend, what unheard of amount of steel, iron, and explosives were hurled at the German front from 1914–1918 in an attempt to break through? Did you know that the amount of material put into action reached almost fantastic numbers, without achieving its goal? This German front of steel-hard men held against this onslaught of total hell for four full years! In the context of our AFRI-COLA Movement, we are in a similar struggle and in a similar situation. Again we are in a great material battle against a systematically organized enemy! Again, there are enough courageous and brave men who are willing and able to resist this assault. It is the task of today's generation of soft drink producers to be ready and have the necessary defenses to prove themselves as a worthy opponent by responding successfully and with a strong counter-offensive.[94]

With Afri-Cola's most common slogan, "Always Refreshing—Good and German," Flach insisted it was the "duty and obligation" of the Third Reich's soft drink industry to organize itself in defense of "the honor of the German profession and trade" by handling his soft drink, the "German Quality Beverage."[95]

However dramatic its rhetoric, Flach's offensive could not go far, for there was no identifiable front line. Coca-Cola GmbH's success had already integrated Coke into the German beverage industry. The Coca-Cola Familie was a German family, and its members were Flach's brethren in the various industry and trade organizations established by the Nazis to coordinate soft drink production. This fact was indisputable after 1935, when Leopold Kretschmann, the Coca-Cola franchise holder from Hof and an early member of the Nazi party, was named an officer in the German association of soft drink producers (Reichsverband der Deutschen Mineralwasserfabrikanten).[96] Therefore, reported Oppenhoff to Atlanta, "Jewish slander . . . is a personal offense against the Concessionaire which we can not prevent him resisting."[97] Although such lawsuits were discouraged by both Atlanta and Essen, at least ten provisional judgments to protect members of the Coca-Cola Familie from "unfair competition" were decreed between 1937 and 1939. Meanwhile, apparently in another attempt to limit the damage from Flach's assertions, Coca-Cola GmbH placed ads in *Der Stürmer*, the notoriously anti-Semitic Nazi periodical published by Julius Streicher.[98]

However, rather than launching a direct counterattack via advertising or legal action, Coca-Cola GmbH's primary reaction was to encourage the Coca-Cola Familie to take the high road of "kingly salesmen." Powers set the standard back in 1934: "The essence of being a 'kingly salesman' is a 'certain something' that does not come from having money or power, and once possessed, it can't be taken away from even the poorest of the poor. This 'certain something' is a sense of moral responsibility that causes the kingly salesman to be as helpful as possible to his co-workers and clients."[99] After justifying Coca-Cola GmbH's efforts to avoid formal legal actions, Oppenhoff called on his fellow Cokemen to be "always diligent about exhibiting model behavior." At the 1937 conference for concessionaires, he noted, "Incorrect conduct by a competitor does not give one the right to respond in kind, for there will never be justice when two fight and both act wrongly."[100] Such sentiments resonated with the Nazis' professed ideal of domestic economic competition. At the same conference, a Nazi official responsible for overseeing the soft drink industry told the Coca-Cola Familie of the "National Socialist performance principle that calls both for the greatest effort in the service of the Volksgemeinschaft from each of us in our own places and for us to try not to diminish economic life with negative criticism of competitors."[101] Coca-Cola Nachrichten elaborated: "Don't complain about increasing competition. . . . One never tries to disparage a competitor. No, the motto should be work harder and perform better."[102]

Ultimately, despite anecdotes of Coca-Cola route salesmen being attacked in bar fights and Afri-Cola's complaints about stolen signs,[103] this battle did little to disrupt the campaign to drench the Third Reich with Coca-Cola's "refreshment." In fact, like the subsequent global "Cola War" with Pepsi, Coke's public relations scuffle with Afri-Cola probably served to sharpen Coke's German marketing efforts and further the overall expansion of the soft drink market. Between 1934 and 1937, while Coca-Cola increased its market share by 11 percent, the overall German soft drink industry grew 44 percent.[104] Noting that the industry had again doubled its turnover by 1941, the Frankfurter Handelsblatt observed in 1942, "Surely thanks also should be given to the Coca-Cola company which in the short time since its establishment in 1929 has become the leading soft drink producer."[105] By this time, not only had the domestic beverage industry come to appreciate Coca-Cola's presence in Germany, but the Nazi state had publicly embraced the soft drink into Hitler's idealized Volksgemeinschaft.

During the summer of 1937, "attempting to market itself as a technologically advanced nation and as a people rooted in timeless tradition," the Third Reich mounted a spectacular trade exhibition that rivaled the concurrent World's Fair in Paris.[106] In Düsseldorf, at the Reichsausstellung "Schaffendes Volk" (the National Exhibition of the "[German] People at Work"), the Nazis sought to demonstrate "how the generation of economic value and the multifarious ramifications of technological progress provide the Volk with what is needed to live, while also uniting with the Volk's cultural achievements to form a harmonious whole."[107] At the opening of the exhibition, Hermann Göring announced, "The intractable goal of the Four-Year Plan [for economic self-sufficiency] is the preservation of German honor and the German way of life. The Schaffendes Volk exhibition in Düsseldorf serves this great endeavor. . . . By conscientiously and extensively applying German innovation and German technology, united with the organizational abilities of the German spirit, to industrial and raw material problems, we not only help ourselves, we show the entire world new economic means and goals."[108]

With its own five hundred–square-meter building near the center of the huge exhibition, along the tracks of the miniature train route and between the pavilions for wood products and the trades, Coca-Cola was thoroughly integrated into Schaffendes Volk's "mirror image of German culture and German commerce."[109] Setting a new standard for Außenverkauf, Coca-Cola GmbH established a "model manufacturing plant" that could wash, fill, and cap four thousand bottles an hour. Nearby, at a sixteen-meter-long service counter, visitors could buy ice-cold Cokes for the standard price of 25 pfennig.[110] After wandering through the huge exhibition, marveling at the wonders of Plexiglas, fifty-ton cranes, JU-86 fighter bombers, synthetic fabrics, wind-powered generators, scale models of highway cloverleafs, and the new technology of television, many of Schaffendes Volk's almost 7 million visitors, including Göring himself, stopped to enjoy "The Pause that Refreshes."[111] While enjoying their drink, not only could guests watch the soft drink being bottled, but they could read display cases, where "statistics, models, and illustrations, coupled with light effects, demonstrated the increasing importance of 'Coca-Cola' to German economic life."[112]

Coca-Cola GmbH's presence at the Schaffendes Volk exhibition prompted a windfall of positive publicity. "We heard from the mouth of visitors countless times that our model manufacturing plant was one of the most interesting displays," reported *Coca-Cola Nachrichten*. "Visitors were impressed to see in what an outstanding and hygienically exemplary method 'Coca-Cola' is produced, and what intelligence, what a spirit of innovation, and what care is required in order to present the public with such a first-class soft drink."[113] Additionally, Coca-Cola's success at Schaffendes Volk was measured in increased sales. Already in June, *Coca-Cola Nachrichten* reported that outside the exhibition, "last month our concessionaire in Düsseldorf achieved the highest percentage of increased Coca-Cola sales in a more than a year. . . . The same effect can be seen in all the areas around Düsseldorf."[114] Soon, Coke wholesalers across the country were reporting that after visiting the exhibition, barkeepers who had refused Coca-Cola for years were now ready to add the soft drink to their menus.[115] Coca-Cola's good name, announced Coca-Cola GmbH, "radiated throughout Germany, as proven by frequent mention of our company's participation in Düsseldorf by the general public in the furthest reaches of the Reich."[116] In the end, the over half a million bottles of Coca-Cola sold at the exhibition were deemed less significant than the publicity, "a seed that will bear fruit for years."[117]

Coca-Cola's integration into the Schaffendes Volk exhibition, and its increasing German sales figures throughout the 1930s, demonstrated that the accusations that it was Jewish/American had little effect. However "foreign" its advertising illustrations, Coke had become firmly rooted in German Trinkkultur thanks to the Coca-Cola Familie of local businessmen that produced and marketed the soft drink. When asked in 1991 if he had encountered anti-American sentiments in the Coca-Cola business, Herr Cohrt, the concessionaire from Kiel, responded, "Actually, not at all during the early years, 1936–1940. I first had to deal with that in 1949 or 1950."[118] Oppenhoff concurred: "Political issues played no appreciable role" in Coca-Cola's development during the 1930s. "This political stuff was not picked up by the general public at all. I mean, they absolutely didn't care. There was no anti-American attitude. . . . Important [to understanding the motives of those Germans behind such attacks] was their role as competitors—they were afraid that they wouldn't be able to sell their own products."[119] Ultimately, despite Flach's efforts to tag Coca-Cola as un-German, it appears that most consumers in the Third Reich saw the soft drink as an affordable taste of the new, more affluent Germany that they were promised in Nazi propaganda.

"Our beverage is a *Volksgetränk* [a drink for all Germans]," declared Coca-Cola GmbH in 1937, "therefore we must tell the *entire Volk* what we have to sell. We want to get our 'sales pitch' out to every last German."[120] With its distribution system fully established, in the late 1930s Coca-Cola GmbH could devote more of its energy and resources to advertising. While the onslaught of materials representing Coca-Cola in the Third Reich never reached the volume found in the United States, the impressive battery of publicity deployed by the Coca-Cola Familie served as an example for the rest of the beverage industry. Staying ahead of the pack, in 1936 Coca-Cola GmbH developed a projector that could present Coke-infused "educational" filmstrips, and, at the 1939 concessionaire conference, the company premiered Coke's first German commercial, an UFA-produced animated color film entitled *Die erfrischende Pause*.[121] Whether at the movie theater, walking down the street, reading a newspaper, commuting to work, or attending a club meeting, Germans were increasingly likely to be reminded to "Trink Coca-Cola." "As an army is comprised of various types of units," noted *Coca-Cola Nachrichten*, "the publicity for a product is made up of various means of advertising."[122]

Unlike in 1935, when the cash-strapped company had downplayed print advertising, Coca-Cola GmbH now devoted significant resources to ads in news-

4. The photograph-based print ads produced by Coca-Cola GmbH in the late 1930s encouraged Germans to take "refreshing" Coca-Cola breaks during both work and play. These appeared in the *Berliner Illustrierte Zeitung* and other periodicals in 1938–1939.

papers and magazines. Rather than the simple line drawings first created by the advertising department in Essen, or the glossy commercial art commissioned by The Coca-Cola Company in Atlanta, Coca-Cola GMBH now produced its own sophisticated, often photograph-based print ads.[123] This development served to further Germanize Coke's image. However, this trend was far from unambiguous. In September 1938, when Coca-Cola GMBH launched its first national ad campaign in Germany's mass-readership magazines, such as the *Münchener Illustrierter Presse* and *Berliner Illustrierte Zeitung*, it did not try to ground Coke deeper into Germany's "blood and soil." Instead, the first full-page Coke magazine ad announced, "Coca-Cola hat Weltruf!" (Coca-Cola is world renowned!).[124] At the same time a series of smaller ads presented basically the same message in *Die Wehrmacht*, the popular illustrated magazine of the German Army.[125] Nonetheless, as the new magazine campaign settled into a series of half-page ads that ran in a variety of periodicals, the "real" photographed people and profiled everyday situations for drinking Coca-Cola appeared more "German" than those in the stylized American illustrations that still dominated Coca-Cola GMBH's poster and billboard ads.[126]

The apparent Germanization of these later ads takes on a new light when reexamined within the context of the debate stirred up by the pursuit of a new concept of Nazi modernity. In his 1996 summary of the debate on "National Socialism and Modernisation," Mark Roseman noted, "The real meat of the controversy and the real value of recent work is that it has irrevocably demonstrated

5. "Protect yourself from fatigue while driving—Refresh yourself regularly with ice-cold Coca-Cola!" Coca-Cola GmbH's version of the "Drink Refreshed" advertising campaign suggested that soft drink consumption was a civic duty. From *Coca-Cola Nachrichten* 4, no. 2 (February 1937): 16–17.

that the Nazis subjectively and objectively operated on the terrain of industrial society." Nonetheless, while the Nazis' infamous agrarian utopianism has been exposed as empty antimodern rhetoric, "it is also clear that Nazi racial policy was by no means just the atavistic irrational fantasy that the earlier wave of historians assumed." However "modern" one classifies Nazi socioeconomic policies (e.g., rationalizing the workplace, establishing pronatalist welfare programs for those deemed part of the Volksgemeinschaft—and the opposite for those who were not), "The central image of the *Volksgemeinschaft*, with its racial foundation, broke with fundamental [liberal/modern] principles of the individual to the collective." As Roseman reminds us, "Freedom was interpreted by many groups in German society as a corporate rather than an individual concept."[127] Reviewing the same controversy, Peter Fritzsche concurred, "The emphasis of [Nazi] social policy was always on the enforcement of discipline in the name of community, not the provision of opportunity for the individual."[128] This shift in emphasis, from the modern world's promise of emancipation to the duty of communal responsibilities, was also manifested in the notion of Erfrischung conjured forth in Coke's German advertising.

In 1937 Coca-Cola GMBH introduced a new brochure and concurrent print advertising that targeted automobile drivers. Depending on whether one is tracking so-called Americanization, Germanization, or modernization, this campaign easily can be read as (1) a direct translation of the American "Drive refreshed" slogan; (2) evidence of Coke's efforts to be part of a German "world of pleasure," considering the pent-up consumer demand for personal automobiles; or (3) evidence of the soft drink's synergy with the forces of "progress." However, closer examination of the brochure also reveals that the concept of "refreshment" could take on new ramifications when contextualized within the Nazi Volksgemeinschaft. Coca-Cola GMBH seems to have suggested that Germans should drink Coke out of a sense of duty:

> Protect yourself from fatigue at the wheel—Refresh yourself regularly with ice-cold Coca-Cola! Nothing is more dangerous for drivers than over-fatigue. Nothing is less excusable than a driver expending all his energy to the point of exhaustion. Life, Health, Happiness and Family are threatened. Hopes, Wishes, Dreams are carelessly gambled. So, refresh yourself during the drive with regular pauses with ice-cold Coca-Cola. Then—truly refreshed—you hold onto your ability to perform, your concentration, your presence of mind. Therefore, from now on: Before the drive, during the drive, after the drive—Drink Coca-Cola.[129]

This connection between refreshment and responsibility was also underscored in Coke's photograph-based print ads produced in 1938 and 1939. Here, unlike their American counterparts, a great many of the representative Coke drinkers are depicted at work. As noted by Alf Lüdtke, photographs of the "honor of labor" were "intensely displayed in the Nazi picture press."[130] In August 1939, a Coca-Cola ad depicted two men in business suits holding bottles of Coke. The text read, "A short break in the negotiations does one good and is often helpful in moving work forward. Tempers calm down, thoughts become clearer—especially when everyone makes the pause a refreshing one with ice-cold Coca-Cola."[131] The photographs in other ads depicted chauffeurs, theater directors, and factory workers enjoying similar refreshing, and responsible, work breaks: "A quick break in the middle of a hard job—that again enlivens the work rhythm."[132] As with the brochure for auto drivers, "die erfrischende Pause" was not a simple private affair. While Coca-Cola ads in Nazi Germany always underscored the soft drink's "delicious and refreshing" qualities, Coke's refreshment was transformed into something one could enjoy in the service of the Volksgemeinschaft.

"If the Nazis were modernizers," observed Peter Fritzsche, "it was less on account of their efficacy in destroying traditional social milieus . . . than of their capacity to manufacture an alternative public sphere in which Germans identified themselves increasingly as *Volksgenossen* (national-comrades)."[133] A similar statement can be made about Coca-Cola: if the soft drink was a means to Americanization, it did this less in terms of offering an escape from Nazi authority than by offering Germans a new, more pleasurable, explicitly consumerist means to express their devotion to the German Heimat and Nazi Volksgemeinschaft. In September 1939, as the war clouds broke over Poland, Max Keith declared, "I am sure that each member of the Coca-Cola Familie is aware of his responsibility to Volk and Fatherland, and that they will do their best to honorably fulfill the responsibilities before them, today and in the future." Contemplating the big picture, he continued, "However things may develop, we can all proudly look back on what we have accomplished, fully aware that our hard work over the recent years has not been in vain because the name and drink 'Coca-Cola' is now and forever firmly anchored within the hearts of millions throughout the Reich."[134]

More subtle and profound than the fantastical "Nazi Coke Adverts" conjured by artists today, the switched polarity of Coke's actual advertising in the Third Reich, and the hard work of the Coca-Cola Familie, integrated the soft drink into Germany's Trinkkultur and the Nazi Volksgemeinschaft. Ultimately, however American the aftertaste, the idea of Coca-Cola transcended both national and ideological differences. Indeed, once World War II had begun, Hitler's Third Reich, like the United States, declared the soft drinks produced by The Coca-Cola Company to be war-essential products. In modern war as in history, "the Pause that Refreshes" was not a trivial matter.

Notes

1. Don Wharton, "Coca-Cola: Its Fame and Fortune," *Reader's Digest*, June 1947, 36.
2. For profiles of Coke's wartime American advertising, see Weiner, "Consumer Culture and Participatory Democracy," and Wrynn, *Coke Goes to War*.
3. *The Coca-Cola Company*, 79.
4. Pendergrast, *For God, Country and Coca-Cola*, 213.
5. E-mail correspondence with the two curators, March 2005. For the "Coca-Cola Nazi Advert Challenge" website, see www.mtcp.co.uk (accessed March 2005). Adopting the word from folklorists, I use the term "Cokelore" to designate the popular, mythologized accounts of Coca-Cola's past found in both "urban legends" and the company's own representation of its history. See Smith, "Contemporary Legends and Popular Culture."
6. *Erlebnis Geschichte: Deutschland vom Zweiten Weltkrieg bis Heute*, 2nd ed. (Bonn: Haus der Geschichte der Bundesrepublik Deutschland, Gustav Lübbe, 2000), 132. For further examples of Coke's iconic status, note the title of Reinhold Wagnleitner's monograph,

Coca-Colonization and the Cold War, and the cover art of Schildt and Sywottek, *Modernisierung im Wiederaufbau*. For analysis of the same, see Mary Nolan, "America in the German Imagination," in Fehrenbach and Poiger, *Transactions, Transgressions, Transformations*, 18; Jeff R. Schutts, "Born Again in the Gospel of Refreshment? Coca-Colonization and the Re-Making of Postwar German Identity," in Crew, *Consuming Germany in the Cold War*, 121–150.

7. These two words, in English, were the title of the exhibition's section on "historical experience." *Faszination Coca-Cola: Einsichten in einen Mythos*, catalogue to the Coca-Cola Exhibit at the Haus der Geschichte, 13 June–16 July 2002 (Essen: Coca-Cola GMBH, 2002).

8. Hans-Dieter Schäfer, "Amerikanismus im Dritten Reich," in Prinz and Zitelmann, *Nationalsozialismus und Modernisierung*, 204–205. See also Schäfer, *Das gespaltene Bewußtsein*.

9. Schäfer, "Amerikanismus," 205. For a discussion of "Resistance without the People?," see Ian Kershaw's historiographical survey, *The Nazi Dictatorship*, 183–217. For a monograph surveying Nazi perceptions of the United States, see Gassert, *Amerika im Dritten Reich*.

10. See, e.g., Kater, "Die Sozialgeschichte und das Dritte Reich. Überlegungen zu neuen Büchern," and Könke, "'Modernisierungsschub' oder relative Stagnation?"

11. Kershaw, *Nazi Dictatorship*, 166.

12. The controversy's two seminal works are Dahrendorf, *Society and Democracy in Germany*, and Schoenbaum, *Hitler's Social Revolution*. For the crest of the 1980s wave, see Zitelmann, *Hitler*, and Prinz and Zitelmann, *Nationalsozialismus und Modernisierung*, from 1991. For surveys of the overall debate, see Schildt, "NS-Regime, Modernisierung und Moderne"; Bernd Weisbrod, "Der Schein der Modernität. Zur Historisierung der 'Volksgemeinschaft,'" in Rudolf and Wickert, *Geschichte als Möglichkeit*, 224–242; Mark Roseman, "National Socialism and Modernisation," in Bessel, *Fascist Italy and Nazi Germany*, 197–229; Fritzsche, "Nazi Modern."

13. On this process more generally, see Schutts, "Coca-Colonization, 'Refreshing' Americanization, or Nazi *Volksgetränk*?" The creolization model was coined by the Swedish anthropologist Ulf Hannerz and has been popularized by the work of the Dutch Americanist Rob Kroes. See Ulf Hannerz, "American Culture, Creolized, Creolizing," in Asard, *American Culture*, 7–30; Kroes, *If You've Seen One, You've Seen the Mall*.

14. Watters, *Coca-Cola*, 198, italics in the original.

15. Nicholson, *Host to Thirsty Mainstreet*, 18.

16. "'Coca-Cola'—Vertrauen aus Dienst und Verantwortung," a reprinted article from *Industriekurier* in *Coca-Cola Nachrichten* 11, no. 12 (1962): 5.

17. "The Pause That Refreshes," *Businessweek*, 27 April 1940, 35; Tedlow, *New and Improved*, 72.

18. "*Ein richtiger Amerikaner*" characterization from an interview with Hubert Strauf, 15 August 1991, contained in "Die Anfangsjahre von Coca-Cola in Deutschland: Eine Dokumentation von Christine Rettenmeier und Stefan Horn," an unpublished collec-

tion of documents and interview transcripts compiled by Coca-Cola GMBH in September 1991, Public Relations Department, Coca-Cola GMBH, Essen.

19. In addition to the author's work, see Olaf Krietemeyer, "Die Marketingpolitik bei der Einführung von Coca-Cola auf dem Deutschen Markt," Diplomarbeit, Business School of the Universität Regensburg, 1993.

20. "Was bewirkt Reklame? Wann und wie sollen wir uns ihrer bedienen?," *Coca-Cola Nachrichten*, 1 July 1935, 3.

21. American figures from Tedlow, *New and Improved*, 83. German figures from "Growth Company Business from 1929 to 1937," in *Germany: A Compilation for the Coca-Cola Company*, ed. Roy D. Stubbs, 423, a spring binder of document excerpts compiled in 1945 and now held by The Coca-Cola Company Archives in Atlanta (hereafter Coca-Cola Archives).

22. Kühles, *Handbuch der Mineralwasser-Industrie*, 21. See also Carl Jacob Bachem, "100 Jahre Verbandssorganisation der deutschen Erfrischungsgetränke-Industrie" (Bonn: Bundesverband der Deutschen Erfrischungsgetränke-Industrie, 1982), a reprint from *Das Erfrischungsgetränk/Mineralwasser-Zeitung* (8 September 1982).

23. See Overy, *The Nazi Economic Recovery*.

24. "German Coca-Cola Business (1938)," in Stubbs, *Germany*, 423.

25. "The Pause that Refreshes" was ranked the third best slogan, and second best advertising campaign, of "The Advertising Century." Garfield, "The Top 100 Advertising Campaigns," 36, with Robyn Griggs, "Coca-Cola Slogan Gives Pause," as a sidebar. See also Watkins, *The 100 Greatest Advertisements*, 138–139.

26. Allen, *Secret Formula*, 18.

27. Tedlow, *New and Improved*, 48. Tedlow is citing Robinson from Watters, *Coca-Cola*, 15.

28. The diversity and abundance of such knickknacks now sustain countless collectors of Coca-Cola memorabilia. Their largest organization, the Atlanta-based Coca-Cola Collector's Club, has over six thousand members in twenty-eight countries. See www.cocacolaclub.org, as well as Munsey, *The Illustrated Guide to the Collectibles of Coca-Cola*; Petretti, *Petretti's Coca-Cola Collectibles Price Guide*.

29. Quote from 1908, cited in Watters, *Coca-Cola*, 227.

30. These terms for a standard categorization of advertising were drawn from a booklet published by The Coca-Cola Company in 1968, "Philosophy of Coca-Cola Advertising," Coca-Cola Archives.

31. Watters, *Coca-Cola*, 218.

32. Williamson, *Decoding Advertisements*, 177.

33. Pasi Falk, "The Genealogy of Advertising," in Sulkunen et al., *Constructing the New Consumer Society*, 81–107.

34. Strauf interview, 15 August 1991, contained in the *Anfangsjahre* compilation. For profiles of Strauf, see the work of Dirk Schindelbeck of the Kultur- und werbegeschichtliches Archiv Freiburg im Breisgau (KWAF): "Magische Formeln. 'Mach mal Pause' — 'Keine Experimente!' Zeitgeschichte im Werbeslogan," in Gries, Ilgen, and Schindelbeck, *"Ins Gehirn der Masse kriechen!,"* 28–39; "Meister der Werbesprüche: Hubert Strauf," *Trödler*

und Sammler Journal, September 2003; as well as Bongard, *Männer machen Märkte*, 161–167; Merkel, *Vorbilder*, 28–39.

35. "History of Coca-Cola in Germany: Interview with Max Keith — 29/30 June 1966," transcript of an interview conducted by Hunter Bell, available at The Coca-Cola Company Archives. An edited version was published in German, *Wie war das damals als Sie anfingen. Ein Interview mit Max Keith* (Essen: Coca-Cola GmbH, ca. 1974).

36. "Was bewirkt Reklame?," *Coca-Cola Nachrichten*, 1 July 1935, 3–5.

37. For a profile of Coke's Santa, see Charles and Staples, *Dream of Santa*. For surveys of Coke's American advertising history, see Munsey, *Illustrated Guide*; Murken-Attrogge, *Werbung — Mythos — Kunst am Beispiel Coca-Cola*; Beyer, *Coca-Cola Girls*.

38. For example, Coca-Cola GmbH received a recommendation that "foreign methods of advertising should not be taken over without alteration. The posters (advertising Coca-Cola) show for the main part typically American scenes. Above all the girl riding. You should not find a head like that here." This quote is from "Advertising in Foreign Countries," an excerpt from a letter from Dr. Walter Fischer to Walter Oppenhoff, dated 10 May 1939, in Stubbs, *Germany*, 239.

39. Interview contained in the *Anfangsjahre* compilation.

40. Samples of new brochures were regularly included in *Coca-Cola Nachrichten*. For this one, see "Der schönste Prospekt des ganzen Jahres — für die Weihnachtszeit," *Coca-Cola Nachrichten*, 1 December 1935, 5.

41. "Karneval und Coca-Cola," *Coca-Cola Nachrichten*, 1 February 1936, 2–3.

42. "Die Neuekarnevals-Postkarte," *Coca-Cola Nachrichten*, 15 January 1937, 13. See also "Neue Prospekte: Karneval / Winter-Olympiade," *Coca-Cola Nachrichten* 3, no. 1 (January 1936): 7; and "Karneval und Coca-Cola," *Coca-Cola Nachrichten*, 1 February 1936, 2–3.

43. For a list of advertising slogans, see Munsey, *Illustrated Guide*.

44. "Leitsprüche für Coca-Cola Leute," *Coca-Cola Nachrichten*, 10 January 1935, 3.

45. "Auch im Siegerland weiß man 'Coca-Cola' zu schätzen," which includes a reprinted article from the *Siegener National-Blatt* entitled "'Trink 'Coca-Cola' und ihr bleibt nüchtern," in *Coca-Cola Nachrichten*, 15 June 1935, 8.

46. "Was bedeutet 'Coca-Cola für den Wirt?," *Coca-Cola Nachrichten*, 1 May 1935, 3.

47. "Ein 5-Punkte-Kunde verkauft 'Coca-Cola' nicht über 25 Pfennig," *Coca-Cola Nachrichten*, 1 December 1935, 2.

48. "Plagt Dich der Katzenjammer," *Coca-Cola Nachrichten*, 10 December 1934, 3.

49. "Der Kleinverbraucher meldet sich: 'Ohne Coca-Cola kann ich nicht arbeiten!,'" *Coca-Cola Nachrichten*, 26 March 1935, 4.

50. "Was bedeutet 'Coca-Cola' für den Wirt?," *Coca-Cola Nachrichten*, 1 May 1935, 4.

51. Keith interview with Bell, 29/30 June 1966.

52. For example, 1935 saw the introduction of Coke billboards with American commercial art illustrations.

53. "Was bewirkt Reklame?," *Coca-Cola Nachrichten*, 15 July 1935, 4.

54. "So werden Trinker gemacht! Messen, Ausstellungen und Massenveranstaltungen," *Coca-Cola Nachrichten*, 1 May 1935, 5.

55. "Welche Bedeutung haben für uns Messen und Ausstellungen?," *Coca-Cola Nachrichten*, 20 April 1937, 7.

56. For example, see Freitag and Pohl, *Das Dritte Reich im Fest*.

57. "Welche Bedeutung," *Coca-Cola Nachrichten*, 20 April 1937, 7.

58. "So werden Trinker gemacht! Nochmals Außenverkäufe," *Coca-Cola Nachrichten*, 15 July 1935, 4.

59. The first issue of *Coca-Cola Nachrichten* included an extensive report on Coke sales in Koblenz during the celebrations over the Saar referendum. See "Einiges über Coca-Cola-Verkauf bei der Saarkundgebung," *Coca-Cola Nachrichten*, 20 October 1934.

60. See "So werden Trinker gemacht! Bericht über die große Leipziger Frühjahrsmesse," *Coca-Cola Nachrichten*, 26 March 1935, 2.

61. Else Bürfent interview, 13 August 1991, contained in the *Anfangsjahre* compilation.

62. See, "Reichsparteitag 1937," *Coca-Cola Nachrichten*, 15 November 1937, 14, and "Auch auf 'd'r Wies'n," *Coca-Cola Nachrichten*, 15 November 1938, 9.

63. "Die Reichsgartenschau 1938 in Essen," *Coca-Cola Nachrichten*, 15 April 1938, 16.

64. It was sponsored by *BZ am Mittag*, the tabloid paper from the Ullstein publishing house. See "3000km Deustchlandfahrt," *Coca-Cola Nachrichten*, 15 June 1937, 12.

65. See the chapter by that title in Mühlbauer, *Rundschreibentext für kritische Situation*, as well as the section on sports in *Faszination Coca-Cola*. In the United States, Coke already had a well-established association with baseball. As one ad slogan stated in 1906, "The Great National Drink at the Great National Pastime."

66. "Mit Motor und Stahlroß um Deutschland," *Coca-Cola Nachrichten*, 15 July 1937, 8–9.

67. Ibid.

68. Author's interview with Walter Oppenhoff, in Cologne, 18 June 1998.

69. Robert Proctor has pioneered the study of this aspect of Nazi health policy. See his *Racial Hygiene* and *The Nazi War on Cancer*.

70. For a historiographical overview, see chapter 4 in Kershaw, *Nazi Dictatorship*.

71. Oppenhoff interview, 18 June 1998.

72. Krietemeyer, "Marketingpolitik," 39, based on lost cassette audiotapes from a 1978 Coca-Cola GMBH interview with several original German Cokemen. Notes from this interview are contained in the *Anfangsjahre* collection.

73. Quoted in Pendergrast, *For God, Country and Coca-Cola*, 218.

74. "Olympische Prospekte 'Sportserie,'" *Coca-Cola Nachrichten*, 1 June 1936, 13.

75. "Benutzen Sie den schönen Olympia-Prospekte," *Coca-Cola Nachrichten*, 15 July 1936, 7.

76. Olympic sales mentioned in the 1978 interview notes, *Anfangsjahre*. In 1936, 1,154,053 cases were sold (Stubbs, *Germany*, 423). See also *10 Jahre Aufbau*, a special issue of *Coca-Cola Nachrichten* from 1939.

77. "Planmässige Arbeit—der Bürge des Erfolges," *Coca-Cola Nachrichten*, 15 November 1936, 12.

78. "Der Geist unserer Arbeit: Vortrag von Hernn Kirchner, Essen," *Coca-Cola Nachrichten*, 1 April 1937, 19.

79. Christian Adt. Kupferberg, "Warum treiben wir Werbung?" Reprint from *Ala-*

Nachrichten- und Beratungsdienst 29 (August–September 1936) in *Coca-Cola Nachrichten*, 15 November 1936, 6.

80. For example, see "Herstellung von Koka-Kola-Grundstoff," the letter to the editor inquiring about the Coca-Cola recipe, and Coca-Cola GMBH's response, in the *Deutsche Destillateur-Zeitung*, 21 March 1936, 147, and 16 April 1936, 189.

81. Stubbs, "Cola-Cola," *Germany*, 53. The company later introduced "Sinalco-Cola."

82. The lawsuit *United States vs. Forty Barrels and Twenty Kegs of Coca-Cola* was filed in 1909 and heard by the U.S. Supreme Court in 1917. It is recounted in most histories of Coca-Cola.

83. Mittelbadischer Brauereiverband GMBH, Niederschrift über die Verbandsversammlung, 24 August 1936, in Bestand 69/199, Karlsruhe Generallandesarchiv.

84. Letter from Parzhamer Venusquelle, Munich, to the Reichsministerium für Ernährung und Landwirtschaft durch das Bayer, 27 April 1937, Staatsministerium für Wirtschaft, Abteilung Handel, Industrie und Gewerbe, MWi 8163 Nr. 13391, Bayerisches Hauptstaatsarchiv.

85. Letter dated 23 January 1937, MWi 8163, Nr. 2910, Bayerisches Hauptstaatsarchiv.

86. The photograph itself apparently had no text. This characterization is from Strauf, *Anfangsjahre*.

87. Afri-Cola still exists, with its most recent market niche as an extra-caffeinated beverage for the rave scene. Its name and other "colonial" iconography alluded to the African origin of kola nut. Although its most remembered marketing came in the late 1960s (with taboo-breaking ads by Charles Wilp and the slogan "Sexy-mini-super-flower-pop-op-Cola—Alles ist in Afri-Cola"), the company has consistently tried to present itself as a German/European alternative to U.S.-based soft drinks. See, e.g., "Africola sieht sich als 'deutsche Alternative,'" *Frankfurter Rundschau*, 19 July 1983, and other clippings in the Afri-Cola file at the Institut der deutschen Wirtschaft in Cologne (IWK), as well as "Karl Flach 60 Jahre," a special issue of *Afri-Post*, 9 January 1965, and *100 jähriges Firmenjubiläum/60. Geburtstag Karl Flach: Ansprachen 8.1.1965 "Flora,"* Köln, a company brochure, both from the collection held at Afri-Cola GMBH, Cologne. For Afri-Cola's current "independent and unique brand character," see www.afri-cola.com.

88. German beverage industry journals also took note of Coke's U.S. success. For example, see "24.7 Millionen Dollar Reingewinn bei der Coca-Cola Co.," *Tageszeitung für Brauerei*, 22, no. 23 (March 1938): 173.

89. Slogans and images from a collection of seven brochures held by Afri-Cola GMBH.

90. For illustrative articles, see, on glasses, "Das 100%ige Afri-Service," *Afri-Post*, April 1937; on coolers, "Eiskasten," *Afri-Post*, March–April 1938; on trucks, "Die erfolgreichsten und billigsten Werbeträger—Ihre Lieferwagen," *Afri-Post*, August 1938; on jingles, "AFRI-Lautsprecherwagen," *Afri-Post*, March–April 1938; and on the business plan, "Afri-Cola Verkaufsschulung in Köln," *Afri-Post*, September 1937, and "Die 12 Gebote, die zum Erfolg führen," *Afri-Post*, April 1937.

91. Stubbs, "Afri-Cola," *Germany*, 45. Actual sales figures for Afri-Cola are unavailable. In June 1939 Nicholson reported that their business was one-third that of Coke's. Stubbs,

Germany, 47. Afri-Cola itself has suggested that its prewar sales were equal to that of Coca-Cola.

92. Stubbs, "Afri-Cola," *Germany*, 43–47.

93. Stubbs, "Kosher Crowns," *Germany*, 164. See also Pendergrast, *For God, Country and Coca-Cola*, and Allen, *Secret Formula*, 246–247.

94. "Steht die Afri-Cola-Front?," *Afri-Post*, September 1937.

95. "1937 — das Jahr der Entscheidung," *Afri-Post*, March 1937.

96. Oppenhoff interview with Mark Pendergrast, 20 April 1991. See also "Die Tagung der Mineralwasser-Industrie in Lübeck," *Coca-Cola Nachrichten*, 1 October 1935, 8, and "Leopold Kretschmann fast 50 Jahre im Dienste des Fachverbandes," *Coca-Cola Nachrichten*, no. 3 (1970): 53.

97. Stubbs, "Jewish Slander," *Germany*, 243.

98. Herman Wündrich, "Wirtschaftswerbung während der NS-Zeit: Versuch einer Analyse," Düsseldorf, 1986. This is an unpublished manuscript obtained from Wündrich's widow.

99. R. R. Powers, "Das 'gewisse Etwas,'" *Coca-Cola Nachrichten*, 20 October 1934, 2.

100. "Der Tagungsbericht," *Coca-Cola Nachrichten*, 1 April 1937, 6–7.

101. Herr Reichsfachgruppenwalter Pg. Gensch, as reported in ibid., 4.

102. "Nicht nörgeln — mehr leisten," *Coca-Cola Nachrichten*, 15 February 1937, 8.

103. The fistfights are mentioned by Allen, *Secret Formula*, 247, and were related second-hand in interviews with Coca-Cola GmbH employees. Afri-Cola's complaints appeared frequently in *Afri-Post*.

104. Max Keith, "Begrüssungsansprache," *10 Jahre Aufbau*.

105. "Die Zukunft der alkoholfreien Getränke," *Frankfurter Handelsblatt*, 17 September 1942, 3, found in EA 398Bü28, Hauptstadtarchiv Stuttgart.

106. While the quote describes Germany's pavilion in Paris, the description is also apt for the exhibition in Düsseldorf. Karen A. Fiss, "The German Pavilion," in Britt, *Art and Power*, 108. See also Frederick T. Birchael, "Vast German Fair Is Built in Secret to Rival Paris Fete," *New York Times*, 26 April 1937, 1. For insight on "Exhibitions and National Identity," see the special issue of *National Identities* 1, no. 3 (1999), as well as Geppert, "Welttheater."

107. Ernst Poensgen, "'Schaffendes Volk,'" *Stahl und Eisen*, 6 May 1937, 466. See also Schäfers, *Vom Werkbund zum Vierjahresplan*.

108. E. W. Maiwald and Richard Geutebruck, eds., *Reichsausstellung Schaffendes Volk — Düsseldorf 1937: Ein Bericht* (Düsseldorf: A. Bagel, 1939), unnumbered introductory page.

109. "Welche Bedeutung," *Coca-Cola Nachrichten*, 20 April 1937, 8.

110. "Coca-Cola auf der Ausstellung 'Schaffendes Volk' in Düsseldorf," *Coca-Cola Nachrichten*, 15 May 1937, 3.

111. Visitors to the Post Office pavilion could "see far" (*fernsehen*, the German word for television) into the exhibition by watching the broadcast from Schaffendes Volk's mobile television trucks. While a photograph of Göring drinking a Coke at Schaffendes Volk was mentioned by Oppenhoff and others, the author has yet to locate a copy.

112. "'Coca-Cola' auf der großen Reichsausstellung," *Coca-Cola Nachrichten*, 15 July 1937, 6.

113. Ibid.

114. "'Coca-Cola' auf der großen Reichsausstellung SCHAFFENDES VOLK Düsseldorf," *Coca-Cola Nachrichten*, 15 June 1937, 7.

115. "Die Preisträgerin im Juni-Wettbewerb an unserm Stand auf der Großen Reichsausstellung 'Schaffendes Volk,'" *Coca-Cola Nachrichten*, 15 July 1937, 2–4.

116. "'Coca-Cola' auf der großen Reichsausstellung," *Coca-Cola Nachrichten*, 15 June 1937, 7.

117. "'Düsseldorf'—Dein Schrittmacher! Folgst Du nach?," *Coca-Cola Nachrichten*, 15 August 1937, 14. See also "Junge, Junge, das macht Eindruck," *Coca-Cola Nachrichten*, 15 December 1937, 10–11. Roughly 8 percent of all the exhibition's visitors took a Coca-Cola pause. In comparison, the larger and more numerous coffee concessions sold 2.7 million cups. Maiwald and Geutebruck, *Schaffendes Volk*, 27.

118. Cohrt interview, *Anfangsjahre*.

119. Oppenhoff interview, 18 June 1998.

120. "Wie sage ich es dem letzten Verbraucher?," *Coca-Cola Nachrichten*, 15 September 1937, 14.

121. See "Diapositiv-Reklame in Lichtspielhäusern," *Coca-Cola Nachrichten*, 1 August 1935, 7, and "Die erfrischende Pause," *10 Jahre Aufbau*.

122. "Ausstellungen und Außenverkäufe," *Coca-Cola Nachrichten*, 15 November 1938, 8.

123. See "'Coca-Cola'-Zeitungsanzeigen," *Coca-Cola Nachrichten*, 15 May 1935, 6.

124. "Im Dienste unserer Werbung!," *Coca-Cola Nachrichten*, 15 September 1938, 19. The ad itself was reproduced on the issue's back cover.

125. "Ja! Coca-Cola hat Weltruf!" ads ran in *Die Wehrmacht* from July 1938 through the end of the year.

126. Drawing from Schäfer, documentary filmmaker Hans-Otto Wiebus determined that the photographed ads had a "very German appearance." *Eiskalt: Coca-Cola im Dritten Reich* (Munich, 1999).

127. Roseman, "National Socialism and Modernisation," 216, 217.

128. Fritzsche, "Nazi Modern," 8.

129. "Der Kraftfahrer-Prospekt," and "Autofahren und 'Coca-Cola,'" *Coca-Cola Nachrichten*, 15 February 1937, 15–16.

130. Alf Lüdtke, "The 'Honor of Labor': Industrial Workers and the Power of Symbols under National Socialism," in Crew, *Nazism and German Society*, 97.

131. "11 Uhr 15 gehts weiter," ad display, *Coca-Cola Nachrichten*, 15 August 1939, 16.

132. Reprint of the factory worker ad from a series of four advertisements reproduced in *Die Leistung* 13, no. 105 (1963): 23.

133. Fritzsche, "Nazi Modern," 7.

134. Max Keith, "An alle unsere Konzessionäre und Mitarbeiter!," *Coca-Cola Nachrichten*, 15 September 1939.

GUILLAUME DE SYON

LUFTHANSA WELCOMES YOU

Air Transport and Tourism in the Adenauer Era

The world is a book and he who stays at home reads only one page," declared the letterhead of the German airline Lufthansa when it began operations anew in 1955. As if to make good on that statement, the government-owned airline went immediately to work to bring people to read (visit) the West German page. From Hamburg, invited groups of journalists and travel agents traveled to Lübeck, Traunsee, Munich, and Heidelberg, among other sites, and enjoyed the best of what the new West German state could offer.[1] The airline and its sponsors hoped that, upon their return, they would publicize how a country which a decade earlier had faced the global wrath of the world was now worth visiting for business and pleasure. The purpose of this essay is to consider the challenges Lufthansa faced after 1955 in offering its passenger services and encouraging foreign tourism in West Germany. It examines the role of the airline in advertising air travel and the role of another governmental agency, the Deutsche Zentrale für Fremdenverkehr (German Central Office for Tourism, DZF), in promoting West Germany as a place of tourism in the late 1950s and early 1960s.[2] Most broadly, this task constituted one element of the overall transformation of West German society in the wake of National Socialism. More specifically, Lufthansa's efforts shaped and reflected the development of a modern form of consumerism and advertising through the sale of air travel. By 1963, the airline, initially limited in its public relations efforts, had become a major purveyor of West Germany's image abroad.

As Susan Strasser has recently observed, semantic problems cloud where exactly consumption begins and ends, often leaving ill defined *what* is produced, advertised, and consumed.[3] The product an airline sells is speedy travel, but advertising this product goes beyond the promise of swift journeying, as air carriers resort to a series of methods ranging from branding to the manufacturing of tradition and emotional appeal. In so doing, they associate the act of flying with far more than simply boarding an aircraft, to include the enticement to travel, the experience onboard, and the experience of arrival and beyond. As Marshall McLuhan hinted decades ago, considerations of everyday life are at play in advertising, which further extend the consumerist realm.

In the case of aviation, the conditions for the transformation of flying into a desirable consumer product first coalesced after 1945. Technology derived from World War II military aviation made aircraft economical to fly. Airlines, whether private or national carriers, used these technological improvements, coming mostly from the United States, to persuade people to take to the air.

While the glamour associated with air travel has today lost most of its luster to crowded, delayed flights, in the first two decades following World War II this was not the case. Flying became, first in the United States, then in Europe, an element of prestige for anyone who could afford it. One dressed for air travel the way one dressed for ocean cruises: in style. Carriers consequently competed in their service offerings, glamorizing the flight experience. They did so using all manner of images, gimmicks, symbols, and gifts. Airline advertising included — and continues to include — the aircraft's livery, the company logo, the flight attendant's uniform, the onboard amenities, and of course the destinations served. In the case of national airlines, before deregulation hit in the late 1970s, carriers were bona fide commercial ambassadors for their respective flags. The appearance of economy seating in 1952 did not immediately affect the quality of service offered, thanks to the price regulation that controlled most ticket sales to scheduled destinations. The place of greatest revenue for all airlines was the North Atlantic, reflecting both the predominant economic power of the United States and its business and political interests in Western Europe. Americans traveled to the "old continent" for a variety of reasons, including economic opportunity, geopolitical imperatives (the U.S. forces stationed there), and historical interest. Such was the case in Germany, where, until 1955, U.S. and several European airlines brought travelers to Frankfurt and Hamburg.[4] Indeed, despite the legacy of World War II, West Germany became a site of tourism.

National Identity and an Airline's Heritage

Following World War II, West Germans faced a considerable challenge in presenting their country as an attractive destination for travel. Much of the country's prewar urban landscape lay in ruins. Especially as the crimes of the Holocaust became widely known, the image of Germans around the world appeared irredeemably ruined. In the years of Christian Democratic political dominance (1949–1969), however, West Germany worked successfully to entice international visitors to Germany, especially businessmen but also tourists eager to see the country's main cities and some of its scenic routes. Though early waves of tourists would combine business and pleasure, by the 1960s tourists (especially Americans) would use their vacation time and the very favorable exchange rate to come and admire a recovering, democratic West Germany.

As Robert Moeller has noted, in the wake of defeat and division, Germans were subjected to foreign political forces that cast the setting of the cold war; nonetheless "West Germans made their own history and created themselves."[5] Constructing a "new" identity required distinguishing West Germany fundamentally from Nazi Germany without sacrificing cultural elements appealing to international visitors. Striking this balance was especially difficult in the 1950s and 1960s, when many outside Germany adhered to the "collective guilt" thesis. Making West Germany *salonfähig* (socially acceptable) ultimately involved chambers of commerce, transportation systems, and advertising expertise. Understanding Germany's campaign to attract foreign tourists therefore requires an analysis of a variety of cultural and political initiatives, including Lufthansa's.

Naturally, the airline itself faced considerable challenges in beginning anew. Founded in 1925, the first incarnation of the state-owned Deutsche Lufthansa functioned throughout the Nazi era, though its assets were seized and incorporated into the transport wing of the German air force in 1939. A few air links within Germany and between it and neutral and allied countries remained, but by the end of the war all of the German airline's flying assets had been dispersed and the Potsdam Protocol banned Germany from participation in civil and commercial aviation.[6] Between 1949 and 1955, however, a series of West German initiatives paved the way for the nation's reentry into the commercial aviation market. These included the creation of a new company, which bought its corporate predecessor's name, but also enjoyed the experience of some of its former managers, as well as the financial largesse of the board overseeing the liquidation of the old Lufthansa, which officially dissolved in 1951.

Flying the "New" Flag

Use of the old Lufthansa's name was a marketing gamble. The old Lufthansa had established a strong reputation in the interwar years for a relatively high degree of reliability (no small feat at the time) and had pioneered many long-distance mail routes around the world. Several of its managers had either declined to join the Nazi party or had been involved in the 20 July 1944 conspiracy against Hitler.[7] This meant that the name and Lufthansa's pre-1933 logo (a stylized flying crane) belonged to the German symbols that, it was hoped, could still prove their worth.[8]

So concerned were the new airline's managers about preserving the positive reputation associated with these symbols that they and the West German Transportation Ministry even went to court in the summer of 1954 to prevent the diffusion of a movie about the rebirth of civil aviation that might antagonize the Allies.[9] The movie told the story of a POW returning from the Soviet Union and working for the new airline, sharing his prewar and war experience with trainees. Although not revanchist as such, the movie did contain footage of Luftwaffe operations and did not make clear that the airline was not a paramilitary organization (a charge often leveled at the old Lufthansa). Although *Der Spiegel* expressed concerns similar to those of the government and Lufthansa's managers, there were no adverse Allied reactions.[10] The film soon disappeared from the screens, and West German civil aviation remained on schedule to resume operations a year later, when the Allies returned sovereignty over its air space to West Germany.[11]

The new Lufthansa still faced substantial difficulties when it began operations on 1 April 1955. First, the Lufthansa board, a mix of economists, lawyers, and government representatives, had to approve the selection of the airline's primary destinations, all of which were abundantly served by competing foreign airlines. Market studies as well as political considerations were required in this case and became reflected in the first international destinations that included such cities as London, Paris, and New York, all considered key to industrial needs but also potential magnets to bring foreign tourists to Germany.[12] Second, as its executive officer, Hans Bongers, recalled, the airline lagged a decade behind other companies in development, with many of these carriers servicing Germany.[13] The Lufthansa fleet of the 1950s, for example, was a hodgepodge of propeller aircraft acquired in a hurry, based on proven track records rather than studied needs.[14] Although this was not unique to Lufthansa (many European airlines experienced the burden of mixed fleets in the postwar years), in the case of the West German airline, fleet acquisition had been shaped by a political commitment to Western machinery, especially British- and American-built planes, as a means of ensuring that the peaceful role of the new airline in a cold war world was clearly under-

1. A Lufthansa Constellation in the 1950s. This type of aircraft became the airline's flagship, and the revised livery design included a German flag. The piston-powered aircraft would soon be dethroned by jets, forcing the airline into costly upgrades to maintain a modern image. Courtesy of Lufthansa.

stood.[15] Lufthansa's rush to acquire aircraft had consequences: after ordering the latest version of the propeller-driven Lockheed Constellation, the airline quickly realized that it would soon have to buy jet aircraft, twice as fast as the Lockheed machines, to remain competitive.[16] Adding to the airline's financial burdens was the training of German pilots. Not only were many surviving crew too old to undergo retraining, but conversion to new Western aircraft involved such technical matters as abandoning the metric system in favor of American measurements, or learning English. Before enough new pilots could be trained, English and American captains would be needed to fly German flagships.[17]

The economic and technical challenges the airline faced, however, were but one part of the equation. To establish its reputation as an efficient company, Lufthansa needed to prove good in-flight service to advertise itself. As internal reports on the airline's early flights show, everything in the field of passenger satisfaction had to be reinvented, from traditions of service to enforcing such positive stereotypes as German punctuality. Early Lufthansa experiences provided numerous examples of minor service lapses. The flight inspector on the first Frankfurt-to–New York flight was dismayed to find that one of the blue-suited flight attendants was wearing beige shoes at a time when commercial flying was very much a matter of style and fashion. Worse, not only was the German beer warm, but it was served in TWA paper cups. The fourteen liters (four gallons) of orange juice loaded for the sixteen-hour flight were quickly consumed, as was all drinkable water, so that short of inhaling hard liquor, the fifty-six passengers had to stay thirsty until they had cleared U.S. immigration.[18] Inspectors on other Lufthansa flights echoed such concerns, especially in cases where invited travel agents had become upset and voiced comparisons aloud: Pan Am provided toothpaste; TWA gave reasons for its delays; there were no souvenirs to be had on board.[19] The inspectors almost uniformly reported two positive things, however: the goodwill of the inexperienced but enthusiastic staff, and the patience of many journalists who were invited on the inaugural flights and whose private comments were duly noted and sent to Lufthansa headquarters for consideration. Furthermore, regardless of the problems encountered, journalistic coverage remained, in the words of one airline official, "extremely useful for the image of Lufthansa."[20]

Within a year, noticeable changes had taken place. As 1956 inspection and financial reports confirm, Lufthansa's situation stabilized remarkably within the space of eighteen months (though it was far from turning a profit). Not only did passenger load factors rise by an overall 15 percent, but service also improved.[21] Tour guides accompanying official guests were even able to capitalize on the notion of "German service" as a definition of quality. For example, on the inauguration of the Stuttgart–London link, three of the four crew members happened to be Swabian (a coincidence). Between the captain's announcements regarding the landscape overflown and the personal comments of the flight attendants, invited travel agents and journalists became convinced that this was a special gesture on the part of the airline intended to offer the expertise of locals who also happened to be airline professionals.[22]

In addition, when foreign officials rather than journalists or travel agents alone were present among the paying passengers (a common occurrence), new prescriptions went immediately in effect. They included press coverage, red carpet greetings, and the playing of the national anthem, inspiring Lufthansa chairman Bongers to inquire dryly whether this meant that the national anthem of each foreign passenger had to be played in such circumstances.[23] Soon, on account of the number of inaugural and special flights it carried out, Lufthansa developed a routine that ensured a smooth operation and the steady development of a positive West German image.

Lufthansa's attitude toward the matter of foreign evaluations of West German hospitality remained ambivalent, however. On the one hand, the airline maintained and updated a list of important journalists and understood that special flights to West Germany would influence the image of the airline and the country.[24] But dealings with foreign representatives and journalists were to remain "unofficial"; the latter's suggestions to airline staff were to be taken into account only as such, not as diplomatic or media demands. This reflected an important element of the airline's mission: Lufthansa's early mission was less about selling Germany diplomatically and culturally than about establishing an efficient airline which might use tourism and culture as a selling point.

Indeed, wooing foreigners to West Germany was obviously not just a matter of reparations, but was also a business proposition that required the creation of a proper marketing image for both the airline and its services.[25] Echoing the attitude of its main shareholder (the West German government), Lufthansa considered its services a form of foreign trade. To compete with foreign airlines for consumer passengers was simply a matter of reclaiming German capital lost in the postwar period.[26] This opinion would become a mantra of Lufthansa's managerial reports until 1964, when the airline turned its first profit. Carrying tourists to their vacation destination was part of the solution, which Lufthansa then boxed into a "German Air Service" association created in 1955, together with the German Railroad, for the purpose of promoting travel abroad.[27]

In defining themes that were suitable for tourism, Lufthansa had to search for ideas that would present its country in a positive light without risk of misunderstanding. Images selected needed to attract both cultural visitors and business travelers.[28] The first travel themes, however, offered strange contrasts. Germany was a country "of engineers and industries, of deep forests, of domes and romanticism": electrical lines and fir trees were depicted side by side with an aircraft flying over them.[29] In constructing its image, Lufthansa sought not only to regain the reputation of its corporate predecessor, but also to play up positive, or at least neutral, elements of the popular image of Germans, such as precision and politeness, to the point of dullness.[30] This odd mix of stereotypes also reflected the West German struggle to search for a new identity that would rely on a safe, pre-1933 past while developing new traits that would characterize West Germany as a peaceful, democratic, and capitalist nation. The only constant in such advertising was that Lufthansa was reopening the "bridge of friendship."

For example, the image of a flight attendant accompanying a small child on his first Lufthansa flight was endearing, but every other airline made use of this theme that emphasized safety and nurture.[31] The evolution of the flight attendant role still requires more study, but generally the woman (and occasional man) serving onboard was portrayed as a caretaker ensuring that the passenger would

LUFTHANSA

2. The Flight Attendant as Mother Figure, ca. 1956. Although such images were legion among all airlines, their repeated use reflected the need to show how safe air transport was. Courtesy of Lufthansa.

not get sick and bringing anything needed to where the person was seated. This emulation of a flying maid was more reminiscent of pre–World War I bourgeois ideals, and the women chosen to work flights reflected this through the work requirement of celibacy (or at least no children). The flight attendant depicted was a maternal figure, but a sexless one, at least in contrast to her counterpart a decade or two later. A more daring use of national and regional German attributes was needed, but this was a difficult endeavor, which sometimes caused heated discussion. One such example of this debate concerned dirndls.

The Dirndl Debate

An early favorite of tourists visiting West Germany in the 1950s was the Oktoberfest.[32] Jolliness all around, albeit with the risk of falling into a drunken stupor, along with the passion for associated souvenirs made it clear to German travel specialists that indigenous dress and tradition could prove the ideal hook for tourists. Lufthansa's marketing department began considering the issue within months of its first flight. Inspired by Japan Airlines' kimono-clad flight attendants and Scandinavian Airlines' "Eskimo suits" for its polar route flights, the dirndl debate, amusing though it will appear here, reflected the serious questions that arose about what constituted a proper West German identity for the airline, and how much it could stress "otherness" in its product barely a decade after World War II.

Imagery of foreign cultures usually requires a human figure in traditional clothing to supplement any other symbol, from architectural motifs to proverbial palm trees. The other is, after all, what modern travel encourages one to experience after leaving the homeland. Whereas print advertising will of course display characters in costumes, it rarely encourages the tourist to interact with such people.[33] On the other hand, the expectation to do so while on a flight might indeed extend the feeling of consuming a German travel experience while also strengthening the airline's image and appeal. The dirndl idea seemed simple enough: rather than the usual staid flight attendant dresses adopted by many airlines in the 1950s, Lufthansa would have its female staff wear southern German dirndls on its North American flights, and possibly some British flights, too.[34] This identification of the "German girl" would of course tease the imagination of the predominantly male clientele, but the returns on playing up to the stereotype would, according to marketing, be tremendous. The reactions that ensued, mostly among male airline managers, ran the gamut from enthusiastic approval to skepticism and outright opposition.

Paramount to all was how a Bavarian dress could be made into a generic German attribute, and the implications of rendering such regional stereotyping national. One of Lufthansa's heads, while stressing that the dirndl, even if worn only in season, was "the one piece that the German clothing industry had contributed to international fashion," worried that adopting the dirndl meant the male pursers and cockpit crew would switch to Lederhosen.[35] Another suggested that the dirndl might not work as well as the kimono did for the Japanese because of its association with more buxom women and its impractical features, like the frills.[36]

Partisans emphasized the need for a toned-down version, distinct from either the "Prussian" or the "Wine Queen" models.[37] Finally, most stressed that the dress, if adopted, should be seasonal and limited to the North American and possibly the British markets. Any use of it on European continental routes, or lines heavily frequented by businessmen or the "good German and European public," would risk demeaning the airline's image; not only was the dirndl not a national dress (one manager noted that wearing a dirndl on a flight to Hamburg would confuse passengers), but flight attendants would risk undermining their authority or upsetting passengers wearing their own dirndls.[38] Despite the mildly positive reaction of midlevel managers to the proposal, executives nonetheless worried that Lufthansa, eager to promote a modern image cleansed of troubled past associations, could not afford to delve into nostalgic uniforms for the sake of a gimmick. Maintaining a low profile was key, and some participants even felt such discussion was an embarrassment to the airline.

Yet two years later, in an apparent reversal of its staid approach to tourism, the Lufthansa managers' annual conference approved of "Operation Dirndl." The airline's newsletter announced that for Oktoberfest 1957, the airline's flight attendants would wear specially designed dirndls, blue for blond women and pink for brunettes. The correspondence surrounding the decision is missing, but the compromise clearly involved limiting the time period and which flights would involve the wearing of the "typically Bavarian dresses" intended to communicate "a bit of the home country" to passengers boarding the selected flights.[39] The promotion was obviously intended to encourage tourism and was one of the first signs of Lufthansa's interest in promoting visits specifically to West Germany.[40] While the dirndl experiment does not appear to have been repeated (the official photograph of the airline's uniforms over four decades does not even record it), it nonetheless signaled the airline's move to interpret and express a West German identity and attract consumers on that basis.

Working with the Deutsche Zentrale für Fremdenverkehr

Even though its development of a West German distinctiveness took time, from its very first flight Lufthansa had flown the flag of the young West Germany. Its German slogan, "Damals bewährt, heute begehrt" (roughly, "Proven yesterday, cherished today"), reflected its incorporation into West German identity. The Bonn government used Lufthansa machines rather than the new Luftwaffe's transport wing well into the 1960s, and an initial aircraft livery without the German flag was quickly revised to include it on airliner tails. Chancellor Adenauer's flights to and from Moscow in 1955, which brought about the final release of all German POWs still in the Soviet Union, illustrate the importance of the airline's image as a national carrier, since one of its planes was specially fitted for the occasion.[41] Yet the airline was not an extension of the Transportation Ministry, as shown in the failures to coordinate business activities with political interests.

When foreign journalists showed up in June 1955 for one of the airline's first transatlantic flights, for example, the governmental press office had no representative on hand to greet them.[42] Later, when the airline was in the market for a new short-range jet, it ignored the chancellery's directive to buy British and opted for a better Boeing design.[43] Not all was friction along such lines, however, as another government office, the Tourism Office (DZF), worked closely with the airline, hoping to benefit from its operations.

Created in 1948 and incorporated soon after into the West German Transportation Ministry, the Tourism Office was an autonomous unit whose mission was to encourage travel to West Germany.[44] To do so, it made abundant use of consular representations but also of private travel agencies and foreign airlines willing to take on advertisements for German tourism. As soon as Lufthansa began operations, the Tourism Office also offered to supply tourism pouches that would include information on sightseeing and accommodations.[45] Although the airline was at first lukewarm about the offer, it soon realized that such "welcome packets" became favored items among foreign passengers flying to West Germany, and their distribution onboard grew. The Tourism Office also oversaw the hotel selection for foreign guests of the airline and the government and footed the bill for some of their entertainment. By 1957, when Lufthansa developed greater interest in the development of tourism in West Germany, an informal agreement existed between the airline and the DZF allowing the latter's staff to use the airline at half-price.[46]

When, however, the DZF offered to incorporate Lufthansa into the board of the agency's governors, the company declined to make membership payments, arguing that it would be more efficient to offer a number of free airline seats to the Tourism Office for use as it pleased. Two years of squabbles between officials on both sides ensued, with other disagreements souring the relationship.[47] The Lufthansa representative in New York City sent irate notes about his counterpart at the DZF there, while shipments of tourism posters and brochures abroad, often sent through Lufthansa at discount, sat in warehouses.[48] The DZF's own financial difficulties (its budget had been reduced by the early 1960s) meant that it was desperate to cash in on its connection with West German land, sea, and air carriers.[49]

Though illogical, the dispute between the DZF and Lufthansa, both of which agreed on the need to bring travelers to West Germany, centered on *how* to and *who* should do it.[50] Both entities reported to the German government, yet their tasks, although overlapping, also profoundly diverged. Indeed, Lufthansa could

3. Two visions of Germany, early 1960s. The brochure on the left reflects Lufthansa's emphasis on the transitory nature of travel, using Germany as a gateway. The one on the right, from the German Tourism Office, emphasizes nostalgia and suggests that Germany is a final destination no matter what means of travel one uses. Courtesy of Lufthansa.

offer travel packages of its own, while the DZF dealt with the whole array of German tourism offices. In the latter case, it might also advertise destinations Lufthansa did not serve, such as West Berlin, a fiefdom of Allied airlines until 1990. Finally, visitors to Germany could come any way they pleased. The DZF wanted only to see them on German soil, and Lufthansa was but one way to get there.

On Lufthansa's side of the equation, the daily flights landing at West German airfields told only part of the story. The airports were hubs: passengers got off the plane, but some never left the transit area, switching to other flights *leaving* West Germany. In fact, to Lufthansa, flying travelers to West Germany was only part of its mission. By 1960 it became as important to transport people to multiple destinations around the world as part of generating airline revenue and developing the image of German service as it was to fly foreigners into West Germany. Some of the airline's international slogans confirmed its vision of travel. Whereas the DZF had successfully marketed a famous "Auf wiedersehen in Germany," Lufthansa stressed that its clientele should "be a traveler . . . not a tourist!"[51]

Lufthansa wanted passengers to see the world, while the DZF wanted tourists in West Germany and felt that the airline, as a heavily subsidized entity, should offer pro bono services to bring VIPs to West Germany only. In apparent contradiction to its wishes, though, the DZF offered its tourism kits and advertising posters to other airlines (a practice established before Lufthansa started operations), thus suggesting that the messenger's identity, that is, Lufthansa, was irrelevant.[52] Eventually, informal discussions between leaders of the airline and the Tourism Office led to a modus vivendi, whereby Lufthansa would recommend what brochures to include in its tourism kits, while the Tourism Office would prepare all information about West Germany on the occasion of inaugural flights. Lufthansa would also be informed of which foreign airlines had received tourism kits.[53]

Lufthansa's role as a provider of foreign tourism would continue not just through the airline's brand, but in its development strategy. Initially shy about its nationality (early posters stressed the company's name and logo but never mentioned Germany), Lufthansa assumed a stronger German identity by the late 1950s. Boarding a Lufthansa plane meant actually entering a constructed West German space, to the point of stereotype. For example, specially designed red seats were an attempt at differentiating the inside of Boeing 707 jet planes from those of other airlines. The German airline was among the first European carriers to fly jets and used the opportunity to name its aircraft after German cities. (The christening of the *Stadt Berlin* by Mayor Willy Brandt garnered international coverage.) This process of "Germanization," symbolic though it was (and far from unique, as most European airlines were doing the same for publicity reasons and to echo the traditions of ocean liners), constituted a further effort to strengthen the airline's national identity despite its Anglo-American fleet.

Parallel moves developed the dimension of the passenger as a consumer. A notable effort at establishing "German service" was the "Senator Klass" (first by any other name), introduced in 1958 as a way to check Pan Am's dominance of transatlantic service to Germany. This move to high-end consumerism required "Senator" planes to be fitted with only thirty-five seats (less than half the usual load) and contributed to attracting a new share of business while improving the

EVERY FRIDAY AT 4 P.M.

. . . a limited number of passengers—never more than thirty-two—embark upon the Senator. This flight of elegance is exclusive with Lufthansa and features the four C's of Comfort, Cuisine, Conviviality and Convenience!

Fly the finest, fastest nonstop flight to Germany. Ask your travel agent to reserve your seat or berth aboard the Senator—De Luxe and First Class only, from New York.

Senator

LUFTHANSA
GERMAN AIRLINES
Offices in the principal cities of the United States and Canada.

4. The Lufthansa Senator class as advertised in the American media in the late 1950s. Although popular with very rich passengers, the full Senator flight was soon displaced by Pan Am's jet service, prompting Lufthansa to rush jets into service. Courtesy of Lufthansa.

airline's reputation.[54] Supplementing this, and despite the fact that German food was not the ideal of culinary connoisseurs, by 1960 Lufthansa's catering department acquired a solid reputation, going to extraordinary lengths to have Westphalian ham at the right temperature and even cold German beer on tap. As for the blue uniforms of 1955, German fashion designer Heinz Oestergard had been called in to redesign them, giving them a more pleasant, less martial look.[55] The airline also entered into an agreement with Daimler Benz to feature some of its models in some airline ads. Meanwhile, the car manufacturer advertised in the United States the opportunity for well-to-do visitors to fly to West Germany to collect their new Mercedes, vacation with it, and have the vehicle shipped home.[56] As for the tourism kits that had been a trademark of onboard service, they now found their way to Lufthansa offices around the world. The result was that rather than having four outlets in North America, the DZF could now count on Lufthansa's forty offices there.[57] The friendship VIP visits also continued, though these were now paid for by cities, Länder, or German industry, as in the case of a Scandinavian delegation to Wolfsburg.[58]

To encourage tourism on paper, however, did not solve the matter of costs. Air travel remained prohibitively expensive despite the introduction of economy fares in 1958 (heavy charter activity would not hit Europe for another decade), thus checking any steady expansion of tourism. Lufthansa was tied to the International Air Transport Association's price structure, a cartel of which most national and noncharter airlines were members, yet it moved to lobby for a review of tariffs on international links to Germany. The result involved the introduction of group rates, attractive to travel agencies. Finally, as part of its general advertising campaign, the airline moved to sponsor the organization of conventions in West Germany and of cultural exhibits abroad.[59] In so doing, it extended the realms of consumerism and advertising. An airline-sponsored art show increased the brand's appeal elsewhere as a quality label. Indeed, flight was not a manufactured good, so drawing consumers out of their households and on their way abroad required a variety of messages. Commercial flight encouraged consumerism but also relied on it in different ways to improve the image of Germany.

By the early 1960s, then, Lufthansa was well on its way to becoming the major advertiser of Germany's image abroad. Initially devoting over 60 percent to the U.S. market, the advertising budget was eventually spread among the European and Asian markets. The funds available largely exceeded those available to the Tourism Office, but the returns justified the large sums invested.[60] In the process, in fact, the airline began displacing the Tourism Office in its mission, offering new, more effective images of the young Federal Republic. These included a new airline livery and trademark advertising campaign appearing in 1963 that would become a classic of airline advertising until the early 1990s, when the airline adopted a new corporate image.[61] It reflected an interest in presenting a modern vision of German service, one which included an acknowledgment of German expertise in technology, but also suggested, at least in American ad campaigns, an apparently novel sense of humor. Taking after the humorous self-deprecating Volkswagen Beetle ads (such as "It's ugly, but it gets you there"), a whole series of witty ads began gracing the pages of American magazines. Though generally well received, they were all considerably toned down in contrast to the 1963 ad that depicted a stern-looking cockpit crew staring at the camera with the slogan announcing that "the friendly Germans" were waiting to fly you safely and efficiently to your destination. The dry humor would hopefully sway potential travelers suspicious of the German airline's nationality; the ad's

The warm, friendly, loveable Germans invite you to fly with them.

Maybe that will be our image in a hundred, or a couple of thousand years. At least, we hope so.

But right now, people love our machines far more than they love us. After all, we're known more for technical abilities than for gay, carefree attitudes.

And there's one time we're glad this is so: when a crew and mechanics are making an airplane ready for flight.

Anyone who takes such good care of you in the sky can't be all bad here on earth.

5. Warm and Friendly ads. While this particular ad backfired, others using humor (and a similar layout, including the Ulm script font) became the backbone of the airline's advertising campaign in the 1960s and 1970s. Courtesy of Lufthansa.

description of the high quality of German technical knowledge concluded, "Anyone who takes such good care of you in the sky can't be all bad here on earth." The ad did not go over as well as planned, and the mixed reaction suggested that while the American public looked far more kindly on Germany than did either the British or the French, the ghosts of World War II were too close to trivialize into a historical spoof.[62]

Flight Advertising and the Selling of a New National Identity

In order to consolidate its new beginnings without invoking the Nazi past, Lufthansa adopted a variety of branding and advertising strategies that emphasized modernity but also called on more positive "national" and "traditional" stereotypes. The careful navigation of this identity terrain continued into the following decades and included the casting of the Lufthansa short-range fleet as European (each plane, though still christened after a German city, became a "Europa-Jet") and the selective use of the airline's technological past in a fiftieth anniversary celebration in 1975 (despite the fact that there was little in common between the pre-1945 and post-1955 entities). Ironically, Lufthansa is probably the only airline that will celebrate two fiftieth anniversaries. The success of the carrier combined with the rehabilitation and reunification of Germany prompted its airline marketing to launch a renewed fiftieth anniversary in 2005 as an effective way to shed all links with the airline's older incarnation. In so doing, it confirmed several aspects of airline consumerism that it had dealt with half a century ago. First, advertising was as much a part of the travel experience as the flight itself and even the experience of the destination. To convince people to board Lufthansa, the airline made emotional as well as rational appeals, playing selectively on stereotypes. The corollary was the development of quality onboard service that would make one want to experience a "piece of Germany" at thirty thousand feet. This search for an experience rather than a tangible good confirms the transformation of a consumerist trend that preceded the mass air transport from the 1970s onward. The Lufthansa branding and advertising sold desires few could afford in the Adenauer era but, in the manner of nineteenth-century bourgeois ideals, all sought to fulfill by traveling, in this case to Germany.

Thus, during the Adenauer era, Lufthansa's role as a purveyor of West German identity abroad evolved to reflect a dual mission of flight and tourism: corporate and national cultures blended for economic and political gains. The influence of the German Tourism Office no doubt played a role in the process, but this was not a straightforward alliance because of the two entities' separate goals. One sold West Germany, the other sold flights there and everywhere else. Flight and tourism had different purposes, with the airline often suggesting that, to paraphrase Robert Louis Stevenson, it was better to travel than to arrive. Yet the very technology of flight and its packaging played an important role in shaping the airline's reputation as well as helping relaunch West German tourism. In the process, it also contributed to the slow, protracted process of the rehabilitation of West Germany.

Notes

1. "Trip to Germany, June 1955," Rosendahl papers, box 77, folders 4 and 5, University of Texas, Dallas.
2. On the early activities of the DZF and its dealings with the German past, see Confino, "Traveling as a Culture of Remembrance."
3. Strasser, "Making Consumption Conspicuous," 762.
4. Sabena and Swissair communiques, 1951, Institut für Stadtgeschichte, Magistratakten (Verkehrs- und Wirtschaftsamt), 7.011: Fremdenverkehr, 1945–1953, Stadtarchiv, Frankfurt.

5. Robert G. Moeller, "Writing the History of West Germany," in *West Germany Under Construction*, 2.

6. For an overview history of Lufthansa and its fleet, see Davies, *Lufthansa*.

7. See John, *Zweimal kam ich heim*.

8. Although the flying crane logo was still painted on fuselages of Lufthansa machines after 1933, it was usually a small patch, having been replaced on aircraft tails with the swastika.

9. Correspondence exchange of August 1954 concerning the movie *Morgengrauen*, B136/9955, Bundesarchiv Koblenz (hereafter BAK).

10. Ibid.

11. On the beginnings of the new Lufthansa, consult Reul, *Planung und Gründung der Deutschen Lufthansa AG*.

12. Höltje, *Der Aufbau der Deutschen Lufthansa*, 5. Speech held 24 March 1961.

13. There were on average 160 flights a week to Frankfurt from North America. See Reuss, *Jahrbuch der Luftfahrt*, 1956–1958 editions.

14. Höltje, *Der Aufbau der Deutschen Lufthansa*, 7–8. For an overview of the fleet, see Davies, *Lufthansa*, 66–73; Hans-Liudger Dienel, "Lufthansa: Two German Airlines," in Dienel and Lyth, *Flying the Flag*, 93–98.

15. Dienel, "Lufthansa," 90–91. On the issue of specific acquisitions and the push by the Lockheed aircraft company to sell its planes, see confidential memoranda of 1955–1956, B136/9955, Bundeskanzleramt, BAK.

16. Bongers, *Deutscher Luftverkehr*, 38.

17. *Der Spiegel*, 25 May 1955, 32; Höltje, *Der Aufbau der Deutschen Lufthansa*, 11; Braunburg, *Die Geschichte der Lufthansa*, 184–187, 191.

18. "DLH 1955 Eröffnungsflüge LH 401/421," confidential report re FRA-NYC 3/4 June, 6 June 1955, Deutsche Lufthansa archives (hereafter DLH).

19. Ibid.; confidential report re: NYC-DUS 9/10 June 1955, 14 June 1955, DLH.

20. Ibid.

21. Based on an average of numbers appearing in Reuss, *Jahrbuch der Luftfahrt 1958*, chapter 4. For example, improvements ranged from an 11 percent increase in passengers on North Atlantic routes (from 39 to 50 percent), to a 25 percent improvement in German domestic transport.

22. "DLH 4/1956 Eröffnungsflüge LH 120/122," undated memorandum re: LH 120 STR-LON, 22 April 1956, DLH. For a less successful endeavor, see "Eröffnungsflüge LH 402/403 und 430/433," memorandum, 1 May 1956. The airline's chartering of a special visit to the Guttenberg medieval castle had been less successful, as it involved dragging the official guests up a steep hill after a four-hour bus ride.

23. Internal memorandum, Bongers to Public Relations Office, 24 October 1958, DLH. On the ceremonies described above, see "Rahmenanweisungen für die Behandlung Ausgehender Eröffnungsflüge," circular memorandum to Lufthansa personnel, 1 October 1958, 2, 4–5, DLH.

24. "LH 402/403 April 1956," internal memorandum from H. Stridde to von Studnitz, 9 March 1956, DLH. Topping the list of important newspapers were the *New York Herald*, the *New*

York Times, *Figaro*, and *Le Monde*. Comments on journalists ranged from "friendly" to "very tough" and even included an "irrelevant to our goals" for Art Buchwald.

25. Hans Baumann, "Fremdenverkehr als Wirtschaftsfaktor," *Der Volkswirt* 6, no. 45 (8 November 1952): 15.

26. Heinz Röhm, "Die Stellung der Bundesrepublik im Weltluftverkehr und der Wiederaufbau der deutschen Lufthansa," *Internationales Archiv für Verkehrswesen* 7, no. 11 (June 1956): 248–259; Bongers, *Es lag in der Luft*, 276.

27. Bongers, *Luft*, 282.

28. Hans Baumann, "Der Luftverkehr als Mittler internationaler Verständigung," *Internationales Archiv für Verkehrswesen* 3, no. 4 (February 1951): 78–80.

29. Lufthansa advertising brochure, ca. 1956, DLH.

30. Dienel, "Lufthansa," 110.

31. Lufthansa poster, ca. 1956, DLH.

32. Koshar, *German Travel Cultures*, 163.

33. O'Barr, *Culture and the Ad*, 83.

34. Lovegrove, *Airline Identity*, 23–27; Omelia and Waldock, *Come Fly with Us!*, 57.

35. "Dienstkleidung" file, correspondence Studnitz to Zobel, 24 November 1955, DLH.

36. "Dienstkleidung" file, correspondence, 25 November 1955, DLH.

37. "Dienstkleidung" file, correspondence Christina Cripps, Hamburg base, to Management, 1 December 1955, DLH.

38. "Dienstkleidung" file, miscellaneous notes, 19 November 1955, 22 November 1955, DLH.

39. *Lufthansa Nachrichten* 76 (August 1957): 1–2, DLH.

40. *Der Lufthanseat*, 21 December 1958, 7. At the 1958 Steuben parade in New York, the airline even sponsored a flower car with its name on it.

41. Bongers, *Luft*, 270.

42. "DLH 1955 Eröffnungsflüge LH 401/421," memorandum of 6 June 1955 from counselor Schirmer of the Federal Press Office, DLH. On that occasion, neither the Press Office nor the German Foreign Ministry had been informed of the visits of U.S. journalists.

43. Correspondence regarding Boeing 737 purchase decision, 1964–1965, B136/9955, BAK.

44. Internal memorandum, 24 July 1952, B231/11, BAK.

45. Miscellaneous correspondence, 1956, file folder "Touristik," DLH.

46. Tourism Office, Chicago branch, to DZF Frankfurt headquarters, 30 April 1957, B231/160, BAK; A. Staks, "Organisation und Arbeitsweise der Deutschen Zentrale für Fremdenverkehr," *Jahrbuch für Fremdenverkehr* 5, no. 2 (summer 1957): 33.

47. Miscellaneous correspondence with DLH, 1958–1959, B231/160, BAK.

48. Miscellaneous correspondence, 1957–1958, file folder "DZF," DLH.

49. Internal memoranda, various dates, 1958–1965, B231/160, BAK.

50. Quarterly reports of DZF offices for 1955, B231/233, BAK. Several offices mention that Lufthansa opened its agency in the same building as theirs.

51. See Lufthansa's advertising campaign in the early 1960s, which included such slogans as "Be a traveler . . . not a tourist!" and the blander "Let Lufthansa show you the world."

52. Letters of DZF to Lufthansa, 31 January 1957, 31 December 1958, 19 February 1959; internal memorandum, German Tourism Office, 16 April 1959, B231/160, BAK.

53. Internal memorandum, German Tourism Office, 16 April 1959, B231/160, BAK.

54. Johenning, "Der Wiederaufbau der kommerziellen Zivilluftfahrt der Bundesrepublik Deutschland nach dem zweiten Weltkrieg," 148.

55. H. J. Becker, *Boeing 707*, 55.

56. Mercedes-Benz ad campaign, 1960–1961, appearing in U.S. magazines (e.g., *National Geographic*, November 1961); Lufthansa campaign ad, 1959, appearing in U.S. magazines (e.g., *Theatre Arts*, September 1959).

57. Wolfgang A. Kittel, *Die Deutsche Lufthansa als Förderer des Fremdenverkehrs nach Deutschland* (Cologne: Lufthansa, 1962) (copy of address, 20 September 1962), 3.

58. "Erröfnungsflug LH 211," 20 April 1959, DLH.

59. Kittel, "Die Deutsche Lufthansa," 6–8.

60. Ibid., 12. In 1960, over 78 percent of American travelers to Germany used air transportation.

61. Bongard, *Fetische des Konsums*, 22–30.

62. Later advertising depictions, emphasizing French cuisine, Scottish Whiskey, and "German flying," worked far better (Lufthansa American ad, *Time*, 1974).

"THE HISTORY OF MORALS IN

THE FEDERAL REPUBLIC"

Advertising, PR, and the Beate Uhse Myth

The Beate Uhse Myth

B eate Uhse's life is often read as a history of Germany's twentieth century. In the words of her biographer, Uta van Steen, "The parallels between her own life and the history of her land astonish, again and again."[1] Upon Uhse's death in 2001, the tabloid *Bild-Zeitung*, like many news outlets, noted the passing of a celebrity whose biography had become a shorthand for German history: "Her success story: it is the history of morals in the Federal Republic."[2] The stations of Uhse's life, paralleling German history, are familiar to Germans.[3] Child of a reformist household in the Weimar years, she got her pilot's license and served in the wartime Luftwaffe. Widowed in the war, she resurfaced as a refugee in Schleswig-Holstein, where she peddled birth control information to desperate women in the "hunger years." Her black market activity grew into an erotica firm, which expanded rapidly during the economic miracle, but which also had to battle the courts and a prudish society. Her struggles contributed to the eradication of the old obscenity laws, and her firm became a giant in the pornography industry. When the Berlin Wall fell, she was there with product catalogues, and her firm quickly expanded eastward. By the end of the century, hers was the first erotica firm on the stock market, and it pioneered the expansion of Web-based pornography.

We can thank Uhse herself for this framing of her life story. In an industry characterized by anonymity and secrecy, Uhse openly identified herself, her firm, and contemporary German history in catalogues starting in the early 1950s. By the beginning of the next decade, the firm was distributing brief biographies of Uhse to journalists. As the media dutifully disseminated the story, Uhse became a celebrity. Over time, this practice evolved into the firm's careful cultivation of the "Beate Uhse Myth," a story that was compelling yet simple enough to become anchored in the public consciousness and take on its own legs as a marketing device.[4] Long accustomed to drawing on Uhse's own accounts of her life, the media's countless retrospectives in the 1990s and beyond all summarized her 1989 "as-told-to" autobiography.[5] We know little about Uhse that she did not tell us herself, and even the common framing of her story as a biography that tells the story of the German twentieth century is Uhse's own. Indeed, the notion that her story *is* "The History of Morals in the Federal Republic" has helped to foster the erroneous belief that Beate Uhse was the only, or at least the most important, erotica firm during the difficult "pioneering" years of the 1950s.[6]

The Beate Uhse Myth eventually far exceeded its initial purpose. For the firm, the Myth began as a means of establishing brand identity. For the West German public, it became a way of understanding history, providing a narrative about their path from Nazism, through hardship and recovery, to a world of pleasure. But if Uhse's biography appears to parallel Germany's, then we should not be surprised if her tellings of her life story changed over the years. After all, Germans' ways of understanding their national history have shifted enormously through the postwar decades.[7] And Uhse had many opportunities to revise her autobiography, since her media were advertising and public relations, not (until 1989) a memoir between hard covers.[8]

Uhse's self-presentation underwent its most remarkable metamorphosis before she emerged as a celebrity in the mid-1960s. In her 1952 product catalogue, Uhse introduced herself as a woman whose marriage and four children sensitized her to women's marital problems during the "rubble years."[9] In her 1963 catalogue, she presented a woman whose courage in the wartime Luftwaffe, culminating in a daring flight out of a besieged Berlin, foreshadowed her courage in battling sexual prudery in reconstruction West Germany.[10] This essay explores this profound shift in Uhse's presentation of herself and German history: from a wife and mother to a highly unconventional woman, from postwar suffering to Nazi-era military prowess. Reflecting Uhse's exquisite instincts as much as any calculated marketing decisions, especially in the early years, Uhse's changing narratives reflected the delicate interplay of sex, gender, social class, and history in establishing respectability in the early FRG.

For millions of West Germans, sexual consumption was a marker of the intimate experience of the journey from Nazi-era optimism through defeat and poverty to recovery. Despite Nazi attacks on sexual "decadence" and reproductive autonomy, Germans had enjoyed erotic art, literature, and popular culture during the flush mid-1930s, and the Wehrmacht had distributed condoms throughout the war. Wartime shortages, however, constrained the circulation of erotic literature, and the collapse of the economy and bureaucracy meant the near disappearance of condoms. The reappearance of basic items like condoms after currency reform helped to mark the end of shortages posing existential threats. Small luxuries, such as lingerie, could symbolize the transition to greater plenty. By roughly 1957, some 8 million West Germans—out of a population of 54 million—were on the mailing lists of mail-order firms for "marital hygiene."[11] Five years later, industry insiders felt that by a conservative estimate, half of West German households had patronized a mail-order erotica firm.[12]

If sexual consumption was part of Germans' "private" experience of the turbulent midcentury, then the Beate Uhse Myth created a shared "public" narrative linking sexuality, history, and consumption.[13] Prior to Uhse's emergence as a public figure, Beate Uhse communicated with customers through product catalogues. Unlike other erotica catalogues, which revealed nothing of the people behind the firm and referred customers to a post office box, Beate Uhse included autobiographical blurbs, photos of the founder and her children, and a street address which customers were invited to visit. Uhse's catalogues emphasized the respectability of the firm, its founder, and sexual consumption. As marketing devices, they were hugely successful, making the firm a major player in the industry in less than a decade. Yet Uhse's autobiographical marketing practice does not reveal the secrets to the sexual needs and fantasies of West Germans in the 1950s; other erotica firms thrived with very different marketing strategies. Furthermore, Beate Uhse's advertising was not just an attempt to attract customers. It also addressed employees and expressed the founder's self-perception. And the outside world with which advertising communicated did not consist only of (potential) customers; it also included the courts and, later, the media. Eventually, public relations became as important as advertising.

The firm's marketing and press offices, the courts, and the media each played a role in hammering out and disseminating the Beate Uhse Myth. Yet in none of these locations was the function of Uhse's biography transparent. This essay thus interprets marketing as an expression of corporate culture and the entrepreneur's sense of self, not just an effort to sell products.[14] It understands the courtroom as a social space, not just a setting where legal issues were resolved.[15]

Recognizing that we cannot know how the public actually interpreted Uhse's story, it focuses on its fascination for journalists, whose dissemination of the Myth confirms at least its appeal to them.[16]

With all audiences, respectability was critical. Yet the terms of respectability were not fixed; they varied by audience, over time, and according to the scale of Uhse's business. Establishing the respectability of a one-woman firm in the hungry late 1940s was not the same as confirming the respectability of a firm with hundreds of employees and millions of customers in the flush early 1960s. Attracting customers, convincing courts of law, and winning over journalists were three different tasks. In some settings, respectability depended mainly on appropriate gendered and sexual behavior. In others, the greater tests concerned social class, entrepreneurial identity, or liberal credentials. By deploying her autobiography to establish respectability in multiple contexts, Uhse revealed complicated perceptions of what was "respectable" about recent German history.

Yet sexual consumption was never *only* about respectability. At the time Uhse introduced the Luftwaffe story, West Germans were increasingly turning to sexual consumption for pleasure even apart from recovery. In those same years, Uhse was making the transition from entrepreneur to celebrity. Where isolated elements of her autobiography had served specific marketing or legal concerns, a neatly packaged biography now became the Beate Uhse Myth. In this context, the Luftwaffe story blended a history of respectability with a story of excitement, thrill, and risk.

With or without Beate Uhse, sexuality and the recent past would have constituted a complicated web for postwar West Germans.[17] But through her personalized marketing and, later, celebrity, Uhse directed what might have been an inchoate set of associations to very distinct images: the female Luftwaffe veteran, the woman of the rubble, the unashamed peddler of erotica. A narrative initially patched together from fragmentary signals of an evolving postwar culture became a seamless story that instructed West Germans to understand the Nazi past, the rubble years, the economic miracle, and sexual liberation as a natural progression—a story strikingly different from that offered by sexual revolutionaries a few years later.

Is Everything All Right in Our Marriage?
Winning Over Customers

When Uhse began her business, she benefited from a large untapped market. Millions wanted better sexual and reproductive lives, and currency reform made small purchases like condoms or a book possible even for those of modest means.

Most potential customers, however, faced barriers of shame to discussing their sexual problems and to purchasing goods related to sex. Beate Uhse's catalogues thus not only presented products; they also assured consumers that their desires were legitimate and that the firm was a trustworthy addressee for their most private concerns.

Yet the catalogues did more than provide customers with a respectable language of sexual consumption. Authored jointly by Uhse and her husband in the early years, catalogues also expressed the founder's self-image and communicated with the firm's personnel. Having started with one woman's black market activity and informed by her husband's business expertise, Beate Uhse retained the feel of a family business for many years; the firm's standing and that of Uhse herself would be hard to separate.[18] In addition, staff had to be compensated for the firm's questionable reputation in its small, remote home city of Flensburg.[19] Beate Uhse accomplished this partly through superior pay and benefits, but also by assuring employees that they were embarked on an important social mission, not a dirty business.[20] Respectable catalogues bound both customers and staff to the firm, and they fulfilled Uhse's own perfectionist drive for advertising materials that she could consider unassailable on aesthetic, technical, and social-philosophical grounds.

With flyers and short catalogues, Uhse built a solid customer base between 1948 and 1951. In 1952, the firm introduced the trope that would become its trademark: the public identification of the firm with the person. In prominent spots in general catalogues for the next fifteen years, the founder introduced herself and her firm. As catalogues grew, so did the frames—from three paragraphs in the 32-page catalogue of 1952 to twelve pages in a 162-page catalogue of 1958.[21] Well into the 1960s, catalogues employed Uhse's biography to link the firm to a feminized history of the recent past and a philosophy of sexuality identifying women as the anchor of companionate heterosexuality.[22] The firm thus drew on the language of Weimar reformers, on popular memories of feminine victimization in the war, and on a broad consensus that the family was crucial to West Germany's defense against Nazism and communism.[23]

The first catalogue to use photography, the 1952 booklet featured on its cover the head of a woman, dramatically lit in the style of Weimar-era expressionism (which had enjoyed a renaissance in early postwar film), staring intently into the camera and implicitly posing the question of the catalogue's title: "Is everything all right in our marriage?" In describing the firm's origins, Beate Uhse's setting was the immediate postwar period. Couples had grown apart, and women's

1. "Is Everything All Right in Our Marriage?" The 1952 catalogue portrayed the customer as a woman worried about her marriage. Courtesy of Beate-Uhse-Stiftung zu Flensburg, Forschungsstelle für Zeitgeschichte in Hamburg.

heavy burdens made pregnancy a disaster. As Uhse explained in her 1952 catalogue, "It's the woman who suffers most from problems in this area" (sexuality). Although she was happily married with four children, a doctor's tales about his patients' problems had inspired her to help married couples in need of advice: "As you can surely imagine, as a woman I can work in this way for women's happiness and the preservation of marriage only with great idealism."[24]

Catalogues through the 1950s presented products in a manner consistent with the goal of saving marriages by improving women's sexual experience. Descriptions of goods continually returned to one point: women suffered because of bad sex. Using the most delicate language and never neglecting the importance of men's own satisfaction, Beate Uhse's catalogues made the following points: Men who rush lovemaking because their minds are cluttered by work disappoint their wives (an erotic novel would get them into the mood). Without contraception, women lived in constant fear of pregnancy and sought unsafe abortions. Anxiety during unprotected sex made women emotionally incapable of orgasm, while withdrawal made it physiologically impossible (couples might choose from a wide array of contraceptives). If a woman appeared "frigid," it was probably because her husband did not know how to make love to her; he might not even know that women, too, are supposed to experience orgasm (they should read a sex manual and perhaps try a device to increase the stimulation the wife experiences during intercourse). Impotence or injury to the genitals might diminish a man's feeling of self-worth, but his wife also suffers if intercourse is no longer possible (he can take a hormone pill for the former or buy a genital prosthetic for the latter). If he climaxed too quickly, he would frustrate his wife, whom nature has equipped to take more time to reach orgasm (an ointment to prevent premature ejaculation might be helpful). The 1952 catalogue did not offer photos of nude women, although subsequent catalogues did. Neither this nor subsequent catalogues stressed condoms' application against sexually transmitted disease, which evoked recent military use and prostitution, settings where men's pleasure was the sole goal.

As the decade progressed, customers and the firm made the transition from recovery to plenty. Covers no longer posed customers' anxious question, Was everything all right in their marriage? Portraying couples happily embracing or talking, they instead optimistically declared, "They're happy!," "The best years of our lives," and "Healthy marriage, happy marriage." Images showed presumptive customers as sometimes content, sometimes worried, but always dressed in style. Creatures of the economic miracle, customers not only expected prompt service and quality products but also had the kind of hectic lives that made it necessary to get a little help in the romance department. Luckily, the equally modern Beate Uhse was there to help. Yet catalogues feminized the image of the entrepreneur behind the efficient firm. Catalogues did not dwell on Uhse's long hours, professional drive, or highly rational decision making. Instead, they featured photos of Uhse and her sons at the beach or washing the car, mentioned her homey touch of sending foreign stamps (from international orders) to children of customers who ordered her "birds and bees" book for children, and — despite her tendency to hire men in top positions — showed a feminized workplace with women answering phones, opening mail, and perusing the firm's library.[25] Linking women's agency with the firm's approach to sexuality, the catalogues explained that "conscientiousness and openness in addressing all problems, courtesy and honest engagement with the cares and concerns of others," had given the firm the "face" that earned it trust and a good reputation.[26]

2. "They're Happy!" The catalogue, ca. 1958, portrayed customers as couples whose path to conjugal harmony was paved with consumption and education. Courtesy of Beate-Uhse-Stiftung zu Flensburg, Forschungsstelle für Zeitgeschichte in Hamburg.

Through the 1950s and into the early 1960s, contraceptives and basic informative books—that is, goods essential to economic and marital stability—dominated sales.[27] Compared to other mail-order firms, which employed a bawdier (and frequently sexist) tone, Beate Uhse had an unusually high number of women's names (approximately 30 percent) on its mailing lists.[28] Still, men dominated the firm's customer base. Beate Uhse did not so much ignore men's desire for pleasure as create a less guilty language for it. Beate Uhse offered an alternative not only to the condemnatory language of decency advocates but also to the "dirty" talk of the military barracks and the pub. The firm's "clean," companionate sexuality surely helped it attract more women than its competitors, but it also provided an amenable language for male sexual pleasure. Using this strategy, the business grew enormously, serving a million and a half customers and employing two hundred people by 1962.[29]

Against this backdrop, which made sexual consumption respectable by inte-

3. Women in the erotica industry. In a feminized workplace, women answer phones, pack customer orders, and respond to queries about personal problems. From *Gesunde Ehe—glückliche Ehe*, Beate Uhse catalogue, ca. 1963. Courtesy of Beate-Uhse-Stiftung zu Flensburg, Forschungsstelle für Zeitgeschichte in Hamburg.

grating Uhse's womanly biography with a language of domestic, companionate eroticism, Uhse's self-presentation in 1963 appears as a bolt from the blue. Here is Uhse's biography, according to the 1963 catalogue: From her unconventional mother, a doctor, she had learned of "the joys and pains of her fellow humans." Always strong-willed, she learned to fly despite her parents' worries and "'stuck by her guns' as a test pilot in the war." Her last flight was a daring escape from a besieged Berlin in April 1945. The postwar story is now a mélange of unordered (and ungendered) images of homelessness, broken existences, endangered marriages, and "the idea of helping people in need of advice." One son makes a meaningful appearance—as an infant, he's with her on that plane out of Berlin—but the husband and other kids have nearly vanished.[30]

If Uhse's respectable biography as a wife and mother had brought such success, why exchange that biography for one that was doubly risky? By evoking images of women far outside traditional roles, the new presentation suggested a radical regendering of the firm and sexual consumption. Furthermore, after over a decade associating sexual consumption with recovery from the postwar crisis, the firm suddenly suggested quite a different historical association: Nazi

Germany. Perhaps changing times and the firm's success emboldened it to take risks. But veterans of the firm, asked in the early years of the twenty-first century about the new marketing strategy of 1963, do not recall feeling encouraged by a more relaxed environment.[31] Rather, they describe a sense of vulnerability. They needed to demonstrate their respectability. Thus they introduced the Luftwaffe story.

In other words, the new biography was just the latest strategy in the effort to establish respectability, an effort that had characterized the firm from day one and was still badly necessary. Such memories raise two questions. First, if business was going so well, why did the firm feel so embattled? Second, if respectability was the answer, why trade a story about civilian wartime suffering, subsequent economic success, and conventional gender roles for a story about military activity and the transgression of gender roles? To answer these questions, we must understand that customers and employees were not the only audience whose positive impressions the firm needed. Long before Uhse became a celebrity, she had a smaller public whose goodwill was essential, regardless of whether of not they bought her products. Uhse learned important early lessons about public relations in her courtroom appearances.

From a Good Family: Winning Over the Courts

In her autobiography, Uhse introduces 1963, the year the Luftwaffe story entered the catalogue, with two stories describing her sense of embattlement. The first concerns the Flensburg Tennis Club's rejection of her application for membership. The second story explains the reasons for "my reputation, my hermaphroditic existence [*Zwitterdasein*] between social disrepute and undeniable success." The explanation consists of a lengthy excerpt from an indictment filed with the Flensburg court.[32]

By the early 1960s, Uhse may have established her respectability with staff and customers, but she had not convinced the judiciary or the Flensburg Tennis Club. By juxtaposing them in her autobiography, Uhse revealed how closely these two groups were linked: both consisted of the local elite. In such circles, respectability referred not only to sexuality and gender, but also to social class. And the elite did not just distinguish according to wealth. It also distinguished between old and new money, between the established bourgeoisie and crass newcomers.

The tennis club episode was isolated, but Uhse was a frequent visitor to the Flensburg courthouse. Legal proceedings were time-consuming, expensive, and risky; the firm could not know then that it would emerge triumphant from its long string of suits. Furthermore, the close association of the firm with its founder made the constant court appearances personally draining: attacks on the firm were attacks on the person. Although distant complainants often filed the initial charges, Uhse had to defend herself in face-to-face confrontations with district attorneys and judges. Establishing respectability in this environment was not the same as writing good catalogue copy for couples in small towns who needed condoms, but it was equally critical to the firm's survival.

The court's first charge was to judge whether particular items or business practices violated statutes on subjects as varied as obscenity, youth endangerment, fraud, and insult. Although this essay cannot detail these legal issues, the rulings had significant implications. If a court ruled an item or a practice illegal, then the whole industry had to alter its practices. Furthermore, such cases tested broad constitutional matters like freedom of expression, commerce, and the unfettered development of the individual's personality.[33]

Courts also, however, evaluated the defendant's character in order to address intent, extenuating circumstances, and likelihood of repeat offense. Legal proceedings were by nature adversarial, but a courtroom in which judges and prosecuting attorneys respected the defendant differed from a courtroom in which they did not. In other words, the courtroom was a social space. Courts did not just evaluate abstracted actions in light of the law; they also established and acted on personal relationships. When a defendant appeared repeatedly before the same small group of district attorneys and judges, as Uhse did, those personal relationships became especially important. Lines like this, from a 1953 judgment, pointed to important victories: "The Court evaluates the defendant's offense mildly. As already stated, the defendant made a good impression on the Court. She presents herself openly and freely, and does not attempt to cover anything up. It could not be established that she acted out of dishonorable motives; rather the contrary."[34]

Who populated the courts? Jurists had been raised in privileged households. University-educated, they belonged to the high ranks of the civil service. They lived in what Germans called "ordered circumstances" (*geordnete Verhältnisse*): their wives were full-time homemakers, their children attended university-prep schools, they lived in nice homes. And they were well established in their careers. In the 1950s, this meant that they had been professionally active during the Nazi period, providing reliable service to the state.

In the transition from Nazi Germany to the Federal Republic, higher civil servants enjoyed a nearly unbroken sense of status, privilege, and reliability. The same was true of the business elite to which Uhse belonged economically, but not socially, by the late 1950s.[35] This self-perception was more important than specifically Nazi sentiments in establishing the culture of respectability that Uhse encountered. This social world did, however, link a history of service to the Nazi state with *Bildung*, a sense of culture and cultivation, learned not only at school but also in the privileged home of one's origin.[36]

Socialized by upper-middle-class standards that were reinforced by Nazi campaigns against "degeneracy," jurists were well versed in stereotypes of asocials, the types of people who presumably peddled condoms from their kitchen table, as Uhse did in the early years. Such a person might be expected to combine low socioeconomic status with moral dissoluteness. Instead, the courts noted Uhse's surprising biography. She had been born to a "good family" on an East Prussian estate. She had enjoyed a good education. She had joined the aristocratic ranks of fliers and had served in the wartime Luftwaffe. Her first husband, likewise a pilot, had fallen in war. After the war, women had sought her advice on sexual matters because they knew her mother had been a physician. In 1949 she had married the son of an established Flensburg shipping family, himself a wounded veteran. They now lived—in ordered circumstances—with their children.[37] Uhse, in short, had far more in common with judges and lawyers than with the "degenerates" and "asocials" whom they associated with obscenity.

The legal implications of Uhse's sociohistorical respectability were not immediately clear. In early trials, her status sometimes constituted an argument that she should have known better. Noting that she targeted physicians and academics for her mailings, an appeals court in 1951 concluded that, due to her "good education and upbringing," Uhse must have known that such recipients would find the catalogues offensive.[38] Yet even as such language condemned Uhse, it also acknowledged her belonging in respectable circles.

Significantly, suggestions that Uhse acted inappropriately *as a woman* dropped out of court proceedings early on. In 1951, the court suggested that her sex made her actions particularly reprehensible; around the same time, a district attorney suggested that she give up her "dirty business" and knit sweaters if she needed to support her family.[39] But subsequent cases did not concern themselves with Uhse's sex. "Dirty talk" was so strongly linked with male voices that Uhse's identification of her careful language with female authorship helped her not just in the marketplace and with employees, but also in the courts, especially once her 1952 catalogue was available as evidence.[40]

By contrast, Uhse's social background and that of her customers never ceased to interest the court. Uhse reiterated both. Aware that elite men condemned sexual consumption among men of the lower orders and women generally, but tolerated it for men of high social status, Uhse repeatedly noted that her customers were professional men—rather like those sitting on the bench.[41] Indeed, Uhse *performed* her status by entering court surrounded by lawyers with long pedigrees and carrying affidavits by expert witnesses with advanced degrees.[42] Such associates helped her to defend against legal charges, but in the spatial environment of the courtroom, they also demonstrated that she kept good company.

The goal, however, was not to establish that success had enabled Uhse to hire good lawyers. This would suggest that Uhse had aimed to make money. In a capitalist economy, this was perhaps a strange accusation, but "profit motive" was evoked frequently in judgments of entrepreneurs selling products whose social value was in doubt.[43] If a "low-class" peddler of sexual consumer goods was "asocial," then a successful peddler of the same goods was an amoral profiteer.[44] A good German entrepreneur, by contrast, was an idealist whose economic activity served the social good.[45]

Uhse argued that her business served the social good, and descriptions of the positive social impact of her products peppered her courtroom testimony. But other elements of her history also helped to establish her as an idealist—and these elements, removed from the world of business, did not need to be argued: they spoke for themselves. Her mother had been a physician. She had grown up on an East Prussian estate. She had served in the Luftwaffe.

In a highly stratified social environment, the Luftwaffe story served many functions, but making Uhse appear unconventional was not one of them. The Luftwaffe story marked Uhse as someone from "old money": flight training was a preserve of the wealthy. It demonstrated that the profit motive did not drive her, since her choice as a young adult had not been for a career in business. It established that she had been a reliable servant to state and *Volk* during the Nazi era, just like the jurists. The Luftwaffe story was one element in a profile of respectability that emphasized social class and political conformity, rather than the sexual and gendered respectability highlighted in Uhse's advertising.

By the late 1950s, Beate Uhse's management knew the Luftwaffe story not only as an anecdote about the founder's youth, but also as an important part of the firm's history—just not a part that was known to customers, because its relevance was in the impression it created on lawyers and judges. But advertising had always been understood holistically at Beate Uhse. Texts that lent confidence to the firm's staff did the same for customers. Advertising materials, presented in court, showed that Uhse did not violate legal proscriptions regarding obscenity. Court rulings led Uhse to alter advertising in ways that, in the eyes of customers who knew nothing of the legal struggles, underscored her discretion.[46] In the firm's experience, language that helped to establish respectability in one environment never hurt in another.

By the time the new catalogue was released in 1963, however, a new actor was joining the mix: the mass media. Through the 1950s, only local newspapers had mentioned Beate Uhse, and then only to relay official reports of trials in curt paragraphs buried in the back pages.[47] By the mid-1960s, Uhse was a fixture in the national media, and she was largely in control of her image. Her biography now did more than introduce an understanding confidant to customers and an honorable entrepreneur to the court. It also presented a celebrity to West Germans with no direct contact to the business. Beate Uhse discovered public relations at just the moment the mass media needed a new language for sex. The result was a match made in heaven, and a new framework for interpreting sexuality and German history.

The Unfettered Development of the Individual:
Winning Over the Press

By the late 1950s, Beate Uhse was confronting an ironic cost of its success. Although it was attracting ever more customers and winning its legal battles, its reputation was, if anything, worsening. In the early years, Beate Uhse had been one of dozens of small, unknown firms. A few years later, the firm was a known quantity not only to its customers, but also to antiobscenity activists (if not yet to the general public). Indeed, the firm's financial and legal successes, combined with Uhse's open association of herself with her firm, prompted ever more complaints; opponents could now attach a name and a face to an industry that had previously been frustratingly elusive, and whose other practitioners remained so. Uhse later claimed that any publicity was good publicity, but at this juncture, the firm's inner circle determined that they needed to take a more active hand in shaping the firm's reputation among noncustomers.[48] In other words, it was time for PR.

But PR was not a purely defensive measure. Even as the firm battled the courts, it was developing ambitions of qualitative change, not just continued growth. So, for example, after attending a direct marketing conference in the United States in 1961 Uhse decided to make Beate Uhse a recognized name brand, a synonym for erotica, as Kleenex is for tissue.[49] This would require educating the general public, not just customers and courts, to associate Beate Uhse with desirable functions.

Organized PR, complete with institutions and specialized professionals, arrived in West Germany (from the United States) only in the 1950s.[50] By the early 1960s, PR had been around long enough that Beate Uhse could draw on established practice, but it was new enough that the firm could benefit by being the first in the industry to engage in it. And PR was a natural fit for this firm that already considered multiple audiences in its advertising: not only customers but also families of potential employees, doctors who might recommend products to their patients or write legal affidavits, and judges who would determine whether the materials were obscene.

Beate Uhse published its first PR brochure no later than 1958.[51] In early 1961, the firm hired Hannes Baiko, who institutionalized PR within the firm by creating a Press Office (Presse-Referat).[52] Baiko was the central figure in crafting the version of Uhse's biography that would be sent out for public consumption, although the entire management team had a hand in crafting all advertising and PR materials. In what appears to have been a partly intuitive, partly calculated process, Uhse and Baiko plucked out of Uhse's biography such valuable tidbits as her mother's history as a doctor, while omitting elements of her background that equally shaped her personality but were less useful from a marketing perspective. The rural childhood, for example, might suggest sex education by barnyard animals; it was omitted. Most fatefully, the firm hammered out a telling of Uhse's Luftwaffe history in which flying was a bit like enlightened sex, although no advertising or PR materials made this comparison explicit, and the firm's management may not have intended it this way. Like better sex, flying was a fantasy of untold millions: few Germans had ever boarded a plane in 1961. Despite its aura of danger, however, in the end it saved the day and even preserved families; the single sentence on Uhse's flying career in an early PR brochure explained that her ability to fly had enabled her to escape a besieged Berlin with her infant son.[53] In other words, taking a few risks would not only make life more exciting, it would actually bring greater security.

By the end of 1961 at the latest, the firm had a PR brochure aimed at a Flensburg audience. The brochure described not only the firm's services to customers all over the country and the world, but also its local impact: its training of a labor force in modern methods of marketing and manufacture, its employment

4. The entrepreneur in domestic guise. The photo appeared in catalogues of the late 1950s and early 1960s and was reprinted in one of the first lengthy articles on Uhse in the local Flensburg press in 1961. *Lustvoll in den Markt* dates it to 1952. Courtesy of Beate-Uhse-Stiftung zu Flensburg, Forschungsstelle für Zeitgeschichte in Hamburg.

of local construction firms in the expansion of its physical plant then under way, its generation of business for the local post office. The brochure also included Uhse's new biography, implicitly informing Flensburgers that they were lucky that postwar dislocations had landed such a dynamic, creative woman in their midst. Another PR brochure, less local in nature, appeared the following year.[54]

The effort paid off. When a case of Beate Uhse's was forwarded to the Constitutional Court in late 1961, the local press departed from its habit of running terse summaries based on court reports. Instead, local papers ran longer stories that were informed by the firm's own materials, and national coverage included biographical information. So inviting was the PR that one reporter actually approached Uhse for an interview—quite possibly a first—and was clearly charmed, describing an unpretentious, down-to-earth entrepreneur, devoting several column inches to the founder's and firm's history, and including a fetching photo of Uhse.[55]

The real breakthrough, however, came when the firm announced a year later that it was opening the world's first "shop for marital hygiene."[56] Uhse had learned in a marketing seminar in the United States that successful mail-order

5. Uhse in uniform, the photo that appeared in *Der Spiegel* in 1965 with the caption "To seventh heaven: Me-109 Pilot Beate Uhse, 1944." Courtesy of Beate-Uhse-Stiftung zu Flensburg, Forschungsstelle für Zeitgeschichte in Hamburg.

firms also had brick-and-mortar shops; and in any case the firm needed to steer the growing stream of curious tourists away from the firm's busy mail-order facilities. (Flensburg was a popular vacation spot and on the route to Denmark, and at this juncture was still better known for its beaches than for its pornography.) It quickly became clear, however, that the firm had stumbled upon a promising new form of commerce in erotica, and it planned additional shops in larger cities, beginning with Hamburg. The first shop's opening attracted notice outside the immediate vicinity and alerted journalists to the fact that Uhse was an articulate, photogenic speaker on sexuality.

Some of the most significant early coverage simply tapped Uhse's sexual expertise and did not concern itself with her prior career: a 1963 series on "sex education for adults" in West Germany's leading women's magazine, a 1966 television broadcast on abortion.[57] But most reports delightedly linked Uhse's first and second careers. With a wink and a nod (and a wartime photograph of Uhse in uniform), West Germany's leading newsweekly, *Der Spiegel*, wrote of the "jet- and marriage-pilot" in 1965: "In the Second World War she ferried the *Jagdmaschinen* Me 109 and Fw 190, the *Sturzkampfbomber* Ju 87, and the *Strahljäger* Me 262 to the front. After the war she helped to steer the German people to seventh heaven."[58]

In part, the press's enthusiastic dissemination of Uhse's dual career simply reflected the fact that this was a good story: it sold papers. But Uhse's story did not just serve the media's commercial interests. It also helped journalists to articulate a relationship between liberalism and sexuality, a relationship that had vexed them through the 1950s and that was becoming yet more complicated in the early 1960s.

The relationship between Germany's midcentury traumas, sexuality, and liberalism had been a frequent, if difficult, theme in the press of the 1950s. Major news organs had sometimes described a satisfactory sex life as part of the battle against totalitarianism or as a strategy for recovering from it. Editorial pages had opposed punitive attitudes toward "victims of war" who had adopted sexually unconventional (but reasonably domestic) strategies to survive hard times: war widows who cohabited rather than marry in order to preserve their pension, for example.[59] News outlets had described returning POWs as rediscovering their individuality in the private (eroticized) sphere of the family after years of forced conformity and anonymity in Soviet prison camps.[60] Sensitive to its own interests, the press had stringently protested censorship in the name of preserving sexual morality, for example, with the 1953 Law Regarding the Dissemination of Youth-Endangering Writings.[61]

But sexuality did not always fit neatly into the battle between liberalism and totalitarianism, whether Nazi or Communist. The Nazi-era tenet that sexuality found its true meaning in its function for the collective found echoes in the Basic Law's declaration that the family was the cell of the state and in subsequent pronatalist policies.[62] Even as the liberal press denounced state intrusion on many sexual matters as assaults on the sovereign individual (and the free press), it legitimized individuals' search for sexual contentment by emphasizing its importance for the common good. Thus returning POWs might find private happiness with wife and children, but in being good husbands and fathers, they also made themselves and their dependents into democratic citizens. When it came to the search for individual pleasure per se, journalists mainly described it as a social problem (e.g., "endangered girls" around military bases) or as a scandal (e.g., the unsolved 1959 murder of Rosemarie Nitribitt, a high-priced call girl whose clients included many members of Frankfurt's business elite).[63]

The bodily comforts of the economic miracle—including a cozy domestic erotic life—provided relief after the misery of the war and the hunger years. Yet reportage on sexuality that acknowledged only this therapeutic function, or which made a liberal position on sexuality important only as a test of other, presumably "larger" matters (like opposition to censorship), remained incomplete: it neglected sexual pleasure and denied good memories of the Nazi years. Lutz Niethammer has described the "good years" of the 1950s as "half-lives," because comfort and material security, which constituted "the controlling principle of meaning, ignore[d] a great part of one's own affective and existential experiences and [could] not integrate them."[64] These nonintegrable experiences had included the thrilling highs and apocalyptic terrors of the Third Reich. As Dagmar Herzog has shown, memories and fantasies of erotic pleasure in Nazi Germany, and not just restrictions on sex, persisted well into the 1950s. Particularly among Christians, this reinforced the conviction that only a more sexually conservative postwar order would bring safety.[65] Yet even in this environment, Maria Höhn emphasizes, local populations could be far more tolerant of the search for pleasure through sex, even outside marriage, than media coverage would suggest.[66]

With the introduction of the birth control pill in 1961, journalists were confronted with the inadequacy of their vocabulary for sexuality. Here was a major news story that was about sex for pleasure, not among marginal populations but among the mainstream, and supported by modern science.[67] For ill-equipped journalists, Uhse appeared at just the right moment, providing a desperately needed vocabulary for sex.

Uhse enabled journalists to tell a sexual story that blended recovery with a search for pleasure beyond healing, a story that made liberalism compatible not just with the sober task of fending off totalitarianism but also with the search for pleasure. The firm's language on sexuality rejected fascism's collective vision in favor of a liberal, individualistic valuation of sexual pleasure, yet it always remained supremely polite and anything but hedonistic. The Luftwaffe story, for its part, evoked pleasurable associations for which the Nazi years, but not the early years of recovery, offered a vocabulary, while excluding aspects of Nazism that signaled danger.

The fantasy of flying evoked a technological modernity linked to sensual corporeality: high speeds, physical risk, freedom from the bonds of the earth.[68] Via her experience, the Luftwaffe story implied, Uhse understood not only suffering and its remedy, comfort, but also thrills, excitement. She had found excitement in service to the state, not while disrupting the social order. But hers were not the threatening thrills of the mass rally, which in their very collectivity were fundamentally fascist and thus dangerous. Rather, they were the individualistic thrills of a flier: in an era of mass institutions and conscription, flying had remained a solo experience and the Luftwaffe an elite club. Uhse's membership in this elite constituted assurance that her brand of excitement had met the exacting standards of very strict masters indeed: the Nazi regime. As the courts had learned, it was hard to reconcile this marker of wealth with images of asocial sexuality. But the press's more breathless language about Uhse's flying blurred strictly socioeconomic criteria of elite status, which might suggest a certain stuffiness, and membership in a well-remembered racial elite that was exciting in its capacity for physical exertion, its mastery of technology, and its sexual virility.

Beate Uhse's catalogues, which accompanied PR brochures in press packets, offered a domestic counterpart to the thrilling corporeality suggested by the Luftwaffe story: a vision of pleasure that was likewise socially responsible yet individualistic, but which, unlike piloting, was accessible to all. Catalogues portrayed customers who sought pleasure for themselves and their intimate partners by curling up with an erotic book, by admiring their partner's body clad in a negligee or wearing a musk perfume, or by having a baby at just the right time. Catalogues harped on products' ability to preserve marriages and could have legitimized erotica by emphasizing the Basic Law's commitment to marriage. But when Beate Uhse cited the Basic Law in the 1963 catalogue, it was to quote the article guaranteeing the unfettered development of the personality.[69] Beate Uhse enabled journalists, whose defense of sexual liberties had required collective goals, to describe the search for individual sexual pleasure as equally legitimized by liberal principles.

The Luftwaffe story also offered a narrative of postwar sexual pleasure that crossed demarcations of gender. Media reference to the war years had usually portrayed a sex-segregated world—men at the fighting front, women at the home front—and discussion of the postwar "sexual crisis" took wartime alienation of the sexes as its starting point. Yet the birth control pill appeared to eliminate the most significant difference between women's and men's sexual experience: the ability of one sex but not the other to enjoy sex without fear of pregnancy. Uhse in uniform suggested a path from war to recovery to pleasure made more plausible by emerging from a more holistically gendered Nazi-era experience. Uhse personified the "Aryan superwoman" whose physicality had enabled her to enjoy romance, bear strong babies, *and* enjoy sport and adventure. But she also knew the military experience that had so powerfully shaped a generation of men. Uhse in uniform thus transformed the common narrative of sexual alienation into a story that more easily progressed from war to healing and then to "seventh heaven."

Uhse in uniform recalled the Nazi era. Yet in its individuality, even within a totalitarian context, the image underscored her claims for a sexuality for a liberal age: individualistic but socially responsible, not hedonistic. At the same time, in its hermaphrodism, it overcame the damaging sex segregation of the war. Finally, it captured a type of excitement that the language of social stabilization and economic recovery had been unable to convey. The integration of legal and commercial concerns, and the merging of various aspects of respectability, are clear in the comments of a veteran of the firm (and her stepson) regarding the new advertising strategy:

> She was trying to get erotica out of the gutter. And [as she presented her-self] she was predestined for this: she was the daughter of a doctor, she came from an estate, she was with the Luftwaffe, she flew, she had three children . . . sometimes four. And she was married, and directed a firm, and so she couldn't be what people imagined about her. Somehow the whole packet, doctor's daughter, daughter of the countryside, test pilot, wife and mother of four children—that was all in all a positive image. And naturally it also made it easier to stand before the court, when one stood there with this whole aura.[70]

Conclusion: Beate Uhse and the Teleology of Sexual Liberation

As the Beate Uhse Myth became well-known, it became an easily referenced shorthand for the passage from Nazism through crisis and recovery to a liberated sexuality. So neatly did it seem to encapsulate German history that it told inspirational and cautionary tales with equal ease. Sexual revolutionaries saw Beate Uhse as personifying the corruptions of sexuality under capitalism, and by extension under a fascism that had not been fully overcome.[71] For antipornography feminists, Uhse showed that both Nazism and the pornography industry profited as a few women liberated themselves at the expense of the many.[72] Compilations excerpted Uhse's autobiography to portray women's strength (Uhse's) and distress (her customers') during the "rubble years."[73] Business texts and newspaper series on entrepreneurs featured Uhse as an icon of the economic miracle.[74] As the Myth became part of the West German vocabulary, it was naturalized. Those who drew on it presented it as a self-contained, logical, and complete story, even as they emphasized different episodes or drew different lessons from it.

To this day, when the Beate Uhse Myth is evoked in reference to the 1950s, it is to illustrate the prudish nature of that decade. The Myth tells us that Uhse had to battle obscenity suits, even as she educated ignorant West Germans about sex, and even as consumer demand demonstrated the need for her goods. But the 1950s was not just the decade in which Uhse's business gained a firm footing. It was also the decade in which Uhse and her staff began to assemble the Myth.

And the Myth was never only about sex; if it were, it would not have become so useful as a shorthand for German history. As diverse aspects of the battle for respectability informed not only Uhse's struggle for her business but also the making of the Myth, they helped to create the vocabulary with which West Germans would later understand the transformations of the mid-twentieth century.

Uhse's sex and family life helped to establish respectability with her customers and staff in the early years of her business. This fact informed the incorporation of feminized stories of her personal life into the Myth: her marriages, her experience as a widow with a young child, her talks with women during the rubble years. Once ensconced in the Myth, such stories highlighted women's strength and vulnerability as important elements of postwar history. But in the courtroom, social standing and responsible entrepreneurship were equally critical elements of respectability. As they were woven into the Myth, they laid the groundwork for Uhse to personify the golden opportunity for newcomers offered by the economic miracle. Older businesses' survival after 1945, sometimes despite participation in Nazi-era atrocities, was not part of this story. Finally, journalists valued Uhse's ability to explain sexual consumption and the quest for pleasure in liberal terms. In the Myth, Uhse became not only a sexual educator and productive entrepreneur, but also a defender of freedom in a fragile democracy.

Within the context of the Myth, the Luftwaffe story was never about an unusual woman's activities in Nazi Germany. Only flight clubs were interested in Uhse's flying career in isolation.[75] And so we should not interpret media fascination with Uhse's Luftwaffe history as an effort to make Nazi-era military service appear harmless, or as any kind of discussion of the Nazi era in its own right. For purveyors of the Myth, the Luftwaffe episode had meaning only in conjunction with the postwar chapters, which themselves reflected a thick layering of concerns of gender, sexuality, class, entrepreneurship, and liberalism in the early Federal Republic. In implying an elevated social status and service to the Volk in the Nazi era, the Luftwaffe story helped to establish an elevated social status and service to the common good in the postwar era. In portraying an individualistic experience of corporeal pleasure even in a totalitarian environment, the Luftwaffe story helped to establish the compatibility of sexual pleasure and liberal individualism. And in connection with Uhse's initiative in addressing women's need for contraception in the rubble years and her resoluteness against those who would shut her down, the Luftwaffe story became a history of self-assuredness, willingness to buck convention, and strength against adversity.

Few elements of the Beate Uhse Myth were unique to it. War movies and popular military magazines recalled the excitement of military activity; images of the "women of the rubble" portrayed women's strength after the war; the myth of the "zero hour" told of a new world in which Germans created wealth and built a democracy. What was unique about the Beate Uhse Myth was that the destination of the trajectory was *sex*. Sexual revolutionaries' theories of sexual liberation required a sharp break with the past.[76] The Beate Uhse Myth required only incremental steps to move from the Nazi era to sexual liberation—energetic and decisive steps, to be sure, but drawing on the same energy and decisiveness that Germans like Uhse had exhibited before 1945. And the incremental nature of the Beate Uhse Myth made its progress inevitable. Sexual revolutionaries' revolution might never occur, or it might never spread beyond a counterculture. The Beate Uhse Myth told of evolution, not revolution: dramatic, leaving a changed world in its wake, but inexorable.

Notes

For their comments on earlier drafts or portions of this material, I thank Irmgard Hill, Robert Moeller, Dirk Rotermund, Wendy Schneider, Johanna Schoen, Jonathan Wiesen, the participants of the 2003 conference "Selling Modernity: Advertising and Public Relations in Modern German History" (Ontario, Canada), members of the "Wine, Cheese, and Gender" group at the University of Iowa, and the anonymous readers of this volume. I am especially grateful to the erotica firms that permitted me to examine their papers, industry veterans who agreed to interviews, consumers and their descendents who made materials available, and Angelika Voß-Louis of the Forschungsstelle für Zeitgeschichte in Hamburg (FZH) for her role in creating an archive and library of West German erotica and sexual science. Page numbers for interviews refer to uncorrected transcripts; tapes and transcripts are at the FZH. Funding from the National Endowment for the Humanities (FA-36988-02), the Howard Foundation, the Obermann Center for Advanced Study at the University of Iowa, and the College of Liberal Arts and Sciences at the University of Iowa supported this research.

1. Van Steen, *Liebesperlen*, 72–73.
2. "Vorher gab es bloss Beischlaf, mit Beate Uhse kam der Sex," BZ, 19 July 2001, 54.
3. Beate Köstlin married Hans-Jürgen Uhse in 1939 and was widowed in 1944. She began her postwar career as Beate Uhse. Her 1949 marriage to Ernst-Walter Rotermund ended in divorce in 1972. Although her legal name (and her identity to friends and family) was Beate Rotermund, the general public knew her as Beate Uhse. I refer to the firm as Beate Uhse and the person as Uhse.
4. Uhse openly describes the Beate Uhse Myth as a marketing device in Uhse, *Lustvoll in den Markt*, 69–72.
5. For example, Monika Siedentopf, "Die Lust-Macherin," *Die Zeit*, 20 March 2003, 28;

Hannelore Hippe, "Nur Fliegen ist schöner: Die Unternehmerin Beate Uhse," MDR (Mitteldeutscher Rundfunk) 1999, broadcast Bayerischer Rundfunk, 25 February 2001; Rupp Doinet, "Grande Dame der niederen Instinkte," *Stern*, 26 July 2001, 40–44. The autobiography is Uhse with Pramann, *Mit Lust und Liebe*. It was later republished with a new final chapter: Beate Uhse with Ulrich Pramann, *Ich will Freiheit für die Liebe* (Munich: List, 2001).

6. On other firms, see Heineman, "The Economic Miracle in the Bedroom." Uhse acknowledges some of her early competitors in passing in *Mit Lust und Liebe*, 114, 121, 152.

7. The literature on "coming to terms with the past" is large; important recent works on the phenomenon outside the memorial setting include Moeller, *War Stories*; Frei, *Vergangenheitspolitik*. On coming to terms with the past in connection with gender and sexuality, see Heineman, "Gender, Sexuality, and Coming to Terms with the Past."

8. By contrast, see Christiane Eifert, "Unternehmerinnen im Nationalsozialismus. Paula Busch und Käthe Kruse blicken zurück," in Schaser, *Erinnerungskartelle*, 117–140.

9. *Stimmt in unserer Ehe alles?*, Beate Uhse catalogue (1952).

10. *Gesunde Ehe — glückliche Ehe*, Beate Uhse catalogue (1963).

11. ". . . Alles Ansichtssache," aus einem Vortrag von W.L., Vereinigung westdeutscher Versandunternehmen (n.d.; ca. 1957), EL 317 I, Bü 2339, Staatsarchiv Ludwigsburg (stAL).

12. Dr. med. E.L., "Statistisches Material aus dem Alltag," talk delivered at the conference "Das Süsse Leben," Evangelische Akademie Tutzing, 7 April 1962, Sammlung Bundesverband Erotik Handel, Hamburg.

13. See Alon Confino's plea for greater integration of "public" and "private" memory in "Telling About Germany."

14. Marchand, *Creating the Corporate Soul*. In the West German setting, see Wiesen, *West German Industry*; Erker, "'A New Business History'?"

15. Berenson, *The Trial of Madame Caillaux*; Taylor, *In the Theater of Criminal Justice*; Robb and Erber, *Disorder in the Court*.

16. On media attraction to personalities and scandal, see Walkowitz, *City of Dreadful Delight*; Schwartz, *Spectacular Realities*. For the West German case, see Schoenbaum, *The Spiegel Affair*; Kruip, *Das "Welt."*

17. Herzog, *Sex after Fascism*.

18. Ernst-Walter Rotermund grew up in a Flensburg shipping family; he returned from a POW camp with a fully formed plan in his head for a mail-order hair tonic business. He was active in Beate Uhse in the early years. On Uhse's control of the firm's image, see Hans Werner Melzer and Bärbel Melzer, interview with author, 9 September 2003; Irmgard Hill, interview with author, 25 February 2003, 68; Dirk Rotermund, interview with author, 10 September 2003, 16.

19. On the significance of the local community to businesses, see Berghoff, *Zwischen Kleinstadt und Weltmarkt*.

20. Uhse, *Lustvoll in den Markt*, 57; Melzer interview, 89, 91; Rotermund interview, 19 June 2003, 12–13; Hill interview, 27.

21. *Stimmt in unserer Ehe alles?*, Beate Uhse catalogue (1952); *Die besten Jahre unseres Lebens: Ein Helfer und Führer für das Liebes- und Eheleben*, Beate Uhse catalogue (1958), 3–14.

22. The following description draws on these general product catalogues. All appeared for many years; these notes give the approximate date of first publication: *Stimmt in unserer Ehe alles?* (1952); . . . *sie sind glücklich!* (1958); *Die besten Jahre unseres Lebens* (1958); *Gesunde Ehe, glückliche Ehe* (1963); *Glückliche Ehe, gesunde Ehe* (1964). Specialty catalogues usually omitted the framing texts; see, however, *Liebe: uralt und immer wieder jung* (1962), 16–17.

23. On Weimar reform, see Grossmann, *Reforming Sex*. On memories of women as victims, see Heineman, "The Hour of the Woman." On hope for the family in the early FRG, see Moeller, *Protecting Motherhood*; Ruhl, *Verordnete Unterordnung*.

24. *Stimmt in unserer Ehe alles?* (1952), back cover. In the 1980s, Uhse revised this portion of her biography to omit the doctor as intermediary and instead emphasize woman-to-woman talks between her and her neighbors. This story appears in Uhse with Pramann, *Mit Lust und Liebe* and subsequent media coverage; it is now the standard tale of the origins of Uhse's business.

25. Stamps in . . . *sie sind glücklich!*, 9; photo of children in *Liebe: uralt und immer wieder jung*, 16; on the 1955 use of photos of her sons, see Uhse, *Lustvoll in den Markt*, photo insert following page 96. See also *Liebe, das schönste Wort auf Erden!*, Beate Uhse catalogue (n.d., ca. 1960).

26. . . . *sie sind glücklich!*, 5. On the "corporate personality," see also Marchand, *Creating the Corporate Soul*, 26–35.

27. Heineman, "Economic Miracle in the Bedroom."

28. 26 November 1960, Hans Giese, Fachwissenschaftliche Gutachten, STAL, EL 317 I / 2343, folio 1024-1035, STAL, The mailing list of Internationales Versandhaus Gisela, another giant that carried a similar line of products, was about 16 percent female; firms that did not carry contraceptives had a yet smaller proportion of female customers. 25 July 1957, Landeskriminalpolizei Hildesheim Tgb. Nr. 3811/57, Vermerk, EL 317 I / 2342, folio 332–339, STAL; W. Pohl, "Der Bezieherkreis unzüchtiger Schriften und Bilder," *Kriminalstatistik* 8 (1954). On problems of interpreting these statistics, see Heineman, "The Economic Miracle in the Bedroom."

29. *Gesunde Ehe—Glückliche Ehe*, 6.

30. Ibid., 5. The colloquialism about the war is even more masculine in the German: "Als Einfliegerin ihren Mann zu stehen."

31. Melzer interview; Rotermund interview, 10 September 2003, 17.

32. Uhse with Pramann, *Mit Lust und Liebe*, 180–182. The indictment quoted here was written no earlier than 1966, but in Uhse's mind it was clearly of a piece with the Flensburg Tennis Club story. Earlier indictments (and judgments) employed language similar to the one Uhse quotes.

33. The courts' handling of obscenity in this era is poorly researched but constitutes part of my larger research on sexual consumer culture in West Germany before the legalization of pornography. For activist and legislative attempts to regulate obscenity and "youth-endangering" materials, see Fehrenbach, *Cinema in Democratizing Germany*; Adelheid von Saldern, "Kulturdebatte und Geschichtserinnerung: Der Bundestag und das Gesetz über die Verbreitung jugendgefährdender Schriften (1952/53)," in Bollenbeck and Kaiser, *Die janusköpfigen 50er Jahre*; Masse, *Prädikat wertlos*.

34. Landgericht Flensburg, 29 September 1953 (5b MS 31/51 NS (IB 67/53)), 18-9/1.2 (I), FZH.

35. Erker and Pierenkemper, *Deutsche Unternehmer zwischen Kriegswirtschaft und Wieder-aufbau*; Wiesen, *West German Industry*. On the Schleswig-Holstein setting, see Godau-Schüttke, *Die Heyde-Sawade-Affäre*; Godau-Schüttke, *Ich habe nur dem Recht gedient*.

36. Volker Berghahn, "Recasting Bourgeois Germany," in Schissler, *The Miracle Years*, 326–340; Rotermund interview, 19 June 2003, 48–49.

37. Not all elements of the biography appear in all judgments, but all listed here appear by 1953. One of the most complete is I. Grosse Strafkammer des Landgerichts in Flensburg, 29 September 1953 (5b MS 179/51 NS (IB 66/53)), 18-9/1.2 (I), FZH.

38. I. Grosse Stafkammer des Landgerichts in Flensburg, 27 September 1951 (5b MS. 31/51), 351/1778 (a), folio 14–15, Landesarchiv Schleswig-Holstein (LASH).

39. Schöffengericht Flensburg, 28 June 1951 (5b MS. 31/51), 351/1778 (a) folio 9, LASH; I. Grosse Strafkammer des Landgerichts in Flensburg (MS 31/51 NS (IB 124/51)), 351/1778 (a) folio 15, LASH; Beate Rotermund to the Generalstaatsanwalt, Schleswig, 28 January 1952, 18-9/1.2 (I), FZH.

40. For example, Landgericht Flensburg, 16 July 1952 (5b MS 179/51 NS (IB 107/52)), 18-9/1.2 (I), FZH; 2. Grosse Strafkammer des Landgerichts in Aachen in der Sitzung vom 28 October 1958 (6 KMS 1/56 / II 146/58), 18-9/1.2 (I), FZH; Uhse, *Lustvoll in den Markt*, 59; Melzer interview.

41. For example, Landgericht Flensburg, 15–16 July 1952 (5 MS. 31/51), 18-9/1.2 (I), 4, FZH. On this phenomenon more generally, see Sigel, *Governing Pleasures*.

42. "Inhaberin eines Flensburger Versandhauses erneut angeklagt," *Kieler Nachrichten* 29 November 1961, 786/2421, folio 89, LASH.

43. For similar themes in trials of some of Uhse's competitors, see I. Strafsenat des Bundes-gerichtshofs in der Sitzung vom 20 November 1962 (I StR 426/62), EL 317 I, Bü 2341, folio 89–92, STAL; Auszug aus einem Urteil des Landgerichts Hamburg betr. die Fa. Haku-Versand (H.K.) in Hamburg, Anlage 2 zum Beisitzerrundbrief Nr. 19 (BPrst) [1962], 351/4020 folio 6–11, especially 11, LASH.

44. Hans W. Müller, "Eindeutige Zweideutigkeiten," *Der neue Vertrieb* 4, no. 67 (February 1952): 49–50.

45. On postwar West German businessmen's efforts to demonstrate their commitment to the social good, see Wiesen, *West German Industry*.

46. Uhse, *Lustvoll in den Markt*, 18–40, 57.

47. Clippings in LASH 351/1778 (a).

48. Uhse, *Lustvoll in den Markt*, 27–28.

49. 3 July 2000 Vortrag, Marketing Club, Bremen, 18-9 / 2.3, FZH. In the early 1960s, the firm also revamped its internal organization, built new facilities, and pioneered storefront shops for erotica.

50. Wiesen, *West German Industry*, 98–118.

51. 7 November 1958, Beate Uhse to the Bundesprüfstelle für jugendgefährdende Schriften, 18-9/1.2, FZH. The brochure mentioned in this letter, *Wir über uns*, does not survive.

52. Edna Nageshkar, "Unser Presse-Referent," *Absender: Beate* 5, no. I (February 1966): 3; "Liebe Mitarbeiter!," *Absender: Beate* 2, no. 2 (April 1963): 1; 18-9, 2.3, FZH.

53. "Der 'unbekannte' Nachbar den Millionen kennen," PR brochure (1961).

54. Ibid.; "Wem interessiert das schon? Wir dachten: zum Beispiel SIE!," PR brochure (1962), both in XIII Dr. 25, Stadtarchiv Flensburg.

55. Veronika [no last name], "Bundesverfassungsgericht soll entscheiden," *Flensburger Presse*, 14 December 1961, 786/2421, folio 93, LASH. See also other clippings in this file and "Jugendschutzgesetz umstritten," *Stuttgarter Nachrichten*, 30 November 1961.

56. Melzer interview, 3 September 2003; Rotermund interview, 19 June 2003, 56; Rotermund interview, 10 September 2003, 11; Uhse with Pramann, *Mit Lust und Liebe*, 166.

57. "Aufklärung für Erwachsene, 5.Teil," *Constanze*, 1 October 1963, 6–9, 52; "Par. 218: Abtreibung," dir. Peter V. Jahn und Peter Nischk, broadcast 1 Deutscher Fernsehen, 24 October 1966.

58. "Beate Uhse: Dieses und jenes," *Der Spiegel* 19, no. 22 (1965): 92–93; "Rapid Turnover on Supermarket for Sex." The Luftwaffe episode also takes a light tone in the youth-oriented *Jasmin*: "Was hält Herr Uhse von Frau Uhse?," *Jasmin* 14, no. 10 (1968): 63–76. Foreign press coverage of the Luftwaffe episode was often more pointed, e.g., "Länsberg, Ullerstam lärare i kontinentens största kärleksskola," *Norrländska Socialdemokraten* 23 November 1966, 1; "Cette Allemande veut pervertir les Francais," [unidentified tabloid], 30 May 1966; George Edwards, "Flying Frau Heads a Sex Empire," *News of the World*, 17 April 1966; all in 18-9/2.1, FZH.

59. Heineman, *What Difference Does a Husband Make*, 169.

60. Moeller, *War Stories*; Frank Biess, "Survivors of Totalitarianism: Returning POWs and the Reconstruction of Masculine Citizenship in West Germany, 1945–1955," in Schissler, *The Miracle Years*, 57–82.

61. For example, the collection of editorials opposing the law in Bayerisches Hauptstaatsarchiv (BAYHSTA), M Inn 92083. On the law, see Saldern, "Kulturdebatte und Geschichtserinnerung"; Maase, *Prädikat wertlos*. On the print media's defense of its liberal privileges (despite its social conservatism), see Hachmeister and Siering, *Die Herren Journalisten*; Schoenbaum, *The Spiegel Affair*.

62. Moeller, *Protecting Motherhood*; Ruhl, *Verordnete Unterordnung*; Niehuss, *Familie, Frau und Gesellschaft*. The commentary to the Basic Law included the formulation "cell of the state."

63. Höhn, *GIs and Fräuleins*; Angela Delille and Andrea Grohn, "Von leichten Mädchen, Callgirls, und PKW-Hetären," in *Hart und Zart: Frauenleben 1920–1970* (Berlin: Elefanten, 1990), 335–339.

64. Lutz Niethammer, "'Normalization' in the West: Traces of Memory Leading Back into the 1950s," in Schissler, *The Miracle Years*, 237–265.

65. Herzog, *Sex after Fascism*.

66. Höhn, *GIs and Fräuleins*; Fehrenbach, *Cinema in Democratizing Germany*, 131–135.

67. For example, "Anti-Baby Pillen," *Der Spiegel*, 26 February 1964, 75–89; Staupe and Vieth, *Die Pille*; Susanne Preuss, "Interview with Beate Uhse," *Stuttgarter Zeitung* (proofcopy), May 1966.

68. Rieger, "Fast Couples"; Fritzsche, *A Nation of Fliers*; de Syon, *Zeppelin!*

69. *Gesunde Ehe—Glückliche Ehe*, inside back cover.

70. Rotermund interview, 10 September 2003, 17; see also Melzer interview, 69. One step-daughter lived with Uhse only briefly.

71. Reiche, *Sexualität und Klassenkampf*, 97; Amendt, *Sexfront*, 157–170.

72. Filter, "Bomber Pilotin und Porno Produzentin."

73. Bastian, *Niemandszeit*; Angela Delille and Andrea Grohn, "Hauptmann der Aufklärung," in Becker, *Wild Women*, 112–118.

74. Siedentopf, "Die Lust-Macherin"; Eglau, *Die Kasse muss stimmen*.

75. "Rangsdorf"; see also clippings in 18-9 / 2.4, FZH.

76. Herzog, *Sex after Fascism*; Ulrike Heider, "Freie Liebe und Liebesreligion: Zum Sexualitätsbegriff der 60er und der 80er Jahre," in *Sadomasochisten*, 91–136; Reimut Reiche, "Sexuelle Revolution: Erinnerung an einen Mythos," in Baier, *Die Früchte der Revolte*.

9

ROBERT P. STEPHENS

"WOWMAN! THE WORLD'S MOST

FAMOUS DRUG-DOG"

Advertising, the State, and the Paradox of

Consumerism in the Federal Republic

E arly in the summer of 1972, "Wowman, the World's Most Famous Drug-Dog" made his grand entrance tucked away in the pages of the children's comic book *Primo*. Though Wowman may have appeared to youngsters as simply a new comic strip featuring a police dog with a strange group of friends and an unusually strong penchant for bones, his significance was in fact far greater. Wowman was a central part of a federal initiative to harness the power of the advertising industry to turn kids off drugs. The first of its kind in Germany, this nationwide antidrug campaign raises significant questions not only about public health and advertising, but also about the problems of rational choice models in public policy.

Research over the past decade has shown the enormous power of consumerism in the postwar period to transform human relationships, to provide new forms of identification, to create new ways of understanding one's place in the world.[1] In Germany, near the end of the 1950s, consumerism gained a new power in people's lives. The government promoted consumerism as a crucial part of citizenship and the key to Germany becoming an "affluent society."[2] By the early 1970s, with the splintering of existing social and political identities that had taken place during the turbulent 1960s, consumerism gained a new power to create complicated micro distinctions as advertisers began to sell "lifestyles." Yet the very success of consumerism after the late 1950s created its own contradictions. The government's increasing reliance on consumerism as the basis of state stability on the one hand, and as the measure of the well-being of the individual on the other, meant that consumerism left the sphere of political control. The antidrug campaign, or more correctly, the failures of the antidrug campaign, laid bare this contradiction.

The success of consumerism in the postwar period drastically increased standards of living and created an unprecedented level of comfort for all Germans. Advertising acted as the engine for the production of consumer desire, convincing consumers of the value of their aspirations and guiding their consumer choices. Yet consumerism was also a Pandora's box. Advertising, the blunt tool of consumerism, had pried open the doors of consumer desire. But when it became evident at the end of the 1960s and in the early 1970s that untamed consumer desire could create very real social problems, the tools of advertising proved woefully inadequate to keep certain desires trapped within the box. The government had championed consumption as the key to a rising gross national product and the advertising industry had promoted a belief that consumption was constitutive of individual identity, yet neither could control the desires unleashed. By examining the 1972 antidrug campaign, this paradox of consumerism comes to the surface. The West German government, locked in an ideological war with its East German foe, promoted a capitalist vision of modernity, but this vision and the instrumental, economic rationality upon which it was based contained contradictions that could not be resolved. When faced with the rising incidence of drug consumption, the government turned to advertising to try to stem the tide, believing that rational actors, educated about the dangers of drug use, would turn their backs on irrational behavior. Yet the failures of the antidrug campaign illustrate the limits of economic rationality, the tension between public health and consumer desire in the postindustrial world, and the erratic power of advertising over consumer behavior.

Advertising and Public Heath Campaigns

The notion of a public health campaign against "problem" consumption certainly was not new by the 1970s. As early as the turn of the twentieth century, the German Association against the Misuse of Spirits (Deutscher Verein gegen den Mißbrauch geistiger Getränke) published temperance tracts, while its successor, the German Association against Alcohol Misuse (Deutscher Verein gegen den

Alkoholmißbrauch), created a comprehensive educational alcohol abuse campaign for industrial workers and their families during the Weimar Republic.[3] The organized temperance movement continued into the National Socialist period, though increasingly alcoholics and drug abusers were seen as "asocial" enemies of the *Volksgemeinschaft*, rather than as spiritually bankrupt or victims of an illness. As Robert Proctor has pointed out, the public campaigns against alcohol abuse intensified during the Nazi period, increasingly focused on new problems such as the dangers of drinking and driving.[4]

Despite their involvement with the temperance movement and, to a certain extent, with the international antidrug movement, Nazi officials directed the bulk of their energies toward antismoking campaigns. Proctor argues that the Nazi authorities attempted to curtail smoking "through a combination of propaganda, public relations, and official decrees."[5] The Reich Health Ministry published antismoking pamphlets and warned schoolchildren publicly about the dangers of smoking. Antismoking campaigners used celebrities to win hearts and minds; images of Hitler, Mussolini, and Franco were used to warn women and children about the dangers of smoking; even sports stars such as the world heavyweight boxing champion Max Schmeling participated in antismoking advertising. Youth organizations like the Hitler Youth and the League of German Girls published their own antismoking tracts.[6] Despite these concerted campaigns against smoking, however, German cigarette consumption continued an inexorable rise until 1942, when the course of the war and increasing shortages led to a rapid decrease in per capita smoking.[7]

For at least a decade after the war, alcohol and tobacco use remained an expensive pleasure. Until the currency reform in 1948, cigarettes, alcohol, and narcotics played significant roles as high-value currency on the black market. Although the wind had gone out of the sails of the Nazi campaign against various vices and the biological worldview that buttressed these campaigns had become officially anathema, the public health system's media campaigns against drinking and smoking showed remarkable continuity, in both substance and personnel. From the end of the war until the 1970s, the major part of the responsibility for dealing with addiction was devolved to various private and parochial groups. The subsidiarity principle enshrined in the federal system of the Federal Republic ensured that although the public health offices of the various Länder would have a role in the prevention and treatment of addiction, the lead was taken by various anti-addiction organizations and private welfare organizations.[8]

The continuity of institutions and personnel ensured a certain continuity of ideas, arguments, and images between the Weimar, Nazi, and postwar periods. Certain aspects of the National Socialist campaigns were offensive enough to be unrepeatable in the postwar period, particularly those that focused on the link between alcohol and tobacco and racial degeneracy. For instance, in a 1941 illustration from the Nazi antismoking periodical *Reine Luft*, alcohol and tobacco are portrayed as the habits of profligate capitalists, Jews, American Indians, Africans, and prostitutes, leaving behind them a trail of burned cities, blood, and skulls. This kind of overtly racist imagery proved unacceptable in the 1950s, but the more common argument from the Nazi period that money spent on ephemeral pleasure like alcohol and cigarettes prevented useful social consumption remained remarkably similar. For example, another 1941 image from *Reine Luft* depicts a smoker letting the trappings of a better life — travel and consumer goods — go up in smoke. Twelve years later, a pamphlet published jointly by the Baden State Association against the Dangers of Addiction (Baden Landesverband gegen die Suchtgefahren) and the Württemberg Office for Public Health for Protection against the Dangers of Addiction (Württemberg Landesstelle für Volksgesundung zur Abwehr der Suchtgefahren) entitled *Can You Pass on It?* includes the same sentiment and a remarkably similar graphic sensibility. The text tells the reader that the 9.5 billion marks spent yearly on tobacco and alcohol would be better spent on four hundred thousand new homes, a message that would have at least seemed persuasive during the housing crisis of the early 1950s. The same kind of consumer goods that were presented in 1941 reappear: a train (the symbol of travel and tourism), a bicycle, and clothing. The message in both images pointed to the economic rationality that lay at the heart of public health campaigns: the purchase of tobacco and alcohol hampers the fulfillment of "proper" consumer desire. Consumption of certain consumer items should be promoted, but the consumption of wasteful, addictive substances serves as a drain on the nation's resources.

These campaigns of the 1940s and 1950s took place before the introduction of "modern" social science techniques to measure the outcomes of public health campaigns. As researchers, we have none of the statistical baggage of later campaigns. The only measure of success or failure still available is the raw statistics on the sale of tobacco and alcohol over the period. From this perspective, the campaigns seem to have been a failure.[9]

The public health campaigns of the 1940s and 1950s give us some perspective on the antidrug campaigns of the 1970s, but in many ways they were quite different, both in terms of the problem addressed and the means of tackling the prob-

1. "Wie kann man daran vorübergehen?" (How can you pass on it?), B142/404, Bundesarchiv Koblenz. A 1953 pamphlet published by a temperance organization in Baden-Württemberg.

lem. First and foremost, the illicit "drug wave" of the 1960s and 1970s was quite unlike the consumption of cigarettes and alcohol. Not only were the speed, hashish, and LSD of the latter period illegal, but they occupied a space in the economy fundamentally different from the corporate world of the tobacco and alcohol industries. This ambiguous status makes the job of historians much more difficult. We do not have an enormous amount of data from companies, industry groups, or the government to gauge the growth of the drug trade or its extent. We are left to generalize. Yet by examining the growth in police seizures and arrests we can sketch the outline of a significant trade. Indeed, it seems safe to conjecture from the evidence that the exponential growth in the drug trade between 1967 and 1972 would have made it the fastest growing sector of the European econ-

Table. Alcohol and Tobacco Consumption in the Federal Republic, 1950–1975

Year	Number of cigarettes per potential consumer (age >15)	Liters of beer per potential consumer	Liters of hard liquor per potential consumer
1950	622	48	1.4
1960	1,619	120	2.4
1970	2,529	184	3.9
1975	2,556	188	3.9

Source: Wolfgang Glatzer, Karl Otto Hondrich, Heinz Herbert Noll, Karin Stiehr, and Barbara Wornal, eds., *Recent Social Trends in West Germany 1960-1990* (Frankfurt: Campus Verlag, 1992), 441.

omy, far outstripping growth in other consumer goods. And by the early 1970s, the drug trade in the Federal Republic was a multibillion-mark industry.[10] This growth was in itself fairly astonishing. Yet perhaps more astounding was that this growth took place in the absence of the offensive arsenal of modern capitalism: the advertising industry. Although the point is obvious, it merits repetition: the drug trade grew without a single TV ad, without radio spots, without print ads, without product tie-ins, without direct mail, coupons, or giveaways.

It is thus particularly interesting that the government turned to the advertising industry to convince consumers not to consume products that showed phenomenal market growth despite the lack of advertising. Why turn to the professional advertising world instead of having the members of the Federal Center for Health Education (Bundeszentrale für gesundheitliche Aufklärung, hereafter BfgA) design and implement the program? Though the answer to this is probably quite complicated, much of the explanation seems to rest with the growth, both in size and sophistication, of the advertising industry between the 1950s and the 1970s. This period saw significant changes in the scope and practice of advertising. Three of the industrywide transformations deserve special mention because they proved important to the design and implementation of public health campaigns and the antidrug campaign in particular: the triumph of the social sciences, the emergence of market segmentation, and the expansion of international advertising.

Transforming the Advertising World

Advertising and, by extension, public health campaigns underwent a radical transformation over the course of the 1950s and 1960s. This was true throughout the industrialized world, and although much of the impetus for this change came from the "consumers' paradise" of the United States, the new inflection of science-driven marketing and advertising spread rapidly on both sides of the Atlantic. Vance Packard's seminal 1957 book *The Hidden Persuaders* pointed to a not-so-secret secret that advertisers had increasingly turned to social psychologists and sociologists to help them "understand" consumers and consequently sell more goods. Perhaps the most important trend in advertising in the postwar period was this shift to approaching consumption as a science, the spread of the belief that desire could be measured and consequently tamed.[11] Though the German advertising agencies were often wary of the danger of "Americanization," the trend toward scientific market analysis emerged during the Weimar period and triumphed during the 1960s.[12] By then, advertising provided a major source of revenue for the German mass media, and while the vast majority of advertising budgets was spent on newspaper and magazine ads, television advertising became an increasingly valuable sector over the course of the 1960s.[13] By 1960, total advertising expenditure reached DM 2.2 billion;[14] this growth continued almost unabated through the decade. The expansion of market research was fed by the growth of advertising revenue, as advertisers demanded proof of the efficacy of advertising on consumer behavior. According to Karin Knop, this increase in accountability led to a strategic move from advertising to "marketing" as German advertising moved toward an Americanized "full-service agency" model.[15] By the 1970s, the advertising industry had become a major economic player in Germany. Social science–driven advertising had become an omnipresent part of everyday lives and, despite the agency of consumers, had become a significant force in shaping consumer desire.

Although the general rise in the "science" of marketing and the growth of the advertising industry played a large role in the consumer revolution of the 1960s, other, more specific changes in the industry played a substantial role in redefining the relationship between consumption and identity. Specifically, in the 1960s advertising theory and practice shifted from appealing to the mass market to market segmentation. Lizabeth Cohen has convincingly shown that after the recession of 1957–1958, a "market segmentation revolution" took place in the U.S. advertising industry. According to Cohen, the economic expansion of the 1950s increasingly brought industries into competition for a limited amount of consumer purchasing power. This crisis forced the advertising and marketing industries to rethink their strategy, which previously had focused on the "average" consumer or the "average" consumer unit, the household. As Cohen puts it, "Executives had come to recognize that future profits—for their advertisers and hence themselves—depended on identifying market uniformity."[16] Over the course of the 1960s, advertisers, aided by social scientists and social psychologists, increasingly divided consumers into quantifiable "lifestyles" and sold the image wrapped in goods.[17] Although much research on market segmentation in Germany still remains to be done, there is ample evidence that the same process was taking place on the Continent at roughly the same time; perusing any mass publication across the 1960s will illustrate this process.[18] Part of this shift toward lifestyle advertising was the result of the growth of youth culture, the student movement, and the various "countercultures." Indeed, as Detlef Siegfried has pointed out, by the late 1950s social scientists saw teenagers as "pioneers in the jungle of the consumer society."[19] Advertisers were forced to adopt new strategies to reach young consumers who had been heavily influenced by critiques of advertising as propaganda.[20] The industry adapted, and by the 1970s, much of the imagery of the counterculture had been appropriated by advertisers, and often, young members of the counterculture helped advertisers reach this seemingly skeptical audience.[21]

In the realm of public health advertising, market segmentation failed to make significant inroads until the 1970s, when public health campaigners began to look to the advertising world for new models of persuasive communication. Public health campaigns then began to target certain lifestyle groups in their research and especially in media campaigns.[22] When the BfgA began its national antidrug campaign in the early 1970s, market segmentation was a guiding principle.

The third major shift in the advertising and marketing industry that greatly affected the early antidrug campaigns was the growth of multinational advertising agencies. Advertising, of course, was well established in the nineteenth century, but it was not until the postwar period that advertising became dominated by enormous global advertising agencies. Victoria de Grazia links the initial expansion of American advertising might across the Atlantic to the growth of the American auto industry in the 1920s. Indeed, she traces the origins of the American advertising expansion to the arrival of the J. Walter Thompson Agency in a number of European cities, including Berlin, in January 1927, to sell General Motors automobiles. By the 1930s, American advertising was ubiquitous in Europe, hawking a growing number of consumer goods from major U.S. concerns.[23] The expansion of the power of JWT and other American firms that followed (N. W. Ayer and Son, H. K. McCann, and Erwin, Wasey and Company, for example) continued into the 1930s and, in many ways, transformed the traditions of European advertising, stimulating the decline of poster advertising and the shift toward an Americanized version of advertising that focused on textual argumentation.[24]

The seizure of power by the National Socialists in 1933 accelerated changes in the advertising business. The Nazi interest in controlling the media led to a rationalization of circulation figures and advertising rates. And while much of the impetus for these changes was the desire to purge "un-German" elements from the media, the paradoxical effect was to create a more "American" form of advertising, as German advertising vigorously adopted textual-based forms of advertising. The war led to a caesura in American advertising as most American firms pulled out of Europe to wait for the end of hostilities.[25]

Although research still needs to be done on the influence of multinational corporations and ad agencies, it seems certain that a significant portion of the advertising revenue growth in the 1960s and 1970s came from and went to multinational corporations. Firms such as JWT returned to Europe after the war and continued expanding in subsequent decades. Perhaps more important, however, over the course of the 1960s and 1970s, all advertisers in Germany, whether multinationals or German-owned firms, borrowed heavily from advertising forms emerging from the United States.[26] When the BfgA began to plan its anti-drug campaign, rather than employing a German-owned firm, it turned to JWT to design the campaign. Even if it had given the contract to a German firm, the results would probably have differed only slightly. By the 1970s, national advertising styles had largely ceased to matter as advertising forms emerging from the United States increasingly became the international norm.[27]

These three innovations of the 1950s and 1960s—psychometrics, market segmentation, and internationalization—coalesced by the early 1970s. The government bureaucracy, though slow to adopt innovations, by the 1970s had realized the need for modern advertising techniques to fulfill its mission of "unselling" drugs. Rather than running the campaign themselves or through private welfare groups, as they had in the past, the federal government turned to the vanguard of consumer capitalism to convince its young citizens not to consume. The remainder of this essay examines how they went about this, the effects of the campaign, and what this example can tell us about larger changes in advertising and the instrumental logic of public bureaucrats in their attempt to sway youth consumer behavior.

The Campaign

After considerable debate and under pressure for specific financial relief from the Länder, on 12 November 1970, the federal government finally published its first "Action Plan for the Struggle against Narcotics Misuse," a properly weighty title for a "comprehensive" plan. The document itself appears unremarkable. Yet it represents a good approximation of the consensus reached on the drug problem in Germany since the beginnings of the so-called drug wave, and it outlined the approach to be taken by the federal government and, to a certain extent, by the Länder, until an upsurge in drug-related deaths at the end of the 1970s. The Action Plan stressed a two-pronged approach to the drug problem. On the one hand, those who "conduct business in illegal drugs and narcotics and make a profit off the endangerment of others, particularly the young, while burdening society with the costs of remedying the damage caused by them," must be punished to the fullest extent of the law. On the other hand, those "who became mixed up in the spell of drugs and narcotics frivolously and imprudently and cannot free themselves from them through their own power" ought to be offered social and medical assistance.[28]

Along with outlining the basic thrust of public policy for those already involved in the drug scene, the Action Plan called for a concerted antidrug campaign in an effort to prevent young people from taking up drug use and to "educate" the young about the "health danger and social harmfulness" of drugs. In order to promote the public health, to rehabilitate the afflicted, to punish the guilty, and, not least, to alleviate the fiscal burden on the Länder, the federal government pledged DM 1.5 million in immediate funding and promised to continue to help shoulder the costs of the drug war in the future. The campaign, as presented in the Action Plan, stressed creating informational materials, purchasing advertising, producing films, supporting various private welfare initiatives, and constructing an educational series for teachers and others in close contact with young people.[29]

When it came to constructing the actual campaign, the BfgA began with a number of presuppositions. "The misuse of drugs is only a symptom of a complex problem, which can have both social and individual-constitutional psychological causes," they argued. "The drug problem must not be allowed to grow in isolation—it must be uncovered at the roots and combated." As important, they realized that the problem needed to be approached deftly, that even young teens often saw messages from the state as inherently repressive and dismissed them out of hand. Likewise, the BfgA concluded that widespread drug use would not disappear just because media messages told young people that drugs were bad for them.[30]

Acting on a tight budget, the BfgA adopted three foundational principles: minimize losses due to nonselective advertising (*minimale Streuverluste*), maximize consumer acceptance, and maximize cost effectiveness.[31] Acting from these principles, the organizers divided the campaign itself into three primary target groups: parents and educators, teens over fifteen years of age, and the principal group, teens ages twelve to fourteen. Having learned the lessons of the 1960s about market segmentation, the campaign planners targeted specific messages and media at each group. For parents, educators, and social workers, a committee headed by Minister for Youth, Family and Health Käthe Ströbel published a brochure entitled *Information on the Drug Problem* (*Informationen zum Drogen-Problem*). For older teens, the BfgA sought to exploit the explosive popularity of pop music celebrities and of music magazines by publishing "interviews" with musicians about the dangers of drugs. Most of the campaign, most of the expense, and most of the media buys were directed to the target group of young teens. The BfgA saw this group of youngsters as the key to the success of the campaign. Viewing the older teens as already jaded by advertising, the media, and personal experience with drug users as well as being overly suspicious of the government and "propaganda," the planners believed that they had to reach the group of "potential drug users" (*potentielle Erstverwender*). Reaching this market, however, seemed more difficult than reaching the older group. One way was through schools, where curricula were set up for teaching drug education.[32] But if the messages disseminated by schools were dismissed by these teens, what other media might prove efficacious? The BfgA settled on the idea of marketing antidrug messages through comic strips and on the radio, both of which offered the promise of reaching this very specific market segment. The messages aimed at each of these three groups were crafted to appeal to their preconceptions and prejudices and pitched at a level appropriate to each.

Now thirty years into the drug wars, most adults have some familiarity with the basics of drugs. This was not the case in the early 1970s. Indeed, even the ignorance of young people in the period is startling. For example, at the end of 1970, the Institute for Applied Social Science in Bonn-Bad Godesburg completed a representative survey of 1,009 Hamburg citizens on the drug problem. When asked if they personally knew someone who had ever consumed drugs, a shocking 81 percent of all respondents claimed they did not know a single user, and the percentage was even higher for those over thirty-five. When asked about their familiarity with certain drugs, the numbers proved as surprising. Only 35 percent of all respondents had heard of heroin, while only 15 percent knew what cocaine was.[33]

The authors of the brochure targeted just this kind of mass ignorance, perceiving it as a hindrance to rational, informed decision making. If parents knew more about drugs, the authors believed, they could help steer their charges down the right path. Children, on the other hand, would be less likely to try drugs in the first place if they were given the "scientific" facts.[34] This kind of instrumental logic, focused on both adults and teens as "rational consumers," permeated the discussions on the drug problem, not only at the BfgA but in the legislature, in the social science literature, and in the more intellectual public press as well. If only people understood the dangers of drugs, they would choose not to use them. In retrospect, this kind of Enlightenment faith that the invisible hand of an informed, rational market could curb demand appears to be as fanciful as the horror stories in the boulevard papers.

Based on a brochure produced by the Senator for Work, Health and Social Welfare in Berlin, the *Information on the Drug Problem* pamphlet was for many their most reliable information on the physiological and psychological actions of specific drugs, particularly when compared with the vitriolic hysteria spewed by the Springer press. The surprisingly measured tone of the brochure conformed to the consensus among the medical profession, the civil service, and the police: that factual information should be emphasized and that scare tactics often proved counterproductive. The BfgA believed that "the assumptions about drugs must be managed by imparting knowledge (professionally correct information about drugs) and by showing the alternatives to drug consumption."[35]

Despite a commitment to Wissenschaft, however, many of the temperance tropes of inevitable organic decay, common since the nineteenth century, emerged as leitmotifs throughout the brochure. Though readers were asked to come to their own conclusions after reading the "facts" contained in the brochure, they were repeatedly faced with clichés. In the letter from Käthe Ströbel, for instance, the minister opens with the recognition that "it is the nature of mankind to seek out new things beyond that which has been reached and is known and therefore to take on a certain risk. Enthusiasm, intoxication and personal ecstasy are not foreign to human nature." This acknowledgment by a major figure in the federal government at the opening salvos of the drug war appears to be quite progressive. Yet after stressing that drug use can be a part of life, she slips

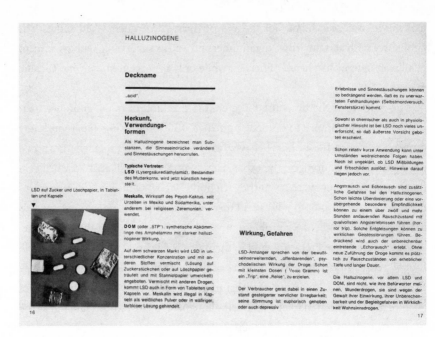

2. Page from *Information zum Drogen-Problem*, B310/236, Bundesarchiv Koblenz. The entry on cannabis products in the first widely distributed drug pamphlet, *Information on the Drug Problem*, produced by the Federal Central Office for Health Education in 1971.

into the familiar mantra of the temperance narrative, the drunkard's progress updated for the hashish generation: "Frequently, all too frequently, these drugs lead directly to illness, to social infirmity [*soziales Siechtum*], and to death."[36]

A similar tone emerges repeatedly throughout the brochure. In the general introduction, after confessing, "We live not only in a mechanized but at the same time a chemical world," the authors conclude with a paragraph so fantastic and spectacular that it deserves quoting at length: "In this 'chemical everyday life' it seems only to be a small step to try drugs that promise a trip with the clouds. This demonstrates the variable risk of these drugs. One risk is the same for all of them: in every case it is a matter of very serious intrusion. With such substances, the brain is forced into such abnormal functions that one can find a comparable state only in the mentally ill. Whoever would like to imagine what this means will reduce the risk of the use of such drugs."[37]

After this introduction, most of the rest of the brochure contains a group-by-group explanation of different drugs, most of which oscillate between demonstrable "facts" (joints = hash cigarettes), politically motivated warnings (claiming that German statistics "confirm" that hashish consumption leads to "hard drug" use), and tepid moralizing (hallucinogens are not "Wunderdrogen" but rather "Wahnsinnsdrogen"—not "miracle drugs" but rather "insanity-inducing drugs").

After the journey through the drug classes, the final two sections give specific examples of the dangers of drugs. The first of the two sections, entitled "Bitter Drug Experience," relates the stories of three young men who learned the lessons of drug use the hard way: a sixteen-year-old apprentice who graduated from hashish to LSD, lost his apprenticeship, and ended up in drug rehab; a twenty-year-old technical draftsman who began using hash with friends but eventually realized the error of his ways and gave it up; and a twenty-year-old loner who left school and his parents' house, joined a commune, and was eventually arrested for robbing a store. The final section contains an interview with a drug addict entitled "Shooting Up Makes You Happy and Dead," first published in *Underground* magazine in 1970. This interview is perhaps the most useful aspect of the brochure, although it is the only part not authored by the committee. The young addict's answer to the question "How would you characterize shooting up? An addiction?," rings much more true and less dogmatic than the rest of the pamphlet: "For me it is a free choice. (!?) Naturally there are people who have been persuaded to do it. I think that's shit. That people don't have any idea where they're leading themselves. I knew where I was leading myself. (?) Of course I'm addicted to drugs, but everyone's addicted to something. I've freed myself from thousands of addictions, and I've traded them for being addicted to drugs."[38]

The added emphasis here is interesting. It is the only place where punctuation is added in the entire brochure, though the punctuation serves not a grammatical function but as a form of commentary. It is as if the editors simply cannot let the addict tell his own story, as if this young man's story is literally incredible. The notion that addiction could be freely chosen is both extraordinarily provocative (!) and incomprehensible (?), while the idea that this young addict could have known where he was leading himself leaves the editors incredulous (?); he must either be disingenuous or self-deluded. In any case, he must not be allowed to speak without some challenge to his authority, without some indication that he is wrong, without some affirmation that addiction is a disease that leads to misery or death. The brochure lives and dies by this contradiction. The creators realize the limits of propaganda; they want to stress the "scientific" facts. Yet the brochure remains an attempt to persuade people not to use drugs. As such, counterarguments or even fragments that do not fit into this archetype must be questioned, confronted, and rejected. In the end, the brochure *is* propaganda, and try as the authors might to bend it into a simple statement of fact, the propaganda function trumps the truth value.

Judged on its own terms, however, the brochure was a success. It did what it set out to do: it provided "scientific" information to the woefully uninformed; it delivered the political message set out in the federal Action Plan; and, perhaps most important, it reached its audience and reinforced preexisting notions (that drugs were an imminent threat to the body and the mind). If the brochure satisfied its authors, its effect on the public was less than satisfactory. According to the market researchers hired by the BfgA, there were a number of significant problems with both the design of the brochure and the execution of the campaign.

After the publication of the brochure, the BfgA engaged the Institute for Market and Advertising Research (Institut für Markt- und Werbeforschung GMBH) in Cologne to research the effectiveness of the brochure on both adults and teens. Not surprisingly, the agency had a different view of the drug problem than the Ministry for Youth, Family, and Health. Rather than treating drugs as a social or cultural peculiarity, they began with the initial assumption that drug consumption "at the basic level cannot be differentiated from other behavior patterns and consumer habits."[39] This presupposition marked a significant departure from the government's approach. The government preferred to place drugs within the area of expertise of the physicians and criminologists, rather than as part of the consumer sciences. After all, consumerism, at least since Ludwig Erhardt's turn as finance minister, had been heralded as fundamentally good; drug consumption could not be seen as a good and, therefore, fell outside of the aegis of consumerism. If the state wanted to force an end to the drug trade, however, advertising and public relations experts were guided by market logic: that drugs were like other consumer goods. If they were products, they had a market, and presumably this market was organized by collective ideas that market researchers could uncover and manipulate. The market analysis stressed the differences between the reception of young people and that of their parents' generation. Parents, the authors reported, tended to receive their information from the media, which had "demonized" drug consumption and consumers. As a result, their conclusions were skewed. Parents believed, for instance, that hashish and amphetamines caused hallucinations, even more so than LSD. Because of their "uninformed way of seeing drugs as equivalent" ("ihre unwissend nivellierende Einschätzung"), parents divided themselves from their children.[40] Young people, on the other hand, proved to be much more informed and received their information from a number of sources (associations, brochures, books, etc.). Indeed, throughout the report young people are praised for being more "enlightened" about drug use than their parents.

The market researchers came to uncomfortable conclusions. They judged the brochure to be a failure. "In summary, we can conclude that the two brochures, in view of the spontaneous impressions, had a significantly weaker reception than comparable advertisements," they declared. "This background should be taken into consideration here since this kind of information is in competition with all the other information flooding consumers every day." In addition to this reminder that antidrug messages had to compete with other media, the most important insight offered to the public health experts by the market researchers was the notion that information is not simply injected into consumers. According to the marketers, the disconnect between what the brochure had to say and what young people were hearing elsewhere led to "cognitive dissonance."[41] For instance, telling teens that hashish was as unsafe as heroin and LSD belied what they already knew. Ultimately, this dissonance led young people to reject everything they were told by the government because the brochure could not come to terms with their own experiences.

The market researchers collected and analyzed data from focus groups made up of both teenagers and adults. One thirty-six-year-old father from the middle class bemoaned the histrionic tone of the brochures, adding the sardonic postscript, "Do the authors actually have children in at-risk ages?" A working mother in her early forties proved to be less skeptical: "They write so well that even the unacquainted are well informed about the issue, we are introduced to the dangers as they actually are." The younger voices, on the other hand, highlighted the cognitive dissonance the researcher emphasized. A middle-class student, age fourteen, pointed out that young people often take drugs to shock their parents. "The experiences in it [the brochure] aren't very frightening. Rather an incitement," she stressed. "Then, there's mother and father falling from their stools when they hear that their kids smoke hash. Some really want that!!"[42]

The final conclusions from the market researchers were damning. Statistically, there was almost no change in opinions after reading the brochures, even immediately after reading it. The researchers questioned whether the brochure in its present form was an efficient medium and suggested that the BfgA should consider lowering their expectations. In summary the Institute concluded:

Without wanting to repeat the individual conclusions in the overall results, here in conclusion we recommend that the theme, composition and realization of the "Anti-Drug Campaign" be fundamentally rethought and a coordinated total strategy developed, which is not only fixated on narcotics but first and foremost also influences the remaining strong public opinion builders in the sense of the planned strategy. Nothing hinders the success of communication more than information that can be contradicted.[43]

In spite of these fundamental reservations, the brochure was published, and by 1973 approximately 2.5 million copies had been distributed. The report by the Institute pointed out many of the problems with the text and layout, but it did not answer other fundamental questions about what happened to the brochure once it found its way out into the world. Two years after the initial design the BfgA undertook a study of the brochure's distribution. They found enormous inefficiencies: groups had received double deliveries or none at all; some had been given far more copies than they could ever use; others could not keep enough in stock. For example, according to their records, the BfgA had delivered thirty-five thousand brochures to the Hamburg Work and Social Welfare Authority. But when they followed up during their distribution research they were told a fantastic story. The social worker charged with the distribution recalled how a large truck had arrived and how the office manager, the truck driver, and he had spent hours unloading boxes, so many that they feared the floor of their office would collapse. The office manager and the social worker then had to decide how they would ever get rid of the enormous number of brochures. They delivered boxes to every office they could think of. In a fit of desperation, the social worker even began taking his two daughters to the main train station in the evenings and handing the brochures out to anyone who would take them. Despite this mammoth effort, he still had many boxes left over. When asked by the interviewer if he thought that there had been 150,000 delivered, he answered, "Yes, at least!"[44]

Yet that explains only part of the distribution problem. What would the consumers do with the brochures? The review gave some examples of rampant skepticism:

> For example, at the Jakob Fugger School they told us that after the brochures were distributed, the majority of them were found in the wastebaskets. One had to approach the distribution of the "Information" brochure to youth with some skepticism: "They can figure out how to use drugs from the brochure." Because of this, the Tempelhof Health Office ended the trial of leaving brochures lying out by the porter's office for

those interested. One had to come to the conclusion that after a time they were being picked up almost exclusively by youth who one would suspect were drug addicts or even dealers.[45]

So not only did distribution fail, but when it worked, the response was often dismissive or ironic. Even when people did read the material and absorb the message, there was no guarantee they would remember it. The instrumental logic of the rational consumer of information proved to be an organizing principle and a fundamental mistake. Given the truth about drugs, different groups could and did come to different conclusions. The brochures could be both informative to parents and a fetish object for young drug consumers; they could be deadly serious or ironically amusing, depending on the readers.

While the brochures fit into a fairly traditional public health model, the BfgA placed the direct advertising campaigns aimed at teens in the hands of the advertising world. Rather than designing and implementing these promotions, as they had the brochure, the BfgA turned the youth campaigns over to the J. Walter Thompson Agency in Frankfurt. The relationship proved to be a complicated one, and the correspondence between the two proves that working together was trying for both sides. The ad agency took over the primary role. They would design mock-ups, send them to the BfgA, and then wait for a critique. When the rules of design and advertising efficiency butted up against the demands of public health, or the public health bureaucracy, the latter inevitably won.

A decision was made early on that the key group was adolescents ages twelve to fourteen. The rationale was that these children were still too young to begin experimenting with drugs, and that if one waited until they were in their later teens, it was already too late, the cognitive dissonance would overwhelm the message of the advertising campaign. Even though JWT decided to focus on the younger group, they did want to reach older teens and particularly those who had begun experimenting with drugs. They believed this market segment, "at-risk" teens, could best be reached by advertising in music magazines. They surmised, quite correctly, that rock music and drugs went hand in hand.[46] In order to reduce the cognitive dissonance, the advertisers at J. Walter Thompson decided to attempt to use the powerful link of drugs and music against itself. Rather than produce the facts about drugs and let those "facts" speak for themselves, like the model used in the brochure, they decided to run interviews with rock stars already associated with drugs explaining why they had quit and why drugs were a dead end. They assembled quite a lineup of artists to take part in the campaign: John Lennon, James Taylor, Grace Slick, Roger Waters from Pink

Floyd, Pete Townshend and Roger Daltrey from The Who, Jon Hiseman, the drummer for Colosseum, and Rosemary Butler from the all-girl quartet Birtha.

The interviews, mostly excerpted from previous interviews, were run from June until December 1972 in a number of popular music magazines (*Musikexpress*, *Popfoto*, *Crash*, *ran*, *Musikboutique*, and *Pop*) and reprinted in school newspapers throughout Germany. These interviews—though the term "interview" normally implies honest, unscripted answers—presented an interesting moral dilemma for the BfgA, if not for the advertising agency. Though it proved to be not much of an obstacle, the dilemma was whether to run the interviews as journalism or as advertising. The crux of the problem rested in the acknowledgment that this material was, in fact, coming from the government. If the young readers of these magazines knew that this was government-sponsored material, would they simply reject it as propaganda? The preface to the documents in the Federal Archive notes specifically that the interviews were run as "editorially created advertisements" (*redaktionell gestaltete Anzeigen*) in order to "secure their acceptance by the target group."[47] The ad agency and the BfgA concluded that playing the interviews as straight news without any acknowledgment that the government was involved, and indeed paying for the media buy, was not a problem that would keep them up at night.[48]

The ethical problems with this are evident. Does the government have a responsibility to citizens to differentiate information from official organs from news and entertainment created in the private sphere? If not, how are citizens to differentiate between entertainment, which may lack the weight of government pronouncements, and propaganda? Or, on an even more cynical note, how are citizens to differentiate between truth and propaganda? In a democratic society that deemed a free press to be the cornerstone of protecting the population from a repetition of tyranny, the notion that the government would purposefully hide government-sponsored information as journalism ought to have raised alarms within the bureaucracy; this seems not to have been the case. I have been able to uncover neither serious debate within the bureaucracy nor any dissent from the publications themselves; the government bought the space, and the magazines published ads as news. Money overcame ethics.

The interviews themselves are fairly predictable, a mixture of general questions and a recitation of how drugs had negatively affected people's lives. Dolf Hartmann's interview with Pete Townshend and Roger Daltrey in December 1972 demonstrates the format at its least subtle. Hartmann notes how much success The Who had in the 1960s and asks Townshend what were the worst times in that decade. Townshend answers predictably: "Oh, we were totally freaked out then. Then the moment came when I couldn't believe in success any longer — and I reached for drugs at the same time. I just sat there forever and asked myself: 'what is it actually all about?' . . . Drugs always lead people to the same thing: bad luck and problems. But drugs can't solve your problems — even when they promise you an answer." Later, Hartmann notes that many musicians have posited a link between drug use and creativity and asks Roger Daltrey about his experience. Daltrey responds, "No! We took speed, smoked hash and 'grass' — but our music never needed it. It's similar to alcohol. You try it, it's good — and then . . ." Hartmann interrupts: "Then perhaps the point comes when there's no longer a way back." Daltrey responds with a final flourish so clichéd that even stoned teens would be hard-pressed to take it seriously: "Sure, I've lost a lot of friends that way."[49]

The interview with John Lennon, a peculiarly excerpted and translated version of Lennon's 1970 interview with *Rolling Stone* magazine, seems less scripted and proves to be more interesting, though the message seems out of place for government-sponsored propaganda.[50] After discussing Lennon's early drug use, the unnamed interviewer (Jann Wenner) asks him what he thinks about his early behavior. Rather than giving the kind of scripted answer evident in The Who's interview, Lennon suggests that drug use is irresponsible when it distracts from revolutionary goals: "Simple. We must recognize realities. There are still class differences, there are still weapons being sold to Africa and blacks murdered on the streets. The people still live in fucking poverty, nothing's changed. Only I've gotten older and a bunch of people are wandering around with long hair. Simple imitation isn't enough. One must think and then act. One must do something. I pulled 'Lucy in the sky' out of the air. 'Power to the people' should replace it."[51]

Though the interview is certainly an antidrug message, it seems peculiar that the German government in the summer of 1972, after the Red Army Faction bombings in May and the arrest of Andreas Baader and Holger Meins in June, would publicly acknowledge its preference for revolution over drug consumption. Certainly the government wanted to reduce, if not end, youth drug consumption, but even Willy Brandt would have taken issue with "Power to the people."

Yet these interviews posed little danger to the pillars of the state, as later market research showed. The follow-up survey of the target segment showed that, other than John Lennon and James Taylor, most of these young teens didn't know the artists. When asked if they had read that any of these artists had quit

Zum Thema Drogen:

JOHN LENNON

«Lucy in the sky» habe ich vom Himmel geholt.

FRAGE: Wann gingen die Beatles tatsächlich kaputt?
John: Nachdem Brian Epstein gestorben war, gab es einen Koller. Paul McCartney wollte an seine Stelle treten und uns führen. Aber was heisst schon führen? Zumal auch noch die Sache mit den Drogen dazukam.
FRAGE: Wie war das mit Deinem ersten Trip?
John: Unser Zahnarzt in London schmuggelte uns bei einem Abendessen in seinem Haus LSD unter. Er tat es uns heimlich in den Kaffee.
FRAGE: Wie lange hast Du dann Trips eingenommen?
John: Jahrelang.
FRAGE: Waren schlechte dabei?
John: Eine Menge, deswegen habe ich ja damit aufgehört. Ich konnte es einfach nicht mehr ertragen.
FRAGE: Hast Du auch andere Drogen genommen?
John: Ja. In der Kunstschule habe ich gesoffen. Dann in Hamburg nahm ich Pillen, die mir halfen, acht Stunden

durchzuspielen, und bei «help» stieg ich auf Hasch um. Ich habe immer Aufputschmittel genommen. Die anderen auch, aber ich nahm wahrscheinlich noch mehr Pillen, mehr von allem, weil ich wahrscheinlich noch verrückter war. Ich war kaputt. Es war ein Ausverkauf.
FRAGE: Wie denkst Du heute darüber?
John: Ganz einfach. Wir müssen die Realitäten erkennen. Es gibt immer noch Klassenunterschiede, es werden immer noch Waffen nach Afrika verkauft und Schwarze auf der Strasse umgebracht. Die Leute leben immer noch in fucking Armut, nichts hat sich geändert. Nur ich bin älter geworden und ein Haufen Leute läuft mit langen Haaren herum. Einfach nachmachen reicht aber nicht. Man muss denken und dann handeln. Man muss was tun.
«Lucy in the sky» habe ich vom Himmel geholt. «Power to the people» soll sie ersetzen.

Dieses Interview erschien in der Zeitschrift „pop" Nr. 6/72

3. "'Lucy in the Sky' habe ich vom Himmel geholt," B310/255, Bundesarchiv Koblenz. Part of a John Lennon interview published in pop magazines in June 1972. The interview was actually an advertisement paid for by the Federal Central Office for Health Education.

using drugs, the responses were abysmal. Only 12 percent of the sample had heard that John Lennon had turned his back on drugs; only 2 percent for James Taylor; and the numbers went down from there. Almost 80 percent of the respondents had not read that any of the named musicians had quit using drugs. The market researchers concluded, "Since the resonance of the ads is low and an amplification in the range is only possible to a limited extent, other alternatives to the ads employed should be discussed as well."[52] The authorities were no doubt disappointed with the failure of the surreptitious propaganda, but they could be thankful that the lack of effectiveness ensured that there would be no demands for "Power to the people."

These interviews were a sideshow to the main thrust of the campaign; the BfgA allocated the majority of the campaign's resources to reaching younger Germans, those who were deemed too young to have had much contact with drugs and who could be influenced by antidrug messages. The difficulty with reaching

4. "Wowman, the world's most famous drug-dog," 310/255, Bundesarchiv Koblenz. The header for the first installment of the federally funded comic book series, *Wowman, the World's Most Famous Drug-Dog*, 1972.

this quite specific market segment was to find a medium that would be as effective and economical as possible. Since 80 percent of youths ages nine to fourteen read comics, the Bfga decided to create a recurring comic strip, place the comic within an established comic book, and produce radio tie-ins to reinforce brand recognition.[53]

The concept that the Bfga and JWT agreed upon seems in retrospect laughable, though perhaps this is not a dreadful characteristic for a comic series. The Bfga pitched the series this way: "The lead character is 'Wowman,' the drug sniffing dog. His characteristic is that as soon as he 'sniffs' drugs, he then becomes powerless; he is then no longer able to help his at-risk friends. This figure should be understood as a parable: Whoever misuses drugs is no longer able to solve the problems that can lead to drug consumption, among other things."[54]

After agreeing on the concept, JWT created mock-ups, which were then critiqued by the Bfga and sent back for revisions. This process went on until the Bfga was satisfied. The final product was a series entitled—without any sense of irony—"The Secret of the Underground Drug Plantation" ("Das Geheimnis der unterirdischen Drogenplantage"). It ran sequentially over several months in *Primo Comic*. Like the interviews, the comics were inserted into other comic strips without any recognition that they had been created by the government and paid for from the public purse.[55]

The story is surprisingly humorous, though not always in the ways intended. The outlines of the story are classic comic book, with a psychedelic, early-1970s twist. Wowman, the world's most famous drug dog (all written in English, presumably for street credibility with ten-year-olds), and his human partner, Hauptwachmeister Knacke, try to foil a plan by the evil head of the drug underworld, Zaster, who looks remarkably like the caricatures of greedy capitalists from the Weimar period, and his hip but evil son, Zaster Jr. This caricature of Zaster as a gangster taps into a much older discourse prevalent in Germany since World War I, in which middlemen, that is, capitalist distributors, act as stand-ins for the problems associated with capitalism. If only the distributors were not so greedy and dangerous, the system would work. Capitalism's failings were not endogenous, but the result of Jews, foreigners, and drug dealers. This kind of logic remained a focal point not only for this campaign, but as a node of agreement in the larger debate over drugs in Germany during the 1970s; the political parties, press, and population could not agree on all aspects of a plan to deal with drugs, but most could agree that if only the traffickers (which often served as a shorthand for foreigners) were captured, drugs would go away.

Our hero, Wowman, has a certain addiction to bones, and when not foiling the plans of Zaster, prefers to sit and chew. The details of the seven-part series are too complicated to discuss in great detail, but the choice of characters is interesting. In the second episode, after Knacke has been tricked into falling into the drug underworld, we are introduced to Wowman's eclectic band of friends—the presumably "at-risk" youths—as they sit around a low table with a large hookah resting on top. The gang of unlikely friends are making tea in the water pipe, the world's first "tea pipe," we're told. Wowman, however, would rather have a "bone pipe" (*Knochenpfeife*). Ali, "the little Muslim," leaves to make a "bone pipe," but falls into the trap laid by Zaster. The others soon follow and fall into the same trap: Rosa, the young socialist; Uwe, the sports expert; Blume and Taube, the hippy pair; Yogi, the Hari Krishna; and Johanna and Johannes, the Jesus Freaks. The rest of the series follows Wowman as he journeys to the underworld to save his partner and his strange group of friends from Zaster's evil plans.[56]

The goal of the series was to convince young people not to use drugs. It certainly portrays the drug kingpins, Zaster and his son, as evil and shows how the at-risk friends ultimately reject drugs. But it remains unclear why the BfgA and JWT believed these comics would be successful at reducing drug consumption. The motley band of characters would have been quite recognizable at the time as stock characters from the counterculture, a panorama of teen culture, from

5. Wowman and his countercultural friends sit around the "tea" waterpipe, 1972, 310/255, Bundesarchiv Koblenz.

the "normal" Uwe, through the socialists, hippies, and religious cult members, and even, surprisingly, Ali as a representation of Turkish immigration, which was connected in the public consciousness with the expansion of drug distribution. All these characters come off as sympathetic, and there is every reason to believe that this might induce drug experimentation rather than hinder it. After all, if Wowman's friends are socialists, hippies, Hari Krishnas, and Jesus Freaks, why would young people not also choose those "types" as models to emulate? Both the BfgA and JWT were aware of the tendency of media portrayals to backfire and provoke curiosity rather than abstinence, but they ultimately could not get around this contradiction. They had to try to "unsell" drug use, and the line between glamorization and demonization proved to be a very thin one.

The J. Walter Thompson Agency designed the campaign to be multifaceted, and the radio spots were meant to work with the comic books. The agency chose Radio Luxemburg to air the spots because of the popularity of this commercial sender with young people. The BfgA claimed that their Wowman spots could reach a potential audience of 1.5 million, 780,000 of whom were between the ages of fourteen and twenty-nine. And though statistics for listeners younger than fourteen were not kept, they estimated that 100,000 to 200,000 members of their target group would hear each spot. The Thompson agency understood the power of the radio medium well and was able to exploit it. The format of the spots followed a set pattern. Each five-minute spot focused on a single problem faced by young people. The audience would be asked to write to Wowman to help him solve the dilemma, and in order to increase listener loyalty, those who wrote in were entered into an album give-away. At the end of the episode, the interviewer reminded listeners that they could follow Wowman's adventures in *Primo Comics*, "available at all newsstands."[57]

The first episode tackles the question "Am I a coward if I don't smoke hash?" The tableau opens with Wowman exclaiming, "Listen up! There are 10 brand new Black Sabbath LPs to win!" Although this might have been a lightly veiled attempt to gain credibility with skeptical listeners, the rationale of telling children not to use drugs and then giving them albums from Black Sabbath, the authors of "Sweet Leaf," seems dubious; it would appear that JWT was creating the kind of cognitive dissonance it was trying to avoid. After the speaker introduces the drug-sniffing dog and Inspector Knacke, the authors take care of one of the sticky problems with their main character by explaining that Wowman had learned to talk at a "special speech laboratory." Knacke, the speaking human, not the speaking dog, then explains what a drug dealer is: "Incidentally, dealers are people who sell secret and illegal drugs. They buy hashish, for example, for relatively little money and then sell it for a lot." The narrator then asks who dealers sell to. "Mainly young people," of course, answers Knacke. The two then go on to discuss the central question: whether those who fail to smoke with friends are cowards. Wowman, unimpressed with the discussion, interjects:

> **Wowman:** You shouldn't talk about things you don't understand. There's nothing better than belonging to a clique of friends that have the same interests, who simply understand each other. And when one then says, come have a toke of my joint you can certainly come into conflict with your conscience.
> **Knacke:** Incidentally, a joint is a hash cigarette.
> **Wowman:** Okay, okay! Something similar happened to me for the first time a few days ago. But before I tell you about it, I suggest that we play some music. And indeed from the LP that you can win today. Black Sabbath, Wow![58]

Up to this point, Wowman has told the children about dealers, reinforced the need for peers, explained what a joint is, and then cut to a Black Sabbath track—and this was considered a prophylaxis against drug consumption.

After the song, Wowman returns to his story about his friend Peter. The scene fades to a flashback. "The music is cool," Peter says. "Now a joint is the only thing missing." Wowman, in a voice-over, explains his weakness for drugs: "And before I could say that I always fall into such a state of powerlessness when I inhale drug smoke, Peter pulled out a joint, lit it and I flipped out." Peter then tries to pass the joint to a young girl. She declines, as does Klaus. Peter tries peer pressure: "Don't talk crap. Take a hit." But Klaus resists the pressure, giving the moral of the tale: "No. I don't have anything against you smoking hash. And you have to accept that I don't smoke it." Peter calls him a coward and shifts his attention to Dieter. The pressure is too much for Dieter. He gives in. Wowman reappears in a voice-over:

> **Wowman:** That's how my friends reacted. I'm interested in how our listeners would have reacted.
> **Narrator:** Yes, dear listeners, simply write on a postcard what you would have done if someone had offered you a joint. Would you have accepted or turned it down? Explain why too. And don't forget to include the return address and your age!
> **Knacke:** Each entry takes part in the raffle for the 10 Black Sabbath LPs.
> **Wowman:** Please write to Wowman, W-O-W-M-A-N, Radio Luxemburg, the final day for entries is. . . . Until next week at the same time!
> **Credits.**
> **Incidentally:** You can read about Wowman's adventures every month in the comics magazine "Primo." "Primo" is available at every kiosk.[59]

A clear focus, material inducements, product tie-ins, listener participation— all these appear to be textbook modern advertising strategies. Yet most of the spots ring hollow. They pile stereotypes on top of clichés, and it is difficult to imagine that the listeners were moved either to take up drugs or to turn them down. Indeed, the whole strategy, to have a talking drug dog convince children to "just say no," seems misguided.[60]

Even so, children did write in to help Wowman solve his friends' problems. Whether it was out of genuine interest or for the free records, one can only speculate. Rita Gross from Niederweiler, for example, wrote to Wowman about the conflict between Rolf and Willy. After explaining why Rolf and Willy failed to understand one another, Rita tells Wowman that he is too simplistic in his thinking:

> Rolf sees drugs as a balm for his mental and emotional pain; in contra-distinction to Willy, who believes that drugs are a harmful poison. He certainly is right about that (because of burning out and so on!!) if he should

succeed in helping his friend. BUT IT REALLY DOESN'T HAPPEN THAT WAY! Willy can't get away with such simple words. He must bring in substantial evidence in order to refute what Rolf thinks about smoking hash. Willy certainly has good intentions with Rolf and definitely also want to help him, but how???

There would be an opportunity to help Rolf, if he did things with many other young people and talked about his problem some time. Then it could be that he allowed himself to be convinced and found an expert in the area of drugs and went into treatment with him. I think Willy is a good example for those who know drug addicts. He tackled the issue wrongly, but it can definitely be changed![61]

It is interesting and significant that Rita reproduces the same kind of instrumental logic that motivated the policymakers in the first place. Like the members of the federal government, Rita believes that if only given the truth about drugs from "experts," individuals would make rational decisions. Michael Fuhr from Gniesenbach also showed sympathy for Willy. Michael opined that Willy should try again to talk to Rolf about his problems, "but without screaming at him at the same time."[62] Most of the few remaining letters, which the BfgA selected as "representative," repeat these themes. They did not keep any dissenting voices, though one could imagine that condemnatory or ironic letters were probably sent. Based on a review of the subsequent market research, however, there may not have been many more letters.

The market research proved unmistakably that the fears that the campaign might backfire and increase the number of young experimenters were unfounded. Almost no one read the comic strips; of those who did, almost no one remembered Wowman; and of those who did remember Wowman, almost no one remembered he was a dog, much less the world's most famous drug dog. Though one ought to be skeptical of statistics, these speak volumes. Of the four main comic books that could have run the series—Primo, Asterix, Micky Maus, and Fix und Foxi—Primo was by far the least read by the target group (Primo 30 percent, Asterix 64 percent, Micky Maus 70 percent, and Fix und Foxi 64 percent). The BfgA and JWT picked the wrong comic book, mainly because it was cheaper. Of the 30 percent that had read Primo in the half-year during which the series ran, only 3 percent had read it "regularly." When Primo readers were asked if they could remember a comic named Wowman, only 3 percent answered in the affirmative, and only 1 percent could identify Wowman as "the dog that sniffs drugs." The market researchers concluded that the campaign had been a failure. "In summary, it can be said that the specific education campaign against youth drug misuse in 1972 only found a very low resonance," they conceded. "A continuation of the campaign in the current form would certainly increase the resonance; however, it is questionable just how much of a decisive increase can succeed."[63] Yet the marketing experts recommended that the BfgA should increase the intensity of the campaign and begin discussing alternative advertisements. Whether the marketers realized the political imperatives would keep the campaign going despite the failures or they simply showed astounding hubris in the face of abject defeat is unclear.

Conclusion

The 1972 youth drug campaign was a failure by any standard. Despite the best intentions of the government and the advertising firm, the campaign failed to reach the hearts and minds of the youth population, much less change them. Indeed, as the emphasis on cognitive dissonance shows, the campaigners were caught in an uphill battle. "Lifestyle," that peculiar object and product of marketing, had emerged over the 1960s and 1970s to offer a hermeneutic device for understanding one's place in the world. For many young people, smoking a joint became a part of how they identified themselves: as antiestablishment, part of a new generation, hip, cool, flipped out. This message came from the media and from interaction with other people their own age. Wowman could do little to alter this fact. The advertisers, despite their wealth of knowledge in how to sell both products and lifestyle, could not unsell drugs.

This episode not only provides insight into the failures of advertising and the failures of government intervention, but it also forces us to ask questions about the instrumental logic that governed state policy in this case. Do individuals act rationally in their own economic or health interests? Does more "factual" information make for better consumers of products and more complicated notions such as health? The logic of advertising that emerged in the postwar period focused on creating micromarkets to which identity could be sold. Health officials borrowed from this model, trusting that the tools of the market could be used to unsell harmful goods, or, conversely, to sell a new model of abstinence. The choices that guided the 1972 antidrug campaign continue to play a prominent role, not only in the "war on drugs" but in other public health issues as well. Governments still believe that given the truth, consumers will make rational decisions. As we can see from this example, the notion of rational consumers may be more illusion than reality.

Notes

1. An excellent review essay of the implications of the new literature on consumerism is Confino and Koshar, "Regimes of Consumer Culture." Another that focuses on periodization is Stearns, "Stages of Consumerism." See also Victoria de Grazia, "Changing Consumption Regimes in Europe, 1930–1970: Comparative Perspectives on the Distribution Problem," in Strasser, McGovern, and Judt, *Getting and Spending*, 59–84.

2. See Wildt, *Vom kleinen Wohlstand*, and his "Plurality of Taste"; also see Carter, *How German Is She?*

3. Wienemann, *Vom Alkoholverbot zum Gesundheitsmanagement*, 340.

4. In 1937, for instance, Heinrich Himmler sent every licensed driver in Germany a letter deploring the habit of drunk driving. Proctor, *The Nazi War on Cancer*, 145.

5. Ibid., 198.

6. Ibid., 199–201.

7. Ibid., 242–244.

8. For instance, in 1947 various temperance organizations (i.e., the Blue Cross, the Good Templars, and the Cross League) banded together to form a federal umbrella organization named the German Main Bureau against the Danger of Addiction (Deutsche Hauptstelle gegen die Suchtgefahren), which was charged with organizing the "struggle against the misuse of addictive substances of whatever kind." This and other organizations specifically formed to combat addiction worked with religious welfare organizations like Caritas and das Diakonische Werk to prevent and treat addiction. See Wienemann, *Vom Alkoholverbot zum Gesundheitsmanagement*, 387.

9. Robert Proctor argues that despite the growth in postwar consumption, and despite the underreporting of cigarettes bought and sold on the black market in the aftermath of the war, there probably was an overall decrease in smoking due to the antismoking campaign. Yet Proctor fails to speculate on the role of the media vis-à-vis the larger cultural shifts in attitude, and the steady rise in smoking over the course of the 1950s and 1960s suggests that any general changes were short-lived. What seems more apparent from the statistical evidence is that increases in both alcohol and cigarette consumption outstripped real growth through much of the 1950s and 1960s. As a result, it seems safe to conclude that the images of substitution of "good" consumer desire for "bad" consumer choices had little effect. Consumers, it seems, wanted their *Genußmittel* as much as, if not more than, other consumer goods.

10. There is no way to measure the extent of the trade. Statistics on seizures and drug prices are notoriously bad and, more often than not, simply made up to serve some political agenda. It is clear, however, that by the early 1970s, literally millions of young Germans had at least tried drugs, and that tens of thousands were regular users.

11. Cohen, *A Consumers' Republic*, 298.

12. Dirk Reinhardt sees the economic expansion of 1925–1928 as the crucial period for the discovery of the consumer and the emergence of *Marktanalyse*, and he notes the establishment of a branch of the J. Walter Thompson Agency in Berlin as the turning point

of the move toward market research. See Reinhardt, *Von der Reklame zum Marketing*, 44–48.

13. Carter, *How German Is She?*, 158–159. See also Christian Steiniger, "Eleganz der Oberfläche: Werbung und die ökonomische Restauration deutscher Normalität," in Faulstich, *Die Kultur der fünfziger Jahre*, 181–198. For the breakdown of spending on various media, see Karin Knop, "Zwischen Afri-Cola-Rausch und dem Duft der großen weiten Welt: Werbung in den sechziger Jahren," in Faulstich, *Die Kultur der sechziger Jahre*, 246. The rapid growth of advertising after the 1948 currency reform led to the formation of the Zentralausschuss der Werbewirtschaft in 1949, and six years later the expansion of market research led to the creation of the Arbeitskreis für betriebswirtschafliche Markt- und Absatzforschung, which acted as an industry group for market research firms such as the widely known Institut für Demoskopie Allensbach as well as the Intermarkt Gesellschaft für Markt- und Meinungsforschung, the latter of which later worked on the antidrug campaign. See International Chamber of Commerce, *Advertising*, D2.

14. International Chamber of Commerce, *Advertising*, D2.

15. Knop, "Zwischen Afri-Cola-Rausch," 244.

16. Cohen, *A Consumers' Republic*, 309–314, 307.

17. On this process in Germany, see Knop, "Zwischen Afri-Cola-Rausch," 246–268.

18. For an example of a German company adopting the lessons of market segmentation, see Harm G. Schröter, "Marketing als angewandte Sozialtechnik und Veränderungen im Konsumverhalten: Nivea als internationale Dachmarke 1960–1994," in Siegrist, Kaelbe, and Kocka, *Europäische Konsumgeschichte*, 615–648.

19. Siegfried, "'Trau keinem über 30'?," 28.

20. Knop, "Zwischen Afri-Cola-Rausch," 242–244.

21. One of the principal arguments in Arthur Marwick's work on the 1960s is that the counterculture itself was widely entrepreneurial. The styles that flourished then and in the early 1970s were largely produced by these young rebels, and, although it remains to be established without a doubt, one can assume that the marketing of these new lifestyles was also significantly influenced by young members of the counterculture, or perhaps graduates of the counterculture who moved on to the corporate world. See Marwick, *The Sixties*, 17.

22. See Ellen A. Wartelle and Patricia A. Stout, "The Evolution of Mass Media and Health Persuasion Models," in Crano and Burgoon, *Mass Media and Drug Prevention*, 19–34.

23. De Grazia, *Irresistible Empire*, 230–232.

24. Ibid., 250–275.

25. Ibid., 275–282.

26. Knop, "Zwischen Afri-Cola-Rausch," 269.

27. This is one of the central arguments of Victoria de Grazia's *Irresistible Empire* (11): that by the 1970s the "Market Empire" had largely triumphed, and although Europe had not become a clone of the United States, it had aligned itself with American consumerism and become part of a larger "White Atlantic."

28. Bundesministerium für Jugend, Familie und Gesundheit, ed., *Dokumente zum Drogen-problem*, 99, 100.

29. Ibid., 100, 103, 106–107. The specific eight-part plan laid out in the federal Action Plan closely resembles the recommendations of Heins Westphal of the Ministry for Youth, Family and Health outlined in a letter to the head of the chancellor's office on 16 July 1970, B/141/37547, Bundesarchiv Koblenz (hereafter BAK).

30. "Vorbemerkung," 1, 2, B310, B310/255, BAK.

31. Ibid., 3.

32. Renate Fuchs et al., *Teilcurriculum für die Klassenstufen fünf bis acht: Zum Drogenproblem* (Cologne: BfGA, 1973), B310/508, BAK.

33. "Meinungen in Hamburg zum Rauschgiftproblem," 1971, Staatliche Pressestelle VI, Institut für angewandte Sozialwissenschaften, Bonn-Bad Godesburg, 135-1 VI, Staatsarchiv Hamburg (hereafter STAH).

34. This campaign bore little similarity to harm reduction strategies. The goal of harm reduction was not just to provide information to users or at-risk youths that might persuade them to avoid drugs but also to give them strategies to use drugs safely if they did not heed the warning. In contrast, the BfGA campaign was an abstinence program; the goal was to prevent drug use altogether. Despite the frequent refrain that they must be scientific or face being ignored by young people, there is a considerable amount of demonization or infantilization of drug users in the campaign.

35. "Vorbemerkung," 3, B310, B310/255, BAK.

36. "Information Drogen-Problem," 3, B310/236, BAK.

37. Ibid., 4.

38. Ibid., 7–21, 25–26, 27.

39. Institut für Markt- und Werbeforschung, "Die Aufklärungsbroschüren 'Information zum Drogenproblem' 'Perspektiven, Aussagen zum Drogenproblem' bei Jugendlichen und Erwachsenen,'" 5, B310/774, BAK.

40. Ibid., 45.

41. Ibid., 79, 31.

42. Ibid., 80–81.

43. Ibid., 106.

44. Walter Dörken, Lothar Gothe, and Marianne Schmid, "Bericht zum Streuweg der Broschüre: Information zum Drogen-Problem" (Cologne: Bundeszentrale für gesundheitliche Aufklärung, [1972]), 24, B310/448, BAK.

45. Ibid., 15–16.

46. On the link between music and drugs, see Bromell, *Tomorrow Never Knows*.

47. "Vorbemerkung," 4, B310, B310/255, BAK.

48. Another case of this type of propaganda portrayed as entertainment occurred when the Office of National Drug Policy made agreements with the networks in the 1990s to pay them for placing antidrug messages in entertainment programming and having some say over scripts. The deal proved to be a public relations fiasco. After the scheme was exposed by Daniel Forbes in *Salon* magazine in January 2000, the news media trounced

Barry McCaffrey and the networks for undermining democracy by sanctioning propaganda. See Forbes, "Propaganda for Dollars." A U.S. trade publication inveighed against this intrusion: "Making editorial choices that have nothing to do with serving readers' interests is the fastest away to piss away their trust. Not making readers privy to glaring conflicts of interests accomplishes the same. It's bad for journalism. Bad for business. It's even bad for the ad makers and media buyers at Bates USA and Ogilvy & Mather, the agencies that took the anti-drug account. Their government-sponsored attempt to blur the line between ads and editorial deserves scorn." Van Bakel, "For Sale: Magazines' Credibility," 4.

49. B310/255, BAK.

50. See Wenner, *Lennon Remembers*.

51. B310/255, BAK. This is a literal translation from the German. The original appears to be a peculiar excerpt from several different paragraphs of the original interview. The staff at J. Walter Thompson apparently borrowed from Lennon for effect rather than precision.

52. Benad, IB3, "Ergebnisse einer Wiederholungsbefragung über Rauschmittelgebrauch bei Jugendlichen—Kurzbericht," B310/247, BAK.

53. "Vorbemerkung," 6, B310, B310/255, BAK.

54. Ibid.

55. Ibid., 7.

56. B310/255, BAK.

57. "Vorbemerkung," 7, B310, B310/255, BAK.

58. B310/255, BAK.

59. Ibid.

60. Ibid.

61. Ibid.

62. Ibid.

63. Benad, 24–26, B301/247, BAK.

10

ANNE KAMINSKY

"TRUE ADVERTISING MEANS PROMOTING

A GOOD THING THROUGH A GOOD FORM"

Advertising in the German Democratic Republic

I s advertising still necessary today?" This was the central question posed by the first issue of the advertising magazine *Neue Werbung*, which was founded in 1954 in the German Democratic Republic (GDR).[1] Although the question was intended to be rhetorical, it just as accurately described the everyday experience for consumers in East Germany. Shaken by a lack of materials and production bottlenecks, marked by rationing, defective goods, long lines, and services in short supply, the world of "real existing socialist" commerce offered little reason for advertising goods and services. "Distribute, Don't Sell" was the motto of daily commerce.

Just a few years after World War II, companies in the Soviet Zone of Occupation (sbz) resumed their advertising activities, which had been interrupted first by the war and then by the immediate postwar task of rebuilding a devastated country. Producers once again began using advertisements in newspapers and magazines, along with direct mail advertising, to present their products and extol their usefulness and attractive prices. These advertisements attempted to evoke familiar products and brands from the prewar period, yet spoke chiefly to the material and financial limitations of East German households, emphasizing above all the products' durability and quality. Product advertising was further stimulated by the establishment of so-called free stores by the state trade organization Handelsorganisation (ho) in November 1948, just a few months after the currency reform in the SBZ. The first HO store offered its goods on Berlin's symbolically charged Frankfurter Allee, later renamed Stalinallee.[2] Here, for the first time, East Germans could buy goods legally without having to use coupons or rationing cards. The prices were fixed slightly below those on the black market in order to soak up the additional cash that was circulating in the GDR through piecework and higher wages. Aside from propping up the GDR's currency and weakening the black market, the HO stores served as a key advertisement for the regime: by displaying concrete proof of the improvements in everyday life made by the party, the stores were supposed to illustrate the "era of achievements" extolled by Walter Ulbricht.[3] Beyond the constant appeals to the population to work longer and harder, the Socialist Unity Party (SED) also had to provide material incentives that showed East Germans that more work would be repaid in the form of attractive consumer goods. The tasks of the HO stores consisted of showing off the promise of consumer plenty and offering it to customers with deep pockets.[4]

The "New Advertising"

Despite the SED's constant evocations of a better future that lay just around the corner, the population of the GDR watched as the party put consumer needs last on its list of priorities. At the Second Party Congress in the summer of 1952, the SED resolved to pour resources into heavy industry and remilitarization, which reversed the policy of increasing consumer goods production that had just been decreed in 1950. The effects of this economic about-face on the daily lives of citizens were glossed over with the now notorious slogan "How we work today is how we will live (and buy) tomorrow." The party advocated reduced consumer spending; the satisfaction of consumer demand was put off until a later, "better" time.

The neglect of consumer goods production also meant that little attention was paid to advertising. Deutsche Werbe- und Anzeigengesellschaft (DEWAG), the GDR's official advertising agency, was founded as a private company in 1945 and put in charge of advertising for industry and commerce in 1949.[5] In line with communist practice, however, DEWAG was responsible for product advertising as well as "visual agitation." In addition to advertising socialist products, DEWAG oversaw the design and production of posters and banners promoting socialism, the SED, and the party's achievements. Nevertheless, party leaders regarded advertising with great suspicion, viewing it as a waste of economic resources and a relic of capitalist economic relations. In the East German planned economy, there should be no need for advertising, which many dismissed condescendingly as "publicity."

In 1953, however, the party leadership's attitude toward advertising changed dramatically, albeit not in the way that officials who scoffed at the idea of product advertising in a socialist system had imagined. During the popular uprising of 17 June 1953, well over 1 million people in over six hundred cities and towns throughout the GDR rose up against the SED dictatorship. Party leaders watched helplessly as unresolved problems in the consumer sector, combined with general discontent over the lack of political liberty, took on a "system-shattering force."[6] The insurrection convinced the SED leadership that it needed not only to make political changes, but also to improve living conditions by inaugurating a "consumer turnaround." The party took two measures. It strengthened its security apparatus to nip future unrest in the bud, and it decided to ease the domestic political situation by continuing with the "New Course," which had been established as official policy prior to the uprising in a last-ditch attempt to make some concessions to consumers. According to the party, the intended aim of the New Course was "to bring about a real improvement in economic and political conditions in the German Democratic Republic in the immediate future and, based on this step, to raise the living standard of the working class and white collar workers significantly."[7] "Improving individual consumption" was the new slogan.

It was not a coincidence that a new journal for advertisers appeared for the first time barely a year after the 1953 uprising. In the first issue, the SED admonished advertising directors to take its idea of "good" advertising to heart. *Neue Werbung* (New Advertising), which was also the magazine's title, was supposed to draw attention to the achievements of the socialist state and communicate them to the population. As Minister of Culture Alexander Abusch declared in an introductory essay, "Even in advertising, we want . . . the unity of goodness and beauty." But socialist advertising was also supposed to distinguish itself clearly from advertising as practiced in the capitalist world by emphasizing the advantages of life under socialism and simultaneously facilitating the distribution of socialist consumer goods. According to the SED leadership, socialist industry would produce the necessary products in the necessary quantities to satisfy the needs of the population. For this reason, it viewed socialist advertising as a medium of information rather than an instrument for encouraging sales. A reference work for advertising photography described the differences between socialist and capitalist advertising this way: "Socialist advertising truthfully informs consumers about the real benefits of goods and services without the exaggeration typical of capitalist advertising. It does not manipulate consumers by trying to convince them that a given product offers additional benefits, such as an increase in prestige. Customers are given information intended to facilitate a fact-based purchasing decision. They should not allow themselves to get carried away by emotionally driven impulse purchases that they may later regret."[8]

But the party leadership's response to the 1953 uprising did not stop at intensifying its efforts to advertise the advantages of socialism. In 1956, the SED founded the Institute for Advertising Techniques. In 1957, it was joined by the Institute for Consumer Needs and Market Research, whose studies aimed to ascertain the needs of consumers and to develop strategies for influencing and managing these needs. The catchphrases were "managing consumer needs" and "educating the new consumer," who would become the new socialist individual. Finally, the GDR broadcast its first televised advertisements in 1959. Under the name *One Thousand Television Tips* (*TausendTeleTips*), the GDR's two television channels aired over four thousand commercials—until advertising was completely banned in 1976.

Educating the New Consumer: The Role
of Advertising under Socialism

As Abusch had emphasized in 1954, one of advertising's most important roles under socialism was to provide tangible proof of the advantages of socialism over capitalism through a large assortment of consumer goods. Looking back at the privations of the immediate postwar period, one author declared in *Neue Werbung*, "We may, however, increasingly consider those times over, and can increasingly display the results of our work for our citizens in shop windows. They are entitled to a continuous supply of everyday necessities, and it is our duty to show them in abundance to our citizens."[9] To attain this ideological and political goal in the most effective manner, advertisers established a direct correlation between the text and consumer goods in ads and created so-called *Stapelschaufenster* (stacked display windows) for displaying the purported abundance of socialist products. Thus, when a product was displayed in a storefront, a text was placed next to it with a slogan, such as "We have the good work of our party to thank for this" or "Socialism makes possible a good life." The sheer amount of products displayed was supposed to repeat the slogan's content; that this method often failed on its own terms is a different question. As the reference work for advertisers put it, "Every effectively decorated storefront [should] reflect the

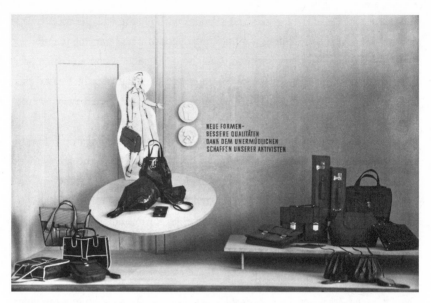

1. "New Forms—Better Quality Thanks to the Untiring Work of Our Activists" (mid-1950s). The presentation of consumer goods in storefront windows was combined with political propaganda. Author's private collection.

GDR's considerable economic achievements" and should support the policies of the party and the state in a striking manner.[10] It no longer sufficed simply to display an item in the store window and trust that customers would recognize that it was attractive. Besides, the product's primary importance no longer lay in its usefulness, as it had at the end of the 1940s. Instead, socialist consumer goods were transformed into harbingers of political and ideological messages.[11] Their political properties were emphasized in advertisements and store windows, where a socialist design or slogan praising the party could be found prominently displayed in the midst of piles of stacked goods. These heaps of goods in storefronts and in ads were meant to demonstrate not simply that consumer goods were increasingly abundant in the GDR, but also that life was increasingly pleasant because of it. Despite the party's promises and the gradual improvements in the supply of goods that it achieved, however, the planned economy never produced enough consumer goods, much less in sufficient diversity. Nevertheless, socialist retailers continued to use stacked display windows until the collapse of the GDR in 1989, often displaying towers of detergent or piles of crackers. Perhaps more important, the GDR struggled with one basic problem throughout its existence: even in the immediate postwar period, East Germans generally believed that life was better in the West.

2. "Our Trust to the Party, Our Work to the Republic!" (mid-1960s). Author's private collection.

By the end of its first decade of existence, the GDR enjoyed a measure of economic stability. Party leaders believed that the time had come to "complete" the construction of socialism in the GDR. The SED grandly decided that its main economic task now consisted of comparing socialism with capitalism on the "consumer front"—a competition that it of course sought to win. The plan was to grow the economy so that by 1961 "the superiority of the socialist order in the German Democratic Republic compared to the leadership of the Bonn government's imperialist forces will be clear and, consequently, our population's per-capita consumption of the most important foods and consumer goods will match and surpass per-capita consumption in West Germany."[12] Because of its ambitious proclamations and very selective points of comparison with the Federal Republic, the SED leadership created exaggerated expectations among East German consumers.[13]

The 1957 party program, with its slogan "Overtake without Catching Up" ("Überholen ohne Einzuholen"), aimed to outdo the Federal Republic by 1961 in per capita consumption of all essential foods and in supplying households with key consumer goods, such as televisions, washing machines, and refrigerators.

The program also fine-tuned what it deemed to be the functions of advertising. The task of advertising, the party emphasized, was to support "socialist development" in the GDR and call attention to the superiority of socialism over capitalism. Infused with political propaganda, advertising had to demonstrate that each new product constituted a victory for socialism in the battle against capitalism. Finally, the party demanded that advertisers implement the principles Abusch had publicized in 1954.

To distribute its message about the superiority of the planned economy, the SED leadership quickly zeroed in on the catalogues of the two mail-order companies, founded in 1955 and 1959, as the perfect advertising medium. With circulations in the hundreds of thousands, their pleasantly packaged messages reached more people than, for example, the party's official organ, the newspaper *Neues Deutschland*. Without a hint of irony, one of the mail-order enterprises had its catalogue announce, "I'm proud to be the catalogue of a socialist mail-order company. As my pages already clearly show, our industrial and agricultural workers are going to make it! By 1961, we will overtake West Germany in per-capita consumption of food and key consumer goods."[14] This advertising line continued inside the catalogue, where the individual products were presented in a way that called attention to their usefulness, to their economic advantages, and to the fact that they were produced by a socialist enterprise.

Economic developments, however, prevented the GDR from achieving its ambitious goal of overtaking West Germany. In fact, the GDR failed even to catch up with West Germany. As a result, the party changed its goals in 1961. Because the SED could find no supply-side solution to the shortage of consumer goods, it decided to focus on a demand-side solution: "consumer education." The party demoted advertising to a secondary role, reduced its budget by half, and changed its mission. Now advertising was expected to help educate East Germans to become economically responsible socialist consumers.

Advertising was now expected to "propagate socialist lifestyles, overcome bourgeois behavior, and influence people's tastes, as well as provide sensible economic information and explain the usefulness of products." Consumer education was understood as advertising "that proceeds from the principles of socialist consumerism . . . to guarantee that the scale and structure of consumption is influenced so that it develops in line with economic limits."[15]

Socialist customers were expected to consume in socialist, rather than "bourgeois," fashion. Simply put, this meant that they should adjust their purchasing preferences to conform to their financial limitations. This entailed giving

3. "A Bouquet for Our Republic!" Cover of the mail-order catalogue for fall/winter 1969. An East German model congratulates the GDR on the occasion of the twentieth anniversary of its establishment and praises the socialist state's accomplishments. Author's private collection.

up habits such as impulse buying, throwing consumer goods away before they had exhausted their usefulness, and the casual wastefulness typical of Western consumerism, all of which was considered morally unacceptable by the SED. This "capitalist consumer behavior" was to be replaced by socialist consumer behavior, which the party defined in terms of socialist consumerism and lifestyles. In particular, this consumer program emphasized a planned and rational purchasing behavior that balanced the regime's material constraints with the population's needs and individual preferences.[16] The party quickly found a scapegoat for the stubborn persistence of "capitalist purchasing habits." Advertising was accused of failing to achieve its mandate, thereby aggravating the GDR's economic woes. Advertising itself was not socialist enough, the SED leadership declared.

Accordingly, advertising was demoted from its previous status as an ideological medium to the status of a "measure for managing consumer needs." The SED's Sixth Party Congress took up this pressing matter in 1963, claiming that advertising's "influence on consumer needs remains quite inadequate. This is particularly true for the measures taken to manage consumer needs, which were never sufficiently aligned with the goals of the plan for supplying the population with consumer goods. In the last few years, neither the assortment of goods, nor price and income policy has contributed sufficiently to the development of socialist lifestyles and consumer habits. In part they even worked against the stable supply of goods and the optimal correlation between consumer goods and disposable incomes."[17]

Shortly afterward, a doctoral dissertation repeated the party's arguments and claimed that advertising had failed to assist the party in glossing over shortages of consumer goods and shaping well-behaved socialist consumers:

> In the last few years, neither the assortment of goods, nor price and income policy has contributed sufficiently to the development of socialist lifestyles and consumer habits. In part they even worked against the stable supply of goods and the optimal correlation between consumer goods and disposable incomes. Nor did advertisements for consumer goods fulfill their task as part of the system of controlling consumer demand. This is partly illustrated by the fact that advertising campaigns were executed sporadically, rather than systematically, and that the implementation of the plan was insufficiently supported by advertising. Several advertising campaigns even promoted capitalist consumer habits, thus inhibiting the development of socialist consumer habits and lifestyles.[18]

Rather than stimulating demand for quality goods, the SED leadership argued that advertising should use clever marketing to convince consumers to buy slow-moving items and snatch up excess production. The problem was, however, that East German consumers based their notion of quality on the products they saw when visiting their relatives in the West. Again and again, the Ministry of Trade and Supply received reports documenting that consumers revealed anarchical purchasing habits redolent of capitalist consumerism. Economic experts criticized hoarding and impulse buying based on whether products were available rather than whether they were needed. Seen in this light, advertisements that encouraged people to buy virtually constituted economic sabotage. Even innocent texts became suspect, such as "We can help with that gap in your wardrobe." More in tune with the SED's didactic proclivities were the advertising characters created to model progressive work methods and behaviors, such as Fredi Frisch (Freddy Fresh), who stood in sharp contrast to Otto Murks (Otto Muck), Peter Penn (Peter Sleepy), and Herr Schlendrian (Mr. Sloppiness). Similarly, Herr Geschmack (Mr. Taste) reined in Frau Mode's (Mrs. Fashion's) uninhibited (i.e., capitalist) propensity to buy.

In the 1960s, the goal of educating customers with the help of advertising underlay many of the studies carried out by the Institute for Market Research. One of the Institute's studies, for example, investigated the need to "provide extensive political and economic justification for advertising priorities, to ensure a uniform rationale for domestic advertising." Such an approach would establish "an essential basis for assuring that advertising corresponds to the specific political and economic requirements of the entire domestic consumer goods market, and that exercising educational influence on the population is more consistently focused on cultivating socialist consumer habits." This had "not always been guaranteed" in the past, when some consumer goods had been advertised even though "increasing their sale was not economically justifiable."[19]

The study identified two "decisive flaws in socialist advertising." First, it determined that "advertising campaigns did not correspond sufficiently to the objectives of the plan. As a rule, these campaigns were not based on a thorough analysis of current political and economic conditions. As a result, consumer needs that could not be satisfied in the current economic climate were created, or those needs were not directed at what was actually in stock." Second, the report argued that advertising required greater central coordination: "Measures taken by individual advertisers frequently overlapped and sometimes even worked against each other. As a result, the financial and material means available for advertising were wasted." As a solution, the report recommended "creating a unified strategy for all advertisers to prevent the promotion of products that are in short supply or that contradict socialist lifestyles."[20]

"Mrs. Fashion and Mr. Taste": Gender and Socialist Advertising

A perfect example of what the party leadership considered poorly conceived advertising was the 1960s "artificially produced sheep" ("Das Schaf in der Retorte") campaign, which was supposed to launch a new line of synthetic textiles to replace the low-quality rayon commonly used as a substitute for costly imports of cotton and silk. Gristen and Wolpryla served as substitutes for wool, Polycon for poplin, Dederon and acetate for silk, Skelan for felt, and Velveton for velvet. These fabrics were popular with East German consumers, not least because they were easy to care for, were wrinkle-resistant, and did not require ironing. As was often the case, however, supply was unable to keep up with demand. Rather than identify the actual cause of the problem, the party's economic experts held advertising responsible for the shortages: "In the first quarter of 1962, for example, industrial enterprises frequently advertised Dederon and cotton on television, even though supplies were not sufficient to satisfy the population's needs, even without the advertisements. Following a television ad for fluffy wool coats made of Dederon, producers did not want to manufacture the coats because they required an excessive use of fabric. But people were already asking for the coats in stores." Once again under fire, those responsible for the advertisement defended themselves, arguing that the campaign had been "aimed at the popularization, not the sale, of the Schaf in der Retorte brand."[21]

If East German politicians and advertisers never quite managed to see eye to eye on product advertising, other advertising techniques emerged that promoted politically desirable lifestyles that could be tied in with specific products. Political exhortations aimed at encouraging East Germans to construct a socialist society linked the creation of modern production methods to the introduction of time-saving consumer goods intended to facilitate shopping and housework. These products were primarily aimed at providing working women with some relief at home and at easing the transition for women about to join the workforce.[22] All manner of kitchen and household appliances played an important role in advertising. "Saving time" was the magic phrase. By presenting these modern shopping and housekeeping conveniences, the press suggested that work and housekeeping were compatible. Women were led to believe that ready-to-wear materials, instant meals, frozen vegetables, and baked goods with preservatives, along with various methods for saving time when shopping, would allow them to complete their housework faster.[23]

An emblematic example was the ad campaign for a pressure cooker, which made use of the usual advertising channels, such as magazines, but also employed the popular comic book *Mosaik* to reach families through their children. Skeptical husbands were reassured that food prepared in the cooker would taste even better than meals cooked in conventional pots. When the cooker went on sale in 1956, wary women were told that they would gain several extra hours of free time per day. In fact, however, a study carried out by the Institute of Market Research determined that at best the time saved by housewives came to just one week per year.

Time and again, the SED promised mechanical solutions that would save women time when cooking as well as washing. In 1956, the mail-order companies introduced what they claimed to be their greatest achievement: a washtub they described as a "washing machine," whose outstanding operating element was a crank for manually stirring the laundry. This device could hardly compete

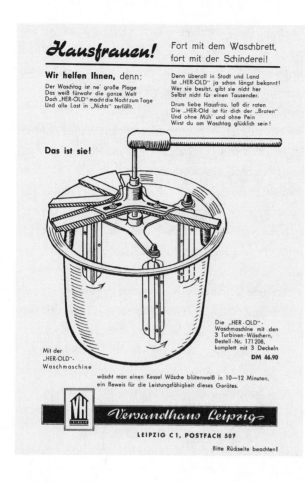

4. "Housewives! Away with washboards, away with drudgery!" (late 1950s). Although automatic washing machines were available by the end of the 1950s in the Federal Republic, which the SED had chosen as its point of comparison, East German industry continued to advertise manual wash basins such as this. To make the gap in living standards between the two Germanies seem less stark, East German authorities counted hand-cranked devices such as this as machines. Author's private collection.

with the automatic washers already on offer in the Federal Republic. But in the race to surpass West Germany, this "machine" could be used to fabricate a statistical victory for the GDR: by counting the washtub as a machine, the GDR would not fall too far behind the West German supply of household appliances.

Even if the appliances had considerably facilitated housework—which they did not—the party leadership could not ignore what its analyses repeatedly revealed: namely, that no amount of advertising could influence production shortages. The shortage of household appliances meant that women were forced to return to older, nonmechanical methods of completing tasks, such as washing clothes in a basin. Because of the shortage of clothing, however, people did not have enough in their wardrobes to go for too long without washing what they did own, which meant in turn that women had to do more washing more frequently. Nor did taking dirty laundry out to professional cleaners solve the problem, since it often took more than four weeks for the cleaners to return the laundry. As the organizers of an official conference on trade concluded, "As long as it still takes four or more weeks to alter and clean clothing . . . women have no choice but to take up their own needles, stand over the washboard themselves, and use up valuable time for these chores."[24] Although the party was aware that production made consumption difficult, and that harried consumers made exhausted workers who could hardly raise production levels, official advertisements continued to suggest that women could use the tremendous amounts of free time they supposedly now had, thanks to the use of modern household technology, to pull their weight in production.

If advertisements for these appliances served the socialist state's goal of convincing women that they had enough time to work and run their households, men were sent a far less progressive message. Even if their wives entered the workforce, socialist ads suggested, it would not affect their domestic comfort. A variety of ads reassured concerned husbands that consumer conveniences made it possible for women to manage their duties at home so economically that they could work without their partner having to take up the slack. In this manner, the SED hoped to reduce potential resistance from men to the mass admission of women into the workforce. Although in the 1950s the party's plans for integrating women into the workforce assumed that men would not be asked to pitch in at home, it soon became clear that "technical household help" alone could hardly offset the multiple burdens on women of caring for children, doing housework, and going to work. Because working women had even less free time, men had to participate in running the household. Within ten years, advertising messages had shifted to reflect the growing responsibility of men at home. In 1971, for example, mail-order catalogues were depicting men in aprons advertising domestic appliances and announcing, "From now on, I'm doing the laundry because my wife is just as entitled to free time and relaxation as I am!"[25]

Toward the end of the 1950s, party and state leaders called on a variety of economic sectors in their bid to surpass the Federal Republic in per capita consumption. But they had quite different ambitions for the fashion and textile industries. The SED's attempts to influence East Germans' fashion sensibilities were not motivated by the goal of surpassing West Germany by supplying consumers with more clothes, shoes, and coats. Quite the opposite: the party sought to constrain consumer demand to ease the burden on the GDR's strained production capacities.

When it suited the party, socialist advertising sought to encourage customers to make purchases. The mail-order catalogue for spring 1961, for example, made use of slogans like "Don't you agree that a new dress is an absolute must for spring?" The catalogue continued by playing on seasonal changes:

> What woman isn't looking forward to the wonderfully warm summer? And the question immediately on everyone's lips is: "What am I going to buy myself this time?" As if it already knew you were waiting, here it is: the new catalogue, eager to give every woman good advice, with styles decorating its pages that are neither extravagant nor plain, styles that have that certain something that takes clothes beyond the everyday look, that makes them chic and desirable. In its variety, this line of clothing epitomizes the fashionable taste and personal touch of our modern woman, who has actively and confidently taken her place in our socialist society.[26]

It soon became clear, however, that retailers did not stock the full range of clothing promoted by these enticing ad slogans and images. Fashion advertising was forced to adjust to this imbalance between supply and demand by promoting the practical clothes that were in stock. Instead of focusing on fashionable clothes, ads in the mid-1960s began directing consumers to purchase clothing that would continue to be in style despite the trends of the fashion industry, highlighting the benefits of durable fabrics that promised long-lasting wear.

To compensate for the GDR's modest fashion statements and short supplies, the party offered ideological justifications. It presented the constant shifts in design characteristic of the capitalist fashion industry as a form of "Western consumer terrorism," which intimidated consumers through its ever-changing styles. In contrast, socialist fashion consciousness resisted capricious trends. As the party noted in its favored formulation, "Changes in fashion, as proposed by the GDR's fashion houses," should occur "continuously and not in fast, abrupt shifts." The SED hoped to exert ideological influence and conserve valuable resources by convincing East German consumers to purchase clothes made of the new fabrics, which constituted 50 percent of the goods available in stores: "The political significance of fashion design is defined by its underlying mission, which is to emphasize the advantages of our socialist society in the competition against capitalism."[27] Between the new, more didactic advertising and the lack of haute couture, consumers were being asked to surrender their purchasing habits and dress styles in favor of practical but unfashionable clothing.

In the 1950s, the party introduced a new fashion ideal in order to realize its ideological and economic goals: the "socialist person, who needs to be clothed." This new ideal was based on the "robustly built" working woman, who took an active part in rural and urban production. The 1 May 1956 edition of the *Bauern-zeitung*, for example, claimed, "Our peasant women" prefer "the somewhat plump type of woman" rather than the slim ideal of "Western fashion." To reinforce this image of the sturdy socialist woman, fashion designers made certain that the majority of the women modeling the latest socialist collections in the 160 fashion shows conducted in rural areas were of the "robust" type. Some economic planners, moreover, genuinely hoped that establishing the robust woman as the universal ideal of beauty would have the economic benefit of reducing demand for female clothing in the middle and long term. They based their assumption on the fact that consumer surveys had supposedly revealed that overweight women would not go along with every trendy change in fashions.[28] In contrast, men were by and large spared educational campaigns to change their dress, since they were generally considered immune to fashion trends and thus less in need of being educated to restrain their shopping impulses. The party's approach to fashion in the 1950s is revealed by the pairing of "Mrs. Fashion" with "Mr. Taste," who kept Fashion's desires in check. Of course, the East German planned economy was no more successful at producing fashionable clothing in sufficient quantity and quality than socialist advertising's didactic attempts to restrict demand were at producing tangible results.

Neither consumers nor manufacturers appreciated the SED's fashion experiments, albeit for very different reasons. Producers refused outright to manufacture oversized clothing because larger sizes required more material. Using more fabric for each item meant that factories produced fewer articles of clothing, which in turn meant factories would not fulfill their production targets. In contrast, a more petite ideal would have helped producers meet their production goals with the same amount of fabric.

By the 1960s, however, stylish young women in elegant clothes and youthful models with cigarettes and portable radios set the tone for fashion in the GDR. Before 1961, women could still be seen rushing to Agricultural Production Cooperative conferences or to plays in the town recreation center dressed in robust peasant dress. But socialist advertising increasingly sought to keep pace with the party's goal of economic and social modernization by presenting slim, urban ideals, which no longer had anything in common with the robust ideal of the worker or peasant woman. Clothing for modern lifestyles in the modern GDR was still supposed to be practical, durable, tasteful, and above all trendy. As ever, it was also expected to be ideologically effective: colorful and optimistic, it was supposed to bear witness to socialist lifestyles and a modern way of life. Unfortunately, these good intentions did not always translate into action. At the end of the decade, the satirical East German magazine *Eulenspiegel* quipped:

> The eager shopper sheds a tear when she takes a closer look at the various textiles. Sacks in dazzling grays or other optimistically dark colors, smocks embellished with sequins or fake brooches, and tacky little numbers all fold their fabric into pleats that violate the plan. And speaking of fabric, it's either very cheap—which is justifiable only for the latest rage, since you can only wear it for one summer anyway—or very expensive. There are almost no clothes whose quality unites ready-to-wear fabrics in appealing colors with timelessly fashionable and respectable cuts. . . . So-called fashion fads are usually out again by the time they've found a brave little tailor here.[29]

West German television and visits from Western relatives ensured that trends in international fashion did not altogether bypass the otherwise insular GDR, even if the party's attempts to keep pace came with ideological baggage. The working woman remained the focal point of fashion propaganda. As the encyclopedia *Die Frau* explained, "Working women who neglect how they dress detract from their dignity," yet it bemoaned the fact that work clothes in the GDR "are unfortunately still the unloved stepchild of the fashion industry." "Boring, unattractive clothes that make women look unappealing and clumsy in the workplace" hardly inspired a love of work. "Instead, the cut and color of work clothes should give women the opportunity to look good in the workplace, but they must also be thoroughly practical (sufficient pockets, no restrictive tucks, no flowing jackets for work at threshing machines, etc.) and durable (especially for women in the country)."[30]

In the 1980s, however, researchers revised their biases about women's fashion consciousness and the related dangers of advertising. One report compiled in 1980, for example, claimed that surveys conducted in the 1960s and 1970s "do not confirm the stereotype that most women believe they need more clothing than they own."[31] As always, the reality was somewhat different: 50 percent of women had trouble finding anything suitable to wear. Often, they could not find clothes available in the size they desired, especially extra large.[32] Actual purchasing patterns also belied the SED's hysterical polemic against "hectic changes in fashions." Most families had just enough clothing to cover their basic needs. Families spent their income on food or saved it for durable goods. For many households, the durability of items—a quality the SED promoted—was an important factor when buying clothes. According to a survey conducted by the Institute for Market Research, the average East German woman in 1964 owned thirty-two items of clothing, including an average of nine dresses and six blouses.[33] By the beginning of the 1970s, however, these numbers had declined to only thirty-one items of clothing on average, including a mere seven dresses and five blouses. Many of these items had not even been purchased from a store, but were homemade. As market researchers put it, making their own clothes was how "a significant number of women [made up for] various flaws in the supply of consumer goods, such as defects in sizes, flaws in the cut and form of ready-made clothing, or unsatisfactory possibilities for combining items."[34] At the same time, the life of each article of clothing varied considerably, in line with earning capacity. Women in the lowest income groups, for example, wore their clothes for an average of ten years, forced to push the limits of natural wear and tear and ignore innovations in fashion. In contrast, women in the highest income groups replaced their clothes every four years. The differences among men were even more striking. Men in the lowest income groups replaced their suits after fourteen years, while men who were better off bought themselves a new suit every four years.[35]

A Political Problem of the First Order

Despite the many setbacks and cutbacks in the plans they had so grandly announced in the 1950s, by the beginning of the 1970s the SED could report successes in at least one area. The supply of food had stabilized, and sufficient amounts of basic foodstuffs were generally available. In fact, the GDR had managed to surpass West Germany in its per capita consumption of butter and fat. The price of overtaking the Federal Republic in butter consumption, however, was a reduction in the supply of cheese and other dairy products—a point the party preferred not to discuss.

Despite this somewhat ambiguous success, the SED was confronted with a new problem. After years of shortages, a "wave of gluttony" (*Fresswelle*) swept the first German workers' and peasants' state. While people's desire for good food after so many years of scarcity and rationing was certainly understandable, no one had anticipated the health problems eating to excess was causing. By 1960, East Germans had successfully eaten their way to the top in the world: by at least one measure, they found themselves in an elite club of industrial nations, including the Federal Republic, whose citizens consumed an average of 33 percent more calories (some 1,000 kilocalories) every day than were necessary. Nutritional researchers warned that the GDR was no longer confronting problems of malnutrition but of hyperalimentation; every fourth adult in the GDR was overweight. The population took in these superfluous nutrients through an excessive consumption of meat, sugar, cakes, alcohol, and sweets, and successfully resisted all attempts to adopt healthy lifestyles and sound eating habits.

The SED decided that it was now time to combat the consequences of the gluttony induced by the German-German eating competition. Initially, the SED proudly tallied up the amount of meat and butter East Germans ate and how much money they spent on these items for comparison with West Germany. When the injurious effects of an unvaried diet that was high in fat content became apparent, however, the party enlisted advertising to persuade people to give up their unhealthy eating habits. As one observer put it, "The population can only effectively be taught to lead a healthy lifestyle if advertising campaigns and scientific information complement each other. Consumers must be encouraged to use products that promote their health through popular-scientific lectures, editorials in the press and trade journals, through individual consultations with doctors, product displays in stores, film advertisements, etc."[36] Strangely enough, the party decided that packaged soups, canned foods, and frozen delicacies would prevent the threat of obesity among workers.

Every possible advertising medium was used to advocate healthy eating habits. Even advertisements for domestic appliances were harnessed to make customers commit to a healthy diet. Pots and pans were introduced whose special coating eliminated the need for grease; steamers accompanied by vegetable-based recipes advocated soups and stews. On television, "The Fish Chef" taught consumers how to prepare fish. Due to a lack of freezers in stores, however, there was hardly any demand for fish through the 1960s, especially since it often took several days to transport fish from the coast to the stores, which hardly increased its attractiveness.

Advertising did not focus only on recognizable products. It also tried to make new products that appeared on the market in the 1970s appeal to wary consumers. The label "optimized nutrition," for example, was developed to signal to consumers that the item was recommended for a healthy diet. Moreover, numerous vegetable-based, low-fat margarines, as well as low-fat cheeses and dietetic foods, were introduced to the market and praised by advertisers.

In practice, however, the GDR's unpredictable economy called the shots. Healthy foods such as fruits, vegetables, and fish, for example, were in short supply and could not be found in stores or in the country's countless cafeterias. As a result, banners created by advertisers to promote healthy foods ended up breeding resentment rather than encouraging people to eat better. Indeed, the supply of fruits and vegetables remained limited through 1989. All efforts to improve the variety available by taking advantage of local fruit and vegetable reserves grown in individuals' small garden plots or through trade with other members of the Council for Mutual Economic Assistance fell short. And even these attempts made sense only during the warm season, when fruits and vegetables were abundant. Although private gardeners delivering their fruit to the central stores did add to the country's tight supplies of fresh produce, they also created new problems. At the beginning of the 1960s, for example, the SED hoped to phase out the traditional activity of making fruit preserves and ease the burden of housework by increasing the availability of prepared and nonperishable foods, including preserved fruits and vegetables. Soon, only hobbyists would still be making preserves. Because food supplies never permanently stabilized, however, making preserves took on increasing importance as a way of supplementing diets. But if private gardeners alleviated the pressure on the GDR's tight supplies of fruits and vegetables, making preserves created tremendous demand for sugar and gelatin, which were essential for making preserves.

At the beginning of the 1960s, East German nutritional experts recognized the fundamental importance of tropical fruits to a healthy diet and noted that these would also benefit the nation's economic health. One study claimed that, "aside from the salutary political effect a sufficient supply of tropical fruits has on consumers, its great economic success consists of its ability to reduce disposable income and demand for many related consumer goods. As a result, there is greater continuity in the circulation of consumer goods and an overall stabilization of the supply situation."[37] Economic experts also believed that tropical fruits could counter the inflationary potential of the population's rapidly growing savings, since people were willing to spend money on tropical fruit. Because consumers were also willing to substitute tropical fruit for other consumer goods, moreover, it would ease demand for other scarce products. However accurate this analysis might have been, economic leaders did not put its recommendations into practice. Bananas and oranges remained rare commodities, since the foreign currency needed to import them was always in short supply. The Institute for Market Research was acutely aware of the multifaceted nature of food shortages and warned the party leadership about the consequences:

> The lack of continuity in the supply of food inhibits the development of a
> socialist consciousness and undermines the population's trust in the state.
> Since food is consumed daily and accounts for more than one third of all
> consumer expenditures, it has become the main criterion by which large

segments of the working population evaluate the standard of living. Guaranteeing a constant, high-quality assortment of goods is thus not exclusively a matter of supply, but also a political issue of the first order. The lack of continuity in supply of food increases the amount of time necessary for shopping and reduces opportunities to curtail it. This lack of a continuous supply is thus at odds with efforts to increase the amount of free time available to working women and to relieve them of unnecessary chores. . . . The inconsistency in the supply of food supports an unbalanced, nutritionally incorrect diet while simultaneously encouraging the increased consumption of alcohol and tobacco. It thus runs counter to the attempts to enforce a correct and healthy diet.[38]

Using Free Time Sensibly

By the end of the 1960s, products increasingly disappeared from advertisements. All too often, the strategy of advertising consumer goods that had been overproduced and thus needed to be sold came to nothing. For one thing, it was impossible to predict which products would become shelf warmers or produced in surplus. For another, even when advertising created demand for certain goods, producers repeatedly proved incapable of turning out sufficient quantities to satisfy popular demand. In all these instances advertising was blamed for the problems. Again and again, advertising was accused of having dedicated itself less to educating consumers than to raising unrealistic expectations. In reality, it was the products featured in advertisements rather than the ads themselves that raised expectations among East Germans, who were then often frustrated when they could not find the goods advertised or had to wait up to several years before the car, the washing machine, or the refrigerator they had ordered was finally delivered.

As products disappeared from advertisements, lifestyles took their place. The range of themes touched upon by advertisers was vast. There were advertisements for apprenticeships and jobs in industry and agriculture, for army service, for occupational health and safety, for health protection, for a healthy diet, and for the employment of women. Increasingly, however, advertising for what was described as a "culturally rich life" moved to the fore. Beginning in the 1960s, the SED leadership became concerned with the consequences of expanded leisure time for its citizens. On the one hand, attention was devoted to whether the increase in free time would result in intensified shopping, especially by women. On the other hand, the party felt impelled to clarify how this free time should be sensibly and constructively spent.

To combine its economic and moral concerns, the SED launched numerous advertising campaigns intended to show consumers how to make sensible use of the free time they could expect to have. To promote the party's priorities, advertising was supposed to recommend ideologically acceptable forms of free time. Just this once, advertisers were allowed to return to old habits and promote new products aggressively. All the same, advertisements for these products had to convey a new lifestyle and leisure spirit, while encouraging ideologically approved activities surrounding the products. For example, advertisers used the slogan "Vacation the Modern Way" to promote camping items, which quickly became available in a variety of assortments. Similarly, slogans such as "For Sun and Relaxation" and "For Tents and Weekends" introduced sunshades, camping beds, and lounge chairs. Initially, the small number of camping accessories produced in the GDR were easy to manage, as were the roughly ten thousand vacationers who visited campsites through the mid-1950s. By 1959, however, the number of campers had risen to 172,000; by 1970, to 500,000. Interest in the outdoors had become a veritable mass movement, as hundreds of thousands of people flocked to the country's campsites during the warm season. The more camping rose in popularity, the more the party augmented the assortment of camping goods. Cameras, sports articles, and camping gear were all used to encourage active outdoor recreation. Sailboats, motorboats, and canoes were produced in great quantities, along with bicycles and roller skates. The special Water Sports and Camping trade show group was founded in 1959 to develop and market new camping gear and leisure goods. Hammocks, sheath knives, camping lanterns, camping stoves, and mess kits were all keyed to leisure activities, emphasizing their healthy and attractive side. Alongside simple and inexpensive camping gear, more expensive luxury items began appearing. The products on offer were soon as diverse as the camping aficionados for whom they were intended. There were serious campers—relatively well-off car owners who kept a second, "outdoor" home so they did not have to forgo a television set, a washing machine, or a full oven—and there were campers who made do with a simple tent.

With the introduction of the five-day work week and longer vacation times in 1965, however, the socialist state felt impelled to regulate more closely what had worked relatively well previously. The SED worried that East Germans, and women in particular, would use their increased leisure time to go shopping and buy up more consumer items that were already in short supply. In an effort to prevent an upsurge in shopping, central authorities stepped up their emphasis on outdoor activities. But the increased use of state-run recreational sites placed a significant burden on state resources; after all, public swimming pools required

5. Family camping (early 1970s). With the introduction of the five-day work week in 1965 the party increasingly considered how the socialist family could spend its newly won free time in a sensible way. Author's private collection.

lifeguards and maintenance crews to keep them open longer. Thus, the reduction of the work week confronted the party with an unpleasant choice between shielding the GDR's inventory of consumer goods by channeling consumer demand toward outdoor activities, or protecting its human and public resources by reducing the availability of outdoor facilities.

In the end, the party felt forced to reverse course and demand that local authorities keep leisure activities under control by shutting down camping and recreational sites, often under the pretext that sanitary facilities were inadequate. Many East Germans were outraged. An official report summarized one complaint to the effect that "the party has suddenly discovered that it is extremely dangerous to camp without toilets that have running water."[39] In Berlin, outdoor pools that had stayed open until 7 p.m. even on weekends before the introduction of the five-day work week now closed at just 2:30 in the afternoon. Even when the GDR recorded economic successes that led to greater consumer sovereignty, the SED could not refrain from trying to exercise control over people's lives.

Although advertising budgets were officially cut by 50 percent in 1961, it was not until 1975 that a complete moratorium was imposed. Advertising directors and government officials had seen too often that advertising was not compatible

Urlaub auf moderne Art

② 36.50

③ 29.80

④ 38.50

⑤ 82.10

① 570.65

6. "Vacation in a Modern Way" (1970s). Advertising was used to stress new products and lifestyles designed to shape the rational and active use of leisure time. Author's private collection.

with an economy marked by scarcity and shortages. Advertisements for products in short supply had only led to further frustration among East Germans. It was better, officials agreed, not to call attention to shortages. Perhaps more important, the SED's original intention—to advertise products that would improve its image—had proven impossible to realize. The population associated the party above all with its failures and blamed it for every shortcoming. Encouraged by advertising to associate products with the party, East Germans held the SED responsible for every missing stick of butter. Worse still, it reflected the party's political messages back onto the products advertised, discrediting socialist consumer goods. As the population of the GDR saw it, Western goods were far superior to Eastern products—and, most important, they were ideologically neutral.

When the Berlin Wall fell in 1989, virtually all socialist products suddenly disappeared from supermarkets. Within a very short period of time, even milk and butter were being imported from the West. Only beginning in 1991 did disappointment with West German democracy lead to a popular return to old East German brands. With the slogan "A Taste of Home," East Germans once again began purchasing familiar products and enjoying old ads. Ironically, the term "honest" was frequently used by advertisers to reintroduce socialist products to East Germans.

Notes

This essay was translated from the German by Jonathan Zatlin.

1. The quotation in this essay's title is from Alexander Abusch, "Zum Geleit," *Neue Werbung* 1, no. 1 (1954): 1, cited in Gries, *Produkte als Medien*, 216.
2. For more on the regime's use of the Stalinallee to promote communism, see Greg Castillo's essay in this volume.
3. Cited in Weber, *Geschichte der DDR*, 198.
4. The press celebrated state stores as a way of undermining the black market, a method of reinvigorating socialist retail, and a means of improving the supply of consumer goods. The state also used the HO stores to crowd out privately owned shops and retail cooperatives by granting HO stores a monopoly on the sale of rationed goods (until rationing was finally abolished in 1958).
5. The Agitation und Propaganda Department of the Central Committee retained ultimate control.
6. Stephan Merl, "Staat und Konsum in der Zentralverwaltungswirtschaft. Rußland und die ostmitteleuropäischen Länder," in Siegrist, Kaelble, and Kocka, *Europäische Konsumgeschichte*, 235.
7. "Der neue Kurs und die Aufgaben der Partei," in *Dokumente der SED* (Berlin: Dietz-Verlag Berlin, 1954), 4: 449.
8. Various authors, *Werbefotografie* (Leipzig: VEB Fotokinoverlag, 1983), 10.
9. Günter Bojny, "Die Aufgaben der Werbeabteilung unter den neuen ökonomischen Verhältnissen," *Neue Werbung*, no. 2 (1955): 1.
10. *Handbuch der Werbung* (Berlin: Verlag Die Wirtschaft, 1968), 318.
11. One of the most striking examples of this association between products and the party's ideological message was the advertisement for Heino men's pants. The politically unacceptable decision to name pants made in the GDR after a popular West German singer resulted not only in the dismissal of the advertisers responsible, but also ensured that in the future consumer goods could not carry names that were more than purely descriptive.
12. *Der Handel im Siebenjahrplan der Deutschen Demokratischen Republik und seine Aufgaben zur weiteren Verbesserung der Versorgung der Bevölkerung: Beschluss des Ministerrats der DDR vom August 1959 zu den Thesen der Handelskonferenz* (Berlin: Zentralkomitee der SED, Abteilung Versorgung und Aussenhandel and Berlin: Ministerium für Handel und Versorgung, 1959), 4.
13. *Diskussion und Entschließungen der Handelskonferenz der SED* (Berlin: Planet-Verlag, 1959); Zielke, "Zur Sozialpolitik in der DDR," 116.
14. *Konsument Katalog*, spring/summer 1959, 2.
15. Anneliese Albrecht, "Die Aufgaben der zentralen staatlichen Organe auf dem Gebiet der sozialistischen Binnenhandelswerbung," *MIM*, no. 27 (1962): 16.
16. *Dein Beruf—dein Leben*, Handel I, no. 4 (Berlin, 1965).

17. Anneliese Albrecht, "Die Funktion und die Aufgaben der Werbung auf dem Konsumgüterbinnenmarkt, die Verantwortung der einzelnen Organe bei der Lösung dieser Aufgaben und die Vorbereitung und Durchführung der Werbemaßnahmen" (Ph.D. dissertation, Leipzig University, 1963), 2.

18. Ibid.

19. Albrecht, "Die Aufgaben der zentralen staatlichen Organe," 22.

20. Ibid., 18.

21. Ibid., 22.

22. See *Programm zur Durchführung von Maßnahmen zur Entlastung der werktätigen Frauen durch den sozialistischen Handel*, SED trade conference (Berlin: Ministerium des Handels, 1959); Günter Manz, *Was darfs denn sein? Was Du vom sozialistischen Handel wissen sollst* (Berlin: Verlag Die Wirtschaft, 1959).

23. Herbert Koch, Waltraud Nieke, and Eberhard Wieland, "Die Erleichterung der Hausarbeit. Konzeption erarbeitet vom Institut für Marktforschung" (1964), 56, DL 102/93, Aussenstelle Coswig, Bundesarchiv Berlin (hereafter BARCHB); Olaf Schmutzler and Werner Bischoff, "Zum Einkaufsverhalten der Haushalte der DDR bei Lebensmitteln," *Mitteilungen des Instituts für Bedarfsforschung*, no. 4 (1968): 11.

24. Zentralkomitee der SED, Abteilung Versorgung und Aussenhandel, *Handelskonferenz der SED* (Berlin: Ministerium für Handel und Versorgung 1959), 40.

25. *Katalog centrum-Versand*, spring/summer 1971.

26. *Katalog konsument-Versandhaus*, spring/summer 1961.

27. Karl Ernst Schubert and Georg Wittek, "Zur Aufgabenstellung des Modeschaffens in der DDR," *Mitteilungen des Instituts für Bedarfsforschung*, no. 2 (1963): 64, 58.

28. Ruth Weichsel, "Die sportlich-legere und kombinierfähige Bekleidung erwirbt die Gunst der Konsumenten," *Mitteilungen des Instituts für Marktforschung*, no. 3 (1971).

29. "Kleider machen Leute," *Eulenspiegel*, no. 15 (1968): 2.

30. *Kleine Enzyklopädie: Die Frau* (Leipzig: VEB Verlag Enzyklopädie Leipzig, 1962), 500.

31. *Aktuelle Informationen zur Mode und Saison*, 1980, 7, unpublished manuscript, DL 102/1572, Aussenstelle Coswig, BARCHB.

32. Weichsel, "Die sportlich-legere," 24.

33. Ibid., 22.

34. Ibid.

35. Ibid., 24.

36. Albrecht, "Die Aufgaben der zentralen staatlichen Organe," 25.

37. *Die Auswirkungen einer bedarfsgerechten Versorgung der Bevölkerung mit Südfrüchten auf die Entwicklung der Nachfrage*, 1980, 7, unpublished manuscript, DL 102/594, Aussenstelle Coswig, BARCHB.

38. *Die künftige Entwicklung der Verbrauchererwartungen an das Sortiment, die Bearbeitung, die Qualität und die Verpackung der Nahrungsmittel*, 1968, 4, unpublished manuscript, DL 102/189, Aussenstelle Coswig, BARCHB.

39. Ibid., 216.

PROMOTING SOCIALIST CITIES AND CITIZENS

East Germany's National Building Program

Exploring the distinctions between capitalist advertising and socialist propaganda, art historian Boris Groys has contrasted "commercial, impersonal art
that responds to and simultaneously strives to manipulate spontaneous consumer demand" with "the art of socialist realism, which markets not things but
ideology . . . free and independent of the potential consumer, since marketing
conditions rule out the possibility that the ideology will not be bought."[1] The
socialist-realist reconstruction of East Berlin as an advertisement for a Stalinist
model of social and economic modernity defies Groys's analysis. In the early
1950s, exploiting divided Berlin's potential as a West-facing "showcase," the
leaders of East Germany's Sozialistische Einheitspartei Deutschlands (SED) initiated a building program that explored the frontiers of what Barbara Kirshenblatt-
Gimblett has called the "political economy of showing."[2] Like the ethnographic
exhibits, heritage spectacles, and world's fairs that are the focus of Kirshenblatt-
Gimblett's scholarship, East German reconstruction planners publicized model
environments as representations of a distinctive way of life. As an advertising
medium, the socialist-realist city "sold" not only ideology, but also the project's
own extravagant price tag. Citizens across the German Democratic Republic
(GDR) had to be persuaded to devote the household cash and volunteer labor
needed to raise monumental stage sets for a public relations campaign that targeted audiences on both sides of the capital city's East-West dividing line.

A newly planned residential street in East Berlin, the Stalinallee, became the
epicenter of redevelopment activity, and as such was freighted with historical
portent. As reported in *Neues Deutschland*, the party daily of the SED, the con-

struction project was to be the proving grounds for an architectural style that, to put it in capitalist terms, would serve as a branding device for the new cities and citizens of postwar German socialism. *Neues Deutschland* called on East German designers to reject modernist architecture, which the party equated with West Germany's Americanization, and instead to emulate their Soviet colleagues' recycling of local aesthetic traditions to come up with a contemporary synthesis, yielding a family of East Bloc styles collected under the rubric of "socialist realism." By contributing to the invention of a new nationalist design idiom, East German architects would confirm their membership in a socialist intelligentsia. Urban reconstruction would nurture other socialist subjectivities as well, according to party newspaper reports. The adoption of Soviet construction techniques by East German labor at the Stalinallee would produce a contemporary proletarian persona: the worker activist. New housing would catalyze a trickle-down model of human transformation, creating residential incubators for the "new people" of East German socialism. As the vortex of an urban renewal program that conflated the remodeling of the capital city with that of its citizens, the Stalinallee's model socialist neighborhood became the protagonist of a cross-referencing cycle of poems, paintings, songs, novels, posters, newspaper articles, documentary films, give-away promotional items, even children's toys—the multimedia tools of a saturation campaign advertising East Germany's National Building Program.

As a state-sponsored promotional idiom, socialist realism displays marked affinities with capitalist advertising. Representations of Stalinism's much heralded "new man," according to Groys, belong to a "typology of the nonexistent," contradicting the apparent realism of Stalin-era aesthetics. Socialist realism is, in short, abstract art, according to Groys. Rather than a hackneyed effort to reproduce reality, its mimetic techniques "focus on the hidden essence of things. . . . Socialist realism is oriented toward that which has not yet come into being but which should be created."[3] Michael Schudson draws an explicit comparison with the iconography of advertising, which he calls "capitalist realism": "It does not claim to picture reality as it is but reality as it should be—life and lives worth emulating. It is always photography or drama or discourse with a message—rarely picturing individuals, it shows people only as incarnations of larger social categories. . . . It focuses, of course, on the new, and if it shows some sign of respect for tradition, this is only to help in the assimilation of some new commercial creation."[4] Socialist realism, much more than a mere stylistic category, also prescribed a distinctive way of seeing. Its hallmark was the superimposition of "a

Berlin · schöner denn je!

Hilf mit am Nationalen Aufbauprogramm der Hauptstadt Deutschlands

1. A model worker-activist looms over architect Hermann Henselmann's design for East Berlin's Weberwiese Tower in a 1952 poster promoting the "National Building Program for Germany's Capital" and its goal of making Berlin "more beautiful than ever!" Courtesy of Institut für Regionalentwicklung und Strukturplanung, Berlin.

better 'soon' on a still imperfect 'now,'" in Sheila Fitzpatrick's memorable gloss.[5] As put into practice by the East German author Jürgen Käding in his prototypic reconstruction chronicle, *Baumeister der Stalinallee* (Master Builders of the Stalinallee): "One should no longer see the rubble in the old way, as if it were just time-worn bricks, rusty steel beams and sooty debris. Look forward, and you see the Stalinallee already there; the domestic palaces of our age of the masses!"[6] This trope, fundamental to East German representations of urban reconstruction, invoked a mode of perception that Katherine Pence has called the "suspended present."[7] It urged citizens to make sense of their ragged postwar surroundings by inhabiting them in the future tense. This characteristic Stalin-era *mentalité* not only celebrated the party's relentless optimism, but also provided an ideological context for the public privation, self-sacrifice, and voluntary labor, which served East Germany's National Building Program as the socialist equivalent of start-up capital.

Cultural Revolution by Decree

As a starting place for Berlin's socialist remodeling, Friedrichshain, just east of the city center, was a logical choice. The working-class quarter had been knotted with factories, tenements, railroad sidings, and slaughterhouse facilities built during the boom years of the late nineteenth century. By 1920 the district had Berlin's highest population density — this in a city infamous as one of Europe's most congested. Bloody street brawls pitting Hitler's SA (Sturmabteilung) against the communist Red Front raged through the precinct in the early 1930s. A small electoral majority carried the Nazi party to victory in Friedrichshain, renamed the Horst Wessel district in memory of a martyred SA youth. Allied bombers caused widespread damage during the war, and in April 1945 much of what survived the air raids was razed to the ground as Soviet tanks and troops fought their way west to Hitler's chancellery. By the war's end, half of Friedrichshain's building stock lay demolished or damaged beyond repair.[8] On 21 December 1949, Stalin's seventieth birthday, state and local officials presided over the renaming of the Frankfurter Allee, the district's primary east–west artery, as the Stalinallee, and set the cornerstone of the boulevard's first modern housing block. *Neues Deutschland*, the SED newspaper, reported that a hundred thousand citizens took part in the festivities, which featured speeches by party leaders and rallies for German-Soviet friendship and culminated in a dazzling nighttime apparition: Stalin's silhouette traced in fireworks beside hissing letters that spelled out the greeting "The working people of all lands send their congratulations."[9] From this point forward, benchmarks in East Berlin's reconstruction would be synchronized with a ritual calendar of Soviet provenance: an alternative chronology advertising the benchmarks of a nation's path to socialism.

The joyful mood reported in East German dailies was not shared by the nation's Minister of Construction, Lothar Bolz. On the day of the inauguration he sent out a memorandum voicing concerns about the modernist reconstruction plan originally developed for municipal authorities by the Institut für Bauwesen (Institute for Building Methods, or IfB), a quasi-autonomous design think-tank. The capital city of German socialism, Bolz insisted, deserved an architecture that would "better express the progress and strengths of our new state than the suggested lowrise housing, reminiscent of . . . Weimar times."[10] Party helmsman Walter Ulbricht agreed. In January 1950, he approved Bolz's proposal to send a planning delegation to the USSR for retraining. Bolz was among the six reconstruction officials who traveled to Moscow that spring, where they absorbed

Soviet approaches to urbanism, housing, and construction, as well as the Stalin-era conviction that these innovations would engender "people who embody the new."[11] A manifesto on urban reconstruction echoing Soviet doctrine, the "Sixteen Principles of City Planning," was written into reconstruction legislation called the *Aufbaugesetz* and passed into East German national law on 6 September 1950. Over the course of the following year, Bolz would wield this manifesto to "propagate dogma, manipulate the vacillating, and unmask opponents," according to Simone Hain's account.[12]

East German architects found plenty to dislike in the new Soviet-sourced reconstruction mandates. Hermann Henselmann, a party member and up-and-coming design talent at the IfB, circulated a withering internal memo on the "Sixteen Principles" in the summer of 1950, declaring its mandates "altogether too dictatorial" and its neoclassical design vocabulary "in a very embarrassing sense colloquialized by Hitler."[13] Henselmann's objections were shared by many of his colleagues. Socialist realism couched its prescribed neoclassical aesthetic in a theory calling for the retrieval of national design traditions associated with social progress. For numerous East German architects, Germany's progressive design legacy was embodied not in Prussian neoclassicism, but in the Bauhaus tradition, which seemed to them to have earned its antifascist credentials by virtue of its Nazi-era suppression. The SED asserted its disagreement in the form of a cultural revolution. "The Battle for a New German Architecture," a component of the broader "Battle against Formalism in Art and Literature" declared by the SED Central Committee in March 1951, was directed by a new centrally managed East German architectural institute called the Deutsche Bauakademie. Its public relations campaign, conducted through the national press, proclaimed the dire state of East German design: "In architecture, which confronts great tasks in the context of the Five-Year Plan, what hinders us the most is the so-called 'Bauhaus-style' and the underlying constructivist, functionalist philosophy of many architects. . . . The point of departure for the majority of architects is abstraction and the mere technical side of building, neglecting the artistic form of the built object and spurning connections to past exemplars." Members of the design intelligentsia were told to learn from their proletarian client base, engage in self-criticism, and report the results in language accessible to working-class readers.[14] As Henselmann learned, these steps were prescriptive, not optional. New modes of aesthetic authority, brought under pressure from a national press campaign, stripped Henselmann of any remaining "bourgeois" illusions, establishing for the architect a socialist persona formulated for mass media dissemination.[15]

Exasperated by Henselmann's intransigence and his design collective's delay in producing a socialist-realist breakthrough for the National Building Program, *Neues Deutschland* published an account of the architectural stalemate. "On Building Style, Political Style, and Comrade Henselmann," penned by the newspaper's editor, Rudolf Herrnstadt, gave the architect one last chance to repent: "What does an artist, who has become disengaged, but is in truth progressive, do? He retreats and in the stillness says of his critics: I'll show these people a thing or two, works with all his strength (political and professional), makes the connection, and finally emerges with work of such beauty and power that it knocks the wind out of yesterday's critics."[16]

Henselmann acquiesced, issuing penitence in built and textual variants. In "The Reactionary Nature of Constructivism," an article published in *Neues Deutschland*, he denounced Bauhaus design in the vocabulary of Stalinist aesthetic discourse, using the long-extinct Russian Constructivist movement as an analogue for German modernism.[17] His architectural contrition, a neoclassical design for the Weberwiese, won unanimous approval from East Berlin's city council. The Weberwiese tower rose to national celebrity even before its construction began. Images of the building appeared on posters and postage stamps and in national periodicals; even toddlers learned to recognize the housing block from its wooden building block replica, complete with miniature workers, residents, and construction machinery, manufactured by a state-owned toy-making firm.[18] Hailed as the nation's first masterpiece of socialist-realist architecture, the Weberwiese was a public relations fraud: a work so ill-proportioned, banal in detailing, and poorly laid-out that, had it not been the National Building Program's firstborn, it would have been condemned as "primitive and schematic," in the language of Stalin-era aesthetic criticism. Henselmann's housing block was a consummate work of art only because the SED wanted one to kick off its advertising campaign for the capital's reconstruction.

A publicity photo taken in 1952 summarizes Henselmann's hard-earned successes as architectural authority and socialist parable. The designer points to the future in Lenin's iconic pose. Flanking construction workers direct their gaze accordingly, wearing optimistic smiles. The heroic triad embodies the unity of the proletariat and its intelligentsia and works compositionally to link unfurled blueprints with the scaffolding of a building in progress. While this advertisement for class harmony can be dismissed as mere propaganda, it conveys Henselmann's epiphany with remarkable economy of expression. The publicity still depicts the happy ending of a socialist-realist drama in which an architect ac-

2. The architect Hermann Henselmann, center, flanked by two construction workers in an East German publicity photo, ca. 1952. Courtesy of Christian Borngräber Archives, Hamburg.

cepts party guidance, learns from Soviet precedent, and is rehabilitated through self-criticism: the cultural revolution's recipe for ideological integration. Henselmann emerged triumphant from "The Battle for a New German Architecture" as the source of two pioneering works created for mass media consumption: a brand-new housing block and a heavily remodeled professional persona.

The Collectivizing Power of Rubble

The SED leadership chose to promote 1952 as the year in which East Germany would vault into a socialist future. Crash programs would collectivize agriculture, expropriate private enterprises, build steel mills, and construct a new capital. *Neues Deutschland* ran the SED Central Committee's breathless proclamation "For the Building of Berlin!" across its front page: "The public will be gripped by building fever . . . the consequences will mount daily before our eyes. Tens of thousands from Berlin, joined by hundreds of thousands from outside Berlin, will clear rubble, lay bricks, forge metal, irrigate, log, reforest, transport, etc., all with the name of the German capital on their lips. . . . The newly risen German capital will become a symbol of the life of the German nation."[19] The SED proposal called for national reconstruction to focus first and foremost on the Stalinallee. A new National Committee for the Building of the German Capital would procure labor, funds, and construction materials, which could not be supplied within the state's Five-Year Plan without undermining previously established economic priorities. Volunteer effort to clear rubble would prepare the building site while supplying recycled construction material. Industrial workers would donate other supplies through labor over and above standing production quotas. A "building lottery" would finance construction. Citizens would be invited to invest 3 percent of their income—to be returned with interest by 1958—for a chance to move into one of one thousand new apartments earmarked for the purpose. The SED urged West Berliners to participate as well, in the interest of creating the future capital city of a unified Germany.[20] These multiple initiatives were to be advanced through a promotional campaign intended to penetrate every facet of East German daily life, from the workplace to home and the public spaces in between.

On the morning of 21 December 1951, Bauakademie architects braved icy winds to assemble for a plein-air conference on "Berlin's first socialist street." As chronicled in Käding's hagiography, *Master Builders of the Stalinallee*, the meeting was of great portent. It could not have been described otherwise, given the fact that it transpired on the dawn of Stalin's seventy-second birthday. Designers unfurled their plans for the first phase of construction: a kilometer-long boulevard of neoclassical housing blocks seven to nine stories high.[21] The ground floor would be lined with restaurants, cafés, and state retail outlets.[22] A first wave of finished apartments had to be ready in time for the new residents to celebrate Stalin's seventy-third birthday. Käding's chronicle portrays the Weberwiese as a nebulous presence that morning, its scaffolding "looming in silhouette through the fog." But the building's function within a master narrative of national reconstruction was clear. If Henselmann's tower design had initiated East Berlin's rebuilding, the Stalinallee would complete the leap to concrete reality. Visitors to this monumental urban fragment would be able to savor a fully realized socialist lifestyle. Walking the broad, shaded sidewalks, gazing into well-stocked shop windows, touring the spacious, well-equipped apartments, citizens from both East and West would undergo a conversion experience. The Stalinallee would be East German socialism's ultimate sales tool: a model of the future built at one-to-one scale.

A public relations barrage coincided with the beginning of public rubble-clearing efforts on 2 January 1952. Hans Jendretzky, a municipal SED leader, drafted the citizen mobilization plan requested by the Politburo. Billboards, posters, and leaflets went up across the city. Newsreels and press photos showed volunteers marching to the site to remove debris side-by-side with national leaders. Agitators at workplaces pressured employees to organize "rubble-clearing brigades" to compete with workers from other enterprises for military-style awards like medals and banners. The East German Women's League for International Woman's Day distributed commemorative scarves adorned with the image of Weberwiese tower: a socialist variant of the give-away promotional novelty. Families were encouraged to keep a "Book of Honor" in which voluntary labor shifts were recorded. They were also asked to donate private household funds; one such scheme involved buying slips of paper for home assembly into a scale model of Henselmann's Weberwiese block. A state radio station programmed music and messages concocted specifically to motivate those removing rubble. Trucks equipped with blaring loudspeakers ensured that the broadcasts could be heard by the volunteers. To popularize socialist work songs and protect citizens from the "pernicious influence of Boogie-Woogie non-culture," the Association of Free German Trade Unions (Freier Deutscher Gewerkschaftsbund) printed up a collection of its favorite music to clear debris by, including "Berlin Will Arise New," "A Million Hands," "Brother, Join In!," and "A Worker Reads Stalin."[23] At the end of the volunteer shifts, movie theaters scheduled free shows for those rubble workers energetic enough to remain upright and alert for another two hours.[24]

As the hills of debris receded, National Committee officers took stock of the results of their public relations campaign. An accounting of setbacks and shortcomings, rather than successes, dominated the minutes of a March 1952 meeting. Brigade leaders from smaller firms had shown up without their associates, but with a pile of collected time cards ready to be stamped. Rubble-clearing volunteers had ridiculed the spectacle of chauffeurs in limousines waiting for party leaders to finish with their debris-removal photo-ops. Complaints about the outdoor music broadcasts included one from a dentist whose patients would no longer sit still, and one from the warden of a local women's prison, whose inmates could not be restrained from dancing. More ominously, counterfeit circulars found in provincial cities encouraged citizens to travel with pick and shovel to Berlin, where free housing and meals were said to await them. Given the national shortage of foodstuffs and residential space and the flood of petitioners seeking residency permits for the capital, the disinformation seemed to be a

3. Frau Pankratz of Weissenfels presents her model of the Weberwiese tower to the secretary of the National Committee for the Building of the German Capital in 1952. The façades are assembled from slips of paper, each representing a 20 Pfennig donation; a completed model contributed 43 marks to the cause.

deliberate attempt to sabotage the reconstruction campaign—a reasonable deduction, given the National Committee's efforts to dispense propaganda, solicit funds, and recruit volunteers in West Berlin.[25]

Another set of concerns involved the "struggle for new labor methods" being waged at construction sites. The SED had planned to use the Weberwiese project as a finishing school for "workers of a new type." German masons were encouraged to adopt Soviet high-speed bricklaying techniques and engage in voluntary speed-ups to raise productivity and reduce construction costs.[26] The National Committee noted that German workers seemed reluctant to increase labor output without a corresponding raise in pay. The committee resolved to address the dilemma fictionally. It commissioned a literary work to popularize the battle for new labor methods and carefully outlined the proposed novel's themes: "The story must show human transformation through changes in economic and material relationships. It must also display the development of people to political maturity."[27] Progress in the construction of the capital city would symbolize the future of East German society and its "new human beings," a socialist-realist promotional message that proved prescient in ways unintended by the SED's literary patrons.

Art in the Service of Socialist Construction

The National Committee entrusted the task of plotting a successful resolution to the conflict between workers and their Marxist-Leninist managers to the "proletarian writer" Theo Harych. A contract driver who had all but abandoned any hope of publishing, Harych elbowed his way into the socialist literary scene with a working-class autobiography that proved surprisingly popular with readers. His credentials as a member of the intelligentsia forged from proletarian stock made him an ideal choice for the National Committee's commission. *Stalinallee*, his first full-fledged attempt in the socialist-realist mode, was said to be firmly rooted in the realities of proletarian life. "As he began the work, he clambered about the building site and became familiar with the life of the construction worker," an East German literary critic later claimed.[28] In fact, the novel was based upon a file stuffed with newspaper articles. Harych organized his clippings into folders corresponding to the novel's major themes, including "new work methods," "activist brigades," "sabotage," and "the Weberwiese tower shapes new people." He lifted characters, events, and plot elements directly from the East German dailies, neatly corroborating Jeffrey Brooks's assertion that socialist realism, as a discursive mode, traces its origins to Stalin-era journalism.[29] The novel's protagonist, an unemployed West Berlin construction worker, meets his love interest, a National Building Program volunteer, during her daring mission into the West to plaster agitprop placards across shop windows (in effect, obstructing capitalist advertising with its socialist equivalent). In rescuing her from arrest, he is plunged into a drama populated by socialist workers, cement mixers, and saboteurs. He eventually repudiates the chromium glitter of capitalism for a life of heroic labor on the Stalinallee. The result is a boy-meets-girl story in which the love interest is driven not by sexual chemistry, but by the magnetic attraction exerted between Stalinist programs for human and urban reconstruction.[30]

Like Harych's novel, party leaders heroized the worker-activist slated to emerge from construction sites at the Stalinallee and Weberwiese. East German labor's rank and file reviled him. Exemplary representatives of this new breed of worker played muse for the new breed of architects, artists, and writers. Henselmann introduced Bertolt Brecht and his lover Ruth Berlau to a hand-picked sample of model proletarians. Berlau reported, "Bert [Brecht] had all the [labor] improvements explained to him, and he blossomed in the presence of this group—older workers, young activists—it was just the elite that Hensel-mann had rounded up."[31] The meeting inspired Brecht's ode "To a Young Stalin-allee Construction Worker," given its provenance, perhaps the quintessential statement of the National Building Program's confluence of revolutionary ardor and individual opportunism, idealism and dishonesty, art and kitsch.[32] Pictorial representation was another medium cultivated in SED public relations efforts, and here, just as in architecture and literature, disabusing the intelligentsia of its penchant for "formalist abstraction" was one of the primary challenges. "Berlin Under Construction," an exhibition held in May 1951, left an art critic for *Neues Deutschland* with "the distressing general impression that most painters and graphic artists approach the grand theme of the building of Germany's capital only in a completely formal and superficial way; that they have not grasped in the slightest the content that is to be expressed. . . . From what planet do these artists come, that they take such twaddle as a representation of our building efforts?"[33] In painting, as in architecture, socialist realism's conflation of fine and applied arts proved frustrating to party ideologues, who repeatedly found them-selves having to coerce artists into producing the aesthetic objects theoretically associated with creativity's liberation from capitalist market forces.

In the interest of improving the representational quality of state-subsidized art, the East German Cultural Fund (Kulturfonds der DDR), charged with financing and managing the Stalinallee's graphic arts commissions, invited art-ists' collectives to the construction site to produce sketches and studies for larger works. The results were presented to Herbert Gute of the Union of Pictorial Artists (Verband Bildender Künstler), who selected what he considered to be the best, proffering Cultural Fund commissions to an instant crop of artists laureate. For the composition *Construction of the Stalinallee* (*Aufbau der Stalinallee*), painter Heinz Löffler was awarded M 2,000. The Arnold-Chemnitzer-Oelsner artists' collective received a windfall of M 50,000, the most generous of the 1952 grants, and a fortune for its time and place. State subventions produced works that in-cluded *Stalinallee*, another *Construction of the Stalinallee*, *A Highrise on the Stalin-allee* (*Ein Hochhaus in der Stalinallee*), *Stalinallee Building Site with View of the Sports Hall* (*Bauplatz Stalinallee mit Blick auf die Sportshalle*), *Topping-out Ceremony on the Stalinallee* (*Richtfest in der Stalinallee*), *Buildings of the Stalinallee with the Weberwiese Tower* (*Bauten der Stalinallee mit Hochhaus Weberwiese*), and more.[34]

Perhaps the most renowned example of the new genre of Stalinallee art was Otto Nagel's *Young Bricklayer of the Stalinallee* (*Junger Maurer der Stalinallee*), a knee-length portrait displayed to great official acclaim at the Third German Art Exhibition held in Dresden in March 1953. An East German art critic explained that Nagel had discovered his model "among the workers building the first socialist street. . . . A young lad, his broad, tender baby-face reveals a man not yet mature, but it is a pleasant, open face inspiring confidence; self-assured, free, proud."[35] This freight train of adjectives describing the worker-activist ideal substantiates Anders Åman's claim that Nagel's portrait is not of a worker, but rather of *the* worker, "the representative of youth and tomorrow, the new man in the making during 'the construction of socialism.'"[36] Nagel's success in painting the visual analogue of a narrative convention was the artist's ticket to fame and, in a more general sense, the foundation for socialist realism's deployment as a representational technology as precisely integrated as anything dreamed up on Madison Avenue.

The Theater of Socialism

It was on Stalin's seventy-third birthday, as foreseen in plans drawn up in 1951, that the first wave of families occupied their new apartments along the Stalinallee. Its buildings stood like "sculpture, isolated in the midst of a cityscape which had just barely been cleared of the wreckage of war," as a contemporary observer described it.[37] The neoclassical façades screened from view the ruinous patchwork of a coexisting urban reality — the one in which the vast majority of East Berliners led daily lives. But from a vantage point bracketed by the continuous row of new apartment blocks, one perceived the new East German capital in its imaginary totality. "Multiply this image by one thousand: the generous appointments of the street, the mechanical comforts of the housing, the attractive shops, social amenities and restaurants," exhorted an East German tract, "and you will get a general idea of the good life in the socialist residential district of the future."[38] The street's inhabitants — the nation's "best patriots," according to a headline — included workers, bureaucrats, members of the intelligentsia, and "outstanding activists, a national award recipient, a Hero of Labor, and two exemplary Teachers of the People."[39] Four-fifths of the Stalinallee's first generation of occupants were working class, but next-door neighbors included the actor Hans Klering, the poet Franz Fühmann, the painter Gabriele Mucchi, and the architect Hermann Henselmann.[40] This was a "demographic composition" in both the statistical and aesthetic sense. The Stalinallee's residential mix conformed to the lexicon of ideal types identified by party doctrine as that of socialism's chosen people.

Media depictions broadcast the Stalinallee's potency as a catalyst for human transformation. In a report about visitors' first impressions, clipped by Harych for his files, a *Neues Deutschland* reporter recounted, "On a tour of the new apartments, Elsbeth Kiengaard, an elderly woman who works as a sales clerk, said, smiling, 'People are conceived clearly here.' And what she meant was clear to everyone. The people who move into these apartments will become different people, will become new people, people who take pride in the work done by their hands."[41]

The street's power to redefine identity extended well beyond that of the proletariat. A feature-length documentary produced by the Deutsche Film AG (DEFA) by splicing together clips from existing newsreels, many shot at Stalinallee inaugural events, endowed the general secretary of the SED Central Committee with a new persona: "Master Builder of Socialism" (Baumeister des Sozialismus). The title, shared by Ulbricht and his eponymous biopic, echoed the designation of the street's architects as "Master Builders of the Stalinallee" and heralded a new "cult of personality" patterned after that of the general secretary's role model, Stalin.[42] The Stalinallee was a monumental branding device: a physical setting that linked socialist construction workers to working-class residents and the street's resident architects to the architect of German Stalinism.

Along the Stalinallee's discursive crossroads, socialist-realist film, journalism, fiction, poetry, painting, sculpture, urbanism, architecture, and interior design intersected. Apartment façades provided surfaces for ornament said to demonstrate the ongoing fusion of all "progressive" design modes. Upper-story exteriors were clad in lustrous cream-colored tiles produced at the Meissen porcelain works, once famous for the china that graced aristocratic tables, now a source of building materials for proletarian palaces. Sheaves of grain, one of the cast ceramic motifs, symbolized the fictive successes of agricultural collectivization. Bas-relief depictions of themes and events like "Berlin's democratic-revolutionary history," "Berlin's workers' movement and its era of struggle," and "the Soviet Union's aid in political, economic and cultural reconstruction" made light work of *Vergangenheitsbewältigung*—the arduous task of coming to term's with German history. Looking out their apartment windows, Stalinallee residents literally learned to live with their nation's past through neatly resolved narratives: the writing was on the wall, so to speak.[43] At the street's sidewalk level, travertine sheathing and Doric columns ennobled state retail outlets. Inside the Stalinallee's watering holes, socialist realism fulfilled its mandate for an art "socialist in content and national in form" through commercial interior decor melding classical elegance with cultural populism. The Haus Budapest Restaurant, with

4. A poster for the "Month of German-Soviet Friendship" in 1952 depicts a phalanx of East German citizens marching down the Stalinallee. Courtesy of Deutsche Historisches Museum, Berlin.

its homespun Magyar embroidery patterns and scraffito folk-art bouquets, and the neighboring Café-Restaurant Warschau (subsequently renamed Bukarest) invoked an even larger socialist composition—the wider world extending outward from the Stalinallee in one direction: east.

Gesamtkunstwerk Stalinallee was also the backdrop for a characteristic genre of socialist-realist performance art. During the festival days of a new ritual calendar, the street's six lanes were sealed off to vehicles and dedicated instead to ideological traffic. Mass processions into the city center demonstrated support for SED policies and announced the emergence of new socialist subjectivities, as depicted in a poster promoting the "Month of German-Soviet Friendship" from 7 November to 5 December, a unit of ideological time that defied the constraining conventions of a Julian calendar. It shows workers and engineers, accompanied by young mothers and their children, processing between the twin sentinels designed by Henselmann to mark the start of the Stalinallee. The adults and children marching toward the socialist future embody the forces of economic production and social reproduction in a rendering so idealized and schematic that their socialist-realist figuration threatens to dissolve, revealing the shimmering ideological essences lurking just beneath the surface.

As "the heart of the new Berlin," the Stalinallee was a tourist destination for sightseers from the two Germanies and abroad. In 1953 the National Building

Program sponsored four thousand tours for organized delegations. By the end of the year, half a million West Germans had visited the street, according to National Committee statistics.[44] The sales pitch presented to capitalist citizens soft-pedaled socialist transformation, sticking to the safer issue of price point. In West Berlin, a two-room apartment went for about DM 130 a month, with utilities raising the total to DM 180. A Stalinallee unit of similar size, including utilities, was pegged at a prewar rental price less than M 60 per month and was fixed at that level for as long as the resident stayed.[45] A West German guestbook comment reads, "The apartments are really beautiful. I wish I could have one, but I live 'over there.' The rent I pay for two rooms and a kitchen, with no private bathroom and a shared hallway, is DM 80.50."[46] Stalinallee propaganda promoted the street's neoclassical architecture as the antithesis of the "proportionless rabbit warrens" of West German apartments in the "American colonial style" — meaning modernism. But to many observers, Western modernism embodied progress.[47] The Stalinallee's socialist-realist monumentality was so effective as its own counterpropaganda that the U.S. Forces Center in West Berlin, taking advantage of mutual treaties guaranteeing free military passage throughout the city for its occupying powers, offered its own daily tour.[48] The sight of convoys of olive drab buses filled with U.S. soldiers was a surreal aspect of daily life on the Stalinallee. "They drive by slowly," intoned an editorial in *Neues Deutschland*, "putting their faces to the windows and making faces. Not for the fun of it: certainly not for fun. One need not decipher the English-language signs on the buses to know that the gentlemen who chew gum as they ride by are Americans."[49] In the cultural cold war, each camp's publicity was quickly mined as raw material for the other's counterpropaganda.

Just as the National Building Campaign reached its crescendo, an adversary more threatening than gum-chewing GIs confronted the SED. As citizens were being asked to donate their cash and volunteer labor to create a neoclassical showcase, state investment in industry was all but eliminating financing for East German consumer goods. The gap between socialist life as lived and publicized reaped a harvest of bitterness and alienation. In the first three months of 1953, with food supplies faltering and morale plummeting, nearly eight thousand East Germans were arrested for infractions like black market transactions or speaking critically of the regime, both punishable by prison sentences. Between fifteen thousand and twenty-five thousand East German citizens fled westward each month.[50] The most remarkable socialist tempo, as it turned out, was not the speed of the Stalinallee's construction, but the rate at which workers were abandoning the nation established in their name.

The uneasy truce between party and proletariat reached a flashpoint on 16 June 1953, just months after Stalin's death. In an unprecedented move, workers from the Stalinallee and another nearby construction site walked off the job to present their grievances at SED headquarters. Heading downtown on foot, they hijacked two sound trucks and, appropriating a National Building Program publicity strategy, broadcast calls for a general strike to be launched the next morning with a mass gathering at the Stalinallee. About 15 percent of the city's workforce—thirty thousand people—came out the following day to join the mass demonstrations. In a carnivalesque inversion of the choreographed rituals beloved by party authorities, protesters carried placards and chanted slogans mocking the SED leadership. As the day progressed, demonstrators trampled national flags, defaced portraits of Stalin, and torched a state retail outlet on Potsdamer Platz in a visceral expression of consumer dissatisfaction.

The following day, 18 June, the protest spread to hundreds of other East German cities and towns. The party remained in power only through the intervention of Soviet tanks. But the revolt that began on construction sites succeeded in demolishing a cycle of myths woven around the capital's reconstruction and citizen self-sacrifice. Harych shelved his unfinished *Stalinallee* manuscript, never to be published.[51] The paean to Ulbricht, *Master Builder of Socialism*, disappeared into a film vault; a single surviving copy came to light four decades later. Nagel's heroic portrait, *Young Bricklayer of the Stalinallee*, now freighted with unintended symbolism, disappeared from the artist's retrospectives, emerging much later under the abbreviated title *Young Bricklayer*, "as if the subject had just been any bricklayer," as Åman notes.[52] By 1961 even the Stalinallee had exchanged its discredited name for the more seemly Karl-Marx-Allee. Stalinism's utopia was proving to be exactly that as it evaporated from official memory, replaced by a reformulated socialist future, represented by a very different urban iconography.

Khrushchev's de-Stalinization appropriated capitalist imagery, echoing the promises of consumer abundance broadcast across Western Europe a decade earlier by the Marshall Plan—ironically, as part of the U.S. strategy to undermine the appeal of socialist self-sacrifice.[53] The new Soviet leader ridiculed the "confectionary" style of palatial apartment blocks built with the approval of his predecessor. Within East Germany's architectural establishment, a spate of reverse defections to modernism soon followed. By 1956, Henselmann felt confident enough about the new trend in socialist architecture to mock the Stalinallee as East Berlin's *Kinderkrankheit*, its "childhood disease."[54] In the early 1960s, the boulevard was finished off in prefabricated concrete apartment slabs, with additional incursions made by movie theaters and parking lots modeled on those found farther west. This was the landscape of a new and improved socialism and the habitat of a novel subjectivity: the socialist mass consumer. The USSR's Seven-Year Plan for 1959–1965 pledged to match the United States in housing supply and consumer goods, some of the latter to be distributed free of charge by 1980, or so the promise went. Soviet braggadocio was echoed in East Germany, where Ulbricht declared at the SED Fifth Party Congress in July 1958 that the nation's standard of living would surpass that of West Germany by the end of 1961. The project to create a socialist consumer society popularized television, the preeminent form of spectatorship in the "golden West." Commercial TV broadcasts transgressed German national borders, providing citizens in the East with a flickering window into the capitalist environments that they could no longer visit—as well as the awareness that their postwar modernist city was a faulty replica. In abandoning the traditionalist aesthetic of socialist realism for a futurist syntax that employed gridded housing blocks, family automobiles, and household plastics as symbols of progress, post-Stalinist reform triggered a new representational crisis. Capitalism's vaunted alternative now shared the same iconography as its reviled antithesis. The party's failure to develop a unique discourse of industrial modernity had turned East Berlin into a Second World knock-off of a First World metropolis. Rather than promoting a fundamentally different political economy, newly built socialist environments advertised the party's failure to make good on the promise of beating the West at its own consumerist game.

Notes

1. Groys, *The Total Art of Stalinism*, 11.
2. Kirshenblatt-Gimblett, *Destination Culture*, 1.
3. Groys, *The Total Art of Stalinism*, 51.
4. Schudson, *Advertising, the Uneasy Persuasion*, 215.
5. Fitzpatrick, *The Cultural Front*, 227.
6. Jürgen Käding, *Baumeister der Stalinallee* (Berlin: Verlag Neues Leben, 1953), 7.
7. Katherine Pence, "The Myth of a Suspended Present: Prosperity's Painful Shadow in 1950s East Germany," in Betts and Eghigian, *Pain and Prosperity*, 142.
8. Bohley-Zittlau et al., *Denkmale in Berlin*, 36–37.
9. "Hunderttausende in der Stalinallee," *Neues Deutschland*, 22 December 1949.
10. Lothar Bolz to Kurt Leibknecht, 21 December 1949, DHI/44476, Stiftung Parteien und Massenorganisationen im Bundesarchiv (hereafter SAPMO-BA).
11. Travel journal entry of Walter Pisternik, 10–12 May 1950, published in Institut für Regionalentwicklung und Strukturplanung (IRS), *Reise nach Moskau*, 61.

12. IRS, *Reise nach Moskau*, 139.

13. Hermann Henselmann, "Vorschläge aus dem Ministerium für Bauwesen vom 5. Juli 1950," DH2 DBA B38/I, SAPMO-BA.

14. "Der Kampf gegen den Formalismus in Kunst und Literatur, für eine fortschrittliche deutsche Kultur. Entschließung des Zentralkomitees der Sozialistischen Einheitspartei Deutschlands auf der Tagung am 15., 16., und 17., März 1951," *Tägliche Rundschau*, 18 April 1951.

15. For a detailed account of this transformation, see Castillo, "Blueprint for a Cultural Revolution."

16. Rudolf Herrnstadt, "Über den Baustil, den politischen Stil und den Genossen Henselmann," *Neues Deutschland*, 31 July 1951.

17. Hermann Henselmann, "Der reaktionäre Charakter des Konstruktivismus," *Neues Deutschland*, 4 December 1951.

18. Heinz Hirdina, *Gestalten für die Serie: Design in der DDR 1949–1985* (Dresden: VEB Verlag der Kunst, 1988), 48.

19. "Vorschlag des Zentralkomitees der Sozialistischen Einheitspartei Deutschlands für den Aufbau Berlins!," *Neues Deutschland*, 25 November 1951.

20. Ibid.

21. East Berlin's Stalinallee has accrued an extensive postunification body of scholarship. The short list includes Durth, Düwel, and Gutschow, *Ostkreuz/Aufbau*; Flierl, "Stalinallee in Berlin"; Engel and Ribbe, *Karl-Marx-Allee*; Tilo Köhler, *Unser die Strasse—Unser der Sieg. Die Stalinallee* (Berlin: Transit, 1993); and Nicolaus and Obeth, *Die Stalinallee*.

22. On the Stalinallee's model of socialist commercial culture, see Johanna Böhm-Klein, "Wohnen, Geschäftsleben und Infrastruktur der Stalinallee," in Engel and Ribbe, *Karl-Marx-Allee*; Katherine Pence, "Schaufenster des sozialistischen Konsums: Texte der ostdeutschen 'consumer culture,'" in Lüdtke and Becker, *Akten*, 91–118; and Pence, "'You as a Woman Will Understand.'"

23. Freier Deutscher Gewerkschaftsbund Gross-Berlin, . . . *und an der Stalinallee. Eine Sammlung neuer Lieder und Texmaterialien zum Nationalen Aufbauprogramm* (Berlin: FDGB Gross-Berlin, 1952), 2–4.

24. Doris Müller, "'Wir bauen die erste sozialistische Straße Berlins.' Die Stalinallee in der politischen Propaganda im ersten Jahr des 'Nationalen Aufbauprogramms Berlin in 1952," in Vorsteher, *Parteiauftrag*, 373–384.

25. "Bericht über die Besprechung am März 1952 mit Frl. Firch vom Aufbau-Komitee," Harych Nachlaß, 12/Mappe 1, Stiftung Archiv der Akademie der Künste, Berlin.

26. "Vorschlag des Zentralkomitees der Sozialistischen Einheitspartei Deutschlands Für den Aufbau Berlins!," *Neues Deutschland*, 25 November 1951.

27. "Bericht über die Besprechung am März 1952 mit Frl. Firch vom Aufbau-Komitee," Harych Nachlaß, 12/Mappe 1, Stiftung Archiv der Akademie der Künste, Berlin.

28. Richard Müller, "Theo Harych—ein schreibender Arbeiter," *Neue Deutsche Literatur* 7, no. 11 (November 1959): 109–110.

29. Brooks, "Socialist Realism in *Pravda*, Read All about It!," 973–991.

30. Theo Harych, "Stalinallee" (unpublished manuscript), Harych Nachlaß, Mappe 9, Stiftung Archiv der Akademie der Künste, Berlin.

31. Ruth Berlau to (Lou) Hans Eisler, undated, Eisler Nachlaß, 5136, Stiftung Archiv der Akademie der Künste, Berlin.

32. Bertolt Brecht, "An einen jungen Bauarbeiter der Stalinallee," in *Gesammelte Werke*, 3: 1003.

33. Heinz Lüdke, "Der Künstler und seine Aussage. Zur Ausstellung 'Berlin im Aufbau,'" *Neues Deutschland*, 6 May 1951.

34. Heinz Löffler, "Aufbau der Stalinallee," in Flacke, *Auftrag*, 70–73.

35. Gerhard Pommeranz-Liedtke, *Otto Nagel und Berlin* (Dresden: VEB Verlag der Kunst, 1964), 88.

36. Åman, *Architecture and Ideology in Eastern Europe*, 191.

37. Flierl, "Stalinallee in Berlin," 79.

38. Herbert Riecke, *Mietskasernen im Kapitalismus, Wohnpaläste im Sozialismus* (Berlin: Verlag Kultur und Fortschritt, 1954), 7.

39. "Den besten Patrioten Schaffen die ersten Wohnungen in der Stalinallee," *Tägliche Rundschau*, 22 December 1952.

40. Nicolaus and Obeth, *Die Stalinallee*, 241.

41. Petra Paal, "Die Bauherren melden sich zum Wort," *Tägliche Rundschau*, 25 May 1952.

42. Heinz Kersten, "Tichtennis mit dem Baumeister," *Der Tagesspiegel*, 18 March 1997.

43. Quoted from minutes of a 1952 meeting discussing the thematic program of Stalinallee ornament, reproduced in Durth et al., *Ostkreuz/Aufbau*, 365–368.

44. Will Jans, "Das Nationale Aufbauprogramm Berlin—Sinnbild eines freilebenden Deutschland," *Tägliche Rundschau*, 1 January 1953.

45. This frequently cited price comparison appears in "Neue Wohnungen—für wen?," *Neues Deutschland*, 12 July 1954; and Grete Groh-Kummerlöw, "Keine Frontbauten—gesunde und billige Wohnungen für die Werktätigen," *Tribüne*, 19 August 1954.

46. Nicolaus and Obeth, *Die Stalinallee*, 240.

47. "Baukünstlerische Grüsse aus dem Land des saülengeschmückten 'sozialistischen Realismus,'" *Baukunst und Werkform* 3, no. 6 (December 1952): 5–6.

48. Impressions of one such tour were recorded by the U.S. Mutual Security Agency's architectural consultant Vernon DeMars in his article "Design behind the Iron Curtain," *Journal of the American Institute of Architects* 19, no. 2 (February 1953): 54–62.

49. Olaf Badstüber, "Wir gingen über diese Straße . . . ," *Neues Deutschland*, 29 November 1953.

50. Ostermann, "New Documents on the East German Uprising of 1953."

51. Harych's last novel, *Im Namen des Volkes* (In the Name of the People), was published posthumously.

52. Åman, *Architecture and Ideology in Eastern Europe*, 191.

53. On the history of West German Marshall Plan consumer spectacles, see Castillo, "Domesticating the Cold War."

54. Böhm-Klein, "Geshäftsleben und Infrastruktur der Stalinallee," 151.

"SERVE YOURSELF!"

The History and Theory of Self-Service

in West and East Germany

n 1973, evolution took another giant leap forward"—from the great apes via
homo erectus, *homo habilis*, and *homo sapiens* to *homo self-service*? In the weeks
I spent writing this essay on the cultural history of self-service, the German
gasoline brand Jet commemorated its own history by unabashedly connecting
itself to the development of mankind. In its advertisement, the low-priced chain
celebrated the introduction of self-service at West German gas stations during
the 1970s and illustrated this apparently epochal event with familiar humanoid
vignettes representing the decisive steps in the history of human phylogenesis:
reaching for the gas nozzle is stylized, not without humor and irony, as the final
and highest stage of human evolution. While this is obviously a clever attention-
grabbing visual metaphor, the advertisement also offers an occasion to reflect on
the cultural implications of self-service: "When we introduced self-serve pump-
ing in Germany in 1973, you took the nozzle into your own hands for the first
time. All on your own! Without any help!"

If one reviews the cultural history of consumption in the nineteenth and
twentieth centuries, there actually appears to be some truth to this exaggerated
interpretation of self-service.[1] The triumph of the self-service principle in Germany during the 1950s and 1960s marked the zenith of a dramatic history of the
development of two social subsystems: consumption and communication. Their
convergence resulted in the formation of a third category of social organization

1973 machte die Evolution nochmal einen gewaltigen Schritt: Selber tanken, Geld verdienen.

Glückwunsch. Sie haben sich ja prächtig entwickelt! Vor ein paar Jährchen noch haben Sie Mammuts mit Steinen beworfen – und heute bestellen Sie einfach irgendwo einen Cheeseburger. Gestern noch präsentierten Sie den Damen als Flirt-Einstieg Ihre Rückenbehaarung, heute säuseln Sie „Darf ich Dir eine Fanta ausgeben?". Den größten Evolutionsschritt aber haben Sie locker in den Siebzigern hingelegt: Denn als wir 1973 das

Selbsttanken in Deutschland eingeführt haben, da haben Sie zum ersten Mal die Zapfpistole selber in die Hand genommen! Ganz allein! Ohne Hilfe! Und dabei festgestellt, dass dadurch der Kraftstoff von JET wieder etwas günstiger wurde

als der von anderen Tankstellen. Das mit dem günstigen Kraftstoff ist bei uns übrigens heute immer noch so. Da haben wir uns seit der Steinzeit kein Stückchen weiterentwickelt.

www.jet-tankstellen.de

DEN REST KÖNNEN SIE SICH SPAREN.

1. "One giant leap for mankind"? Self-service at the gas station. Courtesy of Die Illustratoren/ Christian Kitzmüller (illustrator), Hamburg, 2004.

that is at the crux of society's self-understanding: the process of the *mediatization of product communication*.[2] Mediatization refers to a process by which products themselves are transformed into different kinds of media, permitting a range of actors to exchange information. The term *product communication* denotes here the multitude of communicative acts that products can convey.[3] In Germany, products, especially those with brand names, underwent a process of mediatization that began in the nineteenth century, accelerated in the 1920s and 1930s, and reached completion during the 1960s. This was due in no small part to self-service.[4]

Today there is a consensus among marketing experts that a brand-name product must fulfill two basic functions. In its capacity as a consumer good, the product must meet some material need or desire, and it must also serve as a means of communication. Not only is the product consumed; networks of communicative relationships also form around it. In the context of economic communication, which is what product communication is, the purchasing act has taken on a particular meaning—indeed, *the* decisive meaning. It renders acceptable the "content" of the story that advertising and sales promotion create for each product. This fundamental social, economic, and cultural action is performed by consumers. Those communicative relations and processes directly connected to the purchaser are therefore central not just to economic communication, but also to social communication in general. They foster or hinder predispositions that under specific conditions can lead to the purchase and use of a product.

The introduction of self-service in the 1950s played a decisive role in this process of mediatization. Self-service not only introduced an entirely new structure of communication in retail shops; it also epitomized the product in its dual role as a consumer good and a communicative good. Since then, the character of modern products as media has manifested itself most notably on the shelves of self-service shops. It is here that the product has combined at least three basic communicative functions: the physical carrier function, the nonmaterial semiotic function, and the classic channel function. Products have thus become media, when considered from the perspective of communication theory.[5]

The Takeoff of Self-Service in the Federal Republic of Germany

At the start of the 1950s, the Kaufhof department store chain in West Germany was on the cutting edge of a new sales paradigm. The old sales counters in the large Kaufhof stores had been junked by 1953 and replaced by modern "gondolas." These sales gondolas were oval tables that could be taken apart and, like modular furniture, pushed together into a heart or kidney shape as needed. The interior design of self-service shops was by no means common knowledge in the early 1950s. At these gondolas the saleswomen served their customers "in every direction," the West German newsmagazine *Der Spiegel* explained to its readers. "The tables narrow in a V-shape towards their base, so that the customers can slide their feet under the counters. They are supposed to come as close to the merchandise as possible ('Let the merchandise do the talking')." This would be only the beginning of a "revolution in sales techniques and customer treatment," *Der Spiegel* correctly predicted—a revolution for which Kaufhof's chief executive had found "fantastic role models" during his information-gathering tour of "the American wonderland of mammoth department stores."[6]

Despite his enthusiasm for the United States, Kaufhof's CEO recognized that the American model was transferable to Germany only in a very limited way. The average American wage earner took home the equivalent of DM 1,175 per month, while his West German counterpart took home only DM 325 per month. As of 1953, 58 percent of the German's income still went toward food; for the American, it was only a quarter of his earnings. Compared to the average German earner, the American could thus spend about six times more on manufactured goods.[7] In Germany, by contrast, precisely the shortfall in many household budgets was supposed to stimulate retailers to organize their sales operations more efficiently and to share the resulting savings with their customers. For twenty years, economists had noted that "a person has to stand behind the counter year after year at an annual salary of DM 15,000 to DM 20,000, not to produce goods but just to distribute them to the customer. For the salesperson, half of his working time is pure waiting time."[8]

Despite American encouragement and support, the German retail industry was very hesitant at first to adopt the self-service concept. Initially, consumer cooperatives led the way. Of the first twenty self-service shops that opened in West Germany in 1949–1950, seven belonged to a consumer cooperative.[9] Only in 1957–58 did the new distribution concept achieve a significant breakthrough, and then only after a big promotional push aimed at retailers. At the food industry's 1957 trade fair in Cologne,[10] a special exhibit displayed the most modern forms of store architecture. Nearly forty model shops presented variations on the self-service principle, meaning that products were not kept in a back room but could be handled by the consumer as he or she made the decision whether to purchase an item. And a special show explained the advantages of the key design element of the early self-service store: "the gondola — your best sales assistant."[11] In food retailing alone the changeover to self-service stores now proceeded at a furious pace. While there had been only about 40 self-service stores in this sector in 1951 and just 203 in 1955, by 1960 17,132 self-service stores had been opened. In 1956, these stores' volume share of retail sales made up little more than 4 percent. By 1960, self-service stores made up just under 35 percent of all retail outlets, and this number had risen to 62 percent by 1964.[12] This new form of distributing, presenting, and experiencing products saw inexorable progress. Only in the early 1980s did the rapid decline of the full-service shops level off; the market penetration of self-service stores was now virtually complete.

If the 1950s was a decade characterized by the multiplication of new stores, the 1960s was marked by the expansion of the range of products available. "In 1958, economists counted an average of 998 articles in self-service shops. . . . Thirty years later, in 1988, such shops sold on average 6,000 articles, the larger self-service centers actually averaged 13,000, and the self-service department

„Mutti, hier!"

Nehmen Sie Ihre kleine Tochter an die Hand. Nehmen Sie einen Einkaufswagen. Und lassen Sie sich durch den Konsum ziehen: „Mutti, hier! Mutti, da!" Tausend verschiedene Artikel gibt es im Konsum. Tausendmal gute Ware zu einem vernünftigen Preis. Eine Riesenauswahl: Für erfahrene Hausfrauen. Und für alle, die es noch werden wollen.

Im **KONSUM** kaufen kluge Kunden

2. "Free choice for free citizens." Advertisement for the West German retail chain Konsum, 1965.

stores carried an average of 24,000 products, or 24 times more than their prede-cessors a quarter century earlier."[13] One example of this "explosive product range expansion" was at the union-owned Coop chain, which, despite a recession in the second half of the 1960s, nearly doubled its product range from 1966 to 1969. "Each year about 1,500 new products came on the market, of which about 400 captured a spot on the shelves."[14]

From the outset, customers' experiences with the redesigned salesrooms were overwhelmingly positive. By the 1960s retail chains could even use self-service as a visual advertisement. In 1953, the Karstadt group built a model de-partment store on a prestigious street in Düsseldorf, and customers had noth-ing but praise for the experiment. They lauded the end of waiting for counter service, the improved display of the products, and the ability to make choices free of pressure. They were also happy to avoid quarrels over who was next in line, and they appreciated that they were no longer at the mercy of exhausted and surly saleswomen.[15] That same year, a survey by a market research institute confirmed customers' positive views. Two-thirds of those questioned who had already shopped at a self-service store rated their experiences as "good," offering the following reasons: "convenient," "it's quick," and "no pressure to buy." Twenty percent were undecided, and 13 percent explicitly responded "not good." Those who were dissatisfied found the new shops impersonal, missed the advice of salespeople, and believed they bought more than they had intended. Just 10 percent of those questioned in 1953 wanted "nice sales ladies instead."[16]

Movable shelving and gondolas supplanted the ossified monument of the old shop culture: the sales counter. In 1960, the German sociologist Ernest Zahn greeted the new dynamism and boundless possibilities of self-service with euphoria: "With the disappearance of sales personnel, time has run out for the counter, the ancient sales counter, the symbol of the imaginary boundary between supply and demand, the barrier where commerce was so often an end in itself and a way of passing the time; the price had to be 'negotiated,' the quality inspected, the quantity cumbersomely weighed, measured, or counted, and finally packaged."[17] The counter, which was the site of time-consuming negotiation and a barrier between customers and products, was dismantled. With the communication revolution embodied in the "self-service principle," fundamental changes occurred simultaneously in the temporal and spatial dimensions of product presentation and communication. For contemporaries, saving time was the most compelling argument in favor of the new shopping culture. As the human barrier (the intermediary salesperson) and the material barrier (the distancing counter) were abolished, the customer's relationship to the merchandise became much more direct.

The merchandise now stood on the shelf, and the overall layout of both package and display fostered communication between producer and consumer. Products were permitted "to speak, to offer themselves, and to 'flirt' with the customers. The merchandise now became the initiator, while the salesperson had direct customer contact only when asked for information. Otherwise, the salesperson dealt with the customer solely through the displayed merchandise, assuming the role of an invisible mechanism behind the products. But self-service did not eliminate the salesperson. Instead, it prompted him or her to exit the 'stage' and to work behind the scenes as a 'director' in the stockroom or in the store itself."[18]

With this development, products had to be standardized for placement on the shelves, and at the same time communication had to become more systematic and professional. In order to succeed, products now had to display the qualities of an actor or showman. Henceforth, they would have to become their own media if they wanted to compete effectively in the marketplace. Those best equipped to perform on the stage of the self-service gondolas were the brand-name products, because to some extent they had long, well-rehearsed traditions of communication, which they could now fully reclaim and exploit.

By 1959 the chemical company Henkel had modernized its Persil detergent, a German brand-name product par excellence, to take advantage of the new shopping culture. It updated its typography, which stemmed from the 1920s, and changed its outer form, namely, the packaging. Henkel also added digits to represent the year: "Persil 59" was intended to epitomize progress. The dark green that had been the package's background color since 1907 was lightened considerably, and the logo was given a softer font and oriented diagonally on the package. From now on, Persil appeared in a front-facing package suitable for display on a shelf. And for the first time, a Persil ad campaign was planned not in-house but by an advertising agency.[19] The target group was now young housewives, who—unlike their mothers—had not necessarily grown up with Persil but possibly with Sunil or another competing product. Advertisements and posters showed representatives of a new generation of women, beaming as they held up the Persil package to the viewer.

As the Persil innovations make clear, product communication, among its other functions, reflects broader social mores at distinct historical junctures. At the end of the 1950s, self-service conveyed the powerful message that the postwar period was finally over. The time of privation was past, and a new present was unfolding. Products were to give expression to this new beginning, exemplified by the legions of household appliances that appeared. The new Persil offered the imagery of cosmopolitanism and modernity that advertising increasingly presented at the end of the 1950s.

Though the shopper-*flâneurs* in the 1950s associated this new experience with a feeling of freedom, the increasing abundance of merchandise in the 1960s demanded new communication and consumption skills on the part of the "recipient." This freedom of choice necessitated the internalization of new values. The merchant's expertise and his or her personal ties to the customer could only be partially offset by the communicative performance of the products themselves. The burden that had previously been carried by the merchant now had to be borne by the consumers themselves.[20]

The Takeoff of Self-Service in the German Democratic Republic

In the summer of 1951 the first self-service shop opened in Dresden. A journalist from the *Sächsische Zeitung* reported on the event with requisite optimism and curiosity. "And [what about] non-material values?" he asked. "The young woman already used to the techniques of self-service . . . offers the following answer when I ask her opinion of them: 'But this is our merchandise, anyway. . . . When each person understands this, I would like to ask, why should we *not* help ourselves?'" As this quote demonstrates, the argument for this still experimental means of presenting commodities in the German Democratic Republic (GDR) was guided by a combination of political and practical considerations: when everything belongs to everyone, then virtually everyone must help themselves. From the perspective of the early 1950s, this view was prophetic: "Anyone who thinks through the Dresden experiment . . . will conclude on his own that as these sales techniques become more widespread, the people's democratic consciousness will be elevated."[21] From the viewpoint of the Socialist Unity Party (SED), the degree of self-service available to the consumer served as an indicator of political progress. Nevertheless, nearly a whole decade would pass before self-service achieved a breakthrough in socialist retailing.

The end of food rationing arrived in 1958. The Fifth Party Congress, which met that year, boldly declared that the GDR was on a course toward a bright new future. The Soviet *Sputnik* satellite and "rockets" became ubiquitous allegories of a new, faster-paced era. Euphoric expectations for the next seven years, untrammeled enthusiasm for technology and progress, and breathtaking propaganda of speed played off each other. "At the speed of a rocket toward the victory of socialism" was the prevalent slogan at the end of the 1950s; the Seven-Year Plan was even recast as a "seven-stage rocket."[22] As discussed in Anne Kaminsky's essay in this volume, the party expected that socialism would be firmly established in the GDR within a span of seven years, and with it, a veritable consumer paradise.[23]

Self-service and the products on display were supposed to represent the dawning of a new era. They supported the political goal of narrowing the economic gap between the GDR and the increasingly prosperous Federal Republic of Germany (FRG) within just a few years. According to the SED's expectations, the GDR would "catch up to and overtake" the West by 1961. Walter Ulbricht, SED first secretary, turned to the arena through which the GDR's western neighbors had successfully engendered political and economic loyalty: consumption and product communication. The new socialist society tried to create its own

3. "Save with each penny, each gram, each minute: Self-service is the expression of democratic consciousness." The first self-service shop in Dresden of the East German retail chain Konsum, 1951. Courtesy of Sächsische Landesbibliothek, Staats- und Universitätsbibliothek Dresden, Abteilung Deutsche Fotothek, Dresden.

"consumption era," which it sought to put on display in shop windows, advertisements, and in other forms of "visual agitation."

Such was the political propaganda that attended the arrival of self-service in the GDR. In keeping with the breathtaking political changes, even shopping was supposed to become faster by the tenth anniversary of the GDR's founding on October 7, 1959. In 1956, two experimental self-service department stores opened in Berlin, and additional stores were unveiled during the tenth anniversary celebrations in 1959. By the beginning of October, six thousand East German stores had been converted, partially or completely, to self-service. The Handelsorganisation (HO), the state retail organization, marked the GDR's creation by opening a number of modern self-service shops, such as the Tempo-Tex fabric shop, the first store of this type in Berlin.[24] As of March 31, 1959, there were already 490 shops competing for the customer's favor with the slogan "Help yourself."

Despite their anticapitalist gestures, the East German debates about self-service differed in only minor ways from those in the product-rich West. At the outset of the 1950s, economic planners feared that socialist consumers might lack the maturity and moral steadfastness required for this free access to merchandise. Self-service was not a question of technical equipment, decreed consumer cooperative members in 1951, "but rather an educational challenge for our people. Until self-service has fully arrived, advertising must constantly promote the new sales techniques to customers. Sales managers and salespeople must function as agitators for the customers."[25] At the end of 1966, there were 13,994 self-service grocery stores in the GDR, with 745,000 square meters of sales floor. Self-service stores accounted for just under half of total revenues in food retailing in 1966.

The newspaper *Wochenpost* described the advantages of self-service stores with arguments similar to those heard in the West. This form of presentation seemed at last to be oriented toward the customer, who maintained considerable power in the self-service discourse: "The customer has direct contact with the commodities and can make his selection without influence from the personnel. The customer does not need to feel morally obliged to the salesperson to buy something no matter what. The customer saves time, since the product lines of numerous specialty shops are brought together under a single roof. The customer also need not forgo expert advice in the self-service shop, because the saleswomen working here are just as well-versed in their field as their colleagues in full-service shops."[26]

Under socialism, as in the West, the customer and the merchandise were supposed to take center stage in the self-service process. Accordingly, the merchandise was also supposed to become both the focal point and the communicative partner. However, the shift in the status of merchandise observable in the West met with formidable obstacles in the GDR.

The first stumbling block was the shortfall in the supply of goods. Self-service was introduced into an economy of scarcity, and thus product presentations risked producing an unintended effect: actually highlighting shortages, rather than enabling access to a greater number of goods. The second stumbling block was the GDR's lack of enough cash registers to ring up purchases quickly. Improvements in shopping and the integration of those new goods into the household were supposed to translate the political goal of accelerated efficiency into reality. However, despite such promises, those responsible had to admit that only about 20 percent of the socialist bloc demand for cash registers could be satisfied. In addition, the East German cash register brand, Secura, contributed precious little to efficiency. These registers could not calculate fast enough, and they also lacked coin sorters, change calculators, and change counters. As a result, the registers set up in self-service stores were too few and too slow, so that purportedly fast shopping was frustrated by long waiting times.

The third stumbling block affected all retail stores, but especially the self-service food shops, which depended on clearly visible packaging. Instead, the packaging of all products remained cheaply made and often failed to withstand the shipping process. A bag of flour that had opened before making its way to the shelf simply could not be sold.[27] One of the many consequences of this problem that plagued the GDR's entire economy was that self-service sections remained small, especially in the grocery markets. Though it was common to find sales outlets that combined full-service and self-service departments under a single roof in the 1960s, by the middle of the decade the self-service portion in food market halls constituted, on average, only 55 percent of the store. As one advertiser had put it in 1954, showing his own desire to find social utility for his profession: "Of course, each package must be in a certain proportion to the merchandise's value. But this does not mean that it has to be primitive and unattractive. . . . Even the simple wrappers for butter and margarine, the simple bag of salt can have a pleasing shape and an aesthetic appearance. Particularly in the food industry, we still find packaging where one wonders how they have managed to sleep so obliviously through a half century of advances in advertising art."[28]

In response to this problem, a "packaging regulation" was passed in 1966 that obligated producers to package the merchandise as the last step in the production process. Yet, three years later, nothing had changed substantially; the "packaging question" still kept "self-service from reaching its economic potential."[29] In light of the GDR's packaging troubles, the *Wochenpost* asked whether industry was aware of retailers' desire for presentable merchandise. The advertising director at the HO's head office gave the GDR's leading weekly an unvarnished picture of the merchandise on the shelves of East German shops: "It's been years now! We demand that packaging meet these requirements: it must protect the merchandise and reflect its value; it must make caring for the merchandise unnecessary; it must spell out its price and its usage properties; it must take over the function of the salesperson. With some exceptions, our packaging today falls short of this. The overall appearance of packaging in the department stores is bland and not an effective selling point."[30]

Attractive packaging is a fundamental element of product communication in the self-service business. The theoreticians and functionaries who dealt with retailing in the GDR were well aware of this. They created a thoroughly modern infrastructure for product presentation and communication in the retail sector during the 1960s, but it was never fully utilized. In a society marked by scarcity, marketing and sales remained peripheral to the concerns of most producers.

Fashioning a product as a form of communication with customers served neither the economic nor the ideological interests of socialist manufacturers, nor did it assist them in fulfilling the requirements of the plan, which emphasized quantity, not quality. Because of the irrational incentives of economic planning, however, politicians were unable to motivate producers to accept even a rudimentary notion of merchandise as a message.

The Unleashing of Product Communication in the Federal Republic of Germany

In the history of product presentation in the FRG, the lifting of physical and psychological barriers to consumption emerges as a key theme. Throughout the 1950s and 1960s, traditional forms of product communication still prevented unobstructed access to the product. Nevertheless, these two decades saw a gradual unleashing of the product's communicative power—a process that had both social and cultural dimensions. As we have seen, the most visible expression of this process was the gradual introduction of self-service, which led to the elimination of the service counter and the salesperson behind it. Both came to be regarded as outdated forms of product presentation, which up until then had prevented direct access to the product and regulated the flow of information and merchandise.

During these decades, the *history of communication* unfolded against a background of both an "expansion" and a "concentration" of media offerings.[31] Historians have also spoken of a "media revolution" in the decade after World War II, led most notably by television's emergence as the leading audiovisual medium.[32] Viewed from the perspective of the history of communication, the 1950s saw quantitative and qualitative leaps toward modernization. The *history of consumption* in the 1950s is subject to similar interpretations. Over the course of the decade, both producers and consumers initially counted on the steadily increasing quantity and uninterrupted growth of consumption; on this point, historians have repeatedly cited the example of the so-called wave of gluttony (*Fresswelle*).[33] Precisely in the realm of consumption, however, a process of differentiation and rationalization also took place, which is often interpreted today as a "democratization of consumption" or the "Americanization of consumption."[34]

The *history of product communication and presentation*, which forms a link between these two social subsystems of consumption and communication, underwent similar changes during what was a formative decade for the FRG. The types of media serving the goals of product communication grew more numerous: mail-order catalogues and self-service stores revolutionized product presentation, as did commercial television, which began broadcasting in 1957. Promotional "contact" between customer and commodity expanded with the help of these media. Since then, more and more information about products has reached potential purchasers through channels that are at once more anonymous and more direct than ever before. However, the 1950s revolution in product presentation did not simply consist of an expansion in the range of products or an increase in the volume of product information; it also involved a qualitative transformation. Self-service constituted a new medium of product presentation in which the product became its own medium.[35]

The growth of consumption and communication that unfolded in the years immediately after World War II is best appreciated by returning to the period before 1939. The "democratization" of numerous products in the 1920s and 1930s was a key to this process of mediatization. During these two decades, desires for products were awakened among the masses—desires that would in many cases be satisfied only in the late 1950s and 1960s. We should regard this process not necessarily as the democratization of real purchasing power, but rather as a democratization of product perceptions: as the implementation of consumerist visions. For example, in an attempt to expand its market beyond the very wealthy, the champagne brand Deinhard was advertised as early as the 1920s with the chummy slogan "Deinhard is your champagne!" ("Dein Sekt sei Deinhard!").[36] Under National Socialism the luxury good champagne was supposed to become common property. In proclaiming "Champagne for everyone" Deinhard's advertising campaign indicated that in the *Volksgemeinschaft* (racial community) a *Volkssekt* (people's champagne) was available to all.[37] Of course, the Nazi regime worked to limit the expansion of consumer choice to members of the Volksgemeinschaft. Those who did not belong to this racial elite were not only excluded from German consumer society, but also economically exploited and eventually exterminated. Thus, the dream of "champagne for everyone" was never truly intended for everyone. Even in this racially circumscribed way, however, the foundations of an egalitarian model of consumption continued to be laid. In fact, the popular expectations of sharing in consumer plenty—irrespective of class background or earning power—became so widespread that neither the economic crisis of the late Weimar Republic nor the privations of World War II were able to inhibit them.

The trend toward egalitarian participation in consumption was promoted by key historical events. World War I was the progenitor of momentous social, cultural, and communicative upheavals. The mobilization of the civilian economy for military purposes during the war, for example, necessitated a turn toward "the masses" by means of political propaganda and public relations.[38] The introduction of universal suffrage in 1919 resulted in increased demand for public information and communication, which was satisfied in part by innovations in the field of persuasive communication.

The Weimar Republic saw the expansion of both political propaganda and product advertising.[39] Into the 1930s people could see an expanding consumer horizon, and they experienced the democratizing potential of products in mostly positive terms. Product communication managed to retain the products' uniqueness while building a stable foundation of trust that consumers could later fall back on during the 1940s, when times were precarious and products scarce, and during the 1950s, when the products increasingly became available again.

By the 1960s, self-service had perfected the invitation to an unfettered and lighthearted consumption. During this decade, Western products developed into what communication theory understands as a "medium." With the loss of interpersonal product communication in the retail shop, the product itself took on more power to convey messages. The number of brand-name products increased, and individual goods communicated an ever greater number of meanings. This led to an explosion in product communication during the second half of the 1960s and especially during the 1970s. The mediatization of products, however, has proven a Janus-faced process. The 1960s were distinguished by a growing level of social complexity. On the one hand, the increased ability of brand-name products to communicate with consumers contributed to this complexity. On the other hand, product communication helped assuage accompanying anxieties by producing feelings of trust and safety.[40]

By the 1980s and 1990s, products evoked entire worlds of experience. In a complex "multioption" society, there was a greater need than ever before for intermediaries between subjects. Products had become one instance of such mediation in modern societies. In their deep psychosocial structure, products meet the basic anthropological need for parental care, for security and protection. In the face of the anonymity of postmodern societies, subjects eagerly embrace the products' promise of security.[41]

Limitations on Commodity Communication
in the German Democratic Republic

In contrast to the FRG, the history of product presentation in the GDR reflects the continuing influence of ideological barriers to consumption, despite practical efforts to reduce them at the street level. Party ideologues wanted to create the antithesis of the FRG, particularly in the area of consumption. Marxist-Leninist doctrine envisaged a "cultural society" that would be superior in moral and material terms to the "consumer society" of the West. In opposition to the products of capitalist industry, consumer goods in the East German "cultural society" were defined by their practical utility — their use value — which was supposedly conveyed with the help of transparent and frugal designs.[42] Although Walter Ulbricht's New Economic System briefly permitted new product communication structures, the ideologically motivated barriers to communication remained largely intact throughout the forty-year history of the GDR.[43]

The history of commodity marketing in the GDR also reflects the experience of real shortages, bare shelves, and unsatisfied desires. Consumers, salespeople, store managers, and producers alike were constantly confronted with the experience of scarcity. Shortages of consumer goods constituted an insuperable material threat to any sort of marketing. Where shortages are the main feature of consumer life, there can be no real marketing policy and thus no positive commodity communication. Out of the experience of empty shops a form of product communication was born that had become obsolete in the FRG by the early 1950s: the discourse of scarcity. The experience of scarcity decisively shaped the everyday awareness and behavior of most East Germans. By the mid-1970s, as discussed in detail in Anne Kaminsky's essay, marketing was largely conducted by potential buyers and users themselves; available merchandise was advertised via a whispering campaign.

Despite the Berlin Wall, moreover, the GDR was never a closed society, impervious to outside influence. The simultaneous experience of Eastern shortage and Western abundance, broadcast via television over the Wall, defined product presentation in the GDR. East German consumers constantly compared their country's products and their presentation to their Western counterparts. By the 1980s, East German pensioners returning from trips to West Germany talked about the shelves in Western self-service stores. According to the Ministry for State Security (Stasi), they "stressed, on the one hand the social security [provided by the] GDR; but on the other hand, they offered sometimes effusive descriptions of the voluminous supply of goods in the Federal Republic."[44] According to the Stasi, the returnees glorified the situation in the West, referencing the "overwhelming supply of goods" and the "great cleanliness and neatness in the shops."[45] Western products, with their profusion of meaning, were not only to be found beyond the Wall; they were also omnipresent in the GDR itself: in the hard-currency retail outlets (Intershops), on Western commercial television, and in East German homes, where they were received as gifts from West German family and friends.[46]

Despite the ideological and material impediments to consumption, the GDR also witnessed some attempts to free up product presentation. The Fifth Party Congress in 1958 and the Sixth Party Congress in 1963 set the GDR on a course toward modern product promotion. Advertising in print media, radio, and television experienced a political tailwind, while mail-order companies proudly distributed colorful catalogues.[47] Self-service shops began spreading almost as quickly as in the West. During the 1960s, the GDR developed a culture of sales and consumption oriented toward Western models despite official criticism of capitalism consumerism. Although its progress was often halting, the infrastructure for modern product presentation was nevertheless firmly established in the GDR.

As in the FRG, the 1960s are remembered as the golden years of the GDR. And yet there was a significant difference between a package of Spee that awaited its purchaser on a self-service shelf in the East and a package of Persil on a self-service shelf in the West. The Western product had to prevail against a large number of competitors, while Spee had no real rivals in the East. Persil and its competitors were highly charged with product narratives. Western brands carried multiple meanings and fulfilled the social-psychological needs of their customers.

The GDR brand Spee resonated with East German consumers, though to a much lesser extent than Western packages did for shoppers in the FRG. In part, this was because the limitations on product communication hampered new approaches to branding. Even with a copious supply of goods, the emergence of a distinctive socialist consumer society was inhibited by the SED's anticapitalist philosophy. Socialist products were unable to carry out fundamental social functions as did their Western product counterparts. The mediatization process that made brand-name products into central nodes of social communication was only partially developed in the East. Even the flourishing commodity culture of the East during the 1960s should not be compared to the vibrant product culture of the West because economic structures, the social role of manufactured goods, and their communicative potential were always defined differently. The gradual liberalization of the limitations placed by the SED on consumption did not necessarily lead to a growth in product communication under socialism.

This difference became manifest in the 1970s, when, due to economic considerations, key aspects of commodity culture in the GDR were simply erased by a political stroke of the pen. The commodity and consumption culture was not a priority of the SED leadership. When the party ordered mail-order companies to close and discontinued advertising in 1975, product communication "from above" came to an almost complete halt. Oddly enough, the self-service principle was left untouched by this shift in policy. Even as the party leadership was reining in product communication, however, demand for communication of all kinds was increasing "from below" on the part of the consumers and citizens. During the 1970s, a popular desire for forms of speech that were not regulated by the state, whether they were conversations within the workers' collectives, petitions to public authorities and to the media, or classified ads in East German newspapers and magazines, made itself felt.[48] But party strategists stubbornly ignored the need of party members and the populace for more communication. Starting in the 1970s, there was a simultaneous decrease in the utopian content of political agitation and propaganda aimed at compensating for unfulfilled material desires.[49] Thus, by the 1980s at the latest, the SED could offer consumers neither tangible improvements nor compelling fantasies.

The Future of Self-Service and the Product Media

Even after German unification, the self-service principle has continued to create new ways of expressing itself. Over the next few years, Germans can anticipate self-service concepts that will increase both product communication and the disciplining of the consumer through automation and greater anonymity at the point of sale. Individual aspects of self-service will be technologically perfected and electronically controlled. Thus, the future may belong to a shopping cart that can guide, speak, and calculate. These vehicles of consumption are expected to mutate within a few years from a simple means of transportation to a self-service communication instrument. They will be equipped in the future with electronic devices that call attention to special features and offers on the shelves as one walks past them. It will guide the customer through the tangle of aisles to the shelf where he or she will find the desired product. Moreover, the computer-controlled shopping cart will register and price the chosen products in the basket. And at the checkout counter, the self-service customer of the twenty-first century will pay without cash, by machine, and without any human contact, so that even the cashiers can be eliminated.

In one sense, the self-service principle has revealed itself as but one manifestation of a culture that assigns a maximum number of media functions to products. Our modern product culture gives the customer not only the possibility of participating in the economic process and making informed choices through the purchasing act, but also the opportunity to communicate needs and desires by buying a product.[50] In this context, self-service performs an integral and fundamental service in a system of modern product communication that makes possible expanded forms of cultural expression to consumers, opening up a new arena of self-understanding without which the modern economy is not imaginable.

While the self-service paradigm expands realms of action and unleashes communicative options, it imposes limits as well: the self-service paradigm has placed the scepter (or the nozzle) in the hands of the "customer as the king," but it has eliminated the salesperson in the name of efficiency and will soon make the cashier obsolete. In the future, the point of sale will be deserted—except for the individual shopper. This logic of product presentation has been accompanied not only by additional internalization and disciplining on the part of the "customer king" but also by the impoverishment and isolation of the purchasing act. Though there is still communication at the point of sale, it turns out to be more and more soulless. Might this be the reason that *homo self-service*, seen from the perspective of the year 2004, no longer walks upright like his spear-carrying ancestors, but once again stands slightly stooped?

Notes

This essay was translated from the German by Patricia Stokes and Jonathan Wiesen.

1. For a good overview, see Siegrist, Kaelble, and Kocka, *Europäische Konsumgeschichte*; for the eighteenth to twentieth centuries, see Veyassat et al., *Geschichte der Konsumgesellschaft*, vol. 15; on the fifteenth to twentieth centuries, see Berghoff, *Konsumpolitik*; W. König, *Geschichte der Konsumgesellschaft*.

2. This essay focuses on theses and findings from my comparative dissertation, which was accepted by the Friedrich Schiller University in Jena in 2002 and has been published as a book: Gries, *Produkte als Medien*.

3. On this point, see also Hellmann, *Soziologie der Marke*, 278 n. 121.

4. On the history of this convergence process, see Rainer Gries, "Die Medialisierung der Produktkommunikation: Grundzüge eines kulturhistorischen Entwurfs," in Knoch and Morat, *Kommunikation als Beobachtung*, 113–130.

5. The communications theorist Roland Burkart has developed a catalogue of "conceptual components," which, from the perspective of communication studies as a social science, are intended to be applied to "media." Products as media are capable of fulfilling this ensemble of criteria. See Burkart, *Kommunikationswissenschaft*, 42–44. The systems theorist Siegfried J. Schmidt has drawn up a catalogue of functions that are fulfilled by media in the modern "media culture society." Products also satisfy this catalogue of requirements. See Siegfried J. Schmidt, "Der Umgang mit 'Informationen,' oder: Das Nadelöhr

Kognition," in Tauss, Kollbeck, and Mönikes, *Deutschlands Weg in die Informationsgesell-schaft*, 183–203.

6. "Alles für Frau Piesecke: Warenhäuser," *Der Spiegel* 7, no. 2 (1953): 11–14, 12.

7. Ibid., 13.

8. Ibid.

9. Institut für Selbstbedienung, *Dynamik im Handel*, special edition, October 1988, 12.

10. The trade fair is known as ANUGA: Allgemeine Nahrungs- und Genussmittel-Ausstellung,

11. Wildt, *Am Beginn der "Konsumgesellschaft,"* 179.

12. Lambertz, "Selbstbedienung forcierte Wachstum der Sortimente," 129.

13. Andersen, *Der Traum vom guten Leben*, 61.

14. Ibid.

15. *Der Spiegel* 7, no. 2 (1953): 14.

16. *Der Spiegel* 7, no. 16 (1953): 9. On the "vehemently positive attitude" toward these shops, which were usually rebuilt and newly furnished, see also Wildt, *Am Beginn der "Konsumgesellschaft,"* 191.

17. Zahn, *Soziologie der Prosperität*, 105. The mental power of the counter was displayed in the 1980s, when it was elevated to an icon of a nostalgic ideal of the 1950s. On the use of "found" historical articles (or "spoils") in the 1980s in the FRG, see Gries, Ilgen, and Schindelbeck, *Gestylte Geschichte*, especially 79.

18. Riethmüller, *Selbstbedienung*, 17.

19. Feiter, *80 Jahre Persil*, 61.

20. Self-discipline, which self-service both necessitates and inculcates, has yet to be fully realized. As early as 1954, Karstadt managers marveled at their discovery that shoplifting in a self-service department store, accounting for 0.3 percent of total revenue, was no more prevalent than in a traditionally organized store.

21. "'Bitte, suchen Sie sich Ihre Ware selbst aus!' Erste Verkaufsstelle der Konsumgenossen-schaft Dresden mit Selbstbedienung," *Sächsische Zeitung Dresden*, 6 June 1951.

22. "Arbeitsplan der Agit.-Kommission der gemeinsamen Kommission des Rates des Stadt-bezirkes und des Stadtbezirksausschusses der Nationalen Front Leipzig Mitte zur Vor-bereitung des 10. Jahrestages der Gründung der Deutschen Demokratischen Republik," n.d. [15 June 1959], Stadtverordnetenversammlung und Rat der Stadt (STVUR) 4116, Stadt-archiv Leipzig.

23. On time propaganda in the GDR, see Rainer Gries, "Die runden 'Geburtstage,' künst-licher Pulsschlag der Republik: Zeitkultur und Zeitpropaganda in der DDR," in Gibas et al., *Wiedergeburten*, 285–304.

24. Presse-Informationen, ed. Pressezentrum, "10 Jahre DDR," edition of 3 October 1959, 2.

25. Silke Rothkirch, "Moderne Menschen kaufen modern," in Neue Gesellschaft für Bild-ende Kunst, ed., *Wunderwirtschaft*, 112.

26. Roman Marczikowski, "Viele Körbe sind der Miniläden Tod," *Wochenpost* 15, no. 6 (1968): 8.

27. Ibid.

28. Gerhard Boerger, "Unser Sorgenkind—Die Verpackung," *Neue Werbung* 1, no. 6 (1954): 9.

29. I. Merkel, *Utopie und Bedürfnis*, 206.

30. Roman Marczikowski, "Viele Körbe sind der Miniläden Tod," *Wochenpost* 15, no. 6 (1968): 8.

31. See Jürgen Wilke, "Überblick und Phasengliederung," in *Mediengeschichte der Bundesrepublik Deutschland*, 15–27.

32. Axel Schildt, "Massenmedien im Umbruch der fünfziger Jahre," in Wilke, *Mediengeschichte der Bundesrepublik*, 633. The sociologist Gerhard Schulze has written of a "proliferation of the set of signs" beginning in the second half of the 1950s at the very latest. See Schulze, *Die Erlebnisgesellschaft*, 117.

33. Andersen, "Die Freßwelle" chapter, in *Der Traum vom guten Leben*, 34–88.

34. On the "democratization" of consumption, see Werner Polster, "Wandlungen der Lebensweise im Spiegel der Konsumentwicklung—Vom Dienstleistungskonsum zum demokratischen Warenkonsum," in Voy, Polster, and Thomasberger, *Gesellschaftliche Transformationsprozesse und materielle Lebensweise*, 215–291. On the "Americanization" of German consumption, see Jarausch and Siegrist, *Amerikanisierung und Sowjetisierung in Deutschland*; and Lüdtke et al., *Amerikanisierung*. We are still waiting for a detailed analysis of the process of Americanization in sales and marketing, product leadership, and commercial advertising.

35. See Gries, "Produktverständnisse," chapter 2.1 in *Produkte als Medien*, 53–134.

36. On the history of the Deinhard brand, see Prößler, *200 Jahre Deinhard*; and Gries, "Deinhard Sekt: 'Über alle Zeiten hinweg,'" chapter 4.1 in *Produkte als Medien*, 285–387.

37. One can speak of a "failure of the National Socialist consumer society" only if one interprets the phenomenon of consumption solely in terms of social history and statistics. See W. König, "Das Scheitern einer nationalsozialistischen Konsumgesellschaft."

38. On political mass communication during World War I, see Jeffrey Verhey, "*The Spirit of 1914.*"

39. See Liebert, *Der Take-off von Öffentlichkeitsarbeit*, vol. 5.

40. See Gries, "Versuch einer Historisierung von 'Vertrauen' anhand der Geschichte der Produktkommunikationen," chapter 5 in *Produkte als Medien*, 561–592; and Rainer Gries, "Der Vertrieb von Vertrauen: Überlegungen zu Produktkultur und politischer Öffentlichkeit," in Weisbrod, *Die Politik der Öffentlichkeit*, 261–283.

41. On the process of individualization in developed societies, see, e.g., Jüngst, *Psychodynamik und Stadtgestaltung*.

42. I. Merkel, *Utopie und Bedürfnis*.

43. See Steiner, *Die DDR-Wirtschaftsreform der sechziger Jahre*.

44. 17 November 1986, 1, ZAIG 4165, Bundesbeauftragte für die Unterlagen des Staatssicherheitsdienstes der ehemaligen Deutschen Demokratischen Republik (BStU), Zentralarchiv (ZA).

45. 8 September 1987, 6, ZAIG 4165, BStU, ZA.

46. On the Intershops, see Katrin Böske, "Abwesend anwesend. Eine kleine Geschichte des

Intershops," in Neue Gesellschaft für bildende Kunst, *Wunderwirtschaft*; Volze, "Die Devisengeschäfte der DDR"; and Jonathan R. Zatlin, "Consuming Ideology: Socialist Consumerism and the Intershops, 1970–1989," in Hübner and Tenfelde, *Arbeiter in der SBZ-DDR*, 555–572. On the gifts sent by mail from the West, see Härtel and Kabus, *Das Westpaket*; and Zatlin, *The Currency of Socialism*, chapter 6.

47. See Anne Kaminsky's essay in this volume and her monograph, *Kaufrausch*.

48. On the petitions, see Lüdtke and Becker, *Akten*; I. Merkel, *Wir sind doch nicht die Meckerecke der Nation!*; Oliver Werner, "'Politisch überzeugend, feinfühlig und vertrauensvoll'? Eingabenbearbeitung in der SED," in Timmermann, *Diktaturen in Europa*; and Zatlin, "Eingaben und Ausgaben."

49. See Gries: "'. . . und der Zukunft zugewandt,' Oder: Wie der DDR das Jahr 2000 abhanden kam," in Bünz, Gries, and Möller, *Der "Tag X" in der Geschichte*, 309–333, 375–378.

50. Rainer Gries, "Die Konsumenten und die Werbung: Kulturgeschichtliche Aspekte einer interaktiven Kommunikation," in Hellmann and Schrage, *Konsum der Werbung*, 83–101.

BIBLIOGRAPHY

Allen, Frederick. *Secret Formula: How Brilliant Marketing and Relentless Salesmanship Made Coca-Cola the Best-known Product in the World*. New York: HarperBusiness, 1995.

Åman, Anders. *Architecture and Ideology in Eastern Europe During the Stalin Era: An Aspect of Cold War History*. Cambridge, Mass.: MIT Press, 1992.

Ament, Günter. *Sexfront*. Frankfurt: März-Verlag, 1970.

Andersen, Arne. *Der Traum vom guten Leben: Alltags- und Konsumgeschichte vom Wirtschafts- wunder bis heute*. Frankfurt: Campus Verlag, 1997.

Anderson, Susan C., and Bruce H. Tabb, eds. *Water, Leisure, and Culture: European Historical Perspectives*. New York: Berg, 2002.

Applegate, Celia. *A Nation of Provincials: The German Idea of Heimat*. Berkeley: University of California Press, 1990.

Asard, E., ed. *American Culture: Creolized, Creolizing*. Uppsala: Swedish Institute for North American Studies, 1988.

Aynsely, Jeremy. *Graphic Design in Germany, 1890–1945*. Berkeley: University of California Press, 2000.

Baier, Lothar. *Die Früchte der Revolte: Über die Veränderung der politischen Kultur durch die Studentenbewegung*. Berlin: K. Wagenbach, 1988.

Baranowski, Shelley. *Strength through Joy: Consumerism and Mass Tourism in the Third Reich*. Cambridge, England: Cambridge University Press, 2004.

Bastian, Till. *Niemandszeit: Deutsche Portraits zwischen Kriegsende und Neubeginn*. Munich: Beck, 1999.

Baumann, Hans. "Fremdenverkehr als Wirtschaftsfaktor." *Der Volkswirt* 6, no. 45 (8 Novem- ber 1952): 15.

———. "Der Luftverkehr als Mittler internationaler Verständigung." *Internationales Archiv für Verkehrswesen* 3, no. 4 (February 1951): 78–80.

Baylis, Thomas A. *Technical Intelligence and the East German Elite: Legitimacy and Social Change in Mature Communism*. Berkeley: University of California Press, 1974.

Becker, Bärbel, ed. *Wild Women: Furien, Flittchen, Flintenweiber*. Berlin: Elefanten, 1992.

Becker, Hans Jürgen. *Boeing 707*. Munich: GeraMond, 2001.

Berenson, Edward. *The Trial of Madame Caillaux*. Berkeley: University of California Press, 1992.

———Berghoff, Hartmut. "'Times Change and We Change with Them': The German Advertising Industry in the Third Reich—Between Professional Self-Interest and Political Repression." *Business History* 45, no. 1 (January 2003): 128–147.

———. *Zwischen Kleinstadt und Weltmarkt: Hohner und die Harmonika 1857–1961*. Paderborn: Schoningh, 1997.

———, ed. *Konsumpolitik: Die Regulierung des privaten Verbrauchs im 20. Jahrhundert*. Göttingen: Vandenhoeck und Ruprecht, 1999.

Bessel, Richard, ed. *Fascist Italy and Nazi Germany: Comparisons and Contrasts*. New York: Cambridge University Press, 1996.

Bessel, Richard, and Dirk Schumann, eds. *Life after Death: Approaches to a Cultural and Social History of Europe in the 1940s and 1950s*. Washington, D.C.: German Historical Institute, 2003.

Betts, Paul. *The Authority of Everyday Objects: A Cultural History of West German Industrial Design*. Berkeley: University of California Press, 2004.

Betts, Paul, and Greg Eghigian, eds. *Pain and Prosperity: Reconsidering Twentieth-Century German History*. Stanford: Stanford University Press, 2003.

Beyer, Chris H. *Coca-Cola Girls: An Advertising Art History*. Portland, Ore.: Collector's Press, 2000.

Bluhm, Detlef, ed. *Berliner Warenhäuser: Nachdruck der Erstausgabe von 1908*. Berlin: Fannei und Walz, 1989.

Bohley-Zittlau, Katrin, ed., *Denkmale in Berlin: Bezirk Friedrichshain*. Berlin: Landesdenkmalamt Berlin and Nicolaische Verlagsbuchhandlung, 1996.

Bollenbeck, Georg, and Gerhard Kaiser, eds. *Die janusköpfigen 50er Jahre*. Wiesbaden: Westdeutsche Verlag, 2000.

Bongard, Willi. *Fetische des Konsums*. Hamburg: Nannen-Verlag, 1964.

———. *Männer machen Märkte: Mythos und Wirklichkeit der Werbung*. Frankfurt: Ullstein, 1963.

Bongers, Hans M. *Deutscher Luftverkehr*. Bonn: Kirschbaum, 1967.

———. *Es lag in der Luft*. Düsseldorf: Econ Verlag, 1971.

Brandmeyer, Klaus. *Achtung Marke!* Hamburg: Gruner und Jahr AG, 2002.

Braunburg, Rudolph. *Die Geschichte der Lufthansa*. Hamburg: Rasch und Röhring, 1991.

Brecht, Bertolt. *Gesammelte Werke*. Frankfurt: Suhrkamp Verlag, 1967.

Brenner, Peter J., ed. *Reisekultur in Deutschland: Von der Weimarer Republik zum "Dritten Reich."* Tübingen: Maz Niemeyer Verlag, 1997.

Breward, Christopher. *The Hidden Consumer: Masculinities, Fashion and City life, 1860–1914*. Manchester, England: Manchester University Press, 1999.

Britt, David, ed. *Art and Power: Europe under the Dictators 1930–1945*. London: Hayward Gallery, 1995.

Bromell, Nicholas Knowles. *Tomorrow Never Knows: Rock and Psychedelics in the 1960s*. Chicago: University of Chicago Press, 2002.

Brooks, Jeffrey. "Socialist Realism in *Pravda*, Read All about It! *Slavic Review* 53, no. 4 (winter 1994): 973–991.

Brüggemeier, Franz-Josef, Mark Cioc, and Thomas Zeller, eds. *How Green Were the Nazis? Nature, Environment and Heimat in the Third Reich*. Athens: Ohio University Press, 2005.

Bruhn, Manfred, ed. *Die Marke—Symbolkraft eines Zeichensystems*. Stuttgart: Haupt, 2001.

Buchholz, Wolfhard. "Nationalsozialistische Gemeinschaft 'Kraft durch Freude': Freizeitgestaltung und Arbeiterschaft im Dritten Reich." Ph.D. dissertation, University of Munich, 1976.

Bundesministerium für Jugend, Familie und Gesundheit, ed. *Dokumente zum Drogenproblem mit Information für Eltern und Erzieher*. Düsseldorf: Econ-Verlag, 1972.

Bünz, Enno, Rainer Gries, and Frank Möller, eds. *Der "Tag X" in der Geschichte: Erwartungen und Enttäuschungen seit tausend Jahren*. Stuttgart: Deutsche Verlagsanstalt, 1997.

Burkart, Roland. *Kommunikationswissenschaft: Grundlagen und Problemfelder: Umrisse einer interdisziplinären Sozialwissenschaft*. 4th ed. Vienna: Böhlau Verlag, 2002.

Burke, Timothy. *Lifebuoy Men, Lux Women: Commodification, Consumption, and Cleanliness in Modern Zimbabwe*. Durham, N.C.: Duke University Press, 1996.

Burleigh, Michael. *The Third Reich: A New History*. New York: Hill and Wang, 2000.

Bussemer, Thymian. *Propaganda und Populärkultur: Konstruierte Erlebniswelten im Nationalsozialismus*. Wiesbaden: Deutscher Universitätsverlag, 2000.

Campbell, Joan. *The German Werkbund: The Politics of Reform in the Applied Arts*. Princeton, N.J.: Princeton University Press, 1978.

Canetti, Elias. *Crowds and Power*. Translated by Carol Stewart. New York: Viking Press, 1962.

Carter, Erica. *How German Is She? Postwar West German Reconstruction and the Consuming Woman*. Ann Arbor: University of Michigan Press, 1997.

Castillo, Greg. "Blueprint for a Cultural Revolution: Hermann Henselmann and the Architecture of German Socialist Realism." *Slavonica* 11, no. 1 (April 2005): 31–51.

———. "Domesticating the Cold War: Household Consumption as Propaganda in Marshall Plan Germany." *Journal of Contemporary History* 40, no. 2 (2005): 261–288.

Charles, Barbara F., and Robert Staples. *Dream of Santa: Haddon Sundblom's Vision*. Washington, D.C.: Staples and Charles, 1992.

Church, Roy, and Andrew Godley, eds. *The Emergence of Modern Marketing*. London: Frank Cass, 2003.

Ciarlo, David M. "Rasse konsumieren: Von der exotischen zur kolonialen Imagination in der Bildreklame des Wilhelminischen Kaiserreichs." In *Phantasiereiche zur Kulturgeschichte des deutschen Kolonialismus*, ed. Birthe Kundrus, 135–179. Frankfurt: Campus Verlag, 2003.

The Coca-Cola Company: An Illustrated Profile of a Worldwide Company. Atlanta: The Coca-Cola Company, 1975.

Cohen, Lizabeth. *A Consumers' Republic: The Politics of Mass Consumption in Postwar America*. New York: Knopf, 2003.

Confino, Alon. "Telling about Germany: Narratives of Memory and Culture." *Journal of Modern History* 76, no. 2 (2004): 389–416.

————. "Traveling as a Culture of Remembrance." *History and Memory* 12, no. 2 (winter 2000): 92–121.

Confino, Alon, and Rudy Koshar. "Régimes of Consumer Culture: New Narratives in Twentieth-Century Germany History." *German History* 19 (2001): 135–161.

Connelly, Mark, and David Welch, eds. *War and the Media: Reportage and Propaganda, 1900–2003*. London: I. B. Tauris, 2005.

Crano, William D., and Michael Burgoon, eds. *Mass Media and Drug Prevention*. Mahwah, N.J.: Lawrence Erlbaum, 2002.

Crew, David F., ed. *Consuming Germany in the Cold War*. New York: Berg, 2003.

————, ed. *Nazism and German Society, 1933–1945*. New York: Routledge, 1994.

Dahrendorf, Ralf. *Society and Democracy in Germany*. 1965. New York: Doubleday, 1967.

Damrow, Harry. *Ich war kein geheimer Verführer: Aus dem Leben eines Werbeleiters*. Rheinzabern: Gitzen, 1981.

Daunton, Martin, and Matthew Hilton, eds. *The Politics of Consumption: Material Culture and Citizenship in Europe and North America*. New York: Berg, 2001.

Davies, R. E. G. *Lufthansa: An Airline and Its Aircraft*. New York: Orion Books, 1991.

de Grazia, Victoria. *Irresistible Empire: America's Advance through Twentieth-Century Europe*. Cambridge, Mass.: Harvard University Press, Belknap Press, 2005.

Deichsel, Alexander, ed. *Und alles Ordnet die Gestalt / Hans Domizlaff—Gedanken und Gleichnisse*. Zürich: Kriterion, 1992.

de Syon, Guillaume. *Zeppelin! Germany and the Airship, 1900–1939*. Baltimore: Johns Hopkins University Press, 2002.

Dichter, Ernest. *The Strategy of Desire*. New Brunswick, N.J.: Transaction Publishers, 2002.

Dienel, Hans-Liudger, and Peter Lyth, eds. *Flying the Flag: European Commercial Air Transport since 1945*. New York: St. Martin's Press, 1998.

Diephouse, David. *The Natural History of the German People*. Lewiston, N.Y.: Edwin Mellen Press, 1990.

Doinet, Rupp. "Grande Dame der niederen Instinkte." *Stern*, 26 July 2001, 40–44.

Domizlaff, Hans. *Die Gewinnung des öffentlichen Vertrauens: Ein Lehrbuch der Markentechnik*. Hamburg: Hanseatische Verlagsanstalt, 1939; 2nd ed., Hamburg: Hans Dulk, 1951.

Durth, Werner, Jörn Düwel, and Niels Gutschow. *Ostkreuz/Aufbau: Architektur und Städtebau der DDR*. 2 vols. New York: Campus Verlag, 1998.

Dussel, Konrad. "Wundermittel Werbegeschichte? Werbung als Gegenstand der Geschichtswissenschaft." *Neue Politische Literatur* 42, no. 3 (1997): 416–430.

Edwards, George. "Flying Frau Heads a Sex Empire." *News of the World*, 17 April 1966.

Eglau, Hans Otto. *Die Kasse muss stimmen: So hatten sie Erfolg im Handel*. Düsseldorf: Econ, 1972.

Engel, Helmut, and Wolfgang Ribbe, eds. *Karl-Marx-Allee. Magestrale in Berlin*. Berlin: Akademie Verlag, 1996.

Erker, Paul. "'A New Business History'? Neuere Ansätze und Entwicklungen in der Unternehmensgeschichte." *Archiv für Sozialgeschichte* 42 (2002): 557–604.

Erker, Paul, and Toni Pierenkemper. *Deutsche Unternehmer zwischen Kriegswirtschaft und Wiederaufbau*. Munich: Oldenbourg, 1999.

Etlin, Richard A., ed. *Art, Culture, and Media under the Third Reich.* Chicago: University of Chicago Press, 2002.

Ewen, Stuart. *Captains of Consciousness: Advertising and the Social Roots of the Consumer Culture.* New York: McGraw-Hill, 1976.

———. *PR! A Social History of Spin.* New York: Basic Books, 1996.

Faulstich, Werner, ed. *Die Kultur der fünfziger Jahre.* Munich: Wilhelm Fink Verlag, 2002.

Fehrenbach, Heide. *Cinema in Democratizing Germany: Reconstructing National Identity after Hitler.* Chapel Hill: University of North Carolina Press, 1995.

Fehrenbach, Heide, and Uta G. Poiger, eds. *Transactions, Transgressions, Transformations: American Culture in Western Europe and Japan.* New York: Berghahn, 2000.

Feiter, Wolfgang. *80 Jahre Persil: Produkt- und Werbegeschichte.* Schriften des Werksarchivs, vol. 20. Düsseldorf: Henkel, 1987.

Feldenkirchen, Wilfried, and Susanne Hilger. *Menschen und Marken: 125 Jahre Henkel, 1876–2001* Düsseldorf: Henkel, 2001.

Filter, Cornelia. "Bomber Pilotin und Porno Produzentin." *Emma,* March 1988, 26–31.

Fitzpatrick, Sheila. *The Cultural Front: Power and Culture in Revolutionary Russia.* Ithaca, N.Y.: Cornell University Press, 1992.

Flacke, Monika, ed. *Auftrag: Kunst 1949–1990. Bildende Künstler in der DDR zwischen Ästhetik und Politik.* Berlin: Deutsches Historisches Museum, 1995.

Flierl, Bruno. "Stalinallee in Berlin." *Zodiac* 5 (March 1991): 76–115.

Forbes, Daniel. "Propaganda for Dollars." *Salon,* 14 January 2000, www.dir.salon.com (accessed 30 August 2003).

Frei, Norbert. *National Socialist Rule in Germany: The Führer State 1933–1945.* Oxford: Blackwell, 1993.

———. *Vergangenheitspolitik: Die Anfänge der Bundesrepublik und die NS-Vergangenheit.* Munich: Beck, 1996.

Freitag, Werner, and Christina Pohl, eds. *Das Dritte Reich im Fest: Führermythos, Feierlaune und Verweigerung in Westfalen 1933–1945.* Bielefeld: Verlag für Regionalgeschichte, 1997.

Freud, Sigmund. *Massenpsychologie und Ich-Analyse.* 1921. 4th ed. Vol. 13. Frankfurt: S. Fischer Verlag, 1963.

Friedel, Alois. *Deutsche Staatssymbole—Herkunft und Bedeutung der politischen Symbolik in Deutschland.* Frankfurt: Athenäum Verlag, 1968.

Fritzsche, Peter. *A Nation of Fliers: German Aviation and the Popular Imagination.* Cambridge, Mass.: Harvard University Press, 1992.

———. "Nazi Modern." *Modernism/Modernity* 3, no. 1 (1996): 1–22.

Frommann, Bruno. "Reisen mit 'Kraft durch Freude': Eine Darstellung der KdF-Reisen unter besonderer Berücksichtigung der Auslandsfahrten." M.A. thesis, University of Karlsruhe, 1977.

Garfield, Bob. "The Top 100 Advertising Campaigns." *Advertising Age* 70, no. 13 (1999): 18–41.

Gassert, Philipp. *Amerika im Dritten Reich: Ideologie, Propaganda und Volksmeinung, 1933–1945.* Stuttgart: Franz Steiner Verlag, 1997.

———. "Amerikanismus, Antiamerikanismus, Amerikanisierung: Neue Literatur zur

Sozial-, Wirtschafts- und Kulturgeschichte des amerikanischen Einflusses in Deutschland und Europa." *Archiv für Sozialgeschichte* 39 (1999): 531–561.

Gellately, Robert. *Backing Hitler: Consent and Coercion in Nazi Germany*. Oxford: Oxford University Press, 2001.

Geppert, Alexander C. T. "Welttheater: Die Geschichte des europäischen Ausstellungswesens im 19. und 20. Jahrhundert: Ein Forschungsbericht." *Neue Politische Literatur* 47, no. 1 (2002): 10–61.

Gerlach, Siegfried. *Das Warenhaus in Deutschland: Seine Entwicklung bis zum Ersten Weltkrieg in historisch-geographischer Sicht*. Stuttgart: Steiner, 1988.

Gibas, Monika, Rainer Greis, Barbara Jakoby, and Doris Müller, eds. *Wiedergeburten: Zur Geschichte der runden Jahrestage der DDR*. Leipzig: Leipziger Universitätsverlag, 1999.

Glatzer, Wolfgang, Karl Otto Hondrich, Heinz Herbert Noll, Karin Stiehr, and Barbara Wornal, eds. *Recent Social Trends in West Germany 1960–1990*. Frankfurt: Campus Verlag, 1992.

Godau-Schüttke, Klaus-Detlev. *Die Heyde-Sawade-Affäre: Wie Juristen und Mediziner den NS-Euthanasieprofessor Heyde nach 1945 deckten und straflos blieben*. Baden-Baden: Nomos, 1998.

———. *Ich habe nur dem Recht gedient: Die "Renazifizierung" der Schleswig-Holsteinischen Justiz nach 1945*. Baden-Baden: Nomos, 1993.

Gries, Rainer. *Produkte als Medien: Kulturgeschichte der Produktkommunikation in der Bundesrepublik und der DDR*. Leipzig: Leipziger Universitätsverlag, 2003.

Gries, Rainer, Volker Ilgen, and Dirk Schindelbeck. *Gestylte Geschichte: Vom alltäglichen Umgang mit Geschichtsbildern*. Münster: Verlag Westfälisches Dampfboot, 1989.

Gries, Rainer, Volker Ilgen, and Dirk Schindelbeck, eds. *"Ins Gehirn der Masse kriechen!" Werbung und Mentalitätsgeschichte*. Darmstadt: Wissenschaftliche Buchgesellschaft, 1995.

Grossmann, Atina. *Reforming Sex: The German Movement for Birth Control and Abortion Reform, 1920–1950*. New York: Oxford University Press, 1995.

Groys, Boris. *The Total Art of Stalinism: Avant-Garde, Aesthetic Dictatorship and Beyond*. Translated by Charles Rougle. Princeton, N.J.: Princeton University Press, 1992.

Guenther, Irene. *Nazi 'Chic'? Fashioning Women in the Third Reich*. Oxford: Berg, 2004.

Hachmeister, Lutz, and Michael Kloft, eds. *Das Goebbels-Experiment*. Munich: Deutsche Verlags Anstalt, 2005.

Hachmeister, Lutz, and Friedemann Siering, eds. *Die Herren Journalisten*. Munich: Beck, 2002.

Hagen, Joshua. "The Most German of Towns: Creating the Ideal Nazi Community in Rothenburg ob der Tauber." *Annals of the Association of American Geographers* 94, no. 1 (2004): 207–227.

Hale, Grace Elizabeth. *Making Whiteness: The Culture of Segregation in the South, 1890–1940*. New York, Pantheon Books, 1998.

Hansen, Ursula, and Matthias Bode. *Marketing und Konsum — Theorie und Praxis von der Industrialisierung bis ins 21. Jahrhundert*. Munich: Franz Vahlen, 1999.

Harp, Stephen. *Marketing Michelin: Advertising and Cultural Identity in Twentieth-Century France*. Baltimore: Johns Hopkins University Press, 2001.

Harsch, Donna. *German Social Democracy and the Rise of Nazism*. Chapel Hill: University of North Carolina Press, 1993.

Härtel, Christian, and Petra Kabus, eds. *Das Westpaket: Geschenksendung, keine Handelsware*. Berlin: Christoph Links Verlag, 2000.

Haug, Wolfgang F., ed. *Warenästhetik — Beiträge zur Diskussion, Weiterentwicklung und Vermittlung ihrer Kritik*. Frankfurt: Suhrkamp, 1975.

Heider, Ulrike, ed. *Sadomasochisten, Keusche, Romantiker: Vom Mythos neuer Sinnlichkeit*. Reinbek: Rowohlt, 1986.

Heinelt, Peer. *"PR-Päpste": Die kontinuierlichen Karrieren von Carl Hundhausen, Albert Oeckl und Franz Ronnenberger*. Berlin: Karl Dietz, 2003.

Heineman, Elizabeth D. "The Economic Miracle in the Bedroom: Big Business and Sexual Consumption in Reconstruction West Germany." *Journal of Modern History* 78 (2006): 846–877.

———. "Gender, Sexuality, and Coming to Terms with the Past." *Central European History* 38, no. 1 (2005): 41–74.

———. "The Hour of the Woman: Memories of Germany's 'Crisis Years' and West German National Identity." *American Historical Review* 101, no. 2 (1996): 354–395.

———. *What Difference Does a Husband Make: Women and Marital Status in Nazi and Postwar Germany*. Berkeley: University of California Press, 1999.

Heller, Agnes. *The Theory of Need in Marx*. London: Allison and Busby, 1976.

Hellmann, Kai-Uwe. *Soziologie der Marke*. Frankfurt: Suhrkamp Verlag, 2003.

Hellmann, Kai-Uwe, and Dominik Schrage, eds. *Konsum der Werbung: Zur Produktion und Rezeption von Sinn in der kommerziellen Kultur*. Wiesbaden: Verlag für Sozialwissenschaften, GWV Fachverlage, 2004.

Henatsch, Martin. *Die Entstehung des Plakats*. New York: Olms, 1994.

Herf, Jeffrey. *Reactionary Modernism: Technology, Culture, and Politics in Weimar and the Third Reich*. New York: Cambridge University Press, 1984.

Herzog, Dagmar. *Sex after Fascism: Memory and Morality in Twentieth-Century Germany*. Princeton, N.J.: Princeton University Press, 2005.

Hesse-Freilinghaus, Herta, et al., eds. *Karl Ernst Osthaus: Leben und Werk*. Recklinghausen: Bongers, 1971.

Hilgenberg, Dorothea. *Bedarfs- und Marktforschung in der DDR. Anspruch und Wirklichkeit*. Cologne: Verlag Wissenschaft und Politik, 1979.

Höhn, Maria. *GIs and Fräuleins: The German-American Encounter in 1950s West Germany*. Chapel Hill: University of North Carolina Press, 2002.

Höltje, Gerhard. *Der Aufbau der Deutschen Lufthansa*. Berlin: Deutsche Weltwitschaftliche Gesellschaft, 1961.

Horowitz, Daniel. *The Anxieties of Affluence: Critiques of American Consumer Culture, 1939–1979*. Amherst: University of Massachusetts Press, 2004.

Hübner, Peter, and Klaus Tenfelde, eds. *Arbeiter in der SBZ-DDR*. Essen: Klartext-Verlag, 1999.

Huck, Gerhard, ed. *Sozialgeschichte der Freizeit: Unersuchungen zum Wandel der Alltagskultur in Deutschland*. Wuppertal: Peter Hammer Verlag, 1980.

Institut für Regionalentwicklung und Strukturplanung, ed. *Reise nach Moskau*. Berlin: Dokumentenreihe des IRS, 1996.

International Chamber of Commerce. *Advertising: Conditions and Regulations in Various Countries*. 2nd ed. Basel: Verlag für Recht und Gesellschaft, 1964.

Jarausch, Konrad, and Michael Geyer. *Shattered Pasts: Reconstructing German Histories*. Princeton, N.J.: Princeton University Press, 2003.

Jarausch, Konrad, and Hannes Siegrist, eds. *Amerikanisierung und Sowjetisierung in Deutschland 1945–1970*. Frankfurt: Campus Verlag, 1997.

Jay, Martin. *The Dialectical Imagination: A History of the Frankfurt School and the Institute of Social Research 1923–1950*. Boston: Little, Brown, 1970.

Jeffries, Mathew. *Politics and Culture in Wilhelmine Germany: The Case of Industrial Architecture*. Washington: Berg, 1995.

Johenning, Wilhelm. "Der Wiederaufbau der kommerziellen Zivilluftfahrt der Bundesrepublik Deutschland nach dem zweiten Weltkrieg." Ph.D. dissertation, University of Cologne, 1963.

John, Otto. *Zweimal kam ich heim*. Düsseldorf: Econ Verlag, 1969.

Jüngst, Peter. *Psychodynamik und Stadtgestaltung: Zum Wandel präsentativer Symbolik und Territorialität: Von der Moderne zur Postmoderne*. Stuttgart: Psychosozial Verlag, 1995.

Junker, Detlev, ed. *The United States and Germany in the Era of the Cold War, 1945–1968*. London: Sage, 1979.

Kaminsky, Annette. *Kaufrausch: Die Geschichte der ostdeutschen Versandhäuser*. Berlin: Christoph Links Verlag, 1998.

Kater, Michael H. "Die Sozialgeschichte und das Dritte Reich. Überlegungen zu neuen Büchern." *Archiv für Sozialgeschichte* 22 (1982): 661–681.

Keitz, Christine. *Reisen als Leitbild: Die Entstehung des modernen Massentourismus in Deutschland*. Munich: DTV, 1997.

Kellner, Joachim, Ulrich Kurth, and Werner Lippert, eds. *1945–1995: 50 Jahre Werbung in Deutschland*. Ingelheim: Westermann-Kommunkation, 1995.

Kershaw, Ian. *The Nazi Dictatorship: Problems and Perspectives of Interpretation*. 4th ed. New York: Oxford University Press, 2000.

Kirshenblatt-Gimblett, Barbara. *Destination Culture: Tourism, Museums and Heritage*. Berkeley: University of California Press, 1998.

Kleinschmidt, Christian, and Florian Triebel, eds. *Marketing: Historische Aspekte der Wettbewerbs- und Absatzpolitik*. Bochumer Schriften zur Unternehmens- und Industriegeschichte, vol. 13. Essen: Klartext Verlag, 2004.

Knoch, Habbo, and Daniel Morat, eds. *Kommunikation als Beobachtung: Medienwandel und Gesellschaftsbilder 1880–1960*. Munich: Wilhelm Fink Verlag, 2003.

König, Wolfgang. "Das Scheitern einer nationalsozialistischen Konsumgesellschaft: 'Volksprodukte' in Politik, Propaganda und Gesellschaft des 'Dritten Reiches.'" *Zeitschrift für Unternehmensgeschichte* 48, no. 2 (2003): 131–163.

———. *Geschichte der Konsumgesellschaft*. Supplement to *Vierteljahrschrift für Sozial- und Wirtschaftsgeschichte*. Stuttgart: Franz Steiner Verlag, 2000.

Könke, Günter. "'Modernisierungsschub' oder relative Stagnation? Einige Anmerkungen zum Verhältnis von Nationalsozialismus und Moderne." *Geschichte und Gesellschaft* 20, no. 4 (1994): 584–608.

Kopstein, Jeffrey. *The Politics of Economic Decline in East Germany, 1945–1989.* Chapel Hill: University of North Carolina Press, 1997.

Koshar, Rudy. *German Travel Cultures.* New York: Berg, 2000.

Koszyk, Kurt. *Deutsche Presse 1914–1945.* Berlin: Colloquium Verlag, 1972.

Kratzsch, Gerhard. *Kunstwart und Dürerbund. Ein Beitrag zur Geschichte der Gebildeten im Zeitalter des Imperialismus.* Göttingen: Vandenhoeck und Ruprecht, 1969.

Kriegeskorte, Michael. *Werbung in Deutschland 1945–1965: Die Nachkriegszeit im Spiegel ihrer Anzeigen.* Cologne: DuMont Buchverlag, 1992.

Krietemeyer, Olaf. "Die Marketingpolitik bei der Einführung von Coca-Cola auf dem Deutschen Markt." Diplomarbeit, Business School of the Universität Regensburg, 1993.

Kroes, Rob. *If You've Seen One, You've Seen the Mall: European and American Mass Culture.* Urbana: University of Illinois Press, 1996.

Kruger, Barbara, and Phil Mariani, eds. *Remaking History.* Seattle: Bay Press, 1989.

Kruip, Gudrun. *Das "Welt"-"Bild" des Axel Springer Verlags.* Munich: Oldenbourg, 1999.

Ladwig-Winters, Simone. *Wertheim: Ein Warenhausunternehmen und seine Eigentümer.* Münster: LIT, 1997.

Laird, Pamela Walker. *Advertising Progress: American Business and the Rise of Consumer Marketing.* Baltimore: Johns Hopkins University Press, 1998.

Lamberty, Christiane. *Reklame in Deutschland 1890–1914.* Berlin: Duncker und Humblot, 2000.

Lambertz, Winfried. "Selbstbedienung forcierte Wachstum der Sortimente." *Dynamik im Handel* 31 (October 1988): 126–36.

Landsman, Mark. *Dictatorship and Demand: The Politics of Consumerism in East Germany.* Cambridge, Mass.: Harvard University Press, 2005.

"Länsberg, Ullerstam lärare i kontinentens största kärleksskola." *Norrländska Socialdemokraten,* 23 November 1966, 1.

Lavigne, Marie. *The Socialist Economies of the Soviet Union and Europe.* Trans. T. G. Waywell. White Plains, N.Y.: International Arts and Sciences Press, 1974.

Lears, T. J. Jackson. *Fables of Abundance: A Cultural History of Advertising in America.* New York: Basic Books, 1994.

Leitherer, Eugen. *Geschichte der Handels- und Absatzwirtschaftlichen Literatur.* Cologne: Westdeutscher Verlag, 1961.

Lekan, Thomas, and Thomas Zeller, eds. *Germany's Nature.* New Brunswick, N.J.: Rutgers University Press, 2005.

Liebert, Tobias. *Der Take-off von Öffentlichkeitsarbeit: Beiträge zur theoriegestützten Real- und Reflexions-Geschichte öffentlicher Kommunikation und ihrer Differenzierung. Leipziger Skripten für Public Relations und Kommunikationsmanagement.* Vol. 5. Leipzig: Lehrstuhl für Öffentlichkeitsarbeit, Public Relations an der Universität Leipzig, 2003.

Liebscher, Daniela. "Mit KDF 'die Welt erschließen': Der Beitrag der KDF-Reisen zur Außenpolitik der Deutschen Arbeitsfront 1934–1939." *Zeitschrift für Sozialgeschichte des 20. und 21. Jahrhunderts* 14, no. 1 (1999): 43–72.

Loehlin, Jennifer A. *From Rugs to Riches: Housework, Consumption and Modernity in Germany.* Oxford: Berg, 1999.

Lovegrove, Keith. *Airline Identity, Design and Culture.* New York: TeNeues, 2000.

Lüdtke, Alf, and Peter Becker. *Akten. Eingaben. Schaufenster. Die DDR und ihre Texte: Erkundungen zur Herrschaft und Alltag.* Berlin: Akademie Verlag, 1997.

Lüdtke, Alf, Inge Marssolek, and Adleheid von Saldern, eds. *Amerikanisierung: Traum und Alptraum im Deutschland des 20. Jahrhunderts.* Stuttgart: Steiner, 1996.

Maase, Kaspar. *Prädikat wertlos: Der lange Streit um Schmutz und Schund.* Tübingen: Tübinger Vereinigung für Volkskunde, 2001.

Maier, Charles. "From Taylorism to Technocracy." *Journal of Contemporary History* 5, no. 2 (1970): 27–61.

Marchand, Roland. *Advertising the American Dream: Making Way for Modernity, 1920–1940.* Berkeley: University of California Press, 1985.

———. *Creating the Corporate Soul: The Rise of Public Relations and Corporate Imagery in American Big Business.* Berkeley: University of California Press, 1998.

Marwick, Arthur. *The Sixties: Cultural Revolution in Britain, France, Italy, and the United States, c. 1958–c. 1974.* Oxford: Oxford University Press, 1998.

McClintock, Anne. *Imperial Leather: Race, Gender and Sexuality in the Colonial Contest.* New York: Routledge, 1995.

Meggs, Philip. *A History of Graphic Design.* 3rd ed. New York: Wiley, 1998.

Merkel, Ina. *Utopie und Bedürfnis: Die Geschichte der Konsumkultur in der DDR, Alltag und Kultur.* Cologne: Böhlau Verlag, 1999.

———, ed. *Wir sind doch nicht die Meckerecke der Nation! Briefe an das Fernsehen der DDR.* Cologne: Böhlau Verlag, 1998.

Merkel, Martin. *Vorbilder: 12 Kreative, die das Bild der Werbung bestimmt haben.* Munich: Siegmund, 1988.

Meyer, Paul W., ed. *Begegnungen mit Hans Domizlaff—Festschrift zu seinem 75. Geburtstag.* Essen: Verlag Wirtschaft und Werbung, 1967.

Moeller, Robert G. *Protecting Motherhood: Women and the Family in the Politics of Postwar West Germany.* Berkeley: University of California Press, 1993.

———. *War Stories: The Search for a Usable Past in the Federal Republic of Germany.* Berkeley: University of California Press, 2001.

———, ed. *West Germany Under Construction: Politics, Society, and Culture in the Adenauer Era.* Ann Arbor: University of Michigan Press, 1997.

Mosse, George, ed. *International Fascism: New Thoughts and Approaches.* Beverly Hills, Calif.: Sage, 1979.

Mühlbauer, Georg-Michael. *Rundschreibentext für kritische Situation.* Essen: Eigenverlag, 1993.

Müller, Hans. W. "Eindeutige Zweideutigkeiten." *Der neue Vertrieb* 4, no. 67 (February 1952): 49–50.

Müller, Sebastian. *Kunst und Industrie: Ideologie und Organisation des Funktionalismus in der Architektur.* Munich: Hanser, 1974.

Münch, Wilhelm. "Psychologie der Mode." *Preußische Jahrbücher* 89 (1897): 1–26.

Munsey, Cecil. *The Illustrated Guide to the Collectibles of Coca-Cola.* New York: Hawthorn Books, 1972.

Murken-Attrogge, Christa. *Werbung—Mythos—Kunst am Beispiel Coca-Cola.* Tübingen: Verlag Ernst Wasmuth, 1977.

Neue Gesellschaft für bildende Kunst, ed. *Wunderwirtschaft. DDR-Konsumkultur in den 60er Jahren.* Cologne: Böhlau, 1996.

Nicholson, H. B. *Host to Thirsty Mainstreet.* New York: Newcomen Society, 1953.

Nicolaus, Herbert, and Alexander Obeth. *Die Stalinallee: Geschichte einer deutschen Straße.* Berlin: Verlag für Bauwesen, 1997.

Niehuss, Merith. *Familie, Frau und Gesellschaft.* Göttingen: Vandenhoeck und Ruprecht, 2001.

Nolan, Mary. *Visions of Modernity: American Business and the Modernization of Germany.* Oxford: Oxford University Press, 1994.

O'Barr, William M. *Culture and the Ad: Exploring Otherness in the World of Advertising.* Boulder, Colo.: Westview, 1994.

Omelia, Johanna, and Michael Waldock. *Come Fly with Us!* Portland, Oreg.: Collectors Press, 2003.

Ostermann, Christian. "New Documents on the East German Uprising of 1953." *Bulletin* 5 (spring 1955): 10–21. Washington: Cold War International History Project.

Overy, Richard J. *The Nazi Economic Recovery, 1932–1938.* 2nd ed. Cambridge, England: Cambridge University Press, 1996.

Packard, Vance. *The Hidden Persuaders.* 1957. 16th ed. New York: Pocket Books, 1961.

Patterson, Patrick Hyder. "Truth Half Told: Finding the Perfect Pitch for Advertising and Marketing in Socialist Yugoslavia, 1950–1991." *Enterprise and Society* 4, no. 2 (June 2003): 179–225.

Paul, Gerhard. *Aufstand der Bilder: Die NS-Propaganda vor 1933.* Bonn: Dietz, 1990.

Pence, Katharine. "You as a Woman Will Understand": Consumption, Gender and the Relationship between State and Citizenry in the GDR's Crisis of 17 June 1953." *German History* 19, no. 2 (February 2001): 218–252.

Pendergrast, Mark. *For God, Country and Coca-Cola: The Definitive History of the Great American Soft Drink and the Company That Makes It.* 2nd ed. New York: Basic Books, 2000.

Petretti, Alan. *Petretti's Coca-Cola Collectibles Price Guide.* 11th ed. Radnor, Penna.: Chilton, 2001.

Pinkus, Karen. *Bodily Regimes: Italian Advertising under Fascism.* Minneapolis: University of Minnesota Press, 1995.

Pommerin, Reiner. *Der Kaiser und Amerika: Die USA in der Politik der Reichsleitung 1890–1917.* Cologne: Böhlau, 1986.

Posener, Julius. *Berlin auf dem Wege zu einer neuen Architektur: Das Zeitalter Wilhelms II.* Munich: Prestl, 1979.

Posiadly, Frank. "Imagewerbung für den Staat: Hans Domizlaff (1892–1972)." *Zeitschrift für Politische Psychologie* 3, no. 3 (1995): 275–289.

Prinz, Michael, and Rainer Zitelmann, eds. *Nationalsozialismus und Modernisierung.* Darmstadt: Wissenschaftliche Buchgesellschaft, 1991.

Proctor, Robert. *The Nazi War on Cancer.* Princeton, N.J.: Princeton University Press, 1999.

———. *Racial Hygiene: Medicine under the Nazis.* Cambridge, Mass.: Harvard University Press, 1988.

Prößler, Helmut. *200 Jahre Deinhard, 1794–1994: Die Geschichte des Hauses Deinhard von den Anfängen bis zur Gegenwart.* Koblenz: Deinhard, 1994.

"Rangsdorf: Ein Flugfeld wird sechzig." *Fliegerrevue* 7 (1996): 35–38.

"Rapid Turnover on Supermarket for Sex." *German Tribune* (reprinted in *Süddeutsche Zeitung*), 20 August 1966, 15.

Reiche, Reimut. *Sexualität und Klassenkampf: Zur Abwehr repressiver Entsublimierung.* Frankfurt: Neue Kritik, 1968.

Reinhardt, Dirk. *Von der Reklame zum Marketing: Geschichte der Wirtschaftswerbung in Deutschland.* Berlin: Akademie-Verlag, 1993.

Repp, Kevin. *Reformers, Critics, and the Paths of German Modernity: Anti-Politics and the Search for Alternatives, 1890–1914.* Cambridge, Mass.: Harvard University Press, 2000.

Reul, Georg. *Planung und Gründung der Deutschen Lufthansa AG, 1949 bis 1955.* Cologne: Botermann und Botermann, 1995.

Reuss, Karl-Ferdinand, ed. *Jahrbuch der Luftfahrt.* Mannheim: Südwestdeutsche Verlagsanstalt, 1957–1959.

Richards, Thomas. *The Commodity Culture of Victorian England: Advertising and Spectacle, 1851–1914.* Stanford: Stanford University Press, 1990.

Rieger, Bernard. "Fast Couples: Technology, Gender and Modernity in Britain and Germany during the Nineteen-Thirties." *Historical Research* 76, no. 193 (2003): 364–388.

Riethmüller, Walter. *Selbstbedienung—und wie sie zum Erfolg führt.* Munich: Gehlen Verlag, 1952.

Ringer, Fritz. *Decline of the German Mandarins: The German Academic Community 1890–1933.* Cambridge, Mass.: Harvard University Press, 1969.

Robb, George, and Nancy Erber. *Disorder in the Court: Trials and Sexual Conflict at the Turn of the Century.* New York: New York University Press, 1999.

Rollins, William. *A Greener Vision of Home: Cultural Politics and Environmental Reform in the German Heimatschutz Movement, 1904–1918.* Ann Arbor: University of Michigan Press, 1997.

Ross, Corey. "Mass Politics and the Techniques of Leadership: The Promise and Perils of Propaganda in Weimar Germany." *German History* 24, no. 2 (2006): 184–211.

Rostock, Jürgen, and Franz Zadniček. *Paradies Ruinen: Das KdF-Seebad der Zwanzigtausend auf Rügen.* Berlin: Ch. Links Verlag, 1995.

Rücker, Matthias. *Wirtschaftswerbung unter dem Nationalsozialismus:. Rechtliche Ausgestaltung der Werbung und Tätigkeit des Werberats der deutschen Wirtschaft.* Frankfurt: Peter Lang, 2000.

Rudolf, Karsten, and Christl Wickert, eds. *Geschichte als Möglichkeit: Über die Chancen von Demokratie*. Essen: Klartext, 1995.

Ruhl, Klaus-Jörg. *Verordnete Unterordnung: Berufstätige Frauen zwischen Wirtschaftswachstum und konservativer Ideologie in der Nachkriegszeit, 1945–1963*. Munich: Oldenbourg, 1994.

Sachse, Carola, et al., eds. *Angst, Belohnung, Zucht und Ordnung: Herrschaftsmechanismen im Nationalsozialismus*. Opladen: Westdeutscher Verlag, 1982.

Sandoval, Teresa. "Film Representations of German Holiday Cruises during the Inter-War Years: Between Formation and Propaganda." Paper presented at the "'Tourisms and Histories: Representations and Experiences" conference, University of Central Lancashire, England, 19–21 June 2003.

Schäfer, Hans-Dieter. *Das gespaltene Bewußtsein. Deutsche Kultur und Lebenswirklichkeit, 1933–1945*. Munich: Carl Hanser Verlag, 1981.

Schäfers, Stefanie. *Vom Werkbund zum Vierjahresplan: Die Ausstellung "Schaffendes Volk," Düsseldorf 1937*. Düsseldorf: Droste Verlag, 2001.

Schaser, Angelika, ed. *Erinnerungskartelle: Zur Konstruktion von Autobiographien nach 1945*. Bochum: Winkler, 2003.

Scheer, Thorsten, et al., eds. *City of Architecture, Architecture of the City: Berlin 1900–2000*. Berlin: Nicolai, 2000.

Scheffler, Karl. *Berlin: Ein Stadtschicksal*. Berlin: Fannei und Walz, 1998.

Schenk, Ingrid. "Producing to Consume Becomes Consuming to Produce: Advertising and Consumerism in German-American Relations." In *The United States and Germany in the Era of the Cold War, 1945–1968*, ed. Detlev Junker. London: Sage, 1979.

Schildt, Axel. "NS-Regime, Modernisierung und Moderne: Anmerkungen zur Hochkonjunktur einer andauernden Diskussion." *Tel Aviver Jahrbuch für deutsche Geschichte* 23 (1994): 3–22.

Schildt, Axel, and Arnold Sywottek, eds. *Modernisierung im Wiederaufbau: Die westdeutsche Gesellschaft der 50er Jahre*. Bonn: Verlag W. H. W. Dietz Nachf., 1993.

Schindelbeck, Dirk. "'Asbach Uralt' und 'Soziale Marktwirtschaft': Zur Kulturgeschichte der Werbeagentur in Deutschland am Beispiel von Hanns W. Brose (1899–1971)." *Zeitschrift für Unternehmensgeschichte* 40, no. 3 (1995): 235–252.

Schindelbeck, Dirk, and Volker Ilgen. *"Haste Was, Biste Was!": Werbung für die Soziale Marktwirtschaft*. Darmstadt: Primus Verlag, 1999.

Schindler, Herbert. *Monographie des Plakats: Entwicklung, Stil, Design*. Munich: Süddeutscher Verlag, 1972.

Schissler, Hanna, ed. *The Miracle Years: A Cultural History of West Germany, 1949–1968*. Princeton, N.J.: Princeton University Press, 2001.

Schmidt, Alexander. *Reisen in die Moderne: Der Amerika-Diskurs des deutschen Bürgertums vor dem Ersten Weltkrieg im europäischen Vergleich*. Berlin: Akademie, 1997.

Schmiedchen, Johannes. *Kurzer Beitrag zur Geschichte der deutschen Wirtschaftswerbung—ihrer Männer, ihrer Organisationen, ihrer Presse*. Tübingen: Werkring-Verlag des Werbedienstes GMBH, 1953.

Schmutzler, Olaf, and Werner Bischoff. "Zum Einkaufsverhalten der Haushalte der DDR bei Lebensmitteln." *Mitteilungen des Instituts für Bedarfsforschung*, no. 4 (1968).

Schneeringer, Julia. "The Shopper as Voter: Women, Advertising, and Politics in Post-Inflation Germany." *German Studies Review* 27, no. 3 (October 2004): 476–501.

Schoenbaum, David. *Hitler's Social Revolution: Class and Status in Nazi Germany 1933–1939.* Garden City, N.J.: Doubleday, 1957.

———. *The Spiegel Affair.* Garden City, N.J.: Doubleday, 1968.

Schröter, Harm. "Die Amerikanisierung der Werbung in der Bundesrepublik Deutschland." *Jahrbuch für Wirtschaftsgeschichte* 1 (1997): 94–115.

Schudson, Michael. *Advertising, the Uneasy Persuasion.* New York: Basic Books, 1984.

Schug, Alexander. "Von *Newspaper space salesman* zur integrierten Kommunkationsagentur: Die 120-jährige Entwicklungsgeschichte der Werbeagentur Dorland." *Zeitschrift für Unternehmensgeschichte* 49, no. 1 (2004): 5–25.

———. "Wegbereiter der modernen Absatzwerbung in Deutschland: Advertising Agencies und die Amerikanisierung der deutschen Werbebranche in der Zwischenkriegszeit." *Werkstattgeschichte* 34 (2003): 29–52.

Schulze, Gerhard. *Die Erlebnisgesellschaft: Kultursoziologie der Gegenwart.* Frankfurt: Campus Verlag, 1993.

Schutts, Jeff R. "Coca-Colonization, 'Refreshing' Americanization, or Nazi *Volksgetränk?* The History of Coca-Cola in Germany, 1929–1961." Ph.D. dissertation, Georgetown University, 2003.

Schwartz, Frederic J. *The Werkbund—Design Theory and Mass Culture before the First World War.* New Haven: Yale University Press, 1996.

Schwartz, Vanessa R. *Spectacular Realities: Early Mass Culture in Fin-de-Siècle Paris.* Berkeley: University of California Press, 1998.

Schwarzkopf, Stefan. "Advertising, Mass Democracy and Consumer Culture in Britain, 1919–1951." Ph.D. dissertation, Birkbeck College, London, forthcoming.

———. "They Do It with Mirrors: Advertising and British Cold War Consumer Politics." *Contemporary British History* 19, no. 2 (2005): 133–150.

Semmens, Kristin. *Selling Hitler's Germany: Tourism in the Third Reich.* Hampshire, England: Palgrave Macmillan, 2005.

Siedentopf, Monika. "Die Lust-Macherin." *Die Zeit,* 20 March 2003, 28.

Siegfried, Detlef. "'Trau keinem über 30'? Konsens und Konflikt der Generationen in der Bundesrepublik der langen sechziger Jahre." *Aus Politik und Zeitgeschichte* B45 (2003): 25–32.

Siegrist, Hannes, Hartmut Kaelbe, and Jürgen Kocka, eds. *Europäische Konsumgeschichte: Zur Gesellschafts- und Kulturgeschichte des Konsums 18. bis 20. Jahrhundert.* New York: Campus Verlag, 1997.

Sigel, Lisa Z. *Governing Pleasures: Pornography and Social Change in England, 1815–1914.* New Brunswick, N.J.: Rutgers University Press, 2002.

Smelser, Ronald. *Robert Ley: Hitler's Labor Front Leader.* New York: Berg, 1989.

Smith, Alan H. *The Planned Economies of Eastern Europe.* New York: Holmes and Meier, 1983.

Smith, Paul. "Contemporary Legends and Popular Culture: 'It's the Real Thing.'" *Contemporary Legend* 1 (1991): 123–152.

Sontheimer, Kurt. *Antidemokratisches Denken in der Weimarer Republik — Die politischen Ideen des deutschen Nationalismus zwischen 1918 und 1933*. Munich: Nymphenburger Verlagshandlung, 1962.

Sperber, Jonathan. *"Bürger, Bürgertum, Bürgerlichkeit, Bürgerliche Gesellschaft*: Studies of the German (Upper) Middle Class and Its Sociocultural World." *Journal of Modern History* 26, no. 2 (June 1997): 271–297.

Staupe Gisela, and Lisa Vieth, eds. *Die Pille: von der Lust und von der Liebe*. Berlin: Deutsches Hygiene-Museum, 1996.

Stearns, Peter. "Stages of Consumerism: Recent Work on the Issue of Periodization." *Journal of Modern History* 69 (1997): 102–117.

Steiner, André. *Die DDR-Wirtschaftsreform der sechziger Jahre: Konflikt zwischen Effizienz- und Machtkalkül*. Berlin: Akademie-Verlag, 1999.

Stitziel, Judd. *Fashioning Socialism: Clothing, Politics and Consumer Culture in East Germany*. Oxford: Berg, 2005.

Stöver, Bernd, ed. *Berichte über die Lage in Deutschland: Die Meldungen der Gruppe Neu Beginnen aus dem Dritten Reich 1933–1936*. Bonn: J. H. W. Dietz Nachfolger, 1993.

Strasser, Susan. "Making Consumption Conspicuous." *Technology and Culture* 43, no. 4 (October 2002): 755–770.

Strasser, Susan, Charles McGovern, and Matthias Judt, eds. *Getting and Spending: European and American Consumer Societies in the Twentieth Century*. Cambridge: Cambridge University Press, 1998.

Sulkunen, Pekka, John Holmwood, Hilary Radner, and Gerhard Schulze, eds. *Constructing the New Consumer Society*. London: Macmillan, 1997.

Sywottek, Julia. *Mobilmachung für den totalen Krieg: Die propagandistische Vorbereitung der deutschen Bevölkerung auf den Zweiten Weltkrieg*. Opladen: Westdeutscher Verlag, 1976.

Tauss, Jörg, Johannes Kollbeck, and Jan Mönikes, eds. *Deutschlands Weg in die Informationsgesellschaft: Herausforderungen und Perspektiven für Wirtschaft, Wissenschaft, Recht und Politik*. Baden-Baden: Nomos Verlagsgesellschaft, 1996.

Taylor, Katherine F. *In the Theater of Criminal Justice: The Palais de Justice in Second Empire Paris*. Princeton, N.J.: Princeton University Press, 1993.

Tedlow, Richard. *New and Improved: The Story of Mass Marketing in America*. New York: Basic Books, 1990.

Tietz, Georg. *Hermann Tietz: Geschichte einer Familie und ihrer Warenhäuser*. Stuttgart: Deutsche Verlags-Anstalt, 1965.

Timmermann, Heiner, ed. *Diktaturen in Europa im 20. Jahrhundert — Der Fall DDR*. Berlin: Duncker und Humblot, 1996.

Trentmann, Frank. "Beyond Consumerism: New Historical Perspectives on Consumption." *Journal of Contemporary History* 39, no. 3 (2004): 373–401.

Uhse, Beate. *Lustvoll in den Markt: Strategien für schwierige Märkte*. Planegg: Haufe Mediengruppe, 2000.

Uhse, Beate, with Ulrich Pramann. *Mit Lust und Liebe: Mein Leben*. Frankfurt: Ullstein, 1989.

Van Bakel, Rogier. "For Sale: Magazines' Credibility." *Advertising Agency's Creativity*, 1 April 2000, 4.

van Steen, Uta. *Liebesperlen: Beate Uhse: Eine Deutsche Karriere*. Hamburg: Europäische Verlagsanstalt, 2003.

Verhey, Jeffrey. *"The Spirit of 1914": Militarism, Enthusiasm, and Myth in Germany, 1914–1945*. Cambridge: Cambridge University Press, 2000.

Veyassat, Béatrice, Jon Mathieu, Hannes Siegrist, Jakob Tanner, and Regina Wecker, eds. *Geschichte der Konsumgesellschaft: Märkte, Kultur und Identität. Schweizerische Gesellschaft für Wirtschafts- und Sozialgeschichte*. Vol. 15. Zurich: Chronos, 1998.

Viehöfer, Erich. *Der Verleger als Organisator: Eugen Diederichs und die bürgerlichen Reformbewegungen der Jahrhundertwende*. Frankfurt: Buchhändler-Vereinigung, 1988.

Volkov, Shulamit. *The Rise of Political Anti-Modernism: The Urban Master Artisans, 1873–1896*. Princeton, N.J.: Princeton University Press, 1978.

Volze, Armin. "Die Devisengeschäfte der DDR: Genex und Intershop." *Deutschland Archiv*, November 1991, 1145–1159.

Vorsteher, Dieter, ed. *Parteiauftrag: Ein neues Deutschland. Bilder, Rituale und Symbole der früheren DDR*. Berlin: Deutsche Historisches Museum, 1996.

Voy, Klaus, Werner Polster, and Claus Thomasberger, eds. *Gesellschaftliche Transformationsprozesse und materielle Lebensweise: Beiträge zur Wirtschafts- und Gesellschaftsgeschichte der Bundesrepublik Deutschland (1949–1989)*. Marburg: Metropolis Verlag, 1993.

Wagnleitner, Reinhold. *Coca-Colonization and the Cold War*. Chapel Hill: University of North Carolina Press, 1994.

Walkowitz, Judith R. *City of Dreadful Delight: Narratives of Sexual Danger in Late-Victorian London*. Chicago: University of Chicago Press, 1992.

Ward, Janet. *Weimar Surfaces—Urban Visual Culture in 1920s Germany*. Berkeley: University of California Press, 2001.

"Was hält Herr Uhse von Frau Uhse?" *Jasmin* 14, no. 10 (1968): 63–76.

Watkins, Julian Lewis. *The 100 Greatest Advertisements: Who Wrote Them and What They Did*. New York: Dover Press, 1959.

Watters, Pat. *Coca-Cola: An Illustrated History*. Garden City, N.J.: Doubleday, 1978.

Weber, Hermann. *Geschichte der DDR*. Munich: DTV, 1985.

Weiner, Mark. "Consumer Culture and Participatory Democracy: The Story of Coca-Cola During World War II." *Food and Foodways* 6, no. 2 (1996): 109–129.

Weisbrod, Bernd, ed. *Die Politik der Öffentlichkeit—Die Öffentlichkeit der Politik: Politische Medialisierung in der Geschichte der Bundesrepublik. Veröffentlichungen des Zeitgeschichtlichen Arbeitskreises Niedersachsen*. Vol. 21. Göttingen: Wallstein Verlag, 2003.

Welch, David. "Mobilizing the Masses: The Organization of German Propaganda during World War One." In *War and the Media: Reportage and Propaganda, 1900–2003*, ed. Mark Connelly and David Welch. London: I. B. Tauris, 2005.

———. *The Third Reich: Politics and Propaganda*. 2nd ed. New York: Routledge, 2002.

Wenner, Jann, ed. *Lennon Remembers: The Full Rolling Stone Interviews from 1970*. New York: Da Capo Press, 2000.

Westphal, Uwe. *Werbung im Dritten Reich*. Berlin: Transit, 1989.

Wienemann, Elisabeth. *Vom Alkoholverbot zum Gesundheitsmanagement: Entwicklung der betrieblichen Suchtprävention 1800-2000*. Stuttgart: Ibidem-Verlag, 2000.

Wiesen, S. Jonathan. "Miracles for Sale: Consumer Displays and Advertising in Postwar West Germany." In *Consuming Germany*, ed. David F. Crew, 151-178. New York: Berg, 2003.

————. *West German Industry and the Challenge of the Nazi Past, 1945-1955*. Chapel Hill: University of North Carolina Press, 2001.

Wiggershaus, Rolf. *The Frankfurt School: Its Histories, Theories, and Political Significance*. Cambridge, Mass.: MIT Press, 1994.

Wildt, Michael. *Am Beginn der "Konsumgesellschaft": Mangelerfahrung, Lebenshaltung, Wohlstandshoffnung in Westdeutschland in den fünfziger Jahren*. Hamburg: Ergebnisse Verlag, 1994.

————. "Plurality of Taste: Food and Consumption in West Germany during the 1950s." *History Workshop Journal* 39 (1995): 23-41.

————. *Vom kleinen Wohlstand: Eine Konsumgeschichte der fünfziger Jahre*. Frankfurt: Fischer Taschenbuch, 1996.

Wilke, Jürgen, ed. *Mediengeschichte der Bundesrepublik Deutschland*. Bonn: Bundeszentrale für politische Bildung, 1999.

Willett, John. *The New Sobriety, 1917-1933: Art and Politics in the Weimar Period*. London: Thames and Hudson, 1978.

Williamson, Judith. *Decoding Advertisements: Ideology and Meaning in Advertising*. New York: Marion Books, 1978.

Wrynn, V. Dennis. *Coke Goes to War*. Missoula, Mont.: Pictoral Histories Publishing, 1996.

Zahn, Ernest. *Soziologie der Prosperität*. Cologne: Kiepenheuer und Witsch, 1960.

Zatlin, Jonathan R. *The Currency of Socialism in East Germany: Money and Political Culture*. Cambridge: Cambridge University Press, 2007.

————. "Eingaben und Ausgaben. Das Petitionsrecht und der Untergang der DDR." *Zeitschrift für Geschichtswissenschaft*, 45, no. 10 (1997): 902-917.

————. "The Vehicle of Desire: The Trabant, the Wartburg, and the End of the GDR." *German History*, 15, no. 3 (1997): 358-380.

Zielke, Monika. "Zur Sozialpolitik in der DDR während der Übergangsperiode (1945-1961)." Ph.D. dissertation: Humboldt University, Berlin, 1981.

Zitelmann, Rainer. *Hitler: Selbstverständnis eines Revolutionärs*. Stuttgart: Klett-Cotta, 1989.

CONTRIBUTORS

Shelley Baranowski is a professor of history at the University of Akron in Ohio. In addition to her earlier books on German Protestantism and Prussian agrarian elites, she is the author of *Strength through Joy: Consumerism and Mass Tourism in the Third Reich* (2004). She is currently writing a book for Cambridge University Press that situates Nazism in the broader context of European imperialism.

Greg Castillo is a senior lecturer at the University of Sydney, Australia. His research interests include the legacy of the Bauhaus and the influence of politics on architecture during the cold war. His book, *Cold War on the Home Front: The Propaganda and Politics of Midcentury Domestic Design*, is forthcoming.

Victoria de Grazia is a professor of history at Columbia University and a frequent lecturer at universities abroad. She is the author of various books on fascist Italy, including *Dizionario del Fascismo* with Sergio Luzzatto (2003). She has a long-standing interest in consumer culture, the subject in transatlantic perspective of her recent book, *Irresistible Empire: America's Advance through Twentieth-Century Europe* (2005).

Guillaume de Syon is an associate professor of history at Albright College, Reading, Pennsylvania. He is the author of *Zeppelin! Germany and the Airship, 1900–1939*, and is at work on a history of transatlantic flight and one on German tourism after World War II.

Holm Friebe graduated with a degree in economics from Humboldt University in Berlin, with a focus on economic history and international management. He is currently a doctoral candidate in cultural studies at Humboldt and is writing a dissertation on the history of branding in Germany. He also has his own brand consulting firm in Berlin.

Rainer Gries is a professor of cultural and communications history at the University of Vienna. His research interests include political propaganda, advertising, and product communications in nineteenth- and twentieth-century Germany and Austria. He is the author of numerous articles and books, including *Produkte als Medien. Kulturgeschichte der Produktkommunikation in der Bundesrepublik und der DDR* (2003).

Elizabeth Heineman is an associate professor of history at the University of Iowa. She has written on gender and sexuality in Nazi and postwar Germany, memory, and comparative welfare states; her publications include *What Difference Does a Husband Make? Women and Marital Status in Nazi and Postwar Germany* (1999). Her current research concerns sexual consumer culture before the legalization of pornography.

Michael Imort is an associate professor of geography at Wilfrid Laurier University in Waterloo, Ontario, Canada. His research examines the role of foresters and forestry in German nationalism during the nineteenth and twentieth centuries. He is currently writing a book on the metaphorical use of the forest in naturalizing Nazi ideologies of *Volk*, race, and *Lebensraum*.

Anne Kaminsky received her Ph.D. in 1993 from the University of Leipzig. Since 1998 she has worked at the Stiftung zur Aufarbeitung der SED-Diktatur in Berlin, where she is currently the director. She has published on everyday life history, consumer culture, and questions of memory in East Germany, including *Kaufrausch. Die Geschichte der ostdeutschen Versandhäuser* (1998) and *Wohlstand, Schönheit, Glück. Kleine Konsumgeschichte der DDR* (2001).

Kevin Repp is the curator of modern European books and manuscripts at the Beinecke Rare Book Library. He has written extensively on social and cultural reform in late Imperial Germany, most notably *Reformers, Critics, and the Paths of German Modernity: Anti-Politics and the Search for Alternatives, 1890–1914* (2000), and he is currently nearing completion of a book about Wilhelmine cultural politics and metropolitan landscapes entitled *Berlin Moderns: Art, Politics, and Commercial Culture in Fin-de-Siècle Berlin*.

Corey Ross is a senior lecturer in modern history at the University of Birmingham, England. He has published widely on the history of the GDR, including *The East German Dictatorship: Problems and Perspectives in the Interpretation of the GDR* (2002), has recently coedited a book with Karl-Christian Fuehrer, *Media, Culture and Society in Twentieth-Century Germany* (2006), and is currently writing a social history of the mass media in Germany from the late nineteenth century to 1945.

Jeff Schutts is a history instructor at Douglas College and other schools in Vancouver, British Columbia, Canada. He is currently revising for publication his 2003 Georgetown University dissertation, "Coca-Colonization, 'Refreshing' Americanization, or Nazi *Volksgetränk*? The History of Coca-Cola in Germany, 1929–1961." His other research interests include antiwar dissent within the U.S. military and the role of dramatic and documentary film in public history.

Robert P. Stephens is an assistant professor of history at Virginia Tech. His research focuses on the illicit drug culture in West Germany. Portions of this work have been published in the *Journal of Cultural Research, Consuming Germany in the Cold War* (2003), and most recently in his monograph *Germans on Drugs: The Complications of Modernization in Hamburg* (2007).

Pamela E. Swett is an associate professor of history at McMaster University. She has published on political violence and the collapse of the Weimar Republic and is the author of *Neighbors* *and Enemies: The Culture of Radicalism in Berlin 1929-1933* (2004). Her current research project focuses on advertising in the Third Reich.

S. Jonathan Wiesen is an associate professor of history at Southern Illinois University, Carbondale. He has published on historical memory after World War II, including *West German Industry and the Challenge of the Nazi Past, 1945-1955* (2001). He has recently written about advertising in the Federal Republic of Germany and is currently writing a book about business leaders, consumer culture, and marketing in Nazi Germany.

Jonathan R. Zatlin is an assistant professor of history at Boston University. He has published on public opinion in the GDR, the East German automobile industry, and economic sources of racism in Soviet-style regimes, and is the author of *The Currency of Socialism: Money and Political Culture in East Germany* (2007). He is currently working on a history of Jews and money in modern Germany.

INDEX

Page references in *italics* indicate an illustration.

Abusch, Alexander, 264, 268

"Action Plan for the Struggle against Narcotics Misuse," 239

Adenauer, Konrad, 191, 198

Adorno, Theodor W., 5

advertisements, editorial creation of, 247, 248–50

AEG, 28; Turbine Factory, 38

Afri-Cola, 165–67, *166*, 168, 179n87

Afri-Post, 165, *166*

Aktion Gemeinsinn (Community Spirit in Action), 12

alcohol: black market and, 232; and Coca-Cola, 158–59, 165; consumption of, 235 (table); German thirst for, 154; KdF tours and, 142; temperance movements, 231–33, *234*

Allen, Frederick, 155

Alliance of Advertising Interests, 35

Alliance of Berlin Specialty Stores, 28

Alliance of German Craft Associations, 32

Åman, Anders, 299, 303

American advertising in Germany, 8–9, 12, 61–65, 237–38; slogans in German, 62, 156; for Tietz department store, 30

American-style advertising, 9, 28, 54–56; editorializing style, 55–56; Marchand on, 3; modified for German society, 4–5, 9, 63–65; parallels with Nazi propaganda, 66–72, 127. *See also* editorializing style; United States

American arcadia, 41

Americanization: of consumption, 318; of German advertising, 12, 52–72, 152; of the Old World, 34

American Peril, 34, 41

Analogik (Domizlaff), 82, 94

antidrug campaign (of BfGA): approaches and strategies, 239–40; brochure, 240–47; effectiveness, 245–47, 249–50, 256–57; revolution and, 249; rock musicians' testimonials and, 247–50; target groups for, 240; temperance narrrative of, 242–43; Wowman cartoon, 250–57. *See also* drug trade (illicit)

antirationalism, 82

applied psychology, 82, 84

Arbeiter, Der (Jünger), 83

architecture: "Battle for a New German Architecture," 291; Bauhaus tradition, 291, *292*; commercial, 28–29; Gothic modern, 28–29, 36–37, *38*, 48n29, 49n32;

architecture (*continued*)

modernist, 288, 290–91, 292; neoclassical, 37, 291, 299, 302; *Neues Deutschland* articles on, 292; socialist-realist, 287–88; for Stalinallee, 290–91; for Wertheim department store, 36–37, *38*, 48n29, 49n32. *See also* art

Arnold-Chemnitzer-Oelsner artists collective, 298

art (in advertising): advertisers as artists, 7, 12, 23n20; artistically inspired style, 58; *l'art pour l'art*, 29, 45; critiques of commercial, 42, 44–45; fine vs. commercial, 29, 35–36, 41–42; graphic design and designers, 23n20, 27–29, 44; socialist realism and, 288, 298–99. *See also* architecture; image-based style

artisanal traditions. *See* craft and artisanal traditions

Association for Social Policy, 33, 34

Association of Berlin Artists, 42

Association of German Department and Retail Stores, 33

authoritarianism (German), 5

automobile industry, 237; Chrysler campaign, 65; Volkswagen, 13, 128–29, 138, 196

Ayer and McCann (advertising firm), 54, 237

Baader, Andreas, 249

Baiko, Hannes, 216

Baranowski, Shelley, 19

Barnum, P. T., 28, 46n5

"Battle for a New German Architecture," 291, 293

Bauhaus tradition, 291, 292

Baumeister der Stalinallee (Master Builders of the Stalinallee) (Käding), 289, 294

Beate Uhse (firm), 18, 202–24, *217*, *218*; biographical marketing, 203, 204, 210–11, 216–17; branding, 216; brochures, 216; catalogues, 204, 205, 206–11, 215, 221;

court cases, 211–15, 217; customers, 209, 214; female identification of, 208, 210, 213; links with elite class, 214, 220–21; as local firm, 206, 216–17; parallels with German history, 202, 223; portrayal of women, 206–7, *207*; PR campaign, 215–22; respectability of, 205, 206, 209–10, 214–15, 222; role of Luftwaffe story, 202, 205, 210–11, 213, 218, 220, 223–24; shops, 217–18; staff, 206, *210*, 214–15

Beate Uhse Myth, 203, 222–24

Bedarfsweckung (stimulating consumption), 72

behaviorism, 74n24, 82

Behne, Adolf, 42–43

Behrendt, Walter Curt, 37, 49n32

Behrens, Peter, 38

Berghoff, Hartmut, 75n51, 127, 128

Bergmann tobacco company, 117–19

Berlau, Ruth, 297

Berlin: A City's Destiny (Scheffler), 36

Berlin Commercial College, 44

Berliner Illustrierten Zeitung, 60, *171*

Berlin Olympic Games (1936), 35, 162–63

"Berlin Under Construction" (art exhibition), 298

Berlin Wall, 15–16, 284

Bernhard, Lucian, 28, *41*, 42, *43*, 45, 58

Bildersprache, 66–67

Bildungsbürgertum, 7, 34, 44, 63–64

biologism, 82

Böcher, Hans-George, 87

Bode, Matthias, 79

Bolz, Lothar, 290–91

Bongard, Willi, 79

Bongers, Hans, 185–87, *187*

branding and brand names, 78–98, 308–9; as organism, 85–86; of Beate Uhse Myth, 203, 216; Domizlaff as godfather of, 78; durability of, 3; of heroic founder, 88–89, 97; as means of communication, 308–9, 313, 320; and national-scale marketing,

65–66; natural brand building, 85–89, 88; as producer oriented, 88, 90; product mediatization and, 308–9; as product oriented, 85–86; secondary meanings of, 87–88; in self-service model, 313; of socialist-realist architecture, 287–88; of Stalinallee, 300; of the state, 94–98, 115–16; U.S. brands in Europe, 61. *See also* consumer products

Brandt, Willy, 194

Brecht, Bertolt, 297–98

Brevier für Könige (Domizlaff), 80, 94, 115

Brewers Association of Central Baden, 164

brochures: for Beate Uhse, 216; for BfGA antidrug campaign, 240–47; for Coca-Cola, 156, 163

Brod, Max, 41, 42

Brooks, Jeffrey, 297

Brose, Hans, 13

Brüning, Heinrich, 96, 98, 101n77

Bund deutscher Gebrauchsgraphiker, 58

Bundeszentral für gesundheitliche Aufklärung (BfGA; Federal Center for Health Education), 235, 239–57

Bürfent, Elsie, 161

Burkhardt, Roland, 324n5

Butler, Rosemary, 248

camping equipment, 282, *283*, *284*

Candler, Asa, 158

Canetti, Elias, 102–3, 108, 123

capitalism vs. socialism, 267–68

capitalist advertising, 14–16, 287, 288

capitalist consumption, 268–69, 322

capitalist distributors, 252

capitalist realism, 56, 66, 288

cartoons and comic strips, 135–36, 240, 250–57

cash registers, lack of, 316

Castillo, Greg, 19

Catholic Commercial Associations, 33

Center Party, 35

chain stores, 68

Christian Democratic Union, 184

circulation statistics (newspapers and magazines), 55, 62, 68

class issues: in Beate Uhse's court cases, 211–15; in KdF programs, 129, 135, 142–43

clothing, 11, 271–78

Coca-Cola: alcohol and, 154, 158–59, 165; as American, 153–54, 156–57, 170; association with holiday traditions, 157–58; association with Jews, 164–67, 170; association with pleasure, 155–56; association with sport, 161–63, 178n65; brochure advertising, 156, 163; Coca-Cola Familie, 154; *Coca-Cola Nachrichten*, 157; competitors of, 164–68; concession stands, 160–61, 169–70; creolization of, 153; film advertisements, 170; franchise structure, 153; as German, 151–53, 153–54, 170, 171–74; Germanized advertisements, 156–60, 177; growth of sales, 154–55, 163, 168, 169–70; image-based advertisements, *171*, *173*, 177; "kingly" salesmen, 167–68; local production of, 153, 170; Third Reich government programs and, 164, 167, 168, 171–74

cognitive dissonance, 245, 247, 254

Cohen, Lizabeth, 236

"Cokelore," 174n5

colonialist stereotypes, 20, 26n75

commercial art. *See* art

commodity culture, 322–23

communication, history of, 318

conservative revolution, 79, 89–93

constructivism, 292

consumer-centered approach (to advertising), 56, 60, 71

consumer cooperatives, 310, 311

consumer products: advertisements for abstinence from, 257; association with political messages, 266, *267*, *269*; customer's relationship with, 312; as durable and

consumer products (*continued*)
practical, 262, 275–76, 277–78, 321; GDR
priorities for, 263–64, 302; increasing
availability of, 310–11, 313; labeling and
packaging of, 163, 279, 313, 317, 318–19; as
media, 309; as promise of security, 320;
speaking for themselves, 312–13; standardization of, 312; storefront displays
of, 265–66, *266*; surpluses of, 281; "unselling" harmful goods, 235; vs. aesthetic
or spiritual benefits, 129–30. *See also*
branding and brand names; shortages of
consumer products
consumer research. *See* market research and
analysis
consumers and consumerism: needs managed by advertising, 269–70; power of,
2, 230–31; shoppers-*flâneurs*, 313; social
problems and, 231; wave of gluttony
(*Fresswelle*), 278–79, 318; youth culture
and, 237
consumer society, 3, 321
consumption: Americanization or democratization of, 318, 319–20; capitalist, 268–
69, 322; and communication, 307–8, 318;
definitions of, 182–83; democratization
of, 318, 319–20; history of, 318; ideological barriers to, 320–21; as leisure activity,
282–84; mass, 69, 127; sexual, 204, 206,
219–20; socialist, 268–69, 270–71, 304,
314–18, 321, 322
consumption terror (*Konsumterror*), 13
content vs. form, 117–19
Conti, Leonardo, 163
contraception, 204, 207–8, 220, 221
cooperative stores, 310, 311
craft and artisanal traditions, 12, 31–32,
57–58, 60
Crawford, William, 65
creolization, 153, 175n13
Crowd, The (Le Bon), 83
crowd symbol (*Massensymbol*), 102–3, 123

"cultural society," 321
culture: Kultur vs. Zivilisation, 91, 118;
role in commercial enterprise, 29, 35–
36

Dale, Ernest, 78
Daltrey, Roger, 248–49
Decoding Advertisements (Williamson), 155
defensive advertising, 163, 164
Dehn, Paul, 34
Deinhard champagne, 319
department stores: Karstadt, 311–12, 325n20;
Kaufhof, 309–10; self-service, 309–10;
taxation of, 33; Tietz, 30–31, 37; Wert-
heim, 29, 30, 31–32, 36–37, *38*, 39, 48n29,
49n32
de Syon, Guillaume, 18
Deutsche Arbeitsfront (German Labor
Front), 128–29, 166
Deutsche Arbeitsfront, Die, 136, 137
Deutsche Bauakademie, 291, 294
Deutsche Forstbeamtenzeitung, 105, 118, 119
Deutsche Forstwirt, Der, 105, 110, 111, 112, 113,
121
Deutsche Forst-Zeitung, 105, 120
Deutscher Verein gegen den Alkoholmiß-
brauch (German Association against
Alcohol Misuse), 231–32
Deutscher Verein gegen den Mißbrauch
geistiger Getränke (German Association
against the Misuse of Spirits), 231
Deutsche Werbe- und Anzeigengesellschaft
(DEWAG), 26n71, 263
Deutsche Werbung (German Advertising),
9–10
Deutsche Zentrale für Fremdenverkehr
(DZF; German Central Office for Tour-
ism), 182, 192–97
Deutschlandsfahrt, 161–62
Dialectic of the Enlightenment, The (Hork-
heimer and Adorno), 5
Dichter, Ernest, 5–6

direct marketing, 215–16

Dobbs, Samuel Candler, 155

Domizlaff, Hans, 13, 18, 84–85, 96; advertising profession and, 79–81, 89–90, 91, 92; flag design, 94–96, 95, 98; Nazi propaganda and, 92–93, 115; philosophy of, 80–81, 82–83; at Reemtsma, 80, 82, 86–88, 89; at Siemens, 80, 89; view of salesperson, 89–90

— writings, 78, 79; Analogik, 82, 94; Brevier für Könige, 80, 94, 115; Propagandamittel der Staatsidee, 92, 94, 96, 115; Wie man das öffentliche Vertrauen gewinnt. Ein Lehrbuch der Markentechnik, 78

Döpler the Younger, 28

Dörr (forester), 107, 109

drug trade (illicit): consumerist approach to, 235, 244; growth of, 234–35; public knowledge about, 240–41. See also antidrug campaign

Düesberg, Rudolf, 106–7

Dürer-Bund, 58

East Germany. See German Democratic Republic; Sozialistische Einheitspartei Deutschlands

Edel Steel Works, 142

editorializing style (of advertising), 55–56; German responses to, 62–63; vs. image-based style, 55–56, 58, 70–71, 238; mass psychology and, 59–60; of Nazi propaganda, 67–68, 70–71; Odol advertisement, 57; "reason why" advertising, 155. See also American advertising in Germany; American-style advertising

education: of advertising professionals, 10; of consumers, 265–71

electric signs, 8, 39–40

Elida soap, 73n20

erfrischende Pause, Die, 170

Erhard, Ludwig, 244

erotica, 18, 202–24

Erwin Wasey (firm), 54, 237

European Union, 21, 26n76

Ewiger Wald (Eternal Forest, film), 109

exhibitions and fairs: sponsored by Lufthansa, 196; in Third Reich, 160, 168–70

expressionism, 42

F. Blumhoffer Nachfolger (Bluna), 165

Falk, Pasi, 156

fashion advertising, 11, 271–78

Federal Republic of Germany (FRG), 10–14, 202–24, 232, 236, 238; alcohol and tobacco consumption in, 235 (table); antidrug campaign (1972), 230–31, 239–57; East Germans' perception of, 266, 270, 284, 321–22; GDR's economic competition with, 266, 267–68, 270, 273, 274, 304, 314; national identity, 184, 188–91, 196, 197–98; self-service shopping in, 307, 309–13, 318–20; as site of tourism, 182, 183

films and cinema advertisements: Die erfrischende Pause, 170; Ewiger Wald, 109; Master Builder of Socialism, 300, 303

Fischer, Walter, 177n38

Fitzpatrick, Sheila, 289

Flach, Karl, 165–67

flag (German), 94–96, 95, 98

food: for healthy eating, 162, 278–81; self-service stores and, 310

forest: analogy with Volk, 105–7, 114; army as marching forest, 102, 108–9; as German, 106, 112, 114; as modern vs. romantic, 113; smoking and, 119–21

Forest and Volk (Zentgraf), 107

Forest as Educator, The (Düesberg), 106

forestry journals: articles in, 107; general advertising in, 116–23; professional advertising in, 105, 108–16, 120–21

formalism, 291

form vs. content, 117–19

Förster, Maria, 141

Franco, Francisco, 232

Frankfurter Allee (Berlin), 263, 290

Frankfurt School, 5

Freier Deutscher Gewerkschaftsbund (Association of Free German Trade Unions), 295

Freud, Sigmund, 83, 84

Friebe, Holm, 18

Friedrichshain district (of Berlin), 290

Fritzsche, Peter, 172, 173

Fuchs (forester), 109–11

Fühmann, Franz, 299

full-service agencies, 12, 61, 68, 236

Future (magazine), 30, 44

Futurism, 42

Gebrauchsgraphik, 60

Gemeinschaftswerbung (communal advertising), 13

German Artisans' Congress, 33

German Democratic Republic (GDR): "Battle against Formalism in Art and Literature," 291; "Battle for a New German Architecture," 291; brands after German reunification, 284–85; commodity culture of, 322–23; economic competition with FRG, 266, 267–68, 270, 273, 274, 304, 314; Institute for Market Research, 270–71, 280–81; National Building Program, 288, 289, 292, 301–2, 303; policies on advertising, 16–17, 263–64, 265, 267–71, 283–84; policies on consumer goods, 263–64, 302; post-Stalin period, 303–4; product communication in, 320–23; protests and strikes in, 264, 265, 302–3; rebuilding of East Berlin, 293–97; recreational facilities, 282–84; self-service shopping, 314–18, 322–23; and Sozialistische Einheitspartei Deutschlands (SED; Socialist Unity Party), 14–17, 263–84, 287–304; Western products in, 321–22

German Labor Front (Deutsche Arbeitsfront), 128–29, 166

Gesellschaft Werbeagenturen (Association of Full-Service Advertising Agencies), 12

Gesetz über Wirtschaftswerbung (Commercial Advertising Law, 1933), 104

Gestalt, 83

Gestapo, 135, 142

Gewinnung des öffentlichen Vertrauens (Domizlaff), 13

globalization (of advertising industry), 13, 237–38

Goebbels, Joseph, 92–93, 98, 103–4, 115–16, 152

Goldberger, Ludwig Max, 34

gondola displays, 309, 310

Göring, Hermann, 107–8, 109, 168–69, 180n111

Gothic modern architecture, 28–29, 36–37, 38, 48n29, 49n32

graphic design. *See* art

Grazia, Victoria de, 6, 237

Green Party, 103

Gries, Rainer, 20, 80, 93

Großorganismen (giant organisms), 82, 94

Gross, Rita, 255–56

Group Psychology and the Analysis of the Ego (Freud), 83

Growald, Ernst, 27, 28, 36, 41–44, 66

Groys, Boris, 287

Grundzüge der Psychotechnik (Münsterberg), 82

Guenther, Konrad, 114

"Guidelines for the Design and Execution of Commercial Advertising" (1933), 104

Gustloff, Wilhelm, 138

Gute, Herbert, 298

Hachmeister, Lutz, 98

Hain, Simone, 291

Handelsorganisation (HO), 262–63, 315, 317

Hanewacker tobacco company, 119–20

Hannerz, Ulf, 175n13

Hansen, Ursula, 79

Harden, Maximilian, 30, 44

Hartmann, Dolf, 248–49

Harych, Theo, 297, 300, 303

Haus Budapest Restaurant (Berlin), 300–301

Heineman, Elizabeth, 18

Henkel corporation, 26n75

Henselmann, Hermann, 291–93, 293, 296, 299, 301, 303; design for Weberwiese, 292, 294, 295

Herf, Jeffrey, 93

Herrnstadt, Rudolf, 292

Herzog, Dagmar, 220

Hidden Persuaders (Packard), 5, 236

Hindenberg, Paul von, 97, 98

Hirsch, Harold, 166

Hiseman, Jon, 248

Hitler, Adolf, 92–93, 98, 232

Höhere Reichswerbeschule (Reich Advertising Academy), 10

Hohlwein, Ludwig, 58

Höhn, Maria, 220

Hollerbaum und Schmidt, 27, 40–44

Honecker, Erich, 16–17

Horkheimer, Max, 5

household appliances, 272–74, 313

humor (in advertising), 196–97, 197, 307; cartoons and comic strips, 135–36, 240, 250–57

Hundhausen, Carl, 91

Hupfhauer, Theo, 130

idea organisms (Ideenorganismen), 82

Ilgen, Volker, 80, 93

image-based style (of advertising): for Coca-Cola, 171, 173, 177; vs. editorializing style, 55–56, 58, 70–71; for KdF, 136–37; for Nazi propaganda, 66–67, 70–71, 108–13, 136; posters, 28–29, 39–45, 55–56, 58, 60, 238; reflecting Weimar period, 9; use of

photographs, 171, 173, 264–65, 288, 292, 293. See also art; poster advertising

Imort, Michael, 18

Informationen zum Drogen-Problem (Information on the Drug Problem) (brochure), 240–47, 242

Institute for Advertising Techniques, 265

Institute for Consumer Needs and Market Research, 265

Institute for Market Research (East Germany), 270–71, 280–81

Institut für Bauwesen (IfB; Institute for Building Methods), 290–91

Institut für Markentechnik, 78, 81

Institut für Markt- und Werbeforschung (Institute for Market and Advertising Research, West Germany), 244–46

Institut für Wirtschaftspsychologie, 59

instrumental logic, 241, 257

International Advertising Association, 8, 54

International Air Transport Association, 196

interwar period, 8–9, 52–72, 71–72, 75n51

Italy, KdF tours to, 133, 144, 145

J. Walter Thompson (JWT) (firm): BfGA antidrug campaign and, 238, 247–57; interwar years in Germany, 8–9, 9, 54, 55, 58, 61, 62, 72n10, 237; postwar years in Germany, 12, 238, 247

Jagow, Gottlieb von, 36, 38

Jendretzky, Hans, 295

Jet gasoline, 307, 308

Jews and Judaism: anti-Semitism, 9, 30–31, 32, 104, 118; Coca-Cola associated with, 164–67, 170

Jugend, Die (Youth), 40

Jugendstil, 88

Jünger, Ernst, 83

Junger Maurer der Stalinallee (Young Bricklayer of the Stalinallee) (Nagel), 298–99, 303

Käding, Jürgen, 289, 294

Kaloderma soap, 56

Kaminsky, Anne, 19, 314, 321

Karl-Marx-Allee (Berlin), 303

Karstadt department stores, 311–12, 325n20

Kaufhof department stores, 309–10

Keith, Max, 156, 160, 163, 174

Khrushchev, Nikita, 303

Kiengaard, Elsbeth, 300

Kirschenblatt-Gimblett, Barbara, 287

Klering, Hans, 299

Klinger, Julius, 28, 45

Knapp, Alfred, 8, 72n7

Knop, Karin, 236

König, Theodor, 74n24

Konsum stores, 311

Konsumterror (consumption terror); 13

Kraft durch Freude (KdF; Strength through Joy), 128–46; antimaterialistic philosophy of, 130–34; cruise ships of, 138, 138–39, 142; Gestapo and Sicherheitsdienst surveillance of, 135, 142; image-based advertising, 136–37; leadership, 129, 133, 135; as materialist and consumerist, 129–30, 134–40; participants' accounts of, 135, 141–46; programs of, 128–30; Prora resort, 139–40; racial issues with, 133, 136, 143–44; role in Third Reich, 133–34, 141, 143–44, 145–46; tourism projects, 132–46; women participants in, 136, 137–38, 142–43

Kretschmann, Leopold, 167

Kretzer, Max, 39

Kropff, Hanns, 58, 73n10, 73n20

Kultur, 91, 118

Kulturfonds der DDR (East German Cultural Fund), 298

labeling and packaging, 163, 279, 313, 317, 318–19

Lafferentz, Bodo, 128

Lamberty, Christiane, 23n22

landscape and countryside, 35, 132; Nazi view of nature, 133; unproductive lands, 111–12

Law Regarding the Dissemination of Youth-Endangering Writings (1953), 219

laws: Basic Law, 219; Commercial Advertising Law (1933), 104; Editors Law (1933), 104; on landscape disfigurement (1902 and 1907), 35; Nuremberg Laws on Citizenship and "Blood Protection" (1935), 110; Sterilization Law (1933), 110; on taxation (1901), 33; on youth-endangering writings (1953), 219

League for Homeland Protection, 35, 37–38, 44

League of German Agrarians, 33

Le Bon, Gustave, 59, 83, 84

Lee, Archie, 156

leisure time, 281–84

Leitherer, Eugen, 79

Lennon, John, 247, 249, 250

Lex Wertheim, 33

Ley, Robert, 129–30, 138

lifestyle, 231, 257; healthy diet and, 278–81; socialist, 231; socialist advertisements for, 281

local firms: Beate Uhse, 206, 216–17; Coca-Cola, 153, 170

Löffler, Hans, 298

Lüdtke, Alf, 173

Lufthansa, 18, 182; Constellation, 186; costs and fares, 196; crews and flight attendants, 186, 188–91, 189; dealings with journalists and diplomats, 187–88; and DZF, 192–97; fleet, 185–86; German identity of, 194–95, 196–97; "German" service of, 186–87, 194; identification with Third Reich, 184–85; in interwar years, 184–85; journalistic coverage as advertising for, 187; postwar difficulties of, 185–87; postwar re-creation of, 184; relation to German government, 191–

92; "Senator Klass," 194, *195*; tourism and, 188, 192–97, *193*; use of German stereotypes, 188, 190, 194

Luftwaffe story (Beate Uhse), 202, 205, 210–11, 213, 214

Luther, Hans, 61

"Made in Germany," 3, 12, 22

mail-order catalogues, 318, 322; for erotica, 204, 205, 206–11, 215, 221; in GDR, 268, *269*, 274–75

Mann, Thomas, 91

Marchand, Roland, 3

Markenidee (brand idea), 85–86

Markenpersönlichkeit (brand personality), 85–89, 86, 88

Markentechnik, 81, 83, 85–88, 94–98; vs. advertising, 91–92; as antimodern, 89, 90, 91; and the conservative revolution, 89–93; as product-centered, 85; as secret science, 89

marketing, 13; American vs. Nazi techniques for, 68–69; direct, 215–16; mass, 236; on a national basis, 65–67; in the "provinces," 66; "unselling" harmful goods, 235, 257

market research, 13, 21, 72–73n10, 236; for antidrug campaign, 244–46, 256–57; science of advertising and, 55, 82, 89; in the Third Reich, 67, 70–71; U.S. advertisements in Germany and, 64

market segmentation, 235, 236–37

Marktanalyse (Kropff and Randolph), 73n10

Marshall Plan, 10

mass consumption, 69, 127

Massengehirn (mass brain), 83, 84

Massenseele (mass soul), 83

Massensymbol (crowd symbol), 102–3, 123

masses: crowds and power, 102; as irrational, 59

Masse und Macht (Canetti), 102

mass marketing, 236

mass psychology, 59–60, 82–85, 90, 92

Master Builder of Socialism (film), 300, 303

Mataja, Victor, 40

Matheus Müller German champagne, 25n57

McLuhan, Marshall, 183

media: circulation statistics (newspapers and magazines), 55, 62, 68; Nazi control of, 104–5, 116; postwar, 318; standardization of, 62

mediatization of product communication, 308, 322–23

medium (of advertising): impact of technology on, 21; vs. message, 58

Mein Kampf (Hitler), 59

Meins, Holger, 249

Messel, Alfred, 29, 36–37, 38–39, 45, 49n32

Ministry for State Security (Stasi), 321

Miquel, Johannes, 33

Modern Business, 40, 45

Modern Capitalism (Sombart), 35, 51n53

modernism and modernity, 5; forest as modern vs. romantic, 113; Gothic modern style, 28–29, 36–37, *38*, 48n29, 49n32; reactionary, 93; Stalinist model of, 287; in Third Reich, 112–13, 152–53, 159–60, 171–74

modernist architecture, 288, 290–91, 292

Moede, Walter, 74n23

Moeller, Robert, 184

motivational research, 6

Mucchi, Gabriele, 299

Münsterberg, Hugo, 59, 82

Mussolini, Benito, 232

Nagel, Otto, 298, 303

National Committee for the Building of the German Capital, 294, 296

national economists, 32–33

National Garden Exhibition, 161

National Socialist Association of German Advertising Practitioners, 10

National-Sozialistische Deutsche Arbeiter
Partei (NSDAP; Nazi Party), 9–10, 13–14,
102–23, 127–46. *See also* Third Reich
*Natural History of the German People as a
Foundation for Social Policy* (Riehl), 106
nature, Romantic view of, 133
Nazi propaganda: form vs. content, 117–19;
on health and cleanliness, 130–31, 162–
63; image-based style of, 66–67, 70–71,
108–13, 136; parallels with American-
style advertising, 66–72, 127; parallels
with conservative revolution, 93; parallels with *Markentechnik,* 92–93, 115; racial
issues in, 110–12, 130–32, 137–38; rein-
forcement in advertising texts, 108–13,
122–23; views of socialism and unions,
130. *See also* National-Sozialistische
Deutsche Arbeiter Partei; propaganda;
Third Reich
neoclassical architecture, 37, 291, 299, 302
Neologisms of the World Economy (Dehn), 34
Neues Deutschland, 268, 287–88, 290, 292,
298
Neue Werbung, 16, 262, 264
Neumann, Ernst, 28
Nicholson, H. B., 153
Niethammer, Lutz, 220
Nietzsche, Friedrich, 82–83
Nitribitt, Rosemarie, 219
Nuremberg Laws on Citizenship and
"Blood Protection," 110

Odol mouthwash, 57
Oestergard, Heinz, 195
Oktoberfest, 189
One Thousand Television Tips (*Tausend-
TeleTips*), 265
Oppenhoff, Walter, 162, 164, 166, 168, 170,
177n38
Outfitter, The, 33

packaging, 313, 317
Packard, Vance, 5, 236

Palm cigars, 120–21
Palmolive soap, 65
Pankratz, Frau, *296*
Parzhamer Venus-Quelle, 164
Paul, Bruno, 28
Pein, Ernst, 116
Pein & Pein, 108–16, *110, 111, 112, 113*
Pemberton, John, 155, 158
Pence, Katherine, 289
Pendergrast, Mark, 151
Persil detergent, 313, 322
photographs (in print advertising), *171, 173,*
264–65, 292, *293*
Plutus (newspaper), 44
Pond's cream, 63–65, 76n59
Posener, Julius, 49n32
poster advertising (*Sachplakat*), 28–29, 40,
44–45, 55, 238; for Kaloderma soap, *56;*
for Priester matches, 42, *43;* for Stalin-
allee, *301;* for Stiller shoes, *41. See also*
image-based style
Potsdam Protocol, 184
Powers, Ray Rivington, 154–55, 165
pressure cookers, 272
Priester Match Company, 42, *43*
Printer's Ink (journal), 56
Proctor, Robert, 232
product-centered approach, 70
product communication, 308, 318–20, 323–
24; vs. discourse of scarcity, 321; labeling
and packaging and, 163, 279, 313, 317,
318–19; mediatization of, 308; role of
packaging, 313, 317
professionalization (of advertising), 7, 11–12
propaganda: advertising as, 10, 237; antidrug
campaign literature as, 241–44, 248–50;
research on, 59; unacknowledged, 248,
251–52; during World War II, 10, 120–22.
See also Nazi propaganda
Propagandamittel der Staatsidee (Domizlaff),
92, 94, 96, 115
Psychologie des foules (Le Bon), 59
psychology: of advertising (*Werbepsycholo-*

gie), 59–60, 70–71; applied, 82, 84; mass, 59–60, 82–85, 90, 92; social, 236

psychotechnics, 82

Psychotechnik, 59

public health campaigns, *234*; and advertising industry, 235–38; continuity of, 232–33; failure of, 233

public relations campaigns: for Beate Uhse, 215–22; for Stalinallee, 295–96

racial issues: democratization of consumption and, 319; in KdF programs, 133, 136, 143–44; in Nazi propaganda, 110–12, 130–32, 137–38

radio advertising, 68, 71; for antidrug campaign, 240, 253–56

radio frequency identification (RFID) tags, 21

Radio Luxembourg, 253

Randolph, Bruno, 73n10

reactionary modernism, 93

"Reactionary Nature of Constructivism, The" (Henselmann), 292

recreational activities: camping equipment, 282, *283*, *284*; facilities for, 282–84; sporting events, 161–63, 178n65

Reemtsma, Phillip, 80

Reemtsma tobacco company, 80, 82, 86–88, 89

Reflections of a Non-political Man (Mann), 91

regulation (of advertising): in Berlin, 36; in European Union, 21, 26n76; in Third Reich, 9–10, 69, 104–5, 116, 238; in the United States, 55

Reich Association of Seed Producers and Forest Nurseries, 116

Reich Forestry Office, 107

Reichskulturkammer (Reich Culture Chamber), 104

Reichspropagandaleitung, 76n60

Reichsverband der Deutschen Mineralwasserfabrikanten, 167

Reinhardt, Dirk, 8, 84

Reklame, Die, 69, *96*, *97*

Repp, Kevin, 17

Riehl, Wilhelm Heinrich, 106

Robinson, Frank, 155

rock musicians, 247–50

Rockwell, Norman, 156

Rolling Stone Magazine, 249

Roseman, Mark, 171–72

Ross, Corey, 17, 20, 81, 115

Rotermund, Ernest-Walter, 224n3, 225n18

Royal School of Applied Arts (Berlin), 28

Sachlichkeit (objectivity), 29, 38, 39, 81, 86–87; funky, 39

Sachplakat (object poster), 29, 40–45

salesperson: as agitator for customers, 316; cash registers for, 316; Domizlaff's view of, 89–90; as "kingly," 167–68; in self-service vs. counter-service models, 310, 312

Sanders-Wood, Tracey, 151

Schäfer, Hans-Dieter, 152

Schaffendes Volk exhibition (Düsseldorf, 1937), 168–70

Scheffler, Karl, 36

Scheidemann, Philipp, 141

Schenk, Ingrid, 11

Schindelbeck, Dirk, 80, 93

Schinkel, Carl Friedrich, 37

Schmeling, Max, 232

schöne Dorf (Beautiful Village) project, 132

Schönemann, Friedrich, 91

Schönheit der Arbeit, 130, *131*

Schönheit der Arbeit (Beauty of Labor), 129, 130–34

Schriftleitergesetz (Editors Law, 1933), 104

Schröter, Harm, 11–12

Schudson, Michael, 288

Schultheiss (Berlin brewery), 162

Schutts, Jeff, 18

Schwartz, Frederic J., 81

science (of advertising), 55, 82, 89

Seidels Reklame, 65

self-service shopping, 20, 309–10, *311*, 321–

self-service shopping (*continued*)
22; consumer discipline and, 323; customers' preference for, 311–12; future
development of, 323–24; at gas stations,
307; after German unification, 323–24;
link with consumption and communication, 307–8, 318; as medium of product
presentation, 319; packaging for, 313,
317; socialist views and propaganda on,
314–15; as time-saving, 312, 316
sexuality and sexual consumption, 204, 206,
219–20
shoplifting, 325n20
shortages of consumer products, 302–3;
advertisements reflecting, 10, 26n74,
120–22, 270–71, 275; advertising blamed
for, 271, 281; discourse of scarcity, 321;
and fashion advertising, 273–74; of food,
278–81; non-product advertising, 10, 281;
and self-service shopping, 316, 317–18;
and storefront displays, 265–66, *266. See
also* consumer products
Sicherheitsdienst (SD), 135, 142
Siegfried, Detlef, 237
Siemens, 28, 80, 89
Siemens, Ernst von, 80
Siemens, Werner von, 89
Simplicissimus (magazine), 40
Sinlaco, 164
"Sixteen Principles of City Planning," 291
Slick, Grace, 247
slogans (German translations of), 62, 156
smoking. *See* tobacco companies: and
smoking
social Darwinism, 82
Social Democrats, 33, 34, 95, 141
socialist advertising, 14–16, 271; vs. capitalist
advertising, 264–65, 267–68
socialist consumers and consumption,
268–69, 270–71; vs. consumer society,
321; mass consumer, 304; self-service
shopping for, 314–18; Western orientation of, 322

socialist realism: abandonment of, 303–4;
vs. capitalist advertising, 287, 288; concept of, 287–89; in exterior and interior
design, 300–301; interpretations in the
arts, 288, 297–99, 300–301; and journalism, 297; and the worker activist, 288,
289, 296
social order of the forest, 106–7
social psychology, 236
social sciences, 235, 236
Sombart, Werner, 32–33, 34–35, 44, 51n53
Sontheimer, Kurt, 92
Soviet Zone of Occupation (SBZ), 262–63
Sozialistische Einheitspartei Deutschlands
(SED; Socialist Unity Party), 14–17, 263–
84, 287–304. *See also* German Democratic Republic
Spee detergent, 322
Spengler, Oswald, 82–83
Spitzweg, Carl, 118
sport and sporting events, 161–63, 178n65
Stahl, Fritz, 45
Stalinallee (Berlin), 19, 263; architectural
style, 290–91; in the arts, 296–99; con-
cept and projections for, 287–89, 290,
294–95; public relations and propaganda
for, 295–96, 299–304; residents of, 294,
299–300, 302; as tourist destination,
301–2; volunteer labor and contributions
for, 294, 295, 302
Stalinallee (Harych), 297, 303
Stapelschaufenster (stacked display win-
dows), 265–66, *266*
Steen, Uta van, 202
Stephens, Robert P., 19
stereotypes: of Americans, 57; colonialist,
20, 26n75; German, 188, 190, 194
Sterilization Law (1933), 110
Stevenson, Robert Louis, 198
Stiller shoes, *41*
Stock characters (in advertising), 270–71
storefront displays, 265–66
Strasser, Susan, 182

Strategy of Desire (Dichter), 6

Strauf, Herbert, 156, 157

Streicher, Julius, 167

Strength through Joy. *See* Kraft durch
  Freude

Ströbel, Käthe, 240, 241–42

Sturm (journal), 41

Stürmer, Der, 167

suggestive publicity (*Suggestivwerbung*), 67

Sundblom, Haddon, 156, 157

swastika, 66

symbolism, 28, 39–40

target groups, 85, 240

taxation: of advertising, 33, 104; of department stores, 33; of soft drinks, 154

Taylor, James, 247, 250

technology, 21

Tedlow, Richard, 155

television, commercial, 319, 321

television advertising, 13, 16, 17, 236, 265, 318

temperance movements, 231–33, *234,* 242–43

Tempo-Tex fabric shop, 315

testimonials, 63–64, 67; of rock musicians,
  240, 247–50

Third Reich: advertising regulation, 9–10,
  69, 104–5, 116, 238; Americanization in,
  152; American-style advertising techniques, 66–72, 127; anti-smoking campaigns, 119–21, 232–33; army as marching
  forest, 102, 108–9; civil servants, 212–13;
  as consumer society, 152; control of
  advertising during, 102–23; democratization of consumption, 319; departure of
  U.S. firms during, 67; Deutsche Lufthansa, 184, 185; factories, 130–32; fairs
  and exhibitions, 160–61, 168–70; modernity of, 71, 112–13, 152–53, 159–60, 171–74;
  and Nazi Party, 9–10, 13–14, 102–23, 127–
  46; reflected in Uhse's Luftwaffe story,
  220; sexuality and sexual consumption
  in, 204, 219–20; temperance movement,
  232, 233. *See also* Nazi propaganda

Thomas, Mark, 151, 152

Tietz, Oskar, 30, 33

Tietz department store (Berlin), 30–31, *31,* 37

"To a Young Stalinallee Construction
  Worker" (Brecht), 297

tobacco companies: anti-smoking campaigns and, 119–21, 232–33; Bergmann,
  117–19; Hanewacker, 119–20; Reemtsma,
  80, 82, 86–88, 89; and smoking, 116–23;
  tobacco consumption, 235 (table)

Tomorrow (magazine), 44

tourism: KDF programs, 128, 132–46; role of
  DZF, 182, 192–97; role of Lufthansa, 188,
  192–97, *193;* Stalinallee and, 301–2; vs.
  travel, 193–94, 198

Townshend, Pete, 248–49

"Truth in Advertising" campaign, 54

Uhse, Beate. *See* Beate Uhse (firm)

Uhse, Hans Jürgen, 224n3

Ulbricht, Walter, 16, 19, 263, 290, 300, 304,
  314, 321

Ullstein, Hermann, 100n71

Union of Pictorial Artists, 298

United States: Advertising Council, 12;
  advertising firms in Germany, 8–9,
  12, 61–65, 237–38; Americans' travel to
  Europe, 183; automobile industry, 237;
  Coca-Cola advertising in, 151–52, 155–56;
  Domizlaff's view of, 90–91; German
  views of, 4–5; self-service models in,
  309–10; stereotypes of Americans, 57. *See
  also* American advertising in Germany;
  American-style advertising

Unternehmerstaat, 81

Verbrauchslenkung (steering consumption),
  71–72

Verein der Plakatfreunde, 58

Vershofen, Wilhelm, 1

villages, 132

Voigt, Gerhard, 92

Volk, 105–7, 114

völkisch authors, 105–6

Volksgemeinschaft (racial community), 9, 19, 23n31, 71, 106; common good and, 69–70, 107–8, 109–10, 171–74; democratization of consumption and, 319; mass consumption and, 69

Volksgenossen, 107, 109, 116–23, 174

Volkswagen, 13, 128–29, 138, 196

Wagner, Erich, 142

Wald, Der (art exhibition in Berlin), 114

Ward, Janet, 91

washing machines, 272–74, *273*

Waters, Roger, 247

Watson, John, 63, 74n24

Watters, Pat, 155

wave of gluttony (*Fresswelle*), 278–79, 318

Weberwiese tower (Berlin), 292, 294, 295, *296*, 297

Wehrmacht, Die, 153

Weidenmüller, Hans, 45

Weimar Republic, 8–9, 71–72, 232, 320; Domizlaff's influence during, 78–98

Welt-Reklame Kongress, 72n7

Wenner, Jann, 249

Werbeabgabe (tax on printed advertisements), 104

Werberat der Deutschen Wirtschaft (Advertising Council for the German Economy), 9–10, 13, 104–5, 115–16

Werbeberater (advertising consultants), 68

Werbevermittler (advertising brokers), 68

Werkbund, 7, 58, 81

Wernicke, Julius, 33

Wertheim, Georg, 32

Wertheim department store (Berlin), 29, 30, 31–32; Gothic modern architecture of, 36–37, *38*, 48n29, 49n32

West German Transportation Ministry, 185, 191–92

West Germany. *See* Federal Republic of Germany

Westheim, Paul, 28

Wie man das öffentliche Vertrauen gewinnt (Domizlaff), 78

Wiertz, Jupp, *56*

Wiley, Harvey W., 164–68

Wilhelm II, 32, 85

Wilhelmine era, 6–7, 27–30, 40–45; department stores in, 30–39; government advertising policy, 33, 35; *Jugendstil*, 88

Williamson, Judith, 155

women: in Beate Uhse catalogues, 206–9, *207*; identification with family vs. workplace, 11, 189, 206–8, 272–78, *274*; in Lufthansa advertisements, *189*; in self-service advertising, *311*; in Third Reich advertising, 117, 122, *136*, *137*, 137–38

Woodruff, Robert, 163

worker activist (new worker), 288, *289*, 296–98, 299

World Advertising Congress, 61

World's Fair (Paris, 1937), 168

World War I, 7–8, 133

World War II, 10, 120–22, 151, 174, 183; German advertising during, 118, 120–33; Uhse's Luftwaffe story and, 202, 205, 210–11, 213, 214

Wowman: comic strip, 251–53, *253*; radio spots, 240, 253–56

youth culture, 237

Zahn, Ernest, 312

Zentgraf, Eduard, 107

Zentralausschuss der Werbewirtschaft (Central Federation of the German Advertising Industry), 13

Zivilisation, 91, 118

Pamela E. Swett is an associate professor of history at McMaster University. S. Jonathan Wiesen is an associate professor of history at Southern Illinois University, Carbondale. Jonathan R. Zatlin is an assistant professor of history at Boston University.

Library of Congress Cataloging-in-Publication Data
Selling modernity : advertising in twentieth-century Germany /
edited by Pamela E. Swett, S. Jonathan Wiesen, and Jonathan R. Zatlin;
with a foreword by Victoria de Grazia.
p. cm.
Includes bibliographical references and index.
ISBN 978-0-8223-4047-8 (cloth : alk. paper)
ISBN 978-0-8223-4069-0 (pbk. : alk. paper)
1. Advertising—Germany—History—20th century.
2. Consumption (Economics)—Germany—History—20th century.
3. Consumer behavior—Germany—History—20th century.
I. Swett, Pamela E. II. Wiesen, S. Jonathan. III. Zatlin, Jonathan R.
HF5813.G4S45 2007
659.10943'0904—dc22   2007009342